National Theatre Connections
2024

National Theatre Connections 2024

TEN PLAYS FOR YOUNG PERFORMERS

Age Is Revolting

Shout

Orchestra

Dy Enw Marw/Your Name Is Dead

Kiss/Marry/Push Off Cliff

The Periodicals

Replica

The Sad Club

Wind/Rush Generation(s)

Back in the Day

Edited by
NATIONAL THEATRE

methuen | drama

LONDON • NEW YORK • OXFORD • NEW DELHI • SYDNEY

METHUEN DRAMA
Bloomsbury Publishing Plc
50 Bedford Square, London, WC1B 3DP, UK
1385 Broadway, New York, NY 10018, USA
29 Earlsfort Terrace, Dublin 2, Ireland

BLOOMSBURY, METHUEN DRAMA and the Methuen Drama logo are
trademarks of Bloomsbury Publishing Plc

First published in Great Britain 2024

Introduction copyright © National Theatre, 2024
Resource material copyright © National Theatre, 2024

Age Is Revolting © Abi Zakarian, 2024
Shout © Alexis Zegerman, 2024
Orchestra © Charlie Josephine, 2024
Dy Enw Marw/Your Name Is Dead © Elgan Rhys, 2024
Kiss/Marry/Push Off Cliff © Josh Azouz, 2024
The Periodicals © Siân Owen, 2024
Replica © Titas Halder, 2024
The Sad Club © Luke Barnes, 2019
Wind/Rush Generation(s) © Mojisola Adebayo, 2020
Back in the Day © Yasmeen Khan, 2024

NATIONAL THEATRE and CONNECTIONS typographical font style are used with
the permission of the Royal National Theatre.

The authors have asserted their rights under the Copyright, Designs and Patents Act, 1988,
to be identified as authors of this work.

Cover design by National Theatre Graphic Design Studio

All rights reserved. No part of this publication may be reproduced or transmitted in any form or by any
means, electronic or mechanical, including photocopying, recording, or any information storage or retrieval
system, without prior permission in writing from the publishers.

Bloomsbury Publishing Plc does not have any control over, or responsibility for, any third-party websites
referred to or in this book. All internet addresses given in this book were correct at the time of going to press.
The author and publisher regret any inconvenience caused if addresses have changed or sites have ceased to
exist, but can accept no responsibility for any such changes.

No rights in incidental music or songs contained in the work are hereby granted and performance rights for
any performance/presentation whatsoever must be obtained from the respective copyright owners.

All rights whatsoever in this play are strictly reserved. Application for performance, etc. should be made
before rehearsals begin to the respective playwrights' representatives listed on pages 572–3.
No performance may be given unless a licence has been obtained

A catalogue record for this book is available from the British Library.

A catalog record for this book is available from the Library of Congress.

ISBN: PB: 978-1-3504-5005-9
ePDF: 978-1-3504-5007-3
eBook: 978-1-3504-5006-6

Series: Plays for Young People

Typeset by RefineCatch Limited, Bungay, Suffolk

To find out more about our authors and books visit www.bloomsbury.com
and sign up for our newsletters.

Contents

National Theatre Connections by Kirsten Adam vi
Introduction by Ola Animashawun vii
Connections 2024 Portfolio viii

Age Is Revolting by Abi Zakarian 1
Production Notes 40

Shout by Alexis Zegerman 51
Production Notes 83

Orchestra by Charlie Josephine 95
Production Notes 148

Dy Enw Marw/Your Name Is Dead by Elgan Rhys 159
Production Notes 244

Kiss/Marry/Push Off Cliff by Josh Azouz 259
Production Notes 300

The Periodicals by Siân Owen 311
Production Notes 348

Replica by Titas Halder 359
Production Notes 397

The Sad Club by Luke Barnes 407
Production Notes 434

Wind/Rush Generation(s) by Mojisola Adebayo 449
Production Notes 494

Back in the Day by Yasmeen Khan 511
Production Notes 553

Participating Companies 567
Partner Theatres 570
National Theatre Connections Team 571
Performing Rights 572

National Theatre Connections

Welcome to the Connections 2024 anthology. Connections is the National Theatre's annual nationwide youth theatre festival. Now in its 29th year, Connections gives youth theatres and school groups the unique opportunity to stage new plays that have been written specifically for young people and to perform them at leading theatres across the UK.

We are incredibly fortunate to work with some of the most exciting playwrights working today, and to be able to share ten plays that challenge young people to experience life in someone else's shoes, and transport them to different times, places and emotional landscapes. We are proud that, through this anthology, these plays continue to be permanently available to schools, colleges and youth theatres.

At the beginning of their rehearsal process, companies take part in the Connections Directors' Weekend – an opportunity for the directors to work with the playwright of their chosen play and a leading theatre director. Notes from these workshops accompany the plays in this anthology, giving an insight into the playwrights' intentions, creative inspiration, and tangible techniques and exercises for exploring the text.

In 2024, over 250 companies from across the UK are taking part in Connections, with over 5,000 young people aged 13 to 19 involved in every aspect of theatre-making. Connections is a celebration of the power of young people, and offers them a space to be creative, to express themselves and to connect with other young theatre-makers, both in their local area and across the country.

Connections is not just the National Theatre's programme; it is run in collaboration with fantastic theatres across the UK all of which are equally passionate about youth theatre. Our Partner Theatres work with every company to develop and transfer their production, and we hope the festivals will celebrate the brilliant work that has been created and amplify the voices of young people.

We hope you enjoy this year's plays.

Kirsten Adam
Head of Young People's Programmes
November 2023

Introduction

As I write this, 2024 is now clearly visible on the horizon prompting me to peer hard to see what is apparent, and if it compares favourably with what I would like to see in the immediate future. However things turn out in the next 12 months, one thing is certain: things will change. It is a given. On every level, however you consider it – at home and abroad, personally, inter-personally, political, socially, environmentally, emotionally and intellectually – nothing stays the same. It's a fundamental principle of life, and no two lives are the same.

So, I'm proud to have curated ten plays that encapsulate the dynamics of this fact and the possibilities this provides. The prospect of anything new inspires hope, optimism and renewed faith. So here we have another new collection of plays for a new generation of players, with each and every one of these plays pulsing with a life force, deep and strong enough to light up the world and the lives of all those encountering them. All of them bearing witness to the diversity and complexity of life. Prepare yourself to encounter stories that catapult you back and forth through time to experience being 80, and life in the 80s, that explore the choice to stay silent in a cacophonous world, the compulsion to speak out in an unjust world, reveal how to be content if you're sitting in malcontent, how to retain your humanity, reclaim your authenticity in the face of callous scrutiny and misinformation, present a symphony of tireless endeavour, the pursuit of true friendship and the necessity for allyship.

Ten plays, thousands of ways to play them, countless ways to perceive them, united by one hope – that in some way, somewhere (perhaps even everywhere . . . wouldn't that be a thing of wonder?), they manage to change someone's world for the better and make 2024 a joyful year to remember.

Ola Animashawun
National Theatre Associate and Connections Dramaturg
Autumn 2023

Connections 2024 Portfolio

A note on casting

At National Theatre Connections we think long and hard about every play that we add to the selection. The writers whose plays make up our portfolios offer their plays as stories about humanity. We want the plays to be for everyone, and to tell stories about a wide range of experiences from around the world.

We are proud to continue to offer plays that challenge young people to experience life in someone else's shoes, and transport them to different times, places and emotional landscapes. We encourage our playwrights to keep the casting options for their plays as open as possible. For all plays in the portfolio, all parts can be played by D/deaf and disabled performers and, apart from where the playwright states otherwise, by actors of any gender or ethnicity. If your group doesn't exactly match the apparent casting requirements of a play in terms of race, ethnicity or gender, and you would like to produce it, we would still encourage you to do so. Any queries or changes regarding casting should be checked with the Connections team and we will advize accordingly.

Where locations are specified, rather than being preoccupied with accents, we recommend focusing your energies on finding the emotional truth of these settings.

Synopses

Age Is Revolting *by Abi Zakarian*

Cast size: flexible, with a suggested minimum cast size of 14
Recommended for ages: 13+

Choir is for mad old people, right?
When a group of school kids rebel against their boring music lesson they hit the wrong note and magically transform into their 80-year-old selves – and now live in a care home. Suddenly age, and their understanding of it, feels very relevant as they begin to confusedly navigate their way back to the present; no longer older, but maybe just a little wiser.

Content guidance:
- Some strong language

Shout *by Alexis Zegerman*

Cast size: This play is written to be performed with a large ensemble group, but the minimum suggested cast size is 12
Recommended for ages: 14+

In a world full of words, how can Dana survive when she can't speak? Dana has selective mutism, but that doesn't stop her vivid imagination. *Shout* is a funny, moving play about anxiety, celebrating difference and finding your voice. A play that wonders what exactly it takes to overcome anxiety and mental health issues when you're a teenager. It's not just the noise you make that makes you who you are.

Content guidance:

- Play explores experiences of anxiety disorders
- Moments with characters struggling with poor mental health

Orchestra *by Charlie Josephine*

Cast size: This play is written to be performed with a large ensemble group, but the minimum suggested cast size is 11
Recommended for ages: 13+

A youth orchestra practices during half-term holidays in preparation for a concert. Unexpected events cause them all to interrogate their relationship with success. How do you protect the joy of the process whilst also wanting to be the best? Is striving for artistic excellence worth the pressure of losing soul?

Content guidance:

- In one scene, there is a description of a character taking an overdose

Dy Enw Marw/Your Name Is Dead *gan Elgan Rhys/by Elgan Rhys, mewn cydweithrediad â Leo Drayton/in collaboration with Leo Drayton*

Cast size: This play is written to be performed with a large ensemble group, but the minimum suggested cast size is 13
Recommended for ages: 14+

Maint cast: Mae'r ddrama hon wedi ysgrifennu i'w pherfformio gyda grŵp ensembl mawr, ond y maint isaf cast a awgrymir yw 13
Yn addas ar gyfer oedran: 14+

M has got a new name: another piece in the jigsaw that is his life. We follow him over a day, as he navigates shifting relationships and the challenges and joys of being young and trans. Does the jigsaw ever get completed?

Mae M wedi cael enw newydd: Darn arall yn jig-so ei fywyd. Dilynwn ef dros ddiwrnod, wrth iddo wynebu perthnasoedd ar eu newid a'r heriau a llawenydd bod yn ifanc a thraws. Ydy'r jig-so byth yn cael ei gwblhau?

Content guidance:

- Strong language (a version without strong language is available)
- Domestic violence
- Experience of gender dysphoria

Rhybuddion cynnwys:

- Iaith gref (mae fersiwn heb iaith gref ar gael)

- Trais yn y cartref
- Profiad o ddysfforia rhywedd

There are both Welsh-language and English-language versions *of Dy Enw Marw/Your Name is Dead* available. If you would like a copy of the Welsh language version, or a version without explicit language, please contact connections@nationaltheatre.org.uk

Kiss/Marry/Push Off Cliff *by Josh Azouz*

Cast size: This play is written to be performed with a large ensemble group, but the minimum suggested cast size is nine
Recommended for ages: 14+

A group of friends go camping – but after only one night, one of them is ostracized by the rest of the group and cast out into wilderness for something they said . . . or was it something they did? It's strange and it's about to get stranger as friendships are tested, new alliances formed, trusts are broken and reality is twisted out of shape. The trip becomes a rite of passage, guided by a moral compass that isn't entirely reliable.

Content guidance:
- Strong language
- Sexual references
- Scenes of drug use and distribution
- Scenes of alcoholism and children drinking alcohol

The Periodicals *by Siân Owen*

Cast size: This play is written to be performed with a large ensemble group, but the minimum suggested cast size is eight
Recommended for ages: 14+

Set in the near future, a group of young people live as a feral group of techno-savvy fugitives, living off the land – which is a rubbish dump. They stay out of sight of the authorities, particularly the education authorities, who are desperate to get them back into school because it doesn't look good for them. However, school has lost its allure. When the young people are in school they are overlooked and underestimated – seen as being more trouble than they are worth. So now, for this group, school's out forever.

Content guidance:
- Strong language

Replica *by Titas Halder*

Cast size: This play is written to be performed with a large ensemble group, but the minimum suggested cast size is 12
Recommended for ages: 16+

Something happened on the school trip. One of the class has been replaced by an exact replica of themselves. At least that's what everyone's saying. Once a rumour starts, it can be difficult to remember what is real – or who. Convinced that there is an impostor walking among them, a group of teenagers is determined to root out the intruder. A mystery about friendship, the nature of truth and humanity. When it comes to it, how do you prove that you are a human?

Content guidance:

- Strong language
- Some mildly violent language, used in a sci-fi context

The Sad Club *by Luke Barnes, with music by Adam Pleeth*

Cast size: This play is written to be performed with a large ensemble group, but the minimum suggested cast size is 12
Recommended for ages: 13+

This is a musical about depression and anxiety. It's a collection of monologues, songs and duologues from all over time and space, exploring what about living in this world stops us from being happy and how we might go about tackling those problems.

Content guidance:

- Themes of mental health
- Strong language
- References to sex
- Underage drinking

Wind/Rush Generation(s) *by Mojisola Adebayo*

Cast size: This play is written to be performed with a large ensemble group, but the minimum suggested cast size is eight (with a core group of six) or up to 30, ideally with a mixture of genders
Recommended for ages: 15+

This is a play about the British Isles, its past and its present. Set in a senior common room, in a prominent university, a group of first-year undergraduates are troubled, not by the weight of their workload, but by a 'noisy' ghost. So they do what any group of self-respecting and intelligent university students would do in such a situation: they get out the ouija board to confront their spiritual irritant and lay them to rest, only to be confronted by the full weight of Britain's colonial past in all its gory glory. However, if you think you know about British history, empire, slavery, economics, racism and humanity, then this play might get you to think again. As the planche on the ouija board skates from letter to letter at an ever-increasing speed, the students are catapulted through space and time, witnessing the injustices, incongruities and inhumanity of the past. This is a smorgasbord of genres and styles. Fusing naturalism with physical theatre, spoken word, absurdism, poetry and direct address, this is event theatre that whips along with the grace, pace and hypnotic magnetism of a hurricane.

Content guidance:

- Racially abusive language – including the 'N word'
- Language describing the racially motivated abuse of power and violations and attacks
- References to colonialism
- References to genocide
- References to human rights abuse
- Allusions to gun violence

Back in the Day *by Yasmeen Khan*

Cast size: This play is written to be performed with a large ensemble group, but the minimum suggested cast size is 12
Recommended for ages: 13+

A group of classmates are charged with the responsibility of being their school's well-being champions. In a freak occurrence they are transported back to the 80s via an impromptu and heavily improvised roller disco. Here they discover they're not the only ones with skeletons in the cupboard, and there was more to the 80s than glitterballs and strange haircuts.

Content guidance:

- One moment of strong language

AGE IS REVOLTING

by Abi Zakarian

Abi Zakarian is an award-winning British-Armenian playwright born and raised in Derby, now based in London. Some of her plays include: *Lullaby* at Shakespeare's Globe; *Found,* produced by 45North for their 'Written on the Waves' series of audio plays; *Perfect Myth Allegory* at Jermyn Street for the '15 Heroines' series; *I Am Karyan Ophidian* for the Sam Wanamaker Playhouse at Shakespeare's Globe and *A Thousand Yards* at Southwark Playhouse. Her play *Fabric* won a Scotsman Fringe First award, later touring and also at Soho Theatre, and she won a Vault Festival People's Choice Award for *I Have a Mouth and I Will Scream*. Her play *Mountain Warfare* was a finalist in the 2021/22 Women's Prize for Playwriting, and her play *Worthy Women* was longlisted for the Women's Prize in 2023/24. Along with the playwrights Morgan Lloyd Malcolm and Sampira Al-Fihri, she is a co-founder of the horror theatre company Terrifying Women, and she also created and hosts the UK Armenian Creatives group. Abi Zakarian is currently shooting her first short film, *Pomegranate*, and is under commission with Derby Theatre among others.
abizakarian.com

For Ruth (and Teddy)

Characters

*The **Childhood Toys**, some specifically:*
Hopsy
Albert

Manoukian – *a substitute teacher/carer/mage, middle-age*

*The **Youngers**, some specifically:*
Arpi – *girl*
Mo – *boy or girl or non-binary*
Nina – *girl*
Barney – *boy*

*The **Carers**, early to middle-age*

*The **Elders**, late 70s to late 80s, some specifically:*
Arshaluys – *Arpi's nana*
Bob – *Barney's grandad*
Amoy – *care home elder*

Takush – *Arpi's mum, middle-age*
Barney's **Mum**, *middle-age*
Rachel – *Mo's daughter, middle-age*
Ernie – *Mo's grandson, young teen*

Settings

A classroom
A care home
A waiting room of sorts

A few notes

When the transformation of the young people into their elder selves happens they *do not* change their appearance in any way. No grey wigs or dodgy 'old person' acting, please. Once the transformation happens, they must play their role as if they see each other, and themselves, as their older selves. Think about the changes in our bodies as we age, what attendant conditions both physically and mentally might present themselves and how this might affect the speed at which we do things, how we might navigate space, use objects, eat, etc.

Genders can be changed if preferred, just make sure dialogue fits with pronouns. NB: a non-binary term for a parent is 'par' or grandparent is 'grandy' which can be used in the scene with Mo's daughter and grandchild.

'–' at the end of a line indicates an abrupt cut off or interruption.

Arpi, Takush and Arshaluys are written as Armenian heritage; please know that it is this specific history and heritage being referenced when they speak about their past.

Manookian is pronounced Man-oo-key-an
Sarkissian is pronounced Sarr-kiss-eeyan
Takush is pronounced Tah-koosh
Kchuch is pronounced Keh-chutch
Arshaluys is pronounced Ar-shall-ooze

Age Is Revolting **playlist**

https://open.spotify.com/playlist/0RahcDzPAGXndDslqbhHe9?si=9a538911093e4107

Some of the songs are already used in the play; please choose from others here if you want music for the scene transitions.

Important

The songs referred to in the play are my ideal suggestions *but* for the purposes of legal rights and permissions you may need to find alternatives. If this is the case please try to be as faithful to my original suggestions as possible. Whichever songs are used, whether my original choices or alternatives, you are responsible for securing the necessary rights. There is further advice and guidance from the National Theatre in the Company Handbook which all National Theatre Connections companies receive when performing this play.

An invitation to everyone who takes part in this play

Please talk to any elders in your life – grandparents, family members, friends and community elders, members from social clubs and groups within your community, care homes and local area. Make time to sit down with them and talk. Some suggested things to talk about could be:

- What advice would they give their younger selves? (Use the age you currently are as the example age of their younger selves.)
- How do they think elders' opinions are seen and heard by society?
- What do they wish for the younger generation?
- In what ways do they think the youngers and elders of society are similar?
- What is their favourite childhood memory (up to and including late teenage years)?

and finally

This play is about how we are always ourselves, in every moment of our lives, but how society decides where it thinks we should fit in the world depending on our age, and worth, because of it. It's about identity and memories. It's about looking forward and looking back and maybe meeting somewhere in the middle. But most of all it's about how age is revolting. So please, *revolt*!

Have fun,
Abi
x

For a Long Time I Used to Go to Bed Early

A group of well-worn **Childhood Toys** *(they might be a teddy, or a bunny or some other kind of cuddly animal, or a robot, or anything really) are sitting around a table somewhere mellow and safe. They're playing an amiable game of poker or something similar. Some of the* **Toys** *sing softly in the background: 'Unchained Melody'.*

Toy (*to one of the others*)   Raise ya.

Toy   Yeah yeah.

Toy   I'm out.

Throughout this scene the **Toys** *should find ways to show their wear and tear and use over the years of being loved by a child; e.g. one might wring out tears from an oversized ear, one could be constantly trying to mend a worry hole in their seams, another could be putting stuffing back in themselves, or one might be tightening a joint or screw.*

Toy   So, I heard that Jingles got their call.

Toy   Yeah? Oh that's brilliant! So pleased for them.

Toy   Ay. They've waited so long.

Toy   Bet it was lovely.

Toy   It's always lovely.

Toy (*almost to themselves*)   I can't wait for the day I get the call.

Toy   Ah, don't wish it away. Not for them.

Toy   I know, I know. I just mean . . . I miss mine.

Toy   Ay, I get it. It's been so long for me I can't even remember how long it's been.

Toy   But you never forget *them*.

Toy/s (*they all concur*)   Ah true!
Yeah, so true.
How could we?

Toy (*chuckling, recalling a memory*)   Remember when Fuffty got their call?

Much laughter and nods, etc.

Toy   Oh my days yes!

Toy   That was *so* special! The look on their face . . .

Toy   I almost popped my stitching it was so cute!

Toy   I don't mind this waiting you know –

Toy   – oh *endless* waiting –

Toy   – but knowing it's coming . . . well, makes it all worthwhile.

Toy Ay, that it does.

Toy (*laying their cards*) Ahem . . . royal flush.

Toy/s (*much whooping*) Oh, *mate*!
Nice one
Beginner's luck
Pah!

This good-natured chat continues as the cards are dropped, the pot is gathered, etc.

Suddenly there's a noise, but not harsh like a buzzer or bell. More like a happy trill or zing or something like that.

The **Childhood Toys** *gasp then freeze.*

Scene transitions into a classroom in an average comprehensive school. Choose transition music from the playlist.

Right Here, Right Now

A classroom. Piano in the corner, ignored. Loads of young people. Noise, shouting, laughter, general chaos of class before it starts. They're grouped in those age-old tribes of a thousand John Hughes movies: nerd, cool girls, outsiders, ladsladslads, etc. Bits of music (from phones, singing, etc) can be heard like a massive noisy cycle of musical snippets and blasts. This classroom right now is the moment just before a controlled explosion.

There is one girl, **Nina***, who keeps herself pretty much to herself though. Her rucksack is beside her, a small soft toy (***Hopsy***) pokes out when it is accidentally kicked by some of the young people mucking about.*

Mo *spots it, grabs it and holds it up.*

Mo (*laughing*) Oh my GOD. Look at this!

Nina *frantically tries to grab it off them.*

Nina (*yelling*) Give it back!

Arpi Is that a . . . Beanie Baby? Oh my God no way! Those are for little kids! Whaaaat?

Others gather round, start laughing.

Nina Give me it! Give me it back!

Barney (*to* **Mo**) Aw, mate, so cute – suits you.

Mo (*taunting* **Nina**) We got your teddy? Ahhh, do you cuddle it at night?

Lots of laughter and jeers from everyone.

Arpi Who still has a teddy? God . . .

Mo (*to* **Barney**)   Hey, Barney! Here, catch!

Mo *throws the toy to* **Barney** *who catches it and waggles it aloft as* **Nina** *runs over to him and tries to grab it.*

Arpi   Hey, chuck it here!

Barney *throws it to* **Arpi** *who examines it and pushes* **Nina** *away despite her pleading.*

Arpi (*looking at the label*)   Here we go: *Hopsy.* Hopsy the Bunny Beanie Baby.

More laughter and the toy gets flung about to chants of 'Hopsy bunny' and general taunting as **Nina** *tries in vain to get it back, clearly distressed and angry.*

In walks a substitute teacher: Mr/Miss [whichever prefix is required please use throughout] **Manoukian**.

Manoukian (*over the din*)   OI! OI! OI! YOU LOT SETTLE DOWN NOW!

They all shut up pretty quick. Someone throws the toy at **Nina** *who stuffs it into her rucksack.* **Manoukian** *notices this but doesn't say anything.*

Manoukian   Get to your desks, quickly.

Everyone reverts to lethargy.

Come on, at a pace slightly quicker than glacial please.

They eventually get to their desks.

Thank you. Right. Thanks. OK. I'm your substitute teacher for today; Ms Langton is away –

Arpi   What's up with her?

Manoukian   She's indisposed.

Barney   What does that mean?

Manoukian   It's what adults say when they don't want you to know why they're away.

Barney   Who're you then?

Manoukian   I'm Mr/Miss Manoukian –

Mo   Whaaaat?

Manoukian   Man-ook-ee-yan.

Laughter/noise, but good natured.

Manoukian   Yeah yeah, OK, quieten down. I hope you lot are as vocal when actually singing.

Mo   Choir is jokes. Do we have to do it?

General sounds of agreement from all.

Manoukian   Yes, you do.

Mo Oof, nah. Why tho?

Manoukian You have to do it because it's part of the curriculum and group singing has been shown to foster a healthy and harmonious intersectional experience across all age –

Mo YEAH BUT CHOIR SINGING IS FOR MAD OLD PEOPLE THOUGH.

Laughter, chaos.

Manoukian Define old.

The class quietens.

Mo Whut?

Manoukian Define old. What is 'old'?

Mo *Old* people.

Manoukian To you though. What is old *to you*?

Brief pause, then everyone starts to shout out.

Ninety-five!
Seventy!
Oh my God, like forty! –
Oi my mum's forty-five!
Everyone's ancient!
How old are you, sir/miss?

Manoukian That's irrelevant information. Which one of you said 'it's for mad old people'?

Silencio with a side of tumbleweed.

Must've imagined it then. Seriously, who thinks that though? Mad and old?

Arpi I've seen it on the telly. They get all old people to sing in choirs and that.

Classmate And loads of old people are ma– . . . like they have that thing that makes them forget –

Classmate Yeah but when they sing songs from like old times they know all the words –

Barney Yeah my grandad is like that though; he don't know who I am most times. Calls me Albert.

Laughter, ribbing **Barney**, *calls of 'Albert', etc.*

Barney Nah, don't laugh though. He's . . . it's like –

Classmate Maybe he just doesn't like *you*. Maybe he wanted a grandkid called Albert instead of Barney.

Laughter, more ribbing. **Barney** *looks upset.*

Manoukian Oi. Enough.

Class quietens.

Go on, Barney.

A pause, then **Barney** *continues.*

Barney We go see him, every Sunday afternoon. He's in this place –

Transition into a care home.

Barney *is playing on his phone as his* **Mum** *is chatting about nothing much to her father.* **Grandad** *isn't saying anything.*

Barney (*to audience*) She's talking and talking: about the weather, about Dad being useless, about the new Netflix thing she's not even watching. And Grandad . . . I know he's as bored as me because every now and then he'll laugh really loudly like she's just told a good joke even though she's only wanging on about hot flushes and that, but she ignores it and then his eyes fix on me; really laser focused, not faraway like usual, and he'll go:

Grandad It's a thousand yards to escape, Albert. Nothing more. Nothing less. I tell you: a thousand yards.

Barney And Mum goes:

Mum This is Barney, Dad. Barney. Not Albert. Remember?

Barney And she looks sad then. Grandad glares at her, shakes his head like she's proper lost it and:

Grandad He'll always be Albert to me!

Barney I googled 'a thousand yards'. Like, what's a yard anyway? I thought it was what Americans call their gardens but apparently it's a thing from the war – not the one Grandad was in that my dad says was over a stupid tiny island a million miles away – no, this was the first war like a hundred years ago, and it's when soldiers saw so much horror and death they just sort of shut down their brains; to protect themselves from seeing any more –

Mum (*trying not to show her upset, to* **Grandad**) I love you, Dad. I know you know it's us. Me and Barney. We love you.

Grandad A thousand yards, Albert; that's all. A thousand yards' escape before I'm home.

Barney Then he stares into space again and I wonder who Albert is. I think it's a cool name.

Back to the classroom:

Manoukian (*to* **Barney**) Do you think your grandad's a mad old person, Barney?

Barney Well, no. It's just . . . hard, y'know. When he sort of doesn't know me or Mum.

Arpi My nana lives with us and she goes off on long chats about when she was a kid but my mum's always shushing her –

Classmate My nan's the same.

Classmate My aunties are like this allll the time!

Mo And it's always 'Ooh, you kids today don't know how lucky you are' and 'Back in my day you just got on with it, none of this rubbish about pronouns' –

Barney Yeah, but they did live through some mad stuff . . . wars, no iPhones –

Classmate I hate how everything is always our fault. Like, sure, Grandpa, *we didn't destroy the climate.*

Manoukian You know, all these elders were just like you once.

Mad outcry of 'Nah! No way! As if!'

Manoukian Exactly like you. What, you think you're the only teenagers that ever lived?

Mo (*grandstanding*) Only ones that *mattered* yeah, am I right?

General noise of approval.

Manoukian And you lot are going to be old people one day too, believe it or not.

Classmate Nah. No way. I am *not* gonna get old.

Arpi Well, duh, you're not getting any younger.

Barney It just seems really impossible; to be *that* old.

Manoukian And yet, time happens.

Mo Me? I'm gonna live forever *and* stay this hot.

Laughter, noise, someone throws a crumpled-up bit of paper at **Mo**.

Manoukian Oi! No throwing. Come on, settle down, we need to do some actual singing in this class.

Everyone quiets, grumbles, but order sort of returns until:

Mo (*loudly*) Why tho?

Everyone stops.

Manoukian What exactly do you mean, Mo?

Mo This. It's a bit pointless. If we're just going to end up old and busted.

Barney Ah come on, Mo, let's just –

Mo Shouldn't we be learning more maths or something? Stuff that we can use before we cark it –

Manoukian Both are valid no? Maths *and* choir.

Mo Nah. I don't reckon so. I mean, don't get me wrong, I hate maths and that, but you need it for looking after the spenny. Economy in the bin cause of all them oldsters not giving a stuff about anyone but themselves –

Arpi Science too. We're going to need to fix all the mess they've left; climate change, pollution . . .

Manoukian You think it's all the elder generation's fault?

Barney My mum says I won't be able to buy a house because Grandad's generation were all boomers. She's always going on about how she's gonna be stuck with me till I'm like . . . forty.

General buzz of agreement, chuntering, etc.

Arpi They've got it easy. They just watch telly all day; *Inspector Morse* and adverts for those chairs that tip you out of them –

Mo They've all got pensions, going on cruizes –

Barney I mean, we're not saying it's *all* their fault but –

Manoukian Seems to me that you are though.

Pause.

Don't you think our elders deser –

Mo Why you always saying 'elders'? What even is that? *Old*. We say old people.

Manoukian What do you call the elders in your life?

Arpi Well, like *nana* . . . my nana Arshaluys

Barney (*shrugging*) Grandad's just Grandad.

Classmate All my aunties, we just call them 'aunty'.

Manoukian Nina?

No one notices that **Manoukian** *already knows her name; something* **Manoukian** *also takes note of.*

Nina (*startled*) I dunno. I don't . . . I dunno. . .?

Mo (*a bit louder*) Who cares?

There's an uncomfortable pause. **Mo** *looks a bit uncertain but:*

Mo *Our* time's supposed to be now. There's homes and pensions and all of that stuff for them – they're not worrying about the rest of their lives, are they?

Manoukian How do you know they're not? How do you know the elders in your life aren't as worried about the same things you are?

Arpi My nana never stops talking about stuff that happened years ago to ever think about what I'm interested in!

Mo I've only got one set of grandparents, and they're off in some villa in Spain. Not that I ever get to go there. Dad goes mad if anyone ever mentions them.

Classmate Maybe they don't want to see *you*.

Mo Get stuffed.

Manoukian Alright, take it easy.

Classmate I bet that's why they moved to Spain int it? Get away from you, ha ha.

Everyone laughs, but **Mo** *is angry and upset.*

Mo Yeah, well, they're rubbish grandparents. I'll never be like them. I'll be the best grandparent ever – presents, trips, cash, all of that . . .

Mo *trails off, angry, upset but trying not to show it.*

The others are quieter.

Manoukian (*sensing the upset in* **Mo**) Alright then, come on you lot, that's enough enlightened chit-chat, get in a semi-circle. Pick up a songbook on your way, here, come on . . .

The class grumbles but they grab songbooks from a pile on the teacher's desk and get into a semi-circle formation. **Nina**, *clutching her bag, moves her chair slowly.*

Manoukian (*to class, then to* **Nina**) Come on, look lively. You . . . what's your name?

Nina *doesn't respond.*

Manoukian (*not unkindly*) Name?

Barney She doesn't say much.

Arpi She never says anything.

Manoukian Yes, thank you both –

(*To* **Nina** *again.*) Get your chair please, come on . . .?

Nina *pulls her chair over but still says nothing.*

Arpi Nina. Her name's Nina.

Nina *shoots a look of anger at* **Arpi** *for saying her name.*

Manoukian OK, great. Nina, come on. Semi-circle please.

However it happens **Nina**, **Arpi**, **Mo** *and* **Barney** *all end up sitting next to each other.*

Manoukian Right. Let's do some warm-up shall we?

Grumbles from everyone. A few are still mucking around; unsurprisingly **Mo** *is one of them.*

Manoukian *gets on the piano; it's a bit shonky but they get a decent sound out of it.*

Scales, OK? Here we go: deep breaths in.

Plays a few bars of scales, starts singing; some of the class follow but it is really rubbish.

Manoukian   Let's try again. Get air in those lungs. Stand up, everyone.

The singing is a bit better this time but still not everyone joining in or really trying their best. **Nina** *is not singing at all.*

Manoukian (*clearing throat*)   Maybe we should just get stuck straight into a song.

They flip through the song book, spot a song and smile.

Manoukian   OK, I've got the perfect one . . . page 27 please.

They all find the page, a few groan.

Manoukian *begins playing the piano again; it's the opening tinkly chords to 'Sweet Child O' Mine'.*

Manoukian *looks encouragingly to the class but they're all blank.*

Manoukian (*stopping playing*)   You *must* know this?

Classmate   BORING.

Classmate   This is like an *ancient* song.

Barney (*with disgust*)   My *dad* listens to this stuff.

Manoukian   Oh come on, it's a classic!

Classmate   Nah, it's well rubbish.

Manoukian   Well, it's this or 'Somewhere over the Rainbow'.

More grumbles.

Manoukian   Open your minds and your chords will follow.

Arpi   Oh my God, are you actually for real?

Manoukian   Absolutely. Now, come on, again.

Manoukian *begins to play the piano again, same tinkly intro chords.*

The class starts to sing again. It's still not even half-hearted but most of them attempt to sing except **Mo**, **Barney**, **Nina** *and* **Arpi**.

The piano notes get louder; the classmates who are singing move away until the focus is on **Mo**, **Barney**, **Nina** *and* **Arpi**, *and* **Manoukian**. *The four of them realize something weird is happening and look wildly at each other.*

The dinging of the piano notes gets louder, **Mo**, **Barney**, **Nina** *and* **Arpi** *open their mouths and start hitting one note repeatedly; clearly not of their own volition. They look at each other, panicked, unable to stop singing the note.* **Manoukian** *continues playing/casting their spell until a huge crescendo occurs.* **Mo**, **Barney**, **Nina** *and* **Arpi** *suddenly stop for a split second, then draw in a collective, huge and audible breath before a snap blackout.*

The **Childhood Toys** *enter and change the setting to the care home. The* **Childhood Toys** *gently move and rearrange* **Mo**, **Barney**, **Nina** *and* **Arpi** *to be seated in comfy chairs in the care home lounge.* **Manoukian** *has disappeared, as has all trace of the classroom. The song 'The Old Man's Back Again' by Scott Walker is played/sung by the* **Childhood Toys** *as this takes place and becomes the background noise of a TV/ radio in the care home.*

Absolute Scenes

Interior of a care home for elders; lounge. It's daytime and the telly is on, **Mo**, **Barney**, **Arpi** *and* **Nina** *are dozing in comfy chairs. There are a few other* **Elders** *seated/pottering about. Two* **Carers** *enter carrying med trays and nattering. They observe the scene.*

Carer 1 Hello, all! (*To one of the elder residents.*) Hey, Louella, how are you today, my love?

Louella *might look at the* **Carer** *but doesn't respond.*

Carer 2 Ah, lots of sleeping beauties this morning. Come on, everyone, wakey wakey.

Carer 1 Meds and tea! Anyone need a hand to the loo? We all OK?

General murmurings from the **Elders**, *etc.* **Mo**, **Barney**, **Nina** *and* **Arpi** *are still slumbering.*

Carer 2 (*handing out meds and cups of tea to various residents*) Come on, who wants a cuppa?

Mo, **Barney**, **Nina** *and* **Arpi** *start to wake, groggily taking the tea handed to them and slowly looking around. General hubbub around them continues; the* **Carers** *potter about then leave.*

Nina *remains silent through the following exchanges.*

Mo What the –? Where am –?!

Arpi What's going on? Where am I? What the –!

Barney Where am I? What is this?!

Mo, **Arpi** *and* **Barney** *get up; through their movements we see that there is a physical change in their bodies and abilities to move so freely. It is clear that they no longer see their teenage selves; they have become late seventies/early eighties.*

Barney *is the first to kind of put two and two together. He looks at* **Mo**.

Barney M . . . Mo? Mo Driscoll?

Mo (*looking at him, startled*) Yeah! Who are you?! I don't know you!

Barney (*approaching* **Mo**) It's me. Barney! Barney Rushton!

Arpi Barney?!

They both turn to look at **Arpi**.

Mo Barney? What the –

Arpi Mo?! Mo is that YOU?!

Barney Arpi?

Arpi Ye . . . yes . . . I . . . but . . . I don't . . .?

Mo Who are you?

Barney It's me, Mo! Barney! Your mate from school!

Arpi What's happening? What's happened to us?

Barney I . . . I don't know . . .

Mo (*looking down at their hands*)   WHAT IS WRONG WITH MY HANDS?

Arpi Oh God . . . what do I look like? WHAT DO I LOOK LIKE?

Barney You . . . you . . . I dunno, Arpi . . . something's. . . .

Mo, *meanwhile, has found a large mirror on the wall.*

Mo (*looking at self in horror*)   OH MY GOD!

The other two try to rush over (this is not happening fast). When they get there:

Arpi NOOOOO! WHAT IS HAPPENING?!

Barney I . . . it can't be . . . we're . . . we're . . .

General horror and bewilderment, wailing, total confusion as the three of them come to terms with their new age and appearance. **Nina** *has walked over to join them at the mirror and stares at herself, taking it all in, much calmer than the others.*

Nina (*finally*)   . . . Old.

Pause.

Arpi Nina?!

The **Carers** *arrive back in response to all the noise and fuss.*

Carer 1 (*cheerful*)   Well, you've all woken up!

Mo, **Arpi** *and* **Barney** *turn to the* **Carers** *and all start trying to explain what's going on – this is as predictably chaotic as you'd imagine. The* **Carers** *keep a convo going as this continues.*

Carer 2 Ah really? Goodness, all of you have been having fun, haven't you?

Carer 1 (*to* **Carer 2**)   I've never seen anything like it.

Carer 2 (*louder, to the residents*)   Alright! Alright, please, just . . . could we all just –

Carer 1   Has one of the royals done another interview or something?

Carer 2   Must've. Not seen them so animated for weeks.

Carer 1   You know, maybe Betty passing has upset them?

Carer 2   True. I'll get the counsellor in next week for a group chat –

Arpi (*distressed*)   I want my mum!

Mo   Yeah, I'm pretty sure if we're in here then your mum's dead.

This just makes **Arpi** *more distressed; the* **Carers** *try to calm them down.*

Carer 2 (*shouting out the door, but calmly*)   Bit more help in here please!

As the fuss continues another **Carer** *enters. It's the same actor who plays* **Manoukian***. They head over to where everyone is.*

Carer/Manoukian   Hello, hello! Quite the party we're all having here isn't it?

It's not entirely clear whether **Carer/Manoukian** *knows what's going on; their expression is both jovially knowing and just-another-day.*

Mo, **Arpi** *and* **Barney** *don't even notice it's the same person, while* **Nina** *clearly does and breaks into a massive smile and laughs.*

Carer/Manoukian   Nina! So good to see you up and about!

They set about helping the other **Carers** *get everyone seated.* **Carer/Manoukian** *addresses* **Mo** *who is literally speechless for once.*

Carer/Manoukian (*seating* **Mo** *in a comfy chair*)   Mo! You've got visitors! They'll be here in a few minutes. (*To the other* **Carers** *and the other three.*) Come on, let's get you all to your rooms for a bit of quiet time; think you've all got overexcited over nothing.

The other three are led away, still protesting, as **Mo** *sits confused.*

Rachel, **Mo***'s future daughter enters with her own child,* **Ernie**, *the future grandchild of* **Mo**. **Ernie** *is constantly on his phone but with one ear on the convo. (NB: use pronoun as fits.)*

Rachel   Hello, Mum/Dad! Look, Ernie's come with me today. Say hi to your Nan/Gramps/Grandy Ernie.

Ernie   Hey, Nan/Gramps/Grandy.

Mo   What? Who . . . who are you?

Rachel   It's Ernie, Mum/Dad/par.

Mo   I don't know any Ernie. Who are you?

Rachel   It's me, Rachel. Your daughter.

Ernie   They never remember.

Rachel Get off your phone and talk to your Grandad/Grandma/Grandy.

Mo You're not my daughter/son! I can't have a daughter/son!

Ernie See?

Rachel Ernie! Mum/Dad/par, please, it's me, Rachel.

Mo I don't want you. I'm Mo. I want my mum.

Rachel Please, Mum/Dad/par –

Mo – Stop Saying Mum/Dad/par! I'm Mo. I want to go back to school. I want all this to be over.

Rachel *struggles to contain her upset.* **Ernie** *clocks this.*

Ernie Hey, Gran– er . . . *Mo.* Why don't you tell us about school? Like, memories of it and that?

Mo (*in a rush*) They're *not* memories. It's right now. There's Arpi, and Barney Rushton and another girl, Nina, here too. We were in class; and the teacher was a sub . . . I think we were . . . singing? And now we're here and we're old and it's awful.

Rachel Wha–? Calm down, Mum/Dad/par . . . I don't –

Ernie Wait, you've got friends here?

Mo Yes! From school. They're all here.

Rachel (*a bit brighter, pleased*) Well, you're making friends! That's great, Mum/Dad/par.

Ernie And you're singing? Like, a choir?

Rachel Oh yes! I've seen this sort of thing on telly; a choir for . . . (*Pauses.*)

Mo No! No, you don't understand. Something happen –

Ernie What are you singing? Is it something cool? Can we come listen?

Rachel Ooh yes! Are you doing a show? What a fantastic idea!

Mo What? No! There's no sh–

Ernie Are your mates in it? You singing old stuff or . . . oh my God, *please* let it be Lil Nas X –

Mo SHUT UP!

They both shut up.

Mo Listen. Can you get me out of here?

Rachel (*sad again*) Oh, Mum/Dad/par. We've talked about this before. It's not safe –

Mo I know it's not safe! Look what's happened! School wasn't safe!

Rachel But this is the best place for you.

Ernie   You kept falling over.

Mo   Ohhh, you're not listening to me! I'm trying to explain –

Rachel   You said you liked it here. I thought you were ha–

Mo (*frustrated*)   You don't understand . . .

Rachel   Please don't get yourself upset, Mum/Dad/par.

Mo (*trying to make it make sense, talking to themselves*)   I was at school. I was in class. I was . . . chatting back to the sub . . . we were in . . . choir?

Rachel   I'm so glad you're getting involved in some activities.

Mo   No you don't understand . . . we were all there –

Rachel   Yes! It's good for you. And your friends

Mo *sits, frustrated and angry, as their daughter and grandson jabber away in the background – then a lightbulb appears to ding in their head. They get up from their chair.*

Mo   OH MY GOD . . .

Rachel *and* **Ernie** *stop jabbering, look at* **Mo** *expectantly, a bit confused.*

Mo (*triumphant*)   The choir class!

Pause.

Mo   IT WAS THE FLIPPING CHOIR CLASS!

The **Childhood Toys** *lead a transition into* **Barney**, **Mo**, **Arpi** *and* **Nina** *sat in the care home lounge again. It's now the evening.*

Let It Rain

Barney, **Mo** *and* **Arpi** *sit holding the ubiquitous cups of tea and looking a bit shellshocked.* **Nina** *looks surprisingly content.* **Mo** *is talking very animatedly.*

Mo   – my *daughter* and my *grandkid* are sat there like this is *all completely normal* and every time I try and explain it they're looking at me like I'm mad and . . . and . . . anyway, the point being . . . (*Deep breath.*) I think we've been cursed.

They all look at **Mo** *with varying shades of disbelief.*

Barney   Cursed? Cursed . . . *how*?

Mo   Think about it. What were we all doing right before we ended up like this?

They try. Not successfully. Blank faces, except for **Nina** *who just looks amused.*

Mo   Where were we? Think!

Arpi   I can't remember.

Mo   Yes you can. Come on.

Barney (*thinking hard*)   We were . . . at school . . . in class?

Mo   In class, yes. But *what* class was it?

Arpi   Oh yeah! That's right . . . we were supposed to be doing –

Barney   Choir practice!

Mo   Exactly! And what else?

Barney   I can't remember.

Arpi (*lightbulb moment*)   Ohhhhh . . . we had a sub . . . Mank . . . Mankoupan?

Barney   Mankofran!

Nina   Manoukian. Their name was Manoukian.

Arpi   They made us sing! Like really really loudly and that one note –

Barney   It was like a ringing, a ringing that was like something not normal . . .

Arpi   Ohhh . . . were they a . . . a . . . witch?

Mo   They must've been! It's the only thing I can think of.

Barney   OH MY GOD, they did curse us!

Mo   They cursed us because we were so rubbish at choir!

The three of them are spent; this moment of revelation has knocked them sideways. **Nina** *meanwhile sips her tea.*

Barney   So . . . how do we . . . ?

Mo   I . . . I dunno.

Arpi (*frustrated*)   Arghhh! I just want to go home!

Barney   Let's make a run for it.

Mo   Make a run for it. Haha. Look at the size of my ankles, I ain't running anywhere.

Arpi   Why does *everything* hurt?

Mo   And anyway it's not like we can just walk out is it? The door's locked to stop everyone wandering off.

Arpi   No way. Is this it? We're stuck here?

They descend into an argument as **Nina** *watches on.* **Carers** *enter, go about their rounds, plumping cushions, helping* **Elders***, etc. This conversation takes place against the backdrop of* **Arpi***,* **Mo** *and* **Barney** *arguing.*

Carer 1 (*to* **Carer 2**)   Have you seen Bob?

Carer 2   Went to bed early.

Carer 1   Really? You know, I think . . . maybe he's going soon.

Carer 2 Ah no! Oh I love Bob, such a gent. But that last bout of flu really took it out of him

Carer 1 Shall I call his daughter? Just in case?

Carer 2 No. He'll be right till morning. Tough cookie is our Bob. Besides they were in visiting him only yesterday.

(*Noticing* **Arpi**, **Mo** *and* **Barney** *arguing*.) What is going on with that lot?

Carer 1 (*looking over at them*) Must be something in the water! They've been at it all day.

Carer 2 (*calling over to them*) All alright over there? Mo? Need anything?

They all hush.

Mo Er . . . no thanks . . . we're all . . . er . . . *fine*.

Carer 2 (*to* **Carer 1**, *not unkindly*) I don't trust that Mo. Troublemaker.

Carer 1 Cheeky so and so. Shouldn't knock it though. All your faculties at their age, I'd probably still be giving out to be honest.

They finish their rounds.

Carer 1 I think I'll just pop by Bob's room. Check in, make sure he's comfy.

Carer 2 OK. I'll get a coffee going for when you're done.

Carer 1 Ah thanks, love. See you in a sec.

They leave in opposite directions. Focus back on **Barney**, **Mo**, **Nina** *and* **Arpi**.

Barney So that's it then. We're stuck here.

Mo Cursed.

Nina Yeah, that's not it.

They all look at her.

Nina There's no curse. We just got old.

Mo I didn't get old! We didn't get old! This . . . this isn't . . . who we are –

Nina Why? You think you're not Mo because you've got white hair and wrinkles? That's exactly who you are.

Barney I reckon you actually like it here. Look at you, eating cake, drinking tea.

Arpi (*disgusted*) Watching *Homes Under the Hammer*.

Mo Don't seem like you want to get out of here.

Nina Oh, right. You all want to talk to me now?

They all look at her, nonplussed.

Nina When we were at school, did any of you talk to me?

Silence.

Nina   Was I in any of your WhatsApp chats? Going down to the centre with you?

They are quiet.

Nina   Don't worry. I'm not mad at you. Even when the only time you did notice was to laugh at me and Hopsy.

The others look confused.

Arpi   Hopsy?

Nina   Yeah. And you know what? The fact none of you even remember makes it even worse . . . but maybe you can legit blame old age now.

Nina *pulls out her Hopsy the Bunny Beanie Baby toy.* **Hopsy** *the* **Childhood Toy** *enters simultaneously and joins* **Nina** *to hold their hand/comfort her as she speaks.*

Mo (*laughing, proper snarky*)   Oh my days. The bunny. I'd forgott–

Barney (*angrily*)   MATE.

Mo *shuts up.*

Nina   Hopsy was in my hand when we all woke up here. Just like always. So when you threw her round to each other that day, making fun of me . . .

She stops, upset at the memory.

I know what you all think of me. You think I was stupid? I heard everything you said; 'bout my old clothes, my shoes being Primark and that. And Hopsy . . . you just kicked her about and laughed at me still having a toy at my age.

Nina *gets up/moves and* **Hopsy** *mirrors her movements. They might move around the room/space gathering and tidying things as she speaks.*

(*As* **Nina** *is speaking the below monologue an* **Elder** *(***Bob***) sneaks back into the residents' lounge and settles himself into a chair nearby. They don't notice him.*)

Nina   Listen, I've got no one. Never did have. No one except Hopsy.

Pause.

I don't even remember where they came from – maybe it was some foster parent or a social worker who felt sorry for me. Because all my life I've lived *in* homes; foster homes, children's homes, but never *my* home.

Pause.

Mo, my mind is blown: you got to meet *your kid* . . . your *grandkid*! And, Arpi; I'd watch all the times you'd bring in packed lunches your nana made. I never had recipes special for me, but I think it'd be nice to know there's tastes you remember when you think of your nana.

Pause.

So yeah, I do like it here, and I wish you could understand that it makes no difference to me if I'm fifteen or if I'm eighty. So excuse me if I tell you that I'm tired. Not cos I'm this old lady; years on from that girl you ignored and made fun of because of a stupid old toy. But just that I'm tired and I want to sleep; happy to be fed, happy to have a bed and happy to be *home*.

Pause.

Because when I wake up tomorrow – *however* I wake up tomorrow – it's still me, still here . . . and I'll take that, whatever it is.

She lets that land. **Arpi** *picks up the Hopsy toy and goes to where* **Nina** *is, gently handing it over.*

Mo I'm . . . sorry, Nina. I . . . I was a total numpty.

Nina (*nodding, smiling in acknowledgement of their apologies and understanding*) 'Night.

The others watch her leave. A few moments while they process, then:

Mo (*voice lowered, conspiratorial*) Well, I'm glad she's happy but I still want to get out of here. I'm not staying like this.

Barney But what can we do? No one listens to us.

Mo I don't care. I'm not sticking around to . . . to *die*

Arpi Mo! Don't say stuff like that . . . I don't want to –

Barney What exactly do you think you're gonna do then?

Mo *We're* gonna bust out of here.

Pause.

Barney What? You're kidding? How?

Arpi And what happens if we do get out? Where do we go?

Mo (*voice rising*) I dunno. I'll worry about that after. I just want to get out of here –

Arpi Shhhhush!

Mo (*still louder*) Nah, I'm not shushing. I'm out of here. You in or out?

Arpi *and* **Barney** *look at each other, then at* **Mo**, *just as one of them is about to speak* **Bob** (**Barney**'s *grandpa from the earlier scene*) *who, without them noticing, has been listening in for some time, speaks:*

Bob I'm IN!

They all freak.

Mo Oh my GOD! Who the heck –? How long have you been standing there?

Bob Long enough to hear about the great escape you're planning!

Arpi Oh my God, no! Shouldn't you be in bed or something?

Bob Why? You're still up.

Mo He has a point.

Barney *meanwhile has been regarding* **Bob** *curiously.*

Barney (*to* **Bob**) You . . . I . . . this is so strange . . .

Arpi What Barney? What is it?

Barney I dunno . . . just . . . it's like I . . . like I know you?

Bob (*sticking out his hand to* **Barney**) Bob's the name. Escape's the game.

He salutes them all, smiling broadly.

Arpi Oh my God.

Barney God, this is so weird. I feel like I know you but I . . . I can't remember . . .

Bob Happens all the time, my friend, don't fret about it. More important things to worry about. So, what's the plan?

Mo Plan?

Bob Getting out of here! You do have a plan?

Arpi What? No! Look, you can't . . . you can't come with us –

Bob No man, or woman, left behind!

Mo No, no way. Sir. Bob . . . argh! Listen, you need to . . . to go to bed and just –

Bob I know where they keep the spare night key.

Pause.

Mo What's that now?

Bob The spare night key. I know where it's hid.

Arpi Where?

Bob Oh no, I'm not telling you. I'll *show* you!

He sets off to the main door; they all follow.

Barney (*mumbling to himself*) Why can't I remember?

It's predictably slow and shambolic as **Bob** *leads them to the door where he picks up a small decorative vase nearby, tipping it up to reveal a key.*

Bob Not so daft now, eh?

They gather round as he unlocks the door, pulling it open and triggering a red light and a quiet bell which clearly alerts the **Carers** *who come running.*

Mo (*trying to get out the door; remember, everyone is in their eighties and nothing is moving fast*) Quick, before they –

The **Carers** *start shepherding them all back from the door.*

Carer 1 (*not unkindly*) Bob! Not again!

Bob It wasn't me! It was this lot – they made me do it!

Mo Hold up; you were the one who –

Carer 3 That's enough now, come on, everyone, let's get you to bed –

Bob This is elder abuse!

Carer 1 How about if I get you a slice of malt loaf and a cuppa, Bob?

Bob (*immediately capitulating*) Ooh that'd be lovely!

Carer 2 Right come on, everyone, that's enough excitement for one day. Honestly, I don't know what's got into you all.

Carer 3 You know there's two more doors before you can get out . . .

Barney (*looking at* **Bob**) If I could just remember . . .

Carer 1 (*helping* **Barney** *away*) I know, love, now, let's get you all to bed . . .

They're all led away, still protesting as the lights dim.

The **Childhood Toys** *enter and reset the scene. They might sing as they do so (Cher: 'Turn Back Time').*

A Madeleine's Just a Fancy Name for Lemon Cake

It's the next morning in the care home. Our gang are seated around a table with some of the **Elders** *also there.* **Nina** *is happily eating toast and helping one of the* **Elders** *with their food.*

Mo Dunno why she's so happy.

Arpi Maybe she's hungry, Mo. Just . . . can you just . . .

Mo What? Relax? I don't know about you but I did not have a good night.

Nina Heard about your attempted jailbreak. Bob's thirteenth try apparently.

Arpi He's an absolute danger.

Mo Yeah, well, it was a stupid idea anyway.

Barney It was *your* idea.

Mo Whatever.

Nina Someone's grouchy.

Arpi Can you all just . . . shut up?

Barney I'm so tired. I had to get up four times to pee last night. Took me like twenty minutes each time.

Arpi It's exhausting being old.

Mo Took me an hour to send a text. Stupid busted fingers.

The others all stare at **Mo** *like 'WHAAT?'*

Barney You've got a phone?!

Mo Yeah. Found it in my room last night. It's this random thing with massive buttons and oh my God the smallest screen I could barely read, and it took *forever* to type and I'm starting to understand why old people are so narky all the time because their phones are basically crap.

Arpi Who did you text?

Mo Dee.

Barney Dee? What? Why would you te–

He breaks off suddenly, having a lightbulb moment

Barney Nahh! DEE? Oh, mate. I never –

Arpi Wait, what? You and Dee? Whaaat? How long –

Nina They've been seeing each other for like *months*.

Mo, **Barney** *and* **Arpi** *all stop, stunned at* **Nina** *offering this info.*

Mo You . . . how –?

Nina (*shrugging, munching on toast*) I might be invisible to you lot but I'm not blind.

Arpi *laughs, impressed.*

Barney Did she message back?

Mo Nope. Stupid clown phone.

Arpi OMG. Stop. Maybe you *married* Dee and that's where your daughter came from!

Barney Haha, you married *Dee Dhawan!*

Mo Shut up, God, this is doing my head in.

Arpi Can I borrow the phone, Mo? I want to try and call my mum.

Mo Be my guest.

Nina It won't work.

Arpi Well, it can't hurt to try . . . Mo, can you get it for me?

Mo Mate, in a bit. My legs.

Arpi I just . . . I just want to talk to my mum. I . . . I can't not speak to Nana again. I just *can't* . . .

Nina (*seeing* **Arpi**'s *distress, moving to comfort her*) Hey. It's OK . . . don't . . . please don't –

Arpi My nana . . .

The others are lost, not sure how to comfort her. They're all feeling mad emotions but this is something they can't deal with, as much as they want to help **Arpi***.*

A **Carer** *enters carrying a small dish. Bustles over, bright and cheerful. Sets the dish down on the table.* **Arpi** *looks up, sees what it is, exclaims loudly.*

Carer Special breakfast!

Arpi *is staring at the dish in amazement. The others are totally baffled by what's going on.*

Arpi But . . . this . . . this is manti?

Carer Yes! From the recipe you gave us. Thought we'd surprise you . . . Cook followed the instructions to the letter. We've all tried it and, oh my goodness, it is delicious!

The **Carer** *keeps chattering on as they pass a plate to* **Arpi***, who takes it, stunned.*

Carer I've never had anything like this before. Is it an old family recipe, Arpi?

Arpi *is silent for a moment, then:*

Arpi It's . . . it's my nana's.

A transition to:

Three generations of women in **Arpi***'s family are busy in Nana* **Arshaluys***'s kitchen.* **Arpi** *addresses the audience but* **Takush** *and* **Arshaluys** *speak within the scene.*

Arpi When my Nana Arshaluys and Mama and all my family came to this country, they brought nothing but recipes. That's what Nana Arshaluys told me.

Takush I was your age. Tiny. I was terrified –

Arshaluys I was terrified too. But less of this new world, with so much rain all the time!

Arpi Nana and Granpa fled. Like, literally fled. Not like in a film, where the time jumps quick and then you're here –

Takush No, it was the slowness of our going. And the lie –

Arshaluys Taku! I had to lie, there was no other way –

Arpi I understand. But I can't . . . I can't imagine –

Takush I understand, Mama, I do. But back then I was a little girl, and my life was gone as we sailed on that ship and –

Arshaluys We did what we had to do to keep you safe. I wish –

Arpi I wish my mum could have had the childhood she was meant to have, but then I know she'd not have met dad, or made me or any of this –

Takush I know, Mama, I know. And look at my beautiful Arpi –

Arshaluys It's in our blood, Arpi; to survive. My mama, my papa . . . they fled too, running into the night with a few gold coin –

Arpi Around my mum's neck; that necklace I know one day I'll get.

Takush (*rummaging in a cupboard, finds something*) Mama, *why* do you keep this old kchuch pot?

From this point **Arpi** *is within the scene and talking to her nana and mum.*

Arpi What's a kchuch pot?

Arshaluys Takush! My own daughter! How does the child not know what a kchuch pot is?

Takush Mama. It's just a baking dish.

Arshaluys Just a baking dish?! *Just* a baking dish?! Takush Sarkissian, you watch your mouth. This is not *just* a baking dish –

Takush Mama, you know what I mea–

Arpi (*laughing*) Nah, go on, nana, tell her off!

Arshaluys This is no funny thing, Arpi. This . . . this pot . . .

She holds the dish, runs her hands over it, lost for a moment

Arshaluys This pot is our *history*. It is our *survival*. My own mother –

She falters, **Arpi** *looks at her mum, and* **Takush** *comes over so all three women are seated together, the pot between them.* **Arpi** *takes her nana's hand.*

Arpi Nana, I'm sorry. I didn't mean to laugh.

Arshaluys (*sadly*) I carried this with me all the way. It was all I had left of *my* mother.

Takush Mama . . .

Arshaluys Every meal made in this pot is thousands of miles, do you understand, Arpi?

Tiny pause.

Arpi I do, Nana. I do. Shall . . . shall we make manti together?

Takush Nana is tired, Arpi, let's not –

Arshaluys I'm not tired. Takush!

Takush *and* **Arpi** *are quiet.*

Arshaluys (*more gently*) Please.

Pause.

Let me remember.

Arpi *moves away from the table, out of the scene again.*

Arpi So we listen to her. Mama sighs, but she's not mad or anything. It's really . . . it's really hard to hear some of it. But I'm glad Nana is telling me, because I feel like this is as much a part of me as it is her; remembering all the things she can't ever forget.

30   Abi Zakarian

Transition back to the care home:

Arpi *reaches for the food from the* **Carer**.

Arpi   Thank you.

Carer   That's alright, my love. Hopefully it's like a little bit of home isn't it?

Arpi (*happily eating, smiling broadly, lost in the taste*)   It's just like my nana used to make.

The others all dig in.

The **Childhood Toys** *enter and 'Help the Aged' by Pulp plays as the scene becomes a montage of many days as the four of them get used to life in the care home. We see the carers helping them and we see the routine of their days (mark the passing of each day somehow) until eventually everyone is in chairs.*

Old Familiar Faces

Arpi, **Mo**, **Barney** *and* **Nina** *and lots of* **Elders** *are doing chair tai chi. Some of the* **Childhood Toys** *might be doing it too. One of the* **Carers** *is leading the class. NB: the dialogues of the* **Carer**, **Barney**, **Mo**, **Arpi**, **Nina** *and other* **Elders** *can overlap.*

Carer (*doing the movement 'waterfall'*)   – and raise the arms slowly, and melt down . . . float up. Lovely, nice and gently . . . go as high as feels comfortable . . . that looks perfect, Judy . . . raise slowly . . . and float down. And rest palms on knees and breathe for a moment.

Mo (*to the others who are seated nearby*)   This is surprisingly soothing.

Barney   Right? Four days of this and I can get out of bed in under two minutes now.

Carer   OK. Let's do Fisherman Casts the Net . . .

Arpi   Oh I love this one! Reminds me of Kung Fu Panda –

Mo   You look like Kung Fu Panda –

Arpi   At least I can do Turtle Swims in the Ocean without complaining about how much my knees hurt.

Carer   . . . lift the arms to the side, left hand lowest, right hand highest, and swoop them down and to the other side . . .

Nina   Amoy – they've got the room next to Mo – told me they have to listen to Mo farting all through the night.

They all laugh at **Mo** *who looks indignant*

Mo   I do *not*.

Barney   Yeah you do. It's worse than when you were at school.

Carer   . . . rotate the hands over so the left hand is top and the right hand is bottom and now we sweep the net down to the other side . . . perfect . . . nice and smooth . . .

Arpi   Do you miss school?

Barney   I guess. Not much we can do about it though is there?

Mo   Until we come up with a plan that doesn't involve us moving at high speed or convincing anyone under the age of sixty that we're not all bonkers . . . so, er . . . *never.*

Carer   . . . now let's do the three slow arm circles to end; lift the arms up . . . round and down . . .

Arpi   I still reckon Mr/Miss Manoukian had something to do with it . . .

Carer   . . . three, and then rest the hands on our laps . . . and we're done. Hope your joints feel a bit more soothed . . . those of you who can, pop your chairs to the side, I'll fetch up the rest . . .

They pick up their chairs and move them.

Nina   You could always ask them.

Mo   Ask who?

Nina   Mr/Miss Manoukian.

Mo   You getting confused, Nina? Hopsy been chatting rubbish again?

Nina   They work here.

The other three all stop and stare at her.

Arpi   That's not funny. Nina.

Barney   Wait, are you being serious?

Nina   Mmhmm.

Mo   Is this a joke?

Nina   I'm not joking. I thought you'd clocked them like I had?

Barney   You *are* serious?

Mo   They're actually *here*?

Nina   Yeah. I thought you knew.

Arpi   What? Do you think if we knew we'd be . . . we'd be doing flippin tai chi in chairs?!

Barney   And what do you mean they *work* here? Like . . . like *teaching*?

Nina   No. Like a carer.

Mo   Where are they then? I haven't seen them. Ever. Have you?

Nina   Well, yeah. That first day.

Barney/Mo/Arpi   WHAT?

Nina   They came in when we were all kicking off and that.

Mo   Why didn't you say anything then?!

Nina   I dunno. I thought you'd seen them too . . .

Barney   Do you not think we'd've said something?

Nina *shrugs, a bit sheepishly.*

Mo   Have you seen them again, Nina? Since we've been here?

Nina   No.

Barney   Honestly? You're not holding out on us are you?

Nina   Why would I do that?

Arpi   Because we all know you don't mind being here; you've literally sold your younger self out for unlimited own brand Battenberg slices.

Nina   I swear. I only saw them that one time.

Barney   So where are they?

Mo   How should I know? We'll just have to watch for them. And when they show up again we . . . we . . . grab them!

Arpi   *Grab them*? That's your brilliant idea?

Mo   Well, I dunno!

Arpi   Because I don't know if you've noticed but we're not exactly up to MMA standards, so *grabbing* might not be the best plan we can come up with.

They all sit, a bit stunned. Eventually:

Nina   Look, I'm sorry I didn't say anything sooner. I just . . . thought that sooner or later we'd just . . . I dunno . . . go back?

Tiny pause.

Arpi   I thought that too.

Mo   Well, if we do ever see them again . . . what do we do?

They all sit in silence, thinking.

Barney   Maybe . . . maybe we don't do anything?

As this is going on **Amoy** *approaches them.*

Amoy   (*holding out a card*)   Hello, gang. Would you like to sign this?

Barney   (*distracted*)   What's this?

Amoy   Its a card. For Bob.

Barney (*taking it thinking it's a birthday card*)   Bob? Oh right, *Bob* . . . er, how old is he?

Amoy   Oh dear, no, not his birthday. It's . . . for Bob . . . well, his family. On account of his passing.

They all stop what they're doing, shocked.

Arpi   Bob . . . escape Bob?

Amoy (*laughing*)   Yes, that's him.

Mo   Ah, OK. Well . . . we're really sorry. We didn't know him that well though –

Amoy (*gently*)   Why yes you did! Lovely Bob.

(*Tiny pause after seeing their blank faces.*) Bob Rushton.

Barney (*after a split second*)   I'm sorry? You said Bob . . . *Rushton*?

Amoy   Yes. Bob. Always playing cards. Oh we shall miss –

Barney   But . . . that's . . . Bob . . . Robert . . . my . . .

(*To* **Amoy**.) You're saying he was here? My grandad was *here*?

Amoy   Your grandad? Oh love. Come on now, you know Bob.

Barney   My grandad . . . Robert Rushton.

Amoy   Such a lovely man; always so nicely turned out. Not so many make the effort these days. I blame TikTok.

Barney   When . . . when did he . . .?

Amoy   Pass? Oh, a few days ago. Peaceful. He had a good innings.

Arpi (*realizing*)   Barney. I'm so sorry.

Amoy   You want to sign it?

Mo (*stepping in*)   Yeah, course we will, Amoy. Tell you what, leave it with us.

Amoy   Oh lovely, thank you. Pop it back when you're done. Such a lovely man . . .

Amoy *leaves. The others gather round* **Barney**.

Mo   I'm sorry, mate.

Nina *squeezes* **Barney**'s *shoulder.*

Barney   My own grandad. I didn't recognize him.

Arpi   It's . . . it's weird here . . . the time, and everything, all distorted –

Barney   How could I have not recognized him? (*He trails off.*)

They're all suddenly lost for words until:

Nina   Sign the card.

Barney (*dazed*)   What?

Nina   You should sign the card. He was your grandad after all; you're family.

Arpi   Yes. Nina's right, you should, Barney.

Barney *looks a bit lost.* **Mo** *opens the card to give to* **Barney***, smiles when they look in it.*

Pause.

Mo (*smiles*)   Look . . . look, Barney.

Shows him the card.

Barney (*reading the card, seeing how full it is*)   All these names, all the messages . . .

Nina (*reading from the card over his shoulder*)   'Bob was one of my best friends here; he never stopped smiling . . .'

Arpi   'I would play cards with Bob every day and he'd always let me win on a Thursday . . .'

Mo   'Bob talked about his family every single –'

They break off here, then gather themselves.

'Bob talked about his family every single day. He loved you all so much.'

Arpi *and* **Nina** *comfort* **Barney***.*

Mo   He sounds brilliant, Barney. I wish . . . I wish I'd had a grandad like him.

Barney   They said he went peaceful didn't they?

Nina   Yeah. And it sounds like he was happy.

Arpi   That's important, that he went happy.

They all hug.

Barney (*laughing, gently*)   I only saw him a few days ago. Back when I was . . . before all this happened. Me and Mum visited. It must've been here.

Pause.

I should've paid more attention to him . . . I just wish . . .

He trails off.

Arpi   What? What is it?

Barney (*he starts to write in the card, almost to himself*)   I just wish I'd found out who Albert was . . .

They all look at him, a bit confused.

The **Childhood Toys** *enter and gently reset the scene as day turns to night then to morning again.*

Everything Old Is New Again

Our gang are all sat around a table having a cup of tea.

Mo   How'd you sleep, Barney?

Barney   Not too bad. I actually had a dream about my grandad.

Arpi   My mum always says when she dreams of my grandad it's like he's come to visit her, just to check she's OK. And they're walking on a beach, or in a park or somewhere. Just chatting and that.

Nina   About what?

Arpi   She never remembers. All she remembers is that it was nice to see them for a bit.

Barney   Yeah, it was like that.

Mo   Well, I'm glad you're feeling better, mate.

Arpi   So, what's on the agenda for today?

Nina   Art club.

Mo   Team quiz tonight.

Arpi   Cook's trying out my nana's dolmades recipe for dinner.

As they chat on the **Carers** *come in to clean away the breakfast things. One of them is* **Carer/Manoukian** *but no one notices yet and they keep chatting.*

Barney   You know. If we never go back . . . well, I'm glad I'm in here with you lot.

Pause.

Arpi   Me too.

Mo   Oh great, I have to agree now don't I? Otherwise I'll look like an idiot.

They laugh and carry on chattering.

Nina   Wait, what about me?

The other three stop nattering and look at her.

Nina   Don't you want to know what I feel about staying here?

There's a tiny pause before the others laugh madly, **Nina** *joins in and all we see at this moment is four* **Elders** *living their best life.*

Carer/Manoukian *wipes the table in front of them, smiling.*

Carer/Manoukian (*jovial*)   I see the four musketeers are thick as thieves again. You know, we all think you're plotting a revolution or something?

Mo (*turning to face* **Carer/Manoukian**, *still laughing*)   Yep, that's righ–

Mo *stops sharply, staring at* **Carer/Manoukian**. *The others are all like 'what?'*

Carer/Manoukian   You alright, love?

Nina *looks at* **Carer/Manoukian** *then starts nudging* **Arpi** *and* **Mo** *prods* **Barney**.

Barney (*doing a really rubbish throat-clearing/cough noise*)   Excuse me.

Carer/Manoukian   Yes, Barney, my love?

Barney   It's you, isn't it?

Carer/Manoukian (*kindly, cheerily*)   Yes, love. It is.

Mo   Seriously tho. It's *you*.

Carer/Manoukian (*a little bit slower, but with kindness*)   Yes. It is me.

Arpi   We're right, aren't we?

Carer/Manoukian   I don't think I'm following you, love.

Pause.

Nina   Oh for – . . . look, we know you're Mr/Miss Manoukian. Our teacher . . . well, our sub . . .

Barney   – from school.

Arpi   – we were supposed to be doing choir. Miss Langton was –

Mo   – INDISPOSED!

Barney   – yes! And you did something like –

Arpi   – like magic or a spell on us because . . . because . . . we –

Mo   – we were mucking about, like being absolute –

Nina   – total nightmares, not listening, not singing –

Arpi   – and the sound got louder and louder until –

Barney   – until –

All of Them   – until we got . . .

They flounder. They can't say it, don't know how to. **Carer/Manoukian** *has been listening to them with a gentle smile. Finally:*

Carer/Manoukian   . . . Old?

They all fall silent.

Carer/Manoukian (*pulling up a chair*)   I prefer 'elder' myself. 'Old' is too short a word. Like a full stop, don't you think?

Nina   I prefer 'elder' too. It's like it's got a bit more to give?

They look at her. Then at **Carer/Manoukian**.

Carer/Manoukian   It's a privilege to age I reckon, don't you?

Pause.

They all nod in agreement. **Manoukian** *waits.*

Barney (*clears throat again*)   I . . . I was just saying, that I dreamt of my grandad last night.

Carer/Manoukian   Ah, that's lovely to hear, Barney. Bob was such a wonderful man. The stories he'd tell!

Barney   That's the thing, all the stories he'd tell and I never listened. But, in the dream it was different. I don't remember what we spoke about, just . . . how nice it felt listening to him talk . . . and I . . . I was thinking that maybe it's not the last breath we take that matters. Maybe it's the last breath . . . we *give*.

Arpi (*moved by this, thinking on*)   Yes, like a goodbye note you leave to the world – a great big breath; coming out of your lungs, up into the air, into the sky – forever going . . .

Mo (*seamlessly picking up* **Arpi***'s words*)   . . . made up of all the spit and stuff and everything you ever lived in your life. All the time we were here. All the time we were in the world.

Nina   The last breath we *give*. That's the thing. That's the thing that matters.

Pause.

I know I said I didn't care about being like this, being here . . . but . . . well, I think, maybe things would be . . . maybe *we* would be different now, if we were young again?

They all nod, smiling at each other; they exhale together. A lovely sort of peace settles in the air.

Carer/Manoukian   Oof. That was quite deep wasn't it? Ha.

Pause, clapping hands together.

Tell you what, do you all fancy a sing-song?

They all stare.

Carer/Manoukian   Always makes me feel good. If I've had a long day full of deep thoughts, you know?

Pause.

Mo   You want us to *sing*?

Carer/Manoukian   Oh, Mo, absolutely not.

Tiny pause.

I want *you* to *want* to sing.

Nina   Wait. Hold up. Like . . . choir?

Arpi   Ohhh!

They all look at **Manoukian** *who nods over towards the piano.*

Carer/Manoukian That thing's not been played in years. Could be a bit rusty.

Barney I . . . I think we should. I think we definitely should.

They're all starting to get it.

Arpi But . . . but what'll we sing?

They all look at each other.

Mo (*to* **Carer/Manoukian**) Maybe we just let you play? And see what happens?

Carer/Manoukian That is a very good idea, Mo.

They gather round the piano; maybe the **Childhood Toys** *have wheeled it over.*

Carer/Manoukian (*lifting the lid on the piano*) Do you need a bit of a warm-up?

Pause.

Mo Sir/Miss, we're all pushing eighty-plus, I think we're ready.

Laughter.

Carer/Manoukian Right, then, let's go . . .

Carer/Manoukian *begins to play the piano.*

Everyone takes a huge deep breath; everything glistens. They are ready.

They play the first tinkly chords of 'Sweet Child O' Mine' . . . and **Arpi**, **Barney**, **Nina** *and* **Mo** *realize they know the song. Maybe one of them starts off, or maybe* **Manoukian** *does, leading them into the song which they join in a bit shakily at first but as it continues it grows into something organic and full of life; loud, chaotic, joyful. Gradually the other* **Elders** *notice and move to join them and join in, then the* **Carers**, *and the* **Childhood Toys**. *Everyone in fact. All must sing, however suits them. Song: 'Sweet Child O' Mine' (abridge and arrange as required).*

As they sing the scene transitions back to the classroom and the four friends return to their younger selves. **Manoukian** *returns to being their sub teacher and the whole class is back.* **Barney**, **Nina**, **Arpi** *and* **Mo** *all acknowledge and hug each other. We see them revelling in their return; not older but a little bit wiser.*

It all ends with everyone doing air punches, star jumps or whatever feels right.

END*

*(except not quite, because nothing ever really ends . . .)

Bonus End Credits Scene: The Hero Fold

We're back in the setting from the opening scene (I don't want to say heaven because who knows if such a place exists. So let's just say it's somewhere beyond life; the next adventure) exactly at the moment we left it – the zing/trill sounds and all the **Toys** *freeze for a split second then much excitement:*

Toys   OH! IT'S HAPPENING!
YESSS!
Quick, quick, get ready!

(More of this general chatter.)

The **Toys** *are so happy, they leap up from the table, clapping, excited, preparing themselves for something; sort of getting into a line.*

A door opens where there wasn't a door before.

Bob *walks through it, looking a bit confused, but not scared.*

Bob   Hullo?

The **Toys** *don't speak, but they wait expectantly as one of the* **Toys** *tentatively moves forward.*

Bob (*peering at the* **Toy** *who moved forward*)   Al . . . Albert?

Pause.

(*Quietly.*) Albert? Is that . . . is that *you*?

The **Toys** *part to form a pathway and* **Bob** *and* **Albert** *walk towards each other.*

Bob   Oh, Albert! Oh it *is* you!

Both are joyful to see each other again and fall into a happy embrace.

Bob   After all this time. A thousand years, Albert.

Tiny pause.

I knew I'd see you again.

They are back together again, at last.

Snap to blackout.

(actual) END

Age Is Revolting

BY ABI ZAKARIAN

Notes on rehearsal and staging, drawn from a workshop with the writer, held at the National Theatre, October 2023

How the writer came to write the play

Writer Abi Zakarian explained that she was at a point where several elders in her life were entering a certain stage of life: some were moving into care homes, some had been given difficult diagnoses. She was struck by how we look at elders in society and can never imagine them once being young. She recalled when she herself was young and not being able to imagine herself being older. She mentioned how there are links with how both young people and elders are disenfranchized from society and either have no, or lose their own, agency. In a capitalist society you are seen as valid when you're able to work and earn money and spend that money to keep the economy and capitalist system going. Zakarian was spending quite a lot of time in care homes and found herself thinking: what would it be like to wake up one day in a care home where everyone is treating you like you're 80 but you're actually still 15 years old? And suddenly the concept of you trying to explain that to people is met with 'oh poor you, you're confused again'.

Zakarian made a point that as you grow, you adapt, but at your core you are always *you*. She says that there is a lovely opportunity with this play to enable young people to really think about their elders, their relationships with them and vice versa.

Ice breakers

Exercise: Two Truths, One Lie

1. In groups of six, come up with two truths and one lie.
2. Find a creative way to present/stage the two truths and one lie to the group.
3. Present to the wider group.

The wider group must guess which are the truth and which is the lie.

Exercise: Clap

Lead director Daniel Bailey likes to work with frequencies and energies; he finds it useful to let people speak on how they feel. This is a useful exercise to get everyone on the same frequency. The aim of the exercise is to all try to clap at the same time. Everyone is sat in a circle; this is important to the exercise as everyone should be able to see each other. Everyone is sat with their hands out in front of them ready to clap; the clap is felt rather than predetermined.

Approaching the play

Exercise: Facts and Questions

Facts are the things in the play that are contained in the stage directions. Bailey stated that he will take some of the things the characters say as fact but not always.

To make it fun he'll ask the company to say BIG FACTS. Anyone can call a BIG FACT, then everyone will discuss and ask is it a fact or not? Bailey will sometimes have a trophy that someone can win for collecting BIG FACTS. (*Note: BIG FACTS are just facts!*)

You can then use these facts for building the world. You can either present them to your group or you do the facts and world building with them, depending on time.

The group did the exercise and these are some of the facts they collected:

Facts

- The toys understand our world.
- At some point in their life all the toys have been loved.
- When a character passes, they get reunited with the thing that connects them to a certain age. Like when Bob dies and gets reunited with Albert which was his childhood toy. Like when Jingles gets the call, it's because his human has passed so they are reunited and go to the next realm/adventure.
- There are three realms: the realm where the toys are, the realm where the characters can travel through time and then the present.
- Jingles got their call.
- When they get the call it is a happy/positive thing.
- The toys have an awareness of time, unlike the other characters.
- Music and sound are really important to all the different realms/worlds, in particular to the realm where the toys are, as that's how they know something is happening. (*Side note: Music is so important throughout our lives, from when a baby is in the womb and we play music to them, through to when we play music to people with dementia to help them to connect to a certain time.*)
- When music plays it means something is happening, something is changing.
- The toys are friends/friendly with each other.
- The toys are fixing themselves.
- Hopsy isn't in the realm because Hopsy is really present with Nina.
- The toys are positive.
- The toys are aware, but they don't know when they will get their call.

Questions (some of these were answered in the room by Zakarian and Bailey)

Q: Why poker?
A: Because it's a group activity and it's something based around fun. The idea in the play is that, no matter what age you are, you are still you. It's incongruous to see toys playing poker, a high-stakes game but still fun. Zakarian was also inspired by the series of paintings of dogs playing poker by Cassius Marcellus Coolidge.

Q: Where does the personality of the toy come from? Is it from their person?
A: Yes, they pick it up from their person.

Q: When the toys end up in the realm, is it because they've stopped being played with? Or they're in a storage box? On the front of a lorry?
A: They are in their waiting space. Their main purpose is to be with their human and be played with, so when they aren't being played with, they go into the storage, their waiting space.

Q: How long have the toys been here?
A: It's up to you; you can go for the most dramatic, e.g. two years, or funny, e.g. 'you've been here two minutes'!

Q: Do the toys age like people or does time freeze for them?
A: Their wear and tear is their age; for example, if it's a toy robot and it's missing a part that's when time stopped for them or how they are now. You see the love manifested on them as this wear and tear.

Q: Can a toy exist in two realms?
A: Yes. For example: they might be displayed in a museum but would also be in the realm at the same time.

Q: Is Hopsy a small or life-size toy?
A: It's a choice for you whether Hopsy is life-size or a small toy.

Feeling is understanding – if you can evoke some sort of feeling in an audience they will find an understanding. Your job is to communicate the world and idea of the play. Create the rules of the world so you have clear parameters of how the world of the play functions, what works in the world and what doesn't. Those details and clarity that you and the cast have will give the audience understanding. Be specific with the rules you set in the world; for example, in the present world the toys can hear what's going on but can't interfere unless music plays.

When getting a clear idea of the journey of a play some people unit scenes (which are described in detail in Katie Mitchell's book *The Director's Craft*), some people will note events. Bailey shared that he uses 'shifts' as he finds that term more useful. For example, if a brick gets thrown into the room, that's a shift. Things shift every few sentences or so; think of where the shifts are. It is helpful to think of the script as a map.

Characters

Most of the following information on characters comes from the group reading through 'Right Here, Right Now', p.9 (from when Manoukian enters) to p.13 (before Nina speaks) and asking, 'What do we know about the characters?' The rest was discovered through other conversations throughout the day.

All the young people have an awareness of what's going on around them in the world. They have understanding and they have foresight.

All of them have different ways that they engage with the elders in their life.

Manoukian:

- is always showing some sort of magic; for example, when they first enter, they already know all of the children's names, even without having met them before. The children don't realize this when it happens
- is of the middling age range of the characters in the play
- their name is Armenian for 'child'
- is a supply teacher. (There's a question to ask about how much they have manipulated the situation . . .)

Barney:

- is family oriented
- just wants to be seen and is possibly overshadowed by Mo but seems comfortable with that
- is quite comfortable to be vulnerable as he shares stories about his grandad.

Grandad:

- Grandad has experienced war (but which war? Most likely the Falklands conflict during the 1980s).

Nina:

- is an outsider.

Mo:

- is very outspoken, the ringleader, is on the front foot
- doesn't have any engagement with elders in their life, they have no grandparents

- they don't trust elders because they are disconnected from that age group, whereas the other characters either have grandparents they live with or aunties that they see regularly.

Arpi:

- seems to follow Mo in the beginning of the play.

The Toys:

- are always alive
- there are elements of spirituality and consciousness that you can explore through the toys' characters
- there is a parallel between how the toys are treated and how elders are treated in society; how they are discarded once they are no longer seen as useful
- they want to be reunited with their humans, they have an objective
- they aren't just small toys any more; they are life size. The idea of humans being able to go there and reconnect with these toys gives us the reason why the humans can travel to that realm and why the toys are life size.

Think of the characters' journeys. Maybe they start the play unsure, maybe they find safety in being in agreement with everyone else and by the end of the play they have their own voice. Each character will have their individual journey.

When working on the monologues or any moments when characters are talking to the audience, think of who your audience is for those monologues. For example, are the audience Manoukian? Are they the toys?

Exercise: Characters

Instructions: Walk around the room. Find the spaces and fill them. Think of yourself as one of the students in the school in the play, think of their energy: where do they lead from? Think of the pace that these students move at. How do they greet people? Is it a head nod? Is it a hello? What kind of attitude do they embody? Greet someone as you walk past them.

You could do this exercise when everyone is cast or before. You can go around the group as everyone is walking and ask the characters questions: How are they today? Do they like school? Who they are friends with?

When talking to young people during her research for the play, Zakarian reflected that they are very aware of huge world issues like climate change, not being able to buy a house, etc. It felt like their attitude towards ageing, and their understanding of what 'old' is, is more about not being able to see what will happen in the future due to the state of the world. They always have to be present because there's constant change.

Staging

You can make this play work with any staging and any budget.

The spaces in the script are fixed, but it's up to you how they are realized. It's the essence of the space that is important; you can create it with just chairs and bodies and the words. Challenge yourself to see if you can create the scenes, the moments with minimal things, with only just the essentials that are mentioned in the script.

Bailey made the point that he will often keep actors on stage all the time as he thinks it keeps people present. It's a directorial choice how you stage the characters that are not directly in the scene, but they don't have to be off stage.

To explore the staging, the group looked at ways to stage the scene 'Right Here, Right Now' (p. 8). Bailey invited participants to run through the scene and then asked the wider group: What isn't working? And what can we try to fix it? They then ran through the scene again and asked the same questions. Below is how it played out.

After the first run-through of the scene Bailey made these suggestions:

- Let's try the rule that the toys bring people into the space and take them out.
- Let's try that the students don't have an awareness of the toys, they are just being moved.
- Maybe Manoukian ushers in the toys to show that they have the awareness of them there.
- When Barney is telling them the story, the audience becomes the other students in the class that he's telling the story to.
- Let's play with levels: students go to sit down on the floor so focus is pulled to Barney.
- Let's try not all students sitting on chairs.

They ran the scene again.

What didn't work?

- There are too many people in the care home so our focus isn't clear.

Let's try:

- The shift with the toys bringing in the chairs and moving people: this should happen around Barney so he is the focus.
- Exploring the energy that the toys come in with: there's an excitement in that they've been called upon.

They ran the scene again.

What worked and what didn't work?

- The staging is blocking the audience when they're in the care home.
- It worked that Manoukian became a focus along with Barney.

- It worked that Nina didn't move; it's like she's able to exist in both realms. It gave a hint that she could be Manoukian in the future.
- It became clear that the school kids are actually not ignoring Manoukian; disagreeing with them is engaging with them.

Let's try:
- Non-naturalistic staging when Grandad and Mum come in. Maybe they are sat a distance away from each other instead of being sat next to each other.
- The toys stay present in the scene.
- Toys taking the chairs out of the space instead of rearranging them.
- Have a think about what Grandad's point of focus* is: is he having a conversation in another time in his head until he's talking to Barney?

*Point of Focus: Something that the performer focuses on during the playing of the scene. This can be anything: it can be elemental, it can be physical; for example, it could be that the teacher is going to turn up at any point so the characters can be having a conversation in one part of the room, but they are consistently aware that they are expecting the teacher to come in.

Exercise: Status Line

Bailey uses this exercise if he's trying to figure out staging, or if he wants to add stakes or layers to a scene. Seeing the movement helps him to get ideas with staging where there needs to be movement and where there needs to be stillness. This exercise can also help you to explore and play around with the drama in the scene. You could do this by starting all the characters at a ten and see what happens.

(The group used pages 19–22 for this exercise.)

Write the numbers one to ten on sticky notes or paper (a number on each sticky note or piece of paper so you have ten in total) and put them in a line on the floor with enough space to walk between them. (For this scene they had three lines as there are three characters). Each performer takes place on a line and you run through the scene moving up and down the status line.

Bailey explained that a character's status is affected by what people say about them or to them in the scene. While running the scene, ask actors to think about what they say to other characters and how that might change their status. This game is interesting because they have to think about how their character interprets what is said to them; for example, in this scene some of what Barney is saying, like 'I want all this to be over', is not meant as Rachel hears it.

Here are some of the things that they tried in the exercise:
- Let's try everyone starting at a ten and see where it goes from there.
- Let's try a different position, characters starting on a different line.

- Let's try Mo saying 'Can you get me out of here?' to Ernie, as Mo might connect with Ernie more as they are the same age.
- Let's try starting Ernie and Barney at a ten and Rachel at a one.
- A note to Mo: if you get too angry or too emotional the carers will come and take you away.
- A note to Ernie: try not to engage in the conversation with Mum and Grandad until you absolutely must.
- A note to Rachel: think about how you're managing everyone's emotions.
- Let's try having carers in the scene on the side keeping an eye out.

While doing this exercise, there was a discovery that Ernie finds it easier to hold status in the situation because they know Gramps as an elder and expects and accepts that Gramps won't remember them. Ernie also finds it easier to talk to Mo in their reality. Whereas Rachel is trying to hold onto her parent as she remembers them, which is why she finds it harder to accept Mo as they are now.

The play is cyclical – Mo in the beginning of the play says: 'I won't be like that. I won't be a mad old person.' And, in this scene, they are perceived as just that.

Important: the timing of the play is not a literal 80 years in the future; in this scene we have the music reference of Lil Nas X which says that we are in this contemporary time, so Mo is 80 in this current time.

Exercise: Nina's Monologue

Read the monologue while walking around the space and when you get to a comma or full stop, change direction. At each of those moments, pick an intention for the line. Each of those shifts is a new thought; sometimes it's the same intention but it's a new thought.

Then do the same but don't move around and keep the same energy. Your point of focus is Mo and Arpi. Let's try that your intention is to confront Mo and educate Arpi.

When doing this exercise, you might action each line or you might action sections. Actioning a line involves thinking of a transitive verb that can be done to the other person. For example, 'I punish you'.

If you've got multiple people, you can set them off on their own to do the exercise at the same time. You can ask them questions to get them to think of what their character's intentions might be at different points. If you don't have a lot of time, you could action the text before giving it to the performer.

Exercise: Tightrope – A Peter Brook exercise

Imagine a tightrope in the space. You must get from one side of the tightrope to the other. You must fully imagine the tightrope.

Then add text and perform the text while crossing the tightrope.

Then add another person to cross the tightrope. You will find out how you navigate someone else crossing the tightrope while still performing the text.

Exercise: Ten things about your character

Ask everyone to find ten things their character thinks about themselves and try to keep it positive. It's easy to say that Mo is the naughty one, but does he think that of himself? If you need a shorthand, you can bring those ten things to your group as an offer.

Question and answer with Abi Zakarian and Daniel Bailey

DB shows an answer from Bailey and AK shows an answer from Zakarian.

Q: How do manage the care of any of the young people who may be going through the experience of an elder family member with dementia?
A: (DB) Creating a safe space for me is checking in to see how people are feeling, asking for names and pronouns, and going back to that as they can change at any time. When it comes to the work you need to be receptive to the fact that the work could trigger someone at any point of rehearsal, so it's good if you can have a physical space where the young person can tap out and take a moment. I just always keep the door open for those conversations and handle it with care. There are different ways but I always encourage you to check in and check out.

Q: If there is a student absent from rehearsal, what do you do in that situation?
A: (DB) The truth is that absence is inevitable, so you must plan for it for now. Ask everyone to read all of the play, all of the characters, so that they are familiar with it. You could even cast understudies.

Q: What directorial choice could ruin the play for you?
A: While doing this exercise, there was a discovery that Ernie finds it easier to hold status in the situation because they know Gramps as an elder and expects and accepts that Gramps won't remember them. Ernie also finds it easier to talk to Mo in their reality. Whereas Rachel is trying to hold onto her parent as she remembers them, which is why she finds it harder to accept Mo as they are now.

The play is cyclical – Mo in the beginning of the play says: 'I won't be like that. I won't be a mad old person.' And, in this scene, they are perceived as just that.

Important: the timing of the play is not a literal 80 years in the future; in this scene we have the music reference of Lil Nas X which says that we are in this contemporary time, so Mo is 80 in this current time.

(DB) Honour the shifts in the play. The ebbs and the flows.

Q: How am I going to have enough time for all of this in a very limited rehearsal period?
A: (DB) All of these exercises can be short cut. You can make lots of decisions and bring them into the room. It is a lot of planning; however, that's how you can make the most of your rehearsal time. For the ensemble building, a short game at the beginning always helps.

Q: I'm worried that the Toys will put off the 18-year-olds in my group. How do I introduce the play to them?
A: (AZ) When you're doing a check-in at the start of the session, before you introduce the play, ask them what their favourite childhood toy is/was. Then start by explaining that the play is magical realism.
(DB) Start with questions; it's always helpful to start that conversation.

Q: Can you give us more info on Arpi to understand that character more?
A: (AZ) Of course. It's very much based on my own family. When I was growing up my mum would not let my nana talk much about the things she went through, such as fleeing from the genocide in Armenia; I think to protect herself and us. So Arpi learns to let her nana talk about her past. Arpi's understanding is that in order to move into her future she needs to hear about that past. It's rooted in the idea of not forgetting your past and also understanding that there might be someone in the generation above you that can't access that past yet. It's about how inherited trauma exists in a family.

Q: What if you have a non-binary student playing Mo, what can be used instead of Dad and Gramps?
A: (AZ) If you have a non-binary student playing Mo, you can discuss with them what term they'd like to use instead. You might have a cultural background in the group that has a name that works for both. G can be useful as you can use it for either. Grandy is another option.

Q: How might we go about costuming the toys?
A: (AZ) If someone says that they want to be a bunny, it might be a pair of bunny ears or a full bunny suit. It could be that the toys are all wearing a hoody made of teddy or fleece material; you could think of the texture of toys.
(DB) You could do eyeliner on the face as whiskers. It all depends on the resources you have. You can make it with whatever you have. It can be bare bones or with set.

Q: Does it have to be a piano?
A: (AZ) No, it can be a keyboard or a guitar or whatever instrument is accessible to you and your group.

Q: I'm worried that the kids I work with may feel disconnected to the songs in the song playlist, so can we change it?
A: (AZ) It's fine to get suggestions from the group, but as long as it's from a wide pool and different kinds of music and a mixture of styles. Think of the scenes and the vibe the music is giving. Think of the purpose of the song in that moment. The only song I would like you to use is 'Sweet Child o' Mine.

Q: Is there anything in the kitchen scene that we need to include because of the cultural references?
A: (AZ) No you don't need to have those specific props.

Q: Are there any other roles that can be multi-roled?
A: (AZ) The carers could double up as the toys and classmates. Ernie, Rachel, Barney and Arpi's mum and grandparent could double.

Q: Do you always work through the text in chronological order?
A: (DB) I prefer to but that isn't always possible.

Q: How sensitive do we need to be to the Armenian culture in the play?
A: (AZ) I understand that the majority of you won't have an Armenian participant in the group and that's fine; but representation is important to acknowledge, and representation is something the Armenian community really does not have in the UK, so please take some time to do a little research on Armenian heritage, history, culture and our diaspora, in order that the person playing the characters has an understanding of us.
(DB) Ask: What does the heritage mean to that character? What research are we going to do that adds that extra layer? When I talk about characterization, I'm talking about adding layers.

From a workshop led by Daniel Bailey
With notes by Brigitte Adela

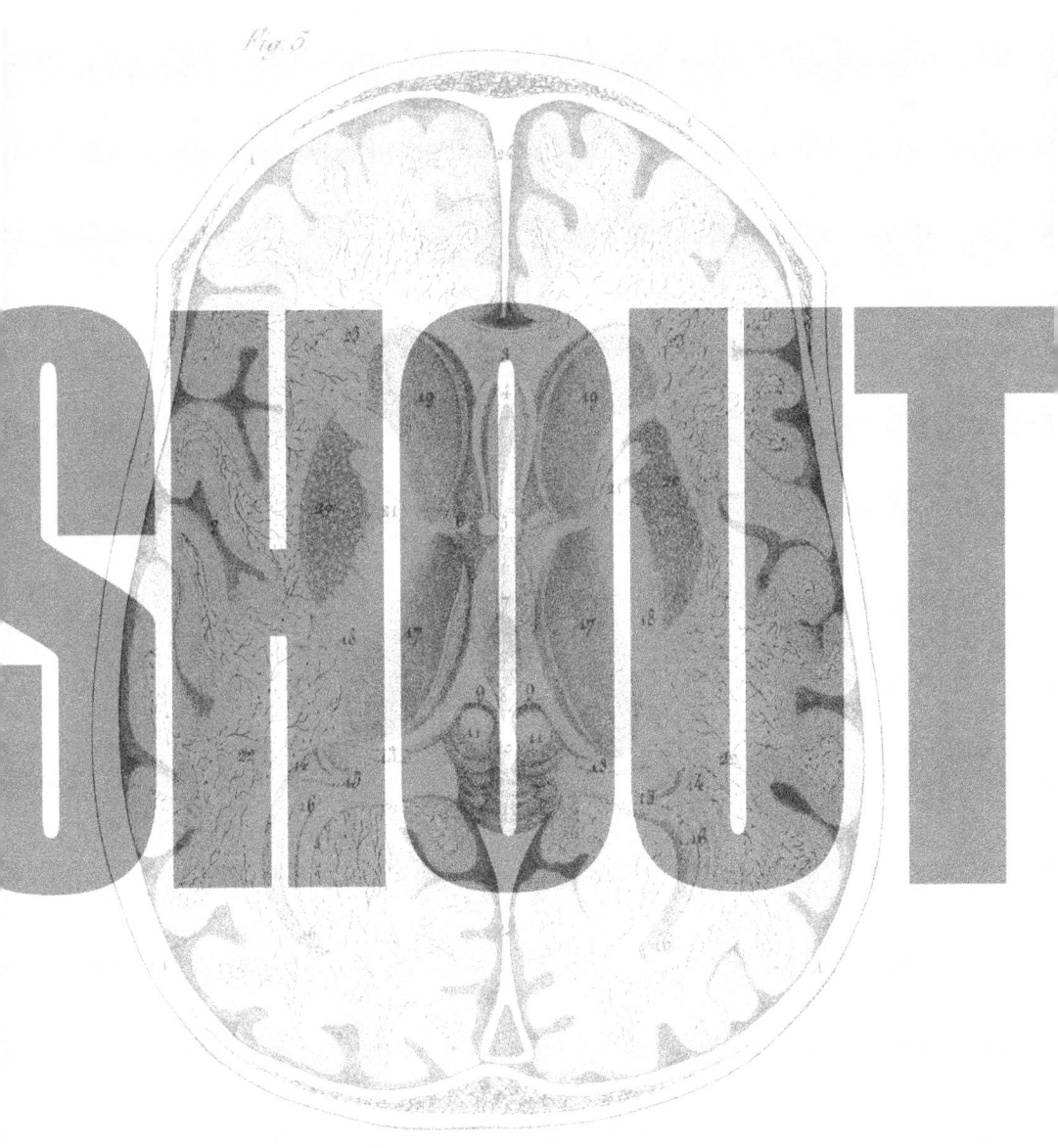

SHOUT

by Alexis Zegerman

Alexis Zegerman's theatre work includes *The Fever Syndrome* and *Lucky Seven* (Pearson Writer in Residence 2008–9) at Hampstead; *Holy Shit* at Kiln; *The Steingolds* (finalist for the Susan Smith Blackburn Prize 2012) at the National Theatre Studio; *Killing Brando* at Òran Mór (A Play, a Pie and a Pint season) and for Paines Plough at the Young Vic; *I Ran the World* for the Royal Court and Flight 5065; and *Marriage and Noise* at Soho Theatre. Alexis Zegerman is currently under commission with Hampstead Theatre and the Manhattan Theatre Club, New York.

Her film work includes the screenplay of *Arthur's Whiskey*, starring Diane Keaton and David Harewood.

Her radio work includes the two comedy series *Mum's on the Run* and *School Runs*, and radio plays are *Déjà Vu* (Prix Europa Special Commendation), *Jump*, *The Singing Butler*, *Are You Sure?* and *Ronnie Gecko* (Richard Imison Award).

Notes

Selective mutism is an anxiety disorder, present in at least one in every 140 children and teenagers. People suffering from selective mutism will not be able to speak in certain or all environments, most commonly school. The disorder is underdiagnosed as it is often mistaken for other things like being shy, depressed or difficult. It presents more commonly in girls than boys.

You will know someone with selective mutism – even if you don't know it.

It is in the nature of the subject matter that the play is designed to be as inclusive as possible. There is ample opportunity for non-speaking roles, movement-only roles, supporting artist roles.

Parts can be multi-roled. The characters in the Calming Room are funny, but please ensure we laugh with them and not at them – they're not to be ridiculed.

Dana *is written for a girl.*

Tristan *is written for a boy.*

All other parts can be played by any gender. If a theatre group wishes for the characters of Dana and Tristan to be gender swapped, or non-binary, this may be entirely possible in consultation with the Connections team and the writer.

The song on page 69 is a suggestion – feel free to change it, but the spirit and energy of what the song conveys in the script should be adhered to. Other song suggestions are listed at the end of the script.

Swearing and curse words can be swapped out for less offensive alternatives – there is a 'no swear' version of the script available from the Connections team.

Selective mutism is the current terminology used, but this may change over time.

Have the confidence and courage to lean into the silences in the play. Hold and embrace the uncomfortableness that can accompany silence.

Technical –

The play is set in a school or sixth-form college. There are chairs all over the stage, which can be moved around to represent each scene's location.

Transitions between scenes are designed to be smooth and fluid.

Text messages, or other digital media in the play, are designed to be said aloud by another actor standing behind the actor who is texting, but feel free to let your imagination go. This goes for all stage directions – they are open to your interpretation, as long as the story and characters' journeys are honoured.

Silence.

Then –

The cast come on chattering, talking, overlapping – certain conversations ping out. The chairs are set up like benches in a school yard. **Dana** *walks through the people, weaves through the noise. Her backpack is heavy. She doesn't look like the hero of our story, or even her own story, but she is. She is silent.*

Student 1   Word.

Student 2   Word.

Student 3   Word.

Student 4   Yeah, I mean –

Student 5   Then he said –

Student 6   Unreal, bruv.

Student 7   Then she said –

Student 6   Oh, my days!

Student 8   LOL.

Student 5   110 per cent.

Student 1   What you doing after school?

Student 2   Why didn't you answer my DM?

Student 3   I'm airing you.

Student 2   Talking to me is a funny way of airing me.

Student 6   Rude.

Student 1   Word.

Dana   Words.

When **Dana** *speaks, she is addressing the audience. This is her interior voice, and nobody on stage can hear her. Only us.*

Dana   Words are coming at you at a thousand miles a second. In the beginning was the word. A sound. A big bang. I speak, therefore I am. And if you're not the loudest voice –

Everyone around her gets louder –

Student 4   110 per cent is not a thing!

Dana (*tries to shout*)   If you don't shout, and scream, and make your mark –

Student 7   She said, 'Girl, you have five seconds to get out of my face' –

Dana   Then how do you get heard?

Student 5   What did she say?

Student 7   She said, 'Suck my –'

Student 6   Rude.

Dana   If you don't speak, do you even exist?

Everyone is silent. Still. A light on **Dana**.

Dana   If a tree falls in the forest, but no one hears it . . . Has it even fallen?

School yard. Everyone is milling in their cliques – doing their various things – TikTok; chatting, plaiting hair. **Dana** *walks through, heading to the school building, head down.*

Viv, *her best friend, runs up to her.*

Viv   Hey, Dana.

Dana *smiles and waves.*

Viv   How are you?

Dana *nods,* 'OK.' *She points to* **Viv** – 'You?'

Viv   I'm good. Apart from the imminent depletion of the tundra's permafrost. And the oceans are absorbing the heat equivalent of five atomic bombs per second. In the selfish, immediate short term, I'm good.
Hey, I've been choreographing this really cool thing for our TikTok channel.

She does a not very cool dance, but it is definitely committed. **Dana** *really enjoys watching her – she gets into it a bit.*

Viv   Oh yeah. Oh yeah. Look at her go. Shut that front door.

The Cool Girls stare at them goofing about.

Maya   Fr-eeeeeeeak

Trinh   Mute.

Viv   Just ignore them.
What time's your appointment with the Admissions Advisor?

Dana *holds up ten fingers.*

Viv   Ah, OK, mine's at eleven. I think I'm definitely going Leeds top choice, then Manchester, then Salford, then the rest are really, like, back-ups if I have a brain haemorrhage during the exam. Which might actually happen in English.

She stops as **Tristan**, *and a group of his friends, walk across the school recreation area, sports bags casually slung over shoulders like they're in* Britain's Next Top Model. **Tristan** *is holding a rugby ball. Everyone stops to stare at* **Tristan**.

Tristan   Go wide.

Tom   Don't smash it into my face.

Sam   His face is his fortune.

Nav   Which is why he's broke.

Tom *runs backwards to catch the rugby ball, and knocks into* **Viv**. *He ignores her. The Cool Girls laugh.*

Viv   Oops, sorry.

Dana *helps her up.* **Viv** *brushes herself off, still staring at* **Tristan**.

Viv   Hey, Tristan.

He walks past her and over to the Cool Girls.

Maya (*to* **Tristan**)   Careful, the Mute is staring at you.

Trinh   Do you think it's catching? Her cow-eye stare will turn you cold-stone mute.

Yaz   F-uh-reeeeeeak.

Viv (*shouts over*)   Privileged douche bags! Instead of getting a car for your birthday, why don't you plant a tree?

Maya (*leaving*)   Why don't you grow some tits?

Viv   Good luck paying for the rising petrol!

Maya   I don't pay it!

Viv   Exactly!

Maya *and* **Tristan** *and the group disappear into the school. The bell rings.*

Viv   I stung her like a bee.

Dana *nods:* **Viv** *really didn't. They walk towards the school steps.*

Viv   Remember our mantra: today is the first day of the rest of our lives.

Dana *smiles, but isn't too sure.*

A chair moves in next to her. Transition into –

Admissions Advisor's *office. The* **Admissions Advisor** *sits on a chair.* **Dana** *sits down on a chair opposite.*

Admissions Advisor   Well, you are restricted by your lack of . . . talking. I'm guessing you'll apply for remote learning only? And then you can always do a voice-text response in tutorials online. Like Stephen Hawking.
Or Siri.
Thing is, Dana. . .You did do extremely well in your GCSEs. You've got a very strong case for applying, well, anywhere. What about University College London, or St Andrews, or Oxbridge?
Ah, but most of these top universities require an interview. Would you . . .?

The **Advisor** *waits for an answer.* **Dana** *shakes her head.*

Admissions Advisor   There may be a case for positive discrimination – Malala got accepted into Oxford after being shot by the Taliban.

Dana *stares at the* **Admissions Advisor***, her eyes nearly rolling out of her head.*

Admissions Advisor   Yes, it's not a reliable parallel, but you do have an EHCP.

Dana *can't say anything. Deflated, the* **Admissions Advisor** *hands her a pile of prospectuses.*

Admissions Advisor   Work on your personal statement. Make your voice heard. And spellcheck, for crying out loud – you have no idea how many applications I see that leave the 'p' out of psychology?

Dana *gets up. The* **Admissions Advisor** *disappears.*

Dana (*to the audience*)   I can't remember the exact day I stopped speaking. Or even why. But I remember people's reactions.
They think I'm being difficult. Or shy. They don't get it. It's not a choice. It's not that I *won't* speak. I literally, physically *can't* speak. I get so anxious –

The **Company** *look at her.*

Dana   My throat tightens.

The **Company** *beat their feet on the floor – ba-boom, ba-boom – like a heartbeat. They move closer. She stands on a chair.*

Dana   I go hot. Palms sweat. Arms tingle.
Words get trapped in my trachea. Face freezes.
My heart beats out my chest. Everything sounds so far away.

The **Company** *close in on her.*

Dana   And then I'm in the sea. Waves of panic overwhelming me. The land getting further and further away.

The **Company** *are the sea – like a wave moving up and down, around her, she reaches up, trying to reach above the water.*

Dana   I try to catch a breath. But I can't. Everything's stuck.

She tries to reach up again, and sinks below the waves.

Suddenly the waves part. The **Company** *set up a classroom around her, chairs facing towards the audience.*

Dana   I'm seventeen, and I speak to exactly the same number of people I spoke to when I was four.
One. My mum. And as you can imagine, that's a double-edged sword.
Two. Myself. Which is having a conversation with someone who gets me. Even if it's someone I don't always like.

She sits down on a chair.

Thing is – nobody wants to be different.

A classroom. A **Classics Teacher** *stands at the front, pointing at two (imaginary) pictures of identical vases on the board. The class looks extremely bored apart from* **Viv** *who is scribbling down notes.*

Classics Teacher   As you can see, these two Attic vases are vastly different. Can anyone tell me the differences between the red-figure Attic vase and the black-figure Attic vase?

Viv*'s hand shoots up.*

Classics Teacher   Anyone else? The red-figure Attic vase . . . and the black-figure Attic vase . . .
Tom?

Tom   Erm . . . one is red and one is black?

Classics Teacher   Yes, anything more refined? . . . technique; function; composition . . .

Dana*'s hand nervously goes up.*

Classics Teacher   Oh, Dana Alford, this is a surprise.

Dana *takes a deep breath, a pause and then she holds up a large card – it has a picture of a toilet on it. The class laugh.*

Maya   Ancient hieroglyphics.

Yaz   Dana needs to go pee pee.

Viv   Shut it.

Trinh   Grow up.

Viv   Your call is important to us, please stay on the line whilst no one gives a shit.

Classics Teacher (*to* **Dana**)   I presume you can't wait. Off you go. Enough disrupting the class.

Dana, *mortified, gets up and leaves the classroom. The classroom dismantles.*

Dana (*to audience*)   An Attic vase originates from the province of ancient Athens. The black-figure vase predates the red-figure vase, but they are basically the same.

She walks along the school corridor.

We pretend to celebrate difference, accommodate it. In reality, we just stick a label on it and put it in a kind of storage unit so it doesn't make the rest of the world look untidy – like my mum does with all her junk stuffed into the top drawer in the kitchen. Let me show you the Calming Room. Also known as the De-escalation Room. The junk drawer of life. Also known as –
The 'Freaks and Geeks' Room.

A number of pupils sit on chairs or on the floor. **Con** *can easily be mistaken for an adult – he's a student, and self-appointed leader.*

Con   Hey, Dana.

Dana *waves.*

Con   Come in. Make yourself super-comfortable. We were just discussing Kierkegaard's take on the frailty of the human condition. Nah, not really, Jono was burping out the hymn 'Jerusalem', but then he followed through at the end, which was fun . . . but messy. There's some newbies here you need to meet. So, let's check in.

Dana *finds a chair and sits.*

Con   OK, attention, freaks and geeks! Dana's in the house. Roll call, please!

Each person says their name and disorder.

Jono   Jono. TikTok tic.

Anita   Anita. Pathological avoidance disorder.

Toni   Toni. Autism.

Pete   Pete. Autism.

Saini   Saini. Autism.

Con   Con. Agoraphobia.

Holly   Holly. I'd rather not say.

Con   Respect.

Mo   Mo. ADHD.

They all turn to **Viv***, who's sitting on a chair.*

Pete   What the hell's she doing in here?

Mo   There's nothing wrong with you.

Viv   I have generalized anxiety about the climate crisis.

Saini   Word!

Con (*pointing at* **Dana**)   Dana, selective mutism. Come into the bosom of our sanctuary.

Pete   Buzoom!

Mo (*to* **Dana**)   Have you started taking the drugs yet?

Dana *shakes her head.*

Toni   She wouldn't be on the same drugs as you – different disorder, different drugs.

Mo   You should take the drugs. They're really good.

Toni   Knucklehead.

Con   Hey, none of that in here.

Mo (*whispers*)   Take the drugs.

Con   This is a safe space. Out there – in the normative world – it's chaos. You gotta start seeing the people out there as freaks.

Pete   Amen.

Jono   They speaketh the truth.

Saini   Word!

Con   They're trying to control us with their therapies, and their Ritalin, in their 'how to be normative' world. Our difference is our safe place.

Jono   It's our superpower.

Anita   That is one messed-up *Avengers'* movie.

Saini   Word!

Holly   Only –

Con (*snaps*)   Only what? (*Then.*) I mean, Holly, go ahead, you have the floor.

Holly   Isn't the whole point that we get out of here?

Con   Excuse me?

Holly   We learn how to move on.

Con   And go where? Where do you want to go?

Jono   KFC.

Con   Nobody is preventing your visit to KFC.

Toni   KFC is dangerous.

Viv   Those are not happy chickens.

Pete (*re* **Viv**)   Why's she here again?

Viv (*overlapping*)   Stuffed full of steroids and antibiotics.

Toni   Once my dog ate a drumstick from KFC, bone splintered in his stomach, Mum had forgotten to renew the pet insurance. That was not a good day

Con (*interrupting*)   OK, everyone, *meditation*. Let's all think about this disruption.

Holly *stops* **Dana** *as she leaves.*

Holly (*whispers*)   There's no Calm Room after this. No De-escalation. You get out into the real world, and there's no SENCO, there's no paediatric psychs, you're out there in the grown-up forest – and you're not like any of the other trees, you're out there, different. And alone.

Mo   Take the drugs.

The **Company** *chant the name of drugs. They run on with a large imaginary skipping rope, and skip into the rope, chanting the drugs, faster and faster, over and over –*

Company

    Sertraline
    St John's wort
    Beta blockers
    Lexapro
    Prozac
    Zoloft
    Celexa
    Valium
    Xanax
    Klonopin
    Sertraline
    St John's Wort
    Beta blockers . . .

Dana *can't run into the skipping rope and join in. She tries. She freezes. The skipping and chanting stop.*

Dana I'm not against drugs – I know they can help. But part of me feels safe with what I know. Safe in being untouched and untouchable. And part of me feels terrified. I'm terrified of changing. And I'm terrified of staying the same.

The School Therapy Room. An over-earnest **Therapist** *sits on a chair, feet planted on the floor, in perfect Alexander Technique positioning.*

Therapist I'm pleased you've made it to our session this week, Dana. We're going to continue with 'fading in'.

Dana (*to the audience*) Fading in is a kind of *exposure therapy.*

Therapist Say, for instance, if you were scared of snakes. 'Ooh . . . snakes are scary.' Which may seem like a completely rational fear but you are extremely unlikely in your lifetime to ever be harmed by a snake. Back to fading in. You start by sitting here, and there's a snake outside the room.

Someone enters on the periphery holding a snake.

In a box, of course. The snake would be in a box.

They put the snake in a pet carrier box.

And you think, 'There's a scary snake outside this room.' But then you slowly carry on doing what you're doing, and soon you completely forget about that snake. You realize, 'Oh, that snake's not hurting me. It's not scary. This is fine. In fact, it's so fine, that snake might be able to move a little bit closer.'

The **Company** *take a step forward, and more people enter holding snakes.* **Dana** *watches them, as they slowly step closer and closer, encircling her, whilst the* **Therapist** *continues.*

Therapist Same with talking. You have an irrational fear of speaking. So we *fade in*. You talk with someone standing outside the room. And, look . . . Nothing bad has happened. You think, 'Oh there's someone outside the room, and maybe they've heard me and that's OK, I haven't *died*.' So they take a step closer –

*The **Company** takes a step closer. **Dana** starts to sweat.*

Dana (*to the audience*)   Is it me, or is it getting very hot in here?

Therapist (*noticing **Dana** panicking*)   You're having a little panic there. That's OK. They can take a step back –

*The **Company** take a step back.*

Therapist   You breathe. Everything settles. And then they keep going.

Dana (*to the audience*)   This can take forever, by the way.

*The **Company** steps closer.*

Dana   And then. . . .

Therapist   You're doing so well.

*The group step closer and closer, closing in on **Dana**.*

Dana   Like a really bad game of Grandmother's Footsteps. . . .

Therapist   No point in giving up now.

Dana (*shouts*)   You suddenly find there's a motherfucking snake staring right at you!

***Dana** stands on a chair, her breathing is fast, she clutches her neck. Everyone disappears, apart from the **Therapist**.*

Therapist   So, that didn't go so well today. Let's try again next week.

*An organ plays the hymn 'Amazing Grace', everyone assembles on chairs in rows for assembly. The **Headteacher** stands at the front, addressing the school.*

Headteacher   Good morning, Stretford Grammar. Firstly, I'd like to say a hearty congratulations to our rugby team, led by captain Tristan Khan, who came top in the Under 18s fixture. Tristan was also named 'Man of the Match'.

Nav (*shouts*)   He's the man!

Someone wolf whistles.

Headteacher   Inappropriate!
Capitalizing on our vertiginous GCSE results, we can expect a bumper crop of top university offers. We can show the North London Collegiates, the Henrietta Barnetts, the Manchester Grammars –[1]

There's a big rival 'boo' from the students.

Headteacher   Ha ha. Yes, indeed –

The 'boos' get louder.

---

1   Put in your own choice of three local schools or colleges here, if you like.

Headteacher Alright. (*Shouts.*) Quieten down! We shall be using a *buddy system* – pairing up sixth formers, to help prepare your personal statements, and work on interview technique.
You shall be going to battle with your peers. And the importance of war is to know thine enemy. Buddy pairs will be pinned to the sixth-form noticeboard after recess.

Maya Hope I'm not paired up with *the Mute*.

Viv (*to* **Maya**) Meathead.

Maya Vegan tits.

Viv What is it with my tits today?

Headteacher Now, please stand and sing hymn number 22 in your hymn books.

The organ plays 'Amazing Grace', people stand and sing as they clear chairs away. **Dana** *stands still amidst all the movement and singing.*

Students (*sing*)

> Amazing grace, how sweet the sound,
> That saved a wretch like me.
> I once was lost –

Dana *joins in, everyone ignores her, their voices peter out until she sings alone.*

Dana (*sings*)

> But now am found.
> Was blind but now I see.

Her voice soars, beautiful, but no one on stage hears it. A lone voice.

> Was blind but now I see.

Someone stands holding a piece of paper – they are the sixth-form noticeboard. Students go up and look at the noticeboard. **Viv** *approaches with* **Dana**; *they look at the list.* **Dana**'s *eyes widen. She walks downstage.* **Viv** *follows her.*

Viv That's really stupid – why didn't they put us together?

Dana *doesn't answer.*

Viv Listen, I can come along. If it's difficult for you.

Dana *shakes her head. She holds up her toilet card.*

Viv Right. Cool. Well, I'll be in the library. If you want to join me. I'm writing a letter to our local MP about fishing quotas. These fish won't save themselves. Well, they would. If they were more sentient.
Oh, and we've got to practize our moves.

Viv *dances.* **Dana** *joins her.*

Viv Go fishies. Go fishies. You're actually dancing like you need the toilet.

Dana *jokingly gives* **Viv** *the finger. They laugh.* **Viv** *dances off.*

Viv Go fishies. Go fishies.

A row of chairs set up to be toilet cubicles. This is the Girls' Bathroom. **Trinh** *sits on the toilet. Next to her* **Dana** *sits in the next cubicle. The gang of Cool Girls stare into the mirror which is the fourth wall, talking out to the audience. They don't know* **Dana** *is there.* **Dana** *can hear everything.*

Maya I can't believe the Mute is paired up with Tristan. (*Putting on lip balm.*) He doesn't need someone with a speech impediment helping him with interview technique. He's walking into Oxbridge on a sport's scholarship.

Yaz Oxbridge isn't a place, moron.

Maya Of course, it is.

Yaz It's two separate places. He can't be in two places at once.

Trinh Guys –

Laura I heard the Mute's applying to Oxford.

Maya Like, not to be offensive, but this is going to reflect really badly on the school.

Yaz It's inclusivity gone mad.

Laura She won't turn up to a meeting with him. She can barely leave home –

Maya I bet she does. She's obsessed with me and Tristan.

Dana *rolls her eyes, shakes her head.*

Maya Always staring at us.

Yaz Is she though?

Maya I can feel those big cow eyes boring into me.

Yaz You think everyone's staring at you. You're a narcissist.

Maya All seventeen-year-olds are narcissists, but thanks for the unwarranted character assassination, bitch!

Trinh Guys!

Yaz He won't turn up to the meeting with her. He's got better things to do.

Trinh Guys! There's no toilet roll.

Laura I heard when she was five, she was crossing the road between Joe & The Juice and Iceland. A car ran her over. It was such an enormous shock, all her hair fell out and her voice stopped working.

Yaz I heard her dad had a heart attack right in front of her, and she tried to give him CPR, she was pumping at his chest like she was in *Holby City*, and by the time the ambulance came, he was dead. She never spoke again.

Dana *slaps her forehead.*

Laura Her dad's alive, you idiot.

Yaz Joe & The Juice has only been on the high street a year!

Maya I heard there are these kids who don't learn how to talk. They grow up without human contact, learn how to behave from wild animals, raised by wolves, living on scraps from the bin. They stare at the moon and howl.

Laura I bet she walks up the hill at night and howls.

She howls. They howl like wolves.

Trinh Guys, I don't know what's going on out there, but there's no toilet roll!

Dana *comes out the toilet. The Cool Girls look at her and stop howling.* **Dana** *passes some toilet roll to* **Trinh** *and runs off.*

The **Company** *enter the stage howling like wolves.* **Dana** *runs through them, running through the forest as we transition to –*

Tristan *waits on stage, alone, his sports bag on the floor. He looks around, sighs, checks his watch –*

He shakes his head. He picks up his bag, and goes to exit. **Dana** *walks on stage, heavy rucksack on her back.*

Tristan We were supposed to meet half an hour ago.

Dana *doesn't say anything.*

Tristan I've got strength training now.

Dana *doesn't say anything.*

Tristan I wasn't gonna come, you know. And now I've gotta go.

Dana *nods. She can't look him in the eye. Frustrated,* **Tristan** *leaves.* **Dana** *stands alone on the stage. Alone. Again. She goes to walk off.*

Tristan *walks back on.*

Tristan I'm gonna get ribbed for not training with the team. That's what teams are all about: turning up.

He puts his bag down.

So how do we do this? How do we – (talk)?

He's getting nothing back from **Dana**.

Tristan This is a bit . . . frustrating.

Dana *pulls a phone out of her pocket. She hands it to him.*

Tristan What?

She points to him. Then she points to the phone.

Tristan Oh, right . . . what? You want me to put my Snap in here?

She nods. He sighs. He puts his number in her contacts. He passes her back the phone.

Dana *starts to type a Snapchat. An actor stands behind* **Dana** *as she types – they are playing* **Dana's Message**. **Dana** *sends the message. There's a 'ping'.* **Tristan** *takes his phone out, and looks at it.*

Dana's Message We can chat. Smiley face.

Tristan *types. An actor –* **Tristan's Message** *– stands behind him.* **Tristan** *sends the message.*

Tristan's Message OK.

Dana *types.*

Dana's Message Sorry I was late.

Tristan *types.*

Tristan's Message Whatever.

Tristan *stops. Taps the phone.*

Tristan's Message Delete. Delete. Delete.

Tristan *types.*

Tristan's Message So what are you applying for?

Dana's Message English. You?

Tristan's Message Same.

Dana*'s eyes widen as she reads the message.* **Tristan** *types.*

Tristan's Message Hey, what's with the face?

Dana's Message It's just my face.

Tristan's Message I got a really strong score in my GCSE English.

Dana's Message You want to do English at Oxford?

Tristan's Message Where are you applying?

Dana's Message (*hesitates*) UCL. Maybe.

Tristan's Message You know you have to interview for UCL?

Dana's Message You know you have to interview for Oxford?

Tristan *looks at his phone, surprized. He stops.*

Tristan I don't actually have to type. I can speak.

Dana *types.*

Dana's Message You shouldn't type. You spelled 'interview' wrong.

Tristan *looks at his phone, scrolls back through the messages.*

Tristan's Message (*reading back*) 'Inter-veiw.'

Tristan *types.*

Tristan's Message   Smart ass.

Dana's Message   Arse. A. R. S. E.

He looks at her, frustrated. He picks up his bag.

Tristan   I don't need to be here –

She waves him 'goodbye'. He looks at her, totally perplexed and frustrated.

Tristan   So why don't you speak?

She looks at him.

Tristan   Why – don't – you – speak?

Dana *gets out her phone, and starts typing.* **Tristan** *starts reading his phone.*

Dana's Message   After my father dropped dead in front of my very eyes, and I failed to resuscitate him even though I have a Bronze level Duke of Edinburgh Award, I was raised by a pack of savage wolves. They called me White Fang Dana –

Tristan   OK –

Dana's Message   And taught me how to hunt with my human paws, and howl at the full moon, but they did not, and could not, teach me how to speak.

Dana *has finished. She stares at him.*

Tristan   OK. I get it. None of my business.

A silence.

Listen, do you want to swap personal statements?

She stands there.

Tristan   If you don't want us to help each other, what are you doing here?

Dana *shrugs.*

Tristan   I know why we're paired-up, OK. You're a whizz at English. You're a wordsmith. And I'm a meathead. That's what you're thinking: I'm a meathead, who's going to walk the interview because I'm one of the top youth rugby players in the county. I'm the top player. But you're right, I can't write as well as you can. So are we gonna help each other out, or what?

Dana *types.*

Dana's Message   You think I'm a *wordsmith*?

Tristan   Ironically, yes.

Dana *reaches into her bag and pulls out a piece of paper – her personal statement. She hands it to* **Tristan**, *barely able to look at him.* **Tristan** *glances at the piece of paper.*

Tristan This just has one sentence on it. That's all you can think to say about yourself?

Dana *shrugs. He takes a piece of paper out of his bag and hands it to her.*

Tristan Let's meet up tomorrow and we can talk this through. Text. Whatever.

Dana *gets her phone out, and writes. A ping.* **Tristan** *looks at his phone.*

Dana's Message   OK.

Tristan *goes to leave. Another ping.*

Dana's Message   Meathead.

He looks at **Dana** *and smiles. She smiles back. He leaves.*

She looks down at **Tristan***'s personal statement. She takes a pen and starts crossing through things.* **Viv** *enters, holding a placard, with 'Walk for the Earth' written on it.*

Viv   Hey, do you want to come to the march in town?

Dana *holds up the piece of paper she's editing.*

Viv   Right. Work. Hey, how did it go with Tristan?

Dana *pulls a face.*

Viv   Yeah, well, the dude's a meathead.

Dana *nods.*

Viv   See ya tomorrow.

Viv *leaves. But* **Dana** *doesn't actually think* **Tristan** *is a meathead.*

The **Company** *march across the stage holding placards. They weave around* **Dana***, each shouting a slogan.*

Company

> Save the Earth.
> Save the trees.
> Save the forests.
> Trees give life.

Dana *puts headphones on, listens to music loudly. We hear the music she can hear; it drowns out the slogan chanters and the* **Company** *turn to trees in the background.*

Tristan *enters. He taps* **Dana** *on the shoulder to get her attention. She takes her headphones off, the music stops.*

Tristan   Hey.

Dana *waves.*

Tristan Thanks for your notes. Harsh. But fair. I would say there is a fine line between confidence and arrogance –

Dana *smiles. She takes her finger and draws an imaginary line across the ground. Then she crosses over the imaginary line.*

Tristan   OK, I may have crossed that line. It's not all arrogance –

She looks at him.

Tristan   I've toned it down. I've even added something about English literature.

She does a mock clap. He smiles. He hands her her personal statement.

Tristan   There wasn't much to go on here. You know you've gotta sell yourself, Dana. This is your one shot to make your mark. You're in competition with everybody else applying . . .

He stops. **Dana** *looks at him: 'What?'*

Tristan   You're really clever. I looked at your results –

She takes the piece of paper from him, embarrassed.

Tristan   You should be applying to Oxford –

Dana *shakes her head.*

Tristan   So . . . what? You're just going to stay here? Do university online?

She shrugs.

Tristan   The whole point of university is that you escape, you meet people, you interact, you get drunk, you throw up. You regret, you make mistakes, you get a job. You work out how to be in the real world. What's the point of all this otherwise?

She looks at him. He stops. A silence between them. He's extremely frustrated. He looks at her headphones.

Tristan   What you listening to?

Dana *shrugs 'nothing much'.*

Tristan *puts his headphones on. He gestures to her phone.*

Tristan   Can I – ?

She hesitates, then hands him her phone. He goes to her music, presses play. Rocks his head around. We don't hear it – just **Tristan** *through the headphones.*

Tristan   OK. Good choice. Angry.

He starts singing the song she's listening to – 'You Oughta Know' by Alanis Morissette.

Tristan (*shouts to* **Dana**)   What? I can't hear you? You're gonna have to speak louder.

Of course, she's not saying anything. She can't help smiling.

Tristan   I've got an idea. You rock out, right? You put your music on loud. I bet you scream, right? Shout it out loud, like nobody's watching?

He puts her headphones over her ears. She looks at him, perplexed.

Tristan You can't hear me with the music playing –

He puts his headphones on.

And I can't hear you.

He whacks the music up loud. He can hear it. **Dana** *can hear it. The song fills the auditorium. He smiles at* **Dana**, *and starts screaming along to the chorus. He gets into it, headbangs.* **Dana** *watches him singing loudly.*

Then **Tristan** *totally commits to the fast, complicated lyrics of the bridge, getting some words wrong, tripping over them –*

Dana *closes her eyes, she starts to sing and shout along, getting more and more into it.*

Tristan *looks at her. He takes off his headphones. He watches her singing aloud, her eyes shut.*

Dana *opens her eyes, she sees* **Tristan** *watching her, headphones off. She covers her mouth, shocked.*

Tristan Dana –

She grabs her stuff.

Tristan Nothing bad happened!

She runs off through the forest.

Tristan Dana!

The Calming Room aka 'Freaks and Geeks' Room – **Con** *is leading the usual suspects in a yoga class. They are all in various, individual states of the tree pose.*

Con And hands raised above and open – like the growing fruit trees of life –

Mo Fruit cakes, more like.

Con Trees do not talk.

And . . . breathe.

Dana *runs in.*

Con Hey, Dana. We're doing yoga practice. Would you like to adopt the tree pose?

Pete You'll be good at this. Trees don't talk.

Saini Word.

Dana *sits down, her heart is thumping in her chest. Her breathing is shallow.* **Con** *looks at her.*

Con Shallow breath?

She nods.

Saini Heart racing?

Anita Tingling arms?

Toni Jelly legs?

Jono Sweaty palms?

Dana *nods.*

Mo Panic attack!

Con Stand back, everyone.
OK, Dana, look at me. Look into my eyes. Focus. Focus. Regulate your breathing. Breathe in and out.

She shakes her head. She can't.

Con Yes, you can.

Mo You can do it, Dana.

Pete You can do it.

Holly Shouldn't we call a nurse?

Con No! What happens in 'Freaks and Geeks', stays in 'Freaks and Geeks'.
(*To* **Dana**.) Look at me –

They breathe with her, in and out –

Con In and out. In and out. You're a tree.
You're a beautiful, individual tree.

Dana (*to the audience*) I don't want to be an individual tree. I want to connect. I want to be able to laugh and love, and be loved back. I want to be able to go to crowded places. And ask for a coffee in Starbucks. And tell my grandma 'I love her' before she croaks. And ask for directions when I'm lost in a dark wood. I want to go to parties, and drink, and throw up –

I want to be able to speak, without throwing up.

Con That's it. She's good. Nothing to see here, folks. Back to downward dog.

They get back to downward dog. As others set up chairs around them.

Con And into sun salutation. Salute the sun.

Mo Hello, sun!

Student 1 Shhhh.

Someone shushes them. The 'Freaks and Geeks' Room breaks up. We're in the school library.

Student 2 Shhhh.   **Student 3** Shhhh.

The **Company** *'shushes' as they sit on chairs, reading books.* **Dana** *sits on a chair in the library, tapping on a computer. The character of* **Dana's Word Doc**, *stands behind the computer, speaking the words* **Dana** *is typing.*

Dana's Word Doc   My name is Dana Alford, this is my personal state –

Dana *taps. Tap. Taps.*

Dana's Word Doc   Delete. Delete. Delete.

Dana *types.*

Dana's Word Doc   My personal heroes are Maya Angelou, Ruth Bader Ginsberg and Little Red Riding Hood – who far from being a victim, was a survivor of parental neglect.

Dana, *frustrated, presses hard on a button.*

Dana's Word Doc   Del-e-e-e-e-e-e-e-e-e-e-e-e-e-te.

Dana (*to audience*)   I've got to make myself stand out, even though I'm already different to everyone else. But I'm not the right kind of different –

Tristan   Dana –

Student 3   Shhhh –

Tristan *walks into the library and sits on the chair next to her.* **Dana** *keeps typing, ignores him.*

Tristan   Hello?

Dana *tries to ignore him, and continues to type.*

Tristan   So I heard your voice. That's a good thing, isn't it? If you can talk to me; you can maybe even talk in an interview. Can you stop typing, it's actually quite rude –

She stops, stares daggers at him and packs up to leave.

Tristan   Don't leave.

Student 1   Shhhh.

Dana *types on the computer.*

Dana's Word Doc   You tricked me into talking –

Tristan   Isn't that what the therapy is? Getting into uni. Being popular. Successful. Surviving this world is one big trick. You want to talk, right?

She gets up.

Tristan   Dana, wait!

Student 2   Shhhhh.

Student 3   Quiet!

Dana *goes to leave.*

Tristan   My mum cleans offices in the Southfield industrial estate. My dad hasn't worked for nearly ten years. I am going to be the first person in my family to go to university. They have huge expectations of me to be a success. Be the best. And I have to be grateful for the opportunities they never had, even though –

Student 4   Shhhh!   **Student 1**   Shhhh!

Tristan   Sometimes I can't be bothered to go training at 7 in the morning –

She stops for a second. Listens to him.

Tristan   I don't want to stand there in the sleet and the mud and have posh boys the size of my dad hurl themselves at me. Sometimes I just want to lie in, and see no one, and order pizza, and watch YouTube. And I know you know how it must feel to try for something, and think you've already failed –

Dana *sits on the chair, and types on the computer.* **Tristan** *reads the screen.*

Dana's Word Doc   No one expects anything of me.

Tristan   That's not true.

Student 2   Shhh!

Tristan (*angrily, to* **Student 2**)   What's your problem?

Student 2   It's a library – that's my problem.

Tristan   You know, that's not true, Dana!

Student 1   Shhhh!

Tristan (*shouts*)   I said, stop shushing me!

Student 4   Quieten down!

Tristan (*screams*)   Ahhhhhhhhhh!

Dana *looks at him – 'What are you doing?'*

Tristan   I'm doing exactly what people aren't expecting. Ahhhhhhhhhh!

Librarian   Stop it, or you'll have to be removed!

Tristan *runs between the chairs of seated people.*

Tristan   Come on. I swear, it feels great! Ahhhhhhhhhhhhhhhhhhhhhhhhhhh!

She hesitates, then –

Dana   Ahhhhhhhhhhhhhhh!

He stands on a chair.

Tristan   Ahhhhhhhh! That's it!

She gets on a chair.

Dana (*howls*)   Ah-wooooooo.

Tristan   Ah-wooooo!

All the students howl.

Viv *walks in and sees* **Dana** *howling with* **Tristan**. *The* **Headteacher** *walks in. Everyone stops howling.* **Dana** *and* **Tristan** *stop howling.*

Headteacher Tristan, I expected better of you! Detention!

Dana – erm, well . . . this is . . . complex . . . Let me think about this.

Viv *looks at* **Dana**, *hurt.* **Viv** *runs off.*

Dana *stays on her chair. The rest of the* **Company** *surround her, moving in closer . . . closer.*

Dana (*to the audience*) My heart's thumping, like it's in my throat. My mouth's dry. The adrenalin rising. Body's in fight or flight. Everything goes quiet, and far away –

The **Company** *are waves surrounding her.*

Dana The waves come. But somehow I stay above water. I gasp for air, and it goes in. Past my throat, and into my lungs. I watch the people on the shore, as I try to find my footing out at sea, but they're not looking. I thought they'd be staring. (*She reaches up to wave above the water.*) I'm waving, but I'm not drowning. 'Dana spoke . . . who gives a crap?'
But to me, it's a tsunami of epic proportions.

Loud music. **Dana** *jumps down from the chair into the human wave. The wave disperses.* **Dana** *stands there watching* **Viv**, *who is practising recording her TikTok dance on her phone, propped up on a chair.*

She ignores **Dana**, *and does the dance defiantly on her own.* **Viv** *mucks up the steps. She goes back, deletes it on her phone. Presses record again. Tries again, even more defiantly.*

Viv You just gonna stand there and watch?

Dana *doesn't say anything.*

Viv What's the matter – cat got your tongue?

Dana *doesn't say anything.* **Viv** *turns her back on her, and dances defiantly to her phone's camera. She stops.*

Viv Why wasn't it me?

Dana *doesn't speak.*

Viv I've done my homework on your condition. I read the books. I tried to do fading in with you. I stuck by you, when everyone else was laughing behind our backs.
Why was it Tristan you spoke to first? Why wasn't it me?

Dana *can't speak. She starts texting on her phone.*

Viv I know, I'm *contaminated*, right? Someone you've got a history of not speaking to. So instead you choose the male saviour? I mean, holy crap, Dana . . . have you been reading too much Jane Austen, or what?

There's a text message 'ping'. **Viv** *picks up her phone and reads.*

Dana Text Message   It means so much to you –

Viv   Of course it does.

Dana Text Message   That's not a question. I know it does. I want to talk so badly, but I don't want to let you down. I don't want to let anyone I care about down. It makes me . . . paralysed.

Viv   So now it's my fault?

A silence. **Dana** *types on her phone.*

Dana Text Message   I guess I spoke to Tristan because I don't care about him. I care about disappointing you.

Viv *is silent. After a moment,* **Viv** *pulls the sleeve of her t-shirt down – her shoulder has a giant plaster on it.*

Dana *looks at her – 'What happened?'*

Viv *peels the plaster back – we don't necessarily have to see what's underneath.*
Dana *looks at* **Viv***, shocked.*

Viv   It's Greta Thunberg.

Dana *types. Ping.*

Dana Text Message   W . . . T . . . A . . . F.

Viv   It'll look more like Greta Thunberg when it heals. Right now, it looks like Boris Johnson.

Dana *looks at her – 'Why?'*

Viv   OK, firstly, Greta Thunberg is a legend. Secondly, she didn't speak. She stopped speaking when she was a kid, for years. She had what you had. And people called her 'shy' and 'difficult' and 'angry.' But she wasn't. She was terrified. And she was in pain. And she took all of that, and she turned it into her superpower. Greta Thunberg is a superhero, Dana.

That's why I did this.

She gestures to her shoulder.

Because it was painful – don't believe what anyone tells you, it really really hurt. Like, I had to tell the guy to stop about two hundred times. And I just wanted to feel that pain that she went through. That you go through, all the time.

There's a long silence between them.

Dana *puts her phone down where* **Viv***'s phone was. She stands back, and dances* **Viv***'s TikTok dance moves from earlier. She stops, tries to remember what* **Viv** *was doing, dances again.*

Viv   Nah, it was like this –

She shows her the dance move.

Dana *copies the dance move.*

Viv Yeah, that's it.

Music rises. They do the dance together.

The Girls' Bathroom. Chairs are arranged like toilet cubicles. The Cool Girls are in a fluster.

Yaz Did you hear? The Mute spoke to Tristan.

Maya I told you she was obsessed.

Laura What did she say.

Yaz She howled at him.

Laura I knew it.

Yaz Not sure we can call her the Mute anymore.

Laura What do we call her?

Yaz Let's call her the 'Wolf'.

Maya That sounds way too cool.

Laura How about 'Diana', Goddess of the Moon? She howls at night.

Yaz Get you, and your classical references.

Laura She still isn't speaking. So you don't have to worry about her seducing Tristan.

Maya I'm not worried.

Yaz Yeah, apparently the freak freaked herself out.

Maya Why do you think I'd be worried?

Laura She's gone even quieter than before.

Maya I'm not worried.

Trinh Maybe us talking about it isn't helping?

They turn and stare at **Trinh** *for a second or two. Chairs start to move . . .*

Maya Why haven't you done your UCAS form?

Trinh I'm weighing up my options.

Laura What options?

Yaz (*leaving*) Oh my God, what did you do to your hair?

Laura (*panics*) Nothing. Why?

Yaz Looks blue.

Laura I used a hair mask.

She touches her hair as the girls exit. The location has morphed to the Calming Room.

Con *is holding court; the other Calming Room regulars listen attentively. It's Personal Statement Day.*

Con   This is it. This is the day to press 'send' on the rest of your life.
Or not.
Soldiers of Difference, it is time to stand up –

They stand.

Con   And bear arms.

They put their arms in the air in the 'tree position'.

Con   Pick up those yoga mats, and be that free, standing alone tree in the forest of life.

Toni   Trees can't really be free – they have roots.

Con (*interrupting*)   Say 'no' to getting on that A-level, university, low-paid entry job, treadmill of Western civilization. Because suddenly you may find yourself living in a shotgun shack. And you may find yourself in another part of the world. And you may find yourself behind the wheel of a large automobile. And you may find yourself in a beautiful house. With a beautiful partner. And you may ask yourself, 'Well, how did I get here?'

Saini   Word.

Mo   That's a song.

Con   What?

Mo   What you just said: it's a song.

Con   No, it's not.

Mo   My parents listen to that song.

Con   Coincidence.

Pete   Thing is, I do sort of want all of that.

Con *stares at* **Pete**. *Beat.*

Con   Did you do it? Did you write your personal statement like *the man* told you to? Did you toe the line?

Pete (*hesitates*)   I did.

Con   Did you use adverbs, and metaphors, and the word 'plethora'?

Pete (*ashamed*)   Twice.

Con   It's not your fault. You've been brainwashed by the normative world.

Pete I haven't been brainwashed. I have an inherited condition.

Con Don't let it define you.

Holly I say, 'Let it define you!'

Mo (*holding up phone*) It's a song by Talking Heads.

They stare at **Con**.

Saini Word.

A few students get up and start to leave.

Con Where are you going?

Holly We've got to present our personal statements.

Some others get up.

Con We're safer in numbers.

Anita We still have to work out how to be part of the world.

Holly In order for them to accept us, we need to accept ourselves. We have to learn to live with who we are.

Jono *gets up.*

Con *Et tu*, Jono?

Jono That's from *Julius Caesar*.

Toni You gotta attribute your citations, dude.

Saini Word.

The classroom. The **Company** *sits. The* **Headteacher** *addresses the class.*

Headteacher This is the first day of the rest of your lives. The day you press send on your university applications. And I would like to invite anybody sitting here, to stand and share their personal statement.
Who'd like to volunteer to go first?

Everyone looks away, no one wants to volunteer.

Headteacher Anyone?

Tristan *stands holding a piece of paper.* **Dana** *stands almost immediately at the same time. The whole class stare at her.*

Headteacher Oh, Dana. Do you need the toilet?

Dana *shakes her head.* **Tristan** *nods at* **Dana** *and he sits down.*

Everyone stares. **Dana** *holds up her personal statement. She takes a deep breath. She goes to read it. Her mouth dries. She rubs her lips together.*

Tom Mute!

Tristan   Shut up!

Yaz   Who's your boyfriend?

Class laugh. **Maya** *looks furious.* **Viv** *smiles at* **Dana**.

Headteacher   Let her speak.

Tristan   Come on, Dana.

Dana *looks at the class. There's a hiss. Someone else hisses.*

Viv *gets up.*

Viv   I can do it for you. If you like?

She takes the piece of paper from **Dana**.

Viv (*reading*)   'My name is Dana Alford. I'm seventeen years old. I could tell you about myself in 550 words – my hobbies, the books I've read, where I see myself in ten years' time. But those words wouldn't actually tell you who I am –'

Nav   Yawn-fest!

Sam *yawns ostentatiously.*

Viv (*continues reading*)   'Over my relatively short life, I've come to realize the way we communicate isn't just about words. It's not just sounds and images –'

Tom (*coughs*)   Bullfrogs!

Viv (*continues*)   'There are things –'

Dana *stands and joins in.*

Viv   . . . we don't see or hear.   **Dana**   There are things we don't see or hear.

Viv *stops. Everyone stares at* **Dana**. *A silence.* **Viv** *hands* **Dana** *her piece of paper.* **Dana** *takes a deep breath and reads on, addressing the class.*

Dana   In a forest, underneath the soil, trees speak to one another. A network of fungi grow underground around their roots. This fungal network is called the Wood Wide Web –

Tom   Loser.

Tristan   I'm warning you –

Dana   This is all true, I saw it on a David Attenborough documentary.

Viv   David Attenborough: legend!

Dana   The trees send messages to other trees through this underground network of connected mushrooms. If they're attacked by predators, they send messages through their roots to warn neighbouring trees. They can share food or nutrients if other trees are hungry or need help. And I believe we can live in a world where human beings are like this too.

We're not in competition with each other for space and light and likes and followers and university places. We're connected in lots of other ways. We can understand each other, without always having to speak.

And lastly I've come to the conclusion that falling down is OK. John Locke was wrong: We're not just solitary trees falling down in a wood with no one hearing. Someone will hear you. Someone will catch you.

They may even join you down there on the forest floor, listening to other trees beneath the ground.

Laura *stands.*

Laura   I pull my hair out. I started twirling it around and around my fingers when I get worried, and now I claw at it. I rip out chunks in my sleep. I have a bald patch underneath.

Sam (*standing*)   I bite my nails. Right down to the cuticle. I don't know why. They started to bleed. So I moved on to my toenails. Now I have a foot infection. I'm on antibiotics.

Trinh   I eat my feelings. I have a lot of feelings.

Maya   I don't eat because I have no feelings.

Nav   I have these thoughts I can't get out my head. Intruding on my brain. They tell me awful stuff. I can't make them go away.

Yaz   I don't have anything wrong with me, and that makes me feel left out. So I pretend that I do.

She gets upset with her confession. People go up to **Yaz** *to comfort her ('Hey'; 'That's OK . . .')*

Mo   I think we're gonna need a bigger 'Freaks and Geeks' Room.

Trinh *talks to the Cool Girls as chairs are put into rows.*

Trinh   I'm not applying to uni.

Laura (*shocked*)   What?!

Trinh   Uni's not the be-all and end-all –

Maya   It's the be-all and end-all.

Yaz   What are you gonna do?

Trinh   I'm gonna be an electrician's apprentice.

She pulls a lightbulb out of her pocket.

I want to make light happen.

She clicks her fingers and there's a flash of lights, like photographs being taken . . . School graduation.

*The **Company** mill around wearing mortarboards after the graduation ceremony.*
***Dana** stands around, in mortarboard, smiling and waving to people.*

Tristan   Hey, Dana, congrats.

She smiles.

Dana   Thanks. I'm sorry you didn't (get in) –

Tristan   Don't be. It's all good. I might come visit. See how the other half live.

*She nods. **Tristan** smiles. There's a silence between them. No words, but an understanding. He leaves.*

Viv *approaches wearing a mortarboard.*

Viv   So, you know I've been totally chill about you talking and all that? I was told, back in Year 7, if you ever did speak to me, I was to put on my cool hat and just act like it was totally normal. Like, not draw attention to it.

So, I've been wearing this cool hat – you see how cool I am? (*She shows off her uncool mortarboard.*) Yeah, well, screw the hat –

Viv *flings the hat off her head and starts dancing like a maniac.*

Viv   Am I drawing attention? Are you embarrassed right now?

Dana *laughs. She dances goofily alongside* **Viv**.

Viv   Oh, yes, that's it. Take it to the bus station. Go, Dana. Go, Dana.

They stop.

Dana   Thanks for being the best of best friends.

Viv   Leeds is 170 miles from Oxford. You have shorter terms than me –

Dana   I'll come visit.

Viv   You'll be OK, won't you?

Dana   Fo sho. I'll call you. If I'm not.

Viv   For what it's worth – you have an amazing voice.

Dana *smiles. The **Company** flood the stage around her.*

Dana *stands on a chair.*

Dana   My name is Dana Alford – and I have a voice.

Music swells. The class encircle her, like before, except . . .

Dana *falls backward off the chair, like a tree falling in the forest, and the other people in the class are there to catch her.*

Blackout.

The End.

For Maya Angelou, Albert Einstein, Greta Thunberg, Lola, and the millions of young people all over the world

who find it difficult to speak.

You are heard.

A note on alternative songs for page 69. Possibilities could be:
'Good 4 U' – Olivia Rodrigo
'So What' – Pink
'Experiment on Me' – Halsey
'Misery Business' – Paramore

Shout

BY ALEXIS ZEGERMAN

Notes on rehearsal and staging, drawn from a workshop with the writer, held at the National Theatre, October 2023

Exercises for use in rehearsals

Exercise: Wide Open

This physical warm-up served as an icebreaker and encouraged the group to explore the space. It also helped them build a vocabulary of movements that could be used later in their staging of different moments from the play.

Lead director Grace Gibson played up-tempo music and gave the group a moment to listen to the beat. She then asked them to:

- walk for a count of eight then jump for a count of eight
- walk for six then jump for six
- walk for four and jump for four
- and finally walk for two and jump for two

– after which the cycle would repeat.

When everyone could complete the cycle of movement confidently, Gibson added new actions, which replaced the jumps, to bring more variety to the sequence. The new cycle was:

- walk for eight, dance for eight
- walk for six, jump on the spot while looking at their hand (as if it was holding a phone) for six
- walk for four, point in the air while gently bobbing on the spot for four
- walk for two, travel around the space for two

As before, the cycle repeated until the whole group could complete it confidently. Gibson then further refined the sequence based on her observations of this emerging movement set piece. She now asked the group to:

- walk for eight, dance on the spot for eight
- walk for six, connect with a partner or partners by placing a hand on the other's shoulder for six
- walk for four, point in the air for four
- walk for two, jump on the spot while looking at a phone for two

Gibson's final instruction was to ask volunteers (those who felt particularly confident with the actions and running order of the latest sequence) to now perform it in reverse: *look at phone for two, point for four, connect for six and dance for eight.* Everyone else completed the cycle in the same order as before.

The overall effect was of a varied and visually striking movement set piece. Each person seemed united in purpose with their peers but were still able to express their individuality, through their direction of travel and their interpretation of each action. The option of performing the sequence in reverse heightened this diversity and provided a bracing counterpoint to the uniformity of each cycle.

Exercise: Change Direction

This physical warm-up encouraged the group to explore the room and engage different parts of their bodies.

Gibson changed the music to a quieter, lower tempo track and asked the group to start walking around the space. When everyone was settled into their walks, she introduced the simple instruction 'Change direction', prompting them to immediately choose a clear new course.

Having practiced this a few times, Gibson asked participants to now lead with their head whenever she called 'Change direction'. She invited them to pay attention to any differences in the quality, size, tempo, duration or sensation of their movements.

Gibson went on to ask the group to change direction leading with their shoulders, their hips and their knees, each time encouraging them to acknowledge any differences in their movement. She also encouraged everyone to make eye contact with their peers, open their awareness of others within the space, and to keep their movements sharp and precize.

Finally Gibson replaced the phrase 'Change direction' with just the name of the leading body part: *Head, Knees, Shoulder, Hips.* When everyone was doing this confidently, she added combinations of multiple body parts – for instance, *Hips and Head.*

Exercise: Stop, Go, Through . . .

Gibson segued directly into this physical collaborative improvisation.

She gave everyone in the group the choice of stopping and starting their movement whenever they wanted. They could also vary their speed, from walking to running.

While the group practiced this, Gibson arranged a few chairs around the space. Group members could now sit or stand on the chairs or floor whenever they chose to stop.

Gibson added a new movement option: whenever individuals saw a gap between two other people, they could accelerate to pass through this space, slowing down afterwards. And a further option: group members could now follow others.

Gibson encouraged the group to avoid falling into repetitive patterns: 'If you find yourself doing one thing, try something else.' She drew attention to their pacing and invited them to experiment with moving very quickly and extremely slowly.

Gibson added one final option, listing all the previous choices mentioned. Group members could now stop, go, speed up to pass through two others, follow and now copy peers.

With these options established, Gibson gave the group an intention: 'What happens if we imagine this is a hostile environment? How does this change how you move?' She continued to offer acting prompts as the game developed into a whole group improvisation: 'How does it change your relationship to space?' 'Are you alone? Are you with other people in this moment?' 'What does it feel like if this becomes a playful environment?'

Gibson gathered the group and asked them to share what they saw and experienced. Their observations and reflections included:

- 'It was a great way to explore the space in a playful but controlled way.'
- 'I'd see someone do something and think "I like that, I'm gonna do that."'
- 'It was really interesting watching individuals within the ensemble – how each person's individuality came through, either on their own or within the clump of people.'
- 'Making eye contact is so simple but it really changes the intention behind a movement.'
- 'The hostile version felt more purposeful.'
- 'It became more powerful and interesting when it became more collaborative.'
- 'You can't help but project story and characters onto different individuals.'

Exercise: Turkey, Turkey, Turkey

Gibson used this icebreaker and language-based concentration game to re-centre the group after a tea break.

She asked the group to stand in a circle and stood in the centre. She explained that she was going to point at each of them in turn going clockwise round the circle. When she pointed at a player, they had to say the next number in the following sequence: *one, two, three, four, five, four, three, two, one, two, three* . . . This continued until everyone had had a turn saying a number.

In the next round, Gibson continued to cue players by pointing at them but instead of moving methodically around the circle, she chose a random order.

Next, she asked players to replace the number two with the name of an animal. An animal cannot be repeated in the same round, e.g., *1, shark, 3, 4, 5, 4, 3, porcupine, 1, zebra, 3* . . . Again she chose players at random.

Subsequent rounds replaced:

- the number 3 with food, e.g. *1, leopard, hummus, 4, 5, 4, lasagne, bear, 1, schnauzer, sandwich* . . .
- the number 4 with the name of a country, e.g. *1, otter, jelly, France, 5, India, pasta, koala, 1* . . .

The game is so called because 'Turkey' is the only word you can use to replace all three numbers – animal, food and country.

Exercise: Pass the Click

This concentration game started with everyone standing in a circle. Gibson demonstrated the basic unit of the game: the first person makes clear eye contact with another player and throws a click at them; the second player clicks to receive the pass then again makes eye contact with another person and throws the click at them.

After the group grew in confidence, Gibson introduced a new element: when she clapped her hands, the group would leave the circle and start moving around the space, all the while continuing to pass the click between them. When she clapped again, the circle reformed, with the click still travelling between players.

It is an effective game to demonstrate how to keep the space alive, to keep the energy passing from person to person, and to recognize that everyone has a responsibility to keep it going.

Applying exercises to the play

Wide Open/Stop, Go, Through . . ./Pass the Click

Gibson took all the discoveries made playing and reflecting on the games and applied these to the script, replacing the click with the first line of the play: 'Word' (p. 54). Players no longer had to 'receive' the pass, only to 'throw' it to the next person by making eye contact and saying the line.

Gibson clapped her hands to cue the breaking of the circle and movement around the space.

Gibson then asked the group to think about the beginning of the play – the atmosphere of the playground at the start of the school day, the means by which news and gossip travel across that space, and the way in which this information is received. Everyone played the game, again breaking the circle and circulating around the space before re-forming the circle once more. The whole group was much more responsive to each other, with individuals interacting non-verbally as well as with speech.

Gibson followed this up with a request for a volunteer. This person would then play the role of Dana, the protagonist from the play. Riffing off the rules of 'Pass the Click', Gibson gave Dana and the rest of the group (now in the roles of school peers) contrasting intentions: Dana has to 'catch' the word; the other students must 'pass' the word amongst themselves but prevent her from 'receiving' it. Informed by the earlier exercises (in particular 'Stop, Go, Through . . .'), the performers had a repertoire of movements and choices to draw on in their interactions with each other and when blocking Dana.

In the subsequent improvisation, Dana moved around and across the circle trying to make eye contact with the different speakers of the line, sometimes inserting herself between them and the person they were trying to address. As the circle dissolved, Dana found the other students turned their backs on her, blocked her path and toyed with her as if they were playing a game of 'Piggy in the Middle'.

For the next improvisation, Gibson asked for a new volunteer to play Dana and gave the character a new intention: rather than try to 'catch' the word, she should instead observe the other students' interactions, as if a David Attenborough-style documentary filmmaker. In this run-through, Dana initially kept her distance from the group, climbing on a chair to observe them from height. As the circle re-formed, she moved to the centre, crouching to make herself as small as possible. When the improvisation was finished, participants made the following observations:

- 'There were moments when you [the volunteer playing Dana] were still and everyone else was moving around you. It's so funny how you focus on the one person who is not doing the same as everyone else.'
- 'How can we give Dana focus? Is it a bright top? Is it to do with speed, is it to do with height?'
- 'How do we play with these elements to bring her in and out of focus?'

Staging technology

Shout is full of references to communication technology used by young people, from TikTok videos to text messages. The writer Alexis Zegerman has even turned some of these technologies into characters in their own right, giving voices to Dana and Tristan's messages on SnapChat and Dana's Word Doc.

Focusing on the section in which Dana and Tristan exchange messages (pp. 65–6: 'So how do we do this? How do we – (talk)?' to 'So why don't you speak?'), Gibson modelled a process for approaching the play's non-naturalistic moments. She started with a couple of seated read-throughs: four volunteers read the speaking roles, a fifth read the stage directions. Gibson drew particular attention to the scene's implied pauses and silences, arising from the characters' awkwardness with each other and the time required to send and receive messages. However, she was also mindful that the scene's rhythm did not become monotonous: once the convention of messaging has been established for the audience, the gap between sending and receiving can be shrunk.

When everyone was more familiar with the dialogue, pacing and shape of this section, Gibson put the scene 'on its feet'. She was especially keen to explore the spatial relationship between Dana and Tristan and between the messages. Over a series of run-throughs, she experimented with different staging options. In one run, Dana and Tristan were very still and grounded while their messages were much more mobile. In another version, Dana had a close collaborative relationship with her messenger while Tristan's was more messy and dysfunctional, reflecting their respective comforts and familiarity with this method of communication. Gibson added performers to expand the two messenger roles into choruses; this unlocked a wide range of expressive possibilities for exploring the human characters' relative status to each other, their competency with the technology and the inherent comedy of the situation.

Gibson took a moment after each run to allow those observing to feedback on what they had just watched: they variously reported enjoying the playfulness and physicality of the different stagings and the potential to use the whole company as Dana and Tristan's message 'factions'. Some directors drew parallels with language interpreters, the daemons from *His Dark Materials* and the emotion characters from *Inside Out*; these references then informed later versions of the staging.

Following these experiments, Gibson led a mind-mapping exercise to gather ideas about how companies might stage the play's striking treatment of digital communication. Offers included presenting the messaging app roles:

- As human-like characters performed by one actor each
- As a chorus, either speaking in unison or with individuals taking a line each. One messenger might have a larger chorus than the other to reflect their respective confidence levels. Chorus members might even defect from one human character to another to show changes in status
- Using projection
- Using lighting – for instance, phone torches or screens to illuminate the character that is messaging
- Using cardboard cutouts of SnapChat Bitmoji or digital avatars
- Using puppetry
- With on-stage microphones
- With voiceover
- With sound design – live or pre-recorded; digital or with instrumentation and vocals

This mind mapping led into them having a go at the scene. There was a conversation about how much tech is necessary here as one director wanted to involve their tech students, which would be great but as long as it contributed to the text rather than distracting from.

Approaching sensitive themes

Exercise: Empowering Headphones

This acting and emotional memory exercise demonstrated an approach to the 'Headphones' scene (pp. 68–9, 'Hey' to 'Dana!'). Ahead of the workshop, Gibson had asked the directors to choose a song that empowered them and to bring it on a phone or personal music player along with headphones. She directed the participants to stand in their own space in the room and respond to their music in whichever way felt natural to them: if they wanted to sing, they could sing; if they wanted to dance, they could dance, etc. After their track finished, they would sit on the floor where they were. Gibson led the group in taking a deep breath in then asked them to shut their eyes and press play.

Gibson repeated the exercise two further times, with half the group responding to their music and the other half observing the variety of different behaviours expressed whilst listening.

Observations included:

- 'It was interesting seeing everyone's different approach to letting go, what that looks like. It made me think about how you approach this with a youth group, say as a group song for a warm-up.'
- 'It felt like it was such a personal thing that I was watching and so individual to people I did not really know – which is really lovely for what that means in the script, because it is a really vulnerable moment.'
- 'It made me think of the private and public self and, for Dana, what is that intersection where they meet.'
- 'Out of the blue people sang moments of the song rather than the whole song. Was it the only part that they remembered or was a part that was really meaningful to them? It made me think whether that would be useful when doing this scene.'
- 'It was quite inspiring and interesting – the difference from comedy to the serious rawness. I think trying to find that balance for an audience that they're comfortable laughing along with Tristan when he's doing it, but when Dana does it it's such a shock.'
- 'I'm interested with how different stimulus – different songs – affect the scene.'

Exercise: Exploring Anxiety

This emotional literacy exercise invited participants to write lists as a means of better understanding and expressing the effects of anxiety. It uses metaphors to, as Gibson put it, 'step slightly outside of it' and find creative ways of having sensitive conversations with young people.

Gibson asked the group members to collect writing materials and sit alone, separate from peers.

She then gave them a series of prompts over an increasingly compressed timeframe:

- 30 seconds to list what anxiety tastes like
- 15 seconds to list the colours of anxiety
- ten seconds to list what anxiety smells like
- ten seconds to list the textures of anxiety
- ten seconds to list the times of day of anxiety

Gibson encouraged the participants to list individual words and short phrases. The compressed duration brought focus to the group and forced the members to think and write quickly and unselfconsciously, as there was no time to deliberate or self-censor.

Afterwards, participants shared items from their lists, including:

Tastes: onions, metallic, sour, bitter, vomit, dry cake, TV static, a pill stuck in your throat

Colours: grey, white, orange, acid green, puke green, blood red, bright lights hazy in the rain

Smells: chemicals, sweat, vinegar, sea water, rotten food, foisty (musty damp), car exhaust, soot

Textures: fizzy, gritty, spiky, sticky, touching a bruize, water pressure, scratchy dry of a wool jumper, wooden lollipop sticks, nail file

Times of Day: 4 am; as I arrive at work; just before I'm eating; 'Sunday Scary'; bedtime; whenever the iPhone alarm goes off; before a journey; the school run

This activity might not be suitable for all companies, and you should make a judgement call based on the young people's needs. Anxiety can be very isolating and (if considered appropriate) this exercise can potentially help young people find connections between their own experiences and those of peers.

Exercise: Body/Texture

Gibson segued directly into the following devising activity.

She asked the participants to gather into groups of six to eight people and gave each group a large piece of paper and pens. She then requested that they divide their paper in half, labelling one half 'Body Parts' and the other half 'Textures'. The groups had three minutes to write a list for the first category, followed by another three minutes for the second category, drawing on their personal lists from the previous exercise.

Next, Gibson asked them to make five pairs from their two lists, with each pair connecting a body part with an anxiety texture. Combinations included:

- Fizzy fingers
- Custard skin lips
- Pins and needles knees
- Paper cut heart
- Shaky lips
- Itchy sternum
- Sandpaper neck
- Gritty teeth
- Heavy chest
- Scratchy shoulder

Gibson then gave the groups ten minutes to devise a repeatable movement sequence from the five pairs. Each group demonstrated their moves to music with a clear beat, heavy bass and a steady, gentle tempo. The movement sequences shared were detailed, delicate and full of contrasts.

Exercise: Staging Scenes

Gibson invited participants to collaborate in small groups to stage either the 'Snake' scene (pp. 61–2, 'Fading in is a kind of exposure therapy' to 'Let's try again next week.') or the 'Waves' scene (p. 74, 'My heart's thumping, like it's in my throat.' to 'But to me, it's a tsunami of epic proportions.'). She encouraged them to draw on all the activities they had participated in that day: the exploratory exercises, vocabularies of gesture and movement, and conversations about technology and anxiety. The groups had 25 minutes to find an ensemble approach to staging these script sections. Gibson asked that they pay particular attention to the pressure put on Dana and the other characters and to the formations of performers on stage.

Examples of the work included:

One group darkened the lights, illuminating Dana with only a phone torch. Taking further inspiration from the 'Staging Technology' discussion, the performers created the encroaching waves through a live vocal soundscape.

Another group took a highly physical approach to staging the 'Waves' scene, lifting Dana across the stage – perhaps inspired by choreography from the earlier 'Body/Texture' exercise.

Another used body percussion to make Dana's accelerating heartbeat, their formation – a slowly shrinking circle – representing the waves closing in on her.

Tackling the 'Snake' scene, one company used choral gesture to create the mass and threat of the reptile, synchronizing their breath to coordinate their movement. The final group used the BSL sign for 'snake' (a clever riff on the play's themes of speech and silence) to communicate Dana's fears.

Question and answer with Alexis Zegerman

Q: Can you explain your thinking behind the mortarboards moment and graduation ceremony? This is quite unusual at the end of sixth form.
A: The scene takes place at some point after the characters have got their exam results, knowing where they are going to university. It's a celebratory moment indicating a new stage in life. Like a prom. The mortarboards are emblematic of a celebration: the characters are 'dressed up' (regardless of what they are actually wearing). I thought putting on a mortarboard is easier than a prom dress, and the hat makes it very obvious what they are celebrating: their exams. And there is one character, Trinh, who is not going to university but is there with a lightbulb. So there is a lot of imagery that is emblematic of where they are in their lives, and where they might be going.

Q: Could it be a celebration event with different costumes or are the mortarboards crucial to that moment?
A: I guess not. Dana's best friend talks of wearing hats so she would need to be wearing some sort of headgear – I guess it could be a baseball cap – and then at the celebratory moment the young people would all need to do something other than throwing their mortarboards up in the air. But yes, that stage direction can absolutely be interpreted as something else, because not every company is going to be able access multiple mortarboards.

Q: What is the timeline that you were thinking of as you were writing the play? Does it cover the whole of sixth form or just a few months?
A: It's basically a school year. This is helpful in terms of Dana's motivation: she is now in her last year of school, after which she would think of herself as an adult. She has got this year to learn whether she is going to have to cope in a speaking world as a non-speaker or whether she is going to overcome her deepest fear.

Q: The play features neurodivergent characters and characters with different mental health challenges. What is the most appropriate way to get young people who may not have experience of these conditions to embody them on stage?
A: Don't play the condition, play the character. Whether they are Student 1 or Student 2 or another numbered rather than named character, each one of them is a person. There are no small parts. Everyone comes on with a history and somewhere that they're going, somewhere that they want to be. Every single person in the 'Freaks and Geeks' Room should have as much of an idea of their character as the actor playing Dana does. Just because she has more words on the page doesn't mean that her character has more internal life than the others. You just have to play the truth of it.

Q: Some of the play's language doesn't fit our performers' accents very well. Are we able to find alternative words or phrases if they do not sit comfortably with our cast?
A: Absolutely. All that matters to me is that the line scans. I want your groups to feel ownership of the play.

Q: When we first meet the 'Freaks and Geeks', what was your intention with the listing of conditions and medications?
A: It's about all the options that are open to Dana. This is Dana's journey from the beginning to the end of this last school year. She is absolutely desperate to fit in – either celebrate her difference (which is very, very hard in a world where everyone talks) or overcome it. The medications are part of that journey: 'I could try the drugs'. It's another option that Dana could try to get to her end goal of living in an adult world. It's another stepping stone. I have left the moment open: you can do a scene change here, movement or dance underscored with music.

Q: To clarify, this list is of medications that are prescribed for anxiety?
A: Not all of those drugs are for anxiety. But they are definitely drugs that might be prescribed to people in the Calm Room.

Q: Do you have a preference as to whether the character's name is pronounced 'DAY-na' or 'DA-na'?
A: No, you should choose whichever best fits your cast's accents. Or whichever is your favourite!

Q: Are you comfortable with certain characters being gender swapped?
A: Absolutely. I don't think there should be any issues other than pronouns, which I am very, very happy for you to change. In fact, when we did the workshop with a young company and Grace Gibson was casting the read-through, she asked, 'Who wants to be the Cool Girls?' and all of the boys' arms went up. It was just an absolute joy that some of the Cool Girls were played by boys.

Q: In terms of stage directions, some playwrights regard them as suggestions and others are clear that 'this is what I want.' Where do you fall on that sliding scale?
A: That's a really good question! Where the stage directions are silences – because it is a play about silence and noise – I would prefer it if these were considered. But in terms of other stage directions, they are just suggestions. Like, no one needs to get plastic snakes out for the 'Fading In' scene – there is a world with prop snakes and a world that uses other amazing, multifaceted means of staging the scene. It's a starting point. Go and play and make it your own.

Q: There is a section where the company shout slogans such as 'Save the Earth', 'Save the trees' and others. Could we add a few similar sentences within that section?
A: You could repeat these slogans and give the same chants to lots of other people. Repeating that list of slogans is absolutely fine, particularly if you have a crowd of people that you would like to keep chanting. That activity earlier ['Wide Open'] when you were walking, jumping and dancing, and some of you were counting a different beat, that sort of thing could absolutely work verbally in this section.

Q: Regarding the music and singing, can you suggest some alternative songs for that moment in the play?
A: There are some suggested alternatives at the end of the script. At the workshop, I asked the young people who their favourite angry, female singer-songwriters are and they were all obsessed with Pink! It was very surprising, a bit retro! There are loads of different songs that give that same energy, so experiment.

Q: Is it important to you that the singer is female?
A: No. I think use whatever song will give your actors that feeling of anger or ownership or that ability to bring the internal external. I get that feeling from listening to the Alanis Morissette track but those other songs that I have listed at the end of the text will do the same.

From a workshop led by Grace Gibson
With notes by Stewart Melton

ORCHESTRA

by Charlie Josephine

Charlie Josephine is an actor and a writer, passionate about making work that centres working-class women and queer people. In summer 2022, their play *I, Joan* opened at Shakespeare's Globe. Recent theatre work includes *Flies* for Boundless *One of Them Ones* for Pentabus and *Birds and Bees* for Theatre Centre. Their previous award-winning plays include *Bitch Boxer* and *BLUSH*. Charlie Josephine's play *Cowbois*, which they co-directed with Sean Holmes, opened at the Royal Shakespeare Company in 2023, and then transferred to the Royal Court in January 2024. They are also currently developing a new feature biopic with Salon Pictures. They are is an associate artist at the NSDF and board trustee at Cardboard Citizens.

Characters/Casting

1st Flute – *any gender.* **2nd Flute** – *any gender.*
1st Clarinet – *any gender.* **2nd Clarinet** – *any gender.* **3rd Clarinet** – *any gender.*
Bass Clarinet – *any gender.*
1st Trumpet – *should be a lad.* **2nd Trumpet** – *should be a lad.* **3rd Trumpet** – *is referred to as 'Mia', with she/her pronouns. Should be a girl.*
1st Trombone – *any gender.* **2nd Trombone** – *any gender.*
Tuba – *any gender.*
Percussion – *any gender.*
Bassoon – *any gender.* **Oboe** – *any gender.*
1st Alto Sax – *is referred to as 'Alyssa', and with she/her pronouns. Should be a girl.*
2nd Alto Sax – *is referred to as 'Nathan', and with he/him pronouns. Could be changed to any name or gender.* **3rd Alto Sax** – *any gender.* **Tenor Sax** – *any gender.*

Notes

I've tried to be as flexible as possible with cast. Most parts could be any gender. And please feel free to question where I've stipulated a specific choice. You could double up parts if you're short of actors. I think 11 actors is probably the smallest cast size (flute, clarinet, two trumpets, trombone, tuba, percussion, oboe/bassoon, three saxophones). I'm imagining just chairs on the stage with no other props. I'd encourage you to find some abstract and gorgeous movement for the performers' bodies during the moments where they're playing music.

A / indicates a fast run onto the next line, almost an interruption.

A /. . indicates where a word can't be found and the actor does something physical to express themself. It could be a small pedestrian gesture or a big abstract movement.

A . indicates where a character should have a line, but is choosing not to speak.

The cast walk on stage, one by one in single file. It's all very, very serious. They sit in their places on plastic chairs, and slowly begin to hold invisible musical instruments. They shuffle invisible music on invisible music stands. They warm up their fingers and take deep breaths. We hear their breathing, all different rhythms and lengths. A cacophony of loud inhales and exhales. The breathing gets faster and louder as they fall into sync with each other. They very slowly rise to their feet. Once all stood they suddenly stop, are still, then sit down as if nothing happened. They speak directly to us.

3rd Alto Sax   I know what you're thinking. But this isn't a school band.

1st Clarinet   Good God no!

1st Trumpet   We're actually really good.

2nd Flute   We're the best in the country.

Bassoon   This is National Wind Youth Orchestra.

Oboe   Or NWYO, for short.

Tuba   That's never caught on.

Oboe   Yes it has!

Tuba   No one says that.

Oboe   Well, I do. When people ask what I'm doing, for the holidays /

1st Clarinet   it's the half term holidays, and we're all here /

3rd Clarinet   in this smelly church hall.

2nd Clarinet   We play together /

3rd Clarinet   every day /

1st Clarinet   for a week.

1st Flute   Hours and hours and *hours*!

2nd Clarinet   Every day, rehearsing for the concert /

1st Trumpet   on Saturday night.

Oboe   When people ask how I'll spend half term, I tell them I'm at NWYO.

Tuba   Oh my God no way!

Oboe   What?

Tuba   I don't tell anyone I'm here.

1st Flute   What? Why?

Tuba   Are you joking? I play the *tuba*!

1st Flute   Yeah?

Tuba   No one cool plays the tuba!

Oboe   But you're the best in the country?!

Tuba   That's even worse!

Oboe   Is it?

1st Clarinet   I don't mind people knowing, but yeah my friends don't wanna, like, come listen or anything. It's not really their style of music.

Bassoon   Yeah same.

1st Trumpet   Yeah. My friends from school are all out, partying and whatever. They're not really into classical music.

Tuba   Oh my God no! I'd die if they found out.

Oboe   That's so weird. I'm proud to be here.

1st Flute   Me too! Not everyone is invited to play in *this* orchestra.

1st Trumpet   Only the *best* in the *country* get to play here.

1st Clarinet   You have to audition, *twice*, to get in.

2nd Flute   And it's not free either.

1st Flute   It's actually quite expensive.

2nd Flute   My mum was quite shocked when they sent through the letter with the fees on it. She can afford it, of course. But still, it's quite expensive.

1st Flute   There's an offer of discount under /

1st & 2nd Flute   'extraordinary circumstances'.

2nd Flute   We have a few of those this year.

1st Flute   One or two.

Everyone looks at **3rd Alto Sax**. *Who tries to front it out, but blushes hard.*

3rd Alto Sax   So?

1st & 2nd Flute   Nothing!

Everyone turns back to us.

1st Flute   We're the Flute section. I'm First.

2nd Flute   Second.

Oboe   Oboe.

Bassoon   Bassoon.

2nd Flute   On the other side is the Clarinets /

1st Clarinet   First.

2nd Clarinet Second. And /

Bass Clarinet Bass Clarinet.

1st Alto Sax Us Saxophones are in the middle. I'm First.

2nd Alto Sax Second.

3rd Alto Sax Third.

Tenor Sax Tenor.

1st Alto Sax The brass are stood behind us /

1st & 2nd & 3rd Trumpet Trumpets.

1st Trumpet First.

2nd Trumpet Second.

3rd Trumpet Third.

1st & 2nd Trombone Trombones.

1st Trombone First.

2nd Trombone And Second.

Tuba Tuba.

1st Alto Sax And behind them is the /

Percussion Percussion section.

Tenor Sax Each section is then broken down into first, second, third, sometimes even fourth parts.

3rd Alto Sax First is the best /

1st Alto Sax obviously. It's the hardest part to play.

2nd Alto Sax If there's a solo then First position gets to play it.

Tenor Sax They're the leader of their section.

3rd Alto Sax They're supposed to be inspiring and supportive but they're usually stuck up and scared and sweaty.

2nd Alto Sax We all want to be First one day.

Tenor Sax Alyssa is First on Alto Saxophone. And the leader of our section.

2nd Alto Sax She doesn't speak much. Just sits quietly, not ever really saying anything, to anyone. She's a brilliant player.

Tenor Sax & 2nd Alto Sax Brilliant.

3rd Alto Sax She sight reads *so* easily /

2nd Alto Sax so easily!

Tenor Sax   Like she knows all the music instantly?!

3rd Alto Sax   She takes music *really seriously*!

Tenor Sax   She's going to be a professional musician.

3rd Alto Sax   Wow!

2nd Alto Sax   Yeah. There's this whole plan.

3rd Alto Sax   Oh right.

Tenor Sax   Her dad's an MP for the Tory party.

3rd Alto Sax   Oh, course he is!

2nd Alto Sax   And he's having an affair with the secretary.

3rd Alto Sax   Oh.

2nd Alto Sax   Everyone knows about it and no one talks about it.

Tenor Sax   Her mum cries all the way through concerts.

2nd Alto Sax   And we all know it's not because she's moved by the music.

3rd Alto Sax   Anyway, Alyssa is brilliant.

Tenor Sax & 2nd Alto Sax   Brilliant!

Tenor Sax   I think certain people play certain instruments. So when someone tells you what they play it's hardly a surprise, sometimes you can just guess. Like all the Oboes are weird.

Oboe   Hey!

2nd Alto Sax   They are the geekiest of all of us.

Oboe   That's maybe true.

3rd Alto Sax   They're really posh. Softly spoken.

1st Flute   They have furry pink bobbles on the end of their pencils.

1st Clarinet   And childish headbands in their hair.

2nd Flute   And they have ill-fitting clothes that come from /

2nd Clarinet   Marks & Spencer?

3rd Alto Sax   Somewhere posh. Why is it that posh people have shit clothes? I'd wear well nice things if I had the money.

1st Trumpet   The Flutes are fit.

3rd Trumpet   They're pretty, and girly and blonde and /

2nd Clarinet   bitchy.

1st Clarinet   The Trumpets always fancy the Flutes.

1st Flute The Clarinets are usually really nice, like all the time.

2nd Alto Sax Their parts are always these mad interlocking chords and scales and rhythms, so when they're working together well it's like they're, like, one organism, like an animal? It's amazing! I find myself watching them the most. Like some weird creature, like a centipede!

1st Flute The Horn section are the most annoying.

1st Clarinet Usually boys with spots and egos and testosterone just oozing out of them.

1st Flute Gross!

3rd Clarinet They talk too much /

1st Flute and are always making The Most Noise in the breaks /

3rd Clarinet and they argue and /

1st Clarinet take the piss out of each other /

2nd Clarinet and they think they're rock stars but they're not /

1st Flute they're really not /

2nd Flute they cry when they get it wrong.

1st Trumpet We don't!

Oboe We usually spend a lot of rehearsal time working out which one of them is out of tune.

Bass Clarinet And then they blush bright red /

Bassoon like tomatoes.

Bass Clarinet And they're mean to each other /

Bassoon laughing.

Oboe And the Flutes flutter and giggle at them.

1st & 2nd Flute We don't!

Bassoon They flirt with each other, across the room /

1st & 2nd Flute oh my gosh! We *don't*!

Bassoon & 2nd Clarinet & Oboe You do!

Oboe It's gross.

Tuba The Percussion lot are in their own world most of the time.

Bass Clarinet Stoned, maybe?

Tenor Sax They jam together during the lunch break and sound amazing.

1st Flute So that's all of us.

Oboe   And Angela.

1st Flute   Oh my God Angela!

1st Trumpet   Ah! Angela!

Oboe   She's our conductor.

1st Flute   She's *wonderful*!

2nd Clarinet   She's got strawberry blonde hair /

2nd Trombone   and big bright eyes /

Tenor Sax   and she wears bright lipstick /

2nd Trumpet   and silk scarfs /

1st Alto Sax   and her cheeks are red from all the wine she drinks /

3rd Alto Sax   and she smokes fags /

1st Clarinet   we all know she smokes /

3rd Clarinet   though smoking is really bad for you.

3rd Alto Sax   Yeah but it makes her voice sound amazing!

Percussion   Yeah!

3rd Alto Sax   Her laugh? It's like this, this gorgeous gaggle, like water going down a drain.

Percussion   Yeah.

1st Trombone   She looks like a cat.

2nd Alto Sax   A big chubby cat /

Oboe   that gives the best ever cuddles /

Percussion   though she's not supposed to touch us because of safeguarding.

Tuba   She knows everything about everyone, somehow you just end up telling her.

Percussion   Yeah.

Tuba   She calls everyone sweetie or sweetheart or darlin'.

2nd Trumpet   And it's blatantly because she's forgotten our names /

Percussion   but it feels nice all the same.

Bass Clarinet   And we know she sneaks off to the pub at lunchtime for a cheeky half /

Percussion   or two.

3rd Alto Sax   And we know when she's hungover /

3rd Clarinet   and when she's having a 'hot flush' /

2nd Trumpet and when she's about to blow her top.

1st Flute She wears too much perfume, and it's like she casts a spell over us /

1st Trumpet she's intoxicating!

2nd Flute Everyone looks up to her like she's their mum.

Bassoon She's basically the reason we come back every year.

They all shift positions.

Oboe Day one is always the same.

1st Trombone Busy car park.

2nd Alto Sax Busy entrance hall.

3rd Trumpet Long sign-in sheets.

3rd Clarinet Awkward goodbyes to parents.

Bass Clarinet Awkward hellos to each other.

2nd Clarinet Oh my God, that's my ex! Hide me, hide me, hi!

Tuba Hi.

2nd Clarinet Hi!

Tuba Hi.

2nd Clarinet Great!

Tuba Yup.

Oboe Ah it's nice to be back!

Bassoon Yeah, it smells the same.

1st Flute Oh hey, nice to see you!

2nd Trumpet Hi!

Bass Clarinet Hi!

Tenor Sax Hi!

2nd Clarinet It's the same set-up /

2nd Trombone every year! And /

2nd Flute every face is familiar.

3rd Alto Sax Except mine.

Everyone stares at **3rd Alto Sax**.

3rd Alto Sax Hi! . . . I'm new.

Everyone is still staring at them.

3rd Alto Sax Okaaaay?!

1st Clarinet Is that /

1st Trumpet yeah /

3rd Clarinet oh /

2nd Trombone yeah, that's /

2nd Flute the one /

1st Flute I was /

2nd Trumpet telling you about /

Bass Clarinet ohh!

Tuba Ohh!

3rd Alto Sax Ohh?

They all slowly move towards **3rd Alto Sax**, *sniffing the air like dogs. Just as it looks like they might pounce on them they all suddenly snap their heads to the front.*

Oboe Angela!

They spring back to their positions and look well behaved. **3rd Alto Sax** *is last to sit down, looking a bit shell shocked.*

1st Alto Sax Angela does these funny little competitions between /

1st Flute the Flute section /

1st Clarinet and the Clarinet section /

Bassoon which always actually makes everyone play better.

Oboe And she's always teasing the boys /

1st Trumpet by which she means the Trumpet section /

1st Alto Sax even though Mia also plays Trumpet. She always forgets and is, like, 'Boys! Oh and Mia!' And Mia blushes and frowns /

3rd Trumpet and hates the patriarchy.

1st Alto Sax Mia is actually really good.

3rd Trumpet Thanks.

1st Alto Sax But she never gets to play First, because the boys take over and play louder, so they get given the hard bits to do /

3rd Trumpet because it's meant to make them behave better. Like if they've got some more responsibility they'll stop messing about, and they'll rise to the challenge, and feel important, because they've been given something to do.

1st Flute So classic.

1st Clarinet Yeah, we all know the teachers' tactics.

2nd Flute Adults are so predictable.

2nd Clarinet Yeah, they do stuff and it's, like, yeah we know what you're doing!

1st Flute Yeah, like I know what this is, but /

1st Flute & 1st Clarinet OK /

2nd Clarinet I'll play along cos it seems to make *you* happy /

2nd Flute yeah, and it'll probably be easier if I just pretend and /

1st Flute & 1st Clarinet go along with it.

2nd Alto Sax When you make a mistake Angela makes a joke and says something like /

3rd Clarinet 'Oh! The saxophones were doing a bit of rewriting in that last section! And though it was interesting, we don't think the composer will be very happy with that, so let's hear it again, and as it's written this time please!'

2nd Alto Sax And then we have to play from bar twenty-two to the end of the phrase /

1st Alto Sax and bar twenty-two is the hardest bit in the piece /

Tenor Sax so we're all panicking!

3rd Alto Sax And we have to play it in front of everyone.

2nd Alto Sax And we do. And it's /

1st Trombone a total car crash!

1st Trumpet A smash of notes /

2nd Trumpet all screaming at each other /

2nd Trombone as they fall down the stairs!

1st Alto Sax Everyone pulls faces /

2nd Alto Sax and laughs /

3rd Alto Sax and one of the Trumpets whistles like /

Tenor Sax *whistles.*

2nd Flute And Angela frowns at them /

2nd Clarinet but her eyes are smiling.

1st Alto Sax And we have to play it /

2nd Alto Sax one /

3rd Alto Sax by /

Tenor Sax   one.

3rd Alto Sax   And of course Alyssa does it perfectly /

1st Alto Sax   yes, I do.

3rd Alto Sax   Then Nathan does it *pretty* perfectly /

2nd Alto Sax   near enough.

3rd Alto Sax   Then I play it, and, and it's /

2nd Alto Sax   embarrassing /

1st Alto Sax   humiliating /

Tenor Sax   awful!

3rd Alto Sax   And Angela says she knows what I'll be doing in my lunch break.

1st Alto Sax   And *everyone* stares.

2nd Alto Sax   And you nod.

3rd Alto Sax   I want to die.

Tenor Sax   And thankfully Angela moves on, and Alyssa /

3rd Alto Sax   glares at me like I've /

1st Alto Sax   let her down personally.

3rd Alto Sax   And Nathan /

2nd Alto Sax   is embarrassed for me /

3rd Alto Sax   but says nothing. And I hate myself for getting it wrong. I feel really stupid.

Tenor Sax   You spent the whole lunch break going over it /

2nd Alto Sax   and over it /

Tenor Sax   and over it.

3rd Alto Sax   I don't even eat! So then later that day when we do that bit again I do it perfectly and loudly and Angela says /

3rd Clarinet   'It's a relief to hear the saxophones have stopped rewriting the music, and are now in fact playing what's written. Perhaps now they could take note of the suggested volume level and not completely blast it!'

1st Alto Sax   And the Flutes titter and smile at Angela /

2nd Alto Sax   and look smug at us like they /

1st Flute   *never* blast it*, ever* /

2nd Flute   they'd never do something /

1st Flute   so *crude*!

Tenor Sax   But it's only cos they *can't* blast it /

2nd Alto Sax   you can't blast *anything* on a flute /

Tenor Sax   Flutes are *stupid.*

3rd Alto Sax *laughs with* **Tenor Sax***. The* **Flutes** *glare at them.* **Tenor Sax** *hides.* **1st Flute** *calls across to* **3rd Alto Sax***. Everyone else stares.*

1st Flute   So, how are you finding it?

3rd Alto Sax   Good yeah. Tough but, yeah, good.

1st Flute *flounces over to the* **Saxophone** *section.*

1st Flute   It's quite a step up from *school* band.

3rd Alto Sax   I don't, play in, we don't have a band at my school.

1st Flute   Oh!

1st Clarinet   Did you audition, to be here?

3rd Alto Sax   Yeah, twice.

1st Flute   Oh! So they *did* audition you?

1st Clarinet *flounces over to the* **Saxophone** *section.*

3rd Alto Sax   Yeah. Twice.

1st Flute   Oh!

1st Clarinet   Yeah, it's a tough process.

1st Flute   Very tough.

1st Clarinet   They don't just let *anyone* in!

1st Flute   No! And of course it's quite expensive.

1st Clarinet   *Quite* expensive!

3rd Alto Sax   .

1st Flute   OK, well, see ya round!

1st Clarinet   See ya round!

1st Flute *and* **1st Clarinet** *flounce back to their positions. When they're alone* **3rd Alto Sax** *speaks to us.*

3rd Alto Sax   My mum phoned to ask about the discount. I begged her not to but she just glared at me. They were really patronizing. I couldn't hear but I could tell by the way my mum's neck went red. It does that when she's embarrassed, and like a bit angry. Like all the words she wants to say but daren't say are sitting in her throat. Stuck in her neck. Makes it go bright red. I watch her holding my breath. She says nothing, then she says *thank you*, and puts the phone down and stares at the wall. I wait, then ask her what happened. She said we got the discount, cos of our circumstances. I ask what circumstances? She says I'm extraordinary. 'You're extraordinary', she goes, really fierce with tears in her eyes. 'You're extraordinary!' I wish I wasn't.

Bass Clarinet   Angela's eyes are all twinkly.

3rd Clarinet   She's really rude /

2nd Clarinet   and really funny /

Bass Clarinet   and we all like her a lot.

3rd Clarinet   We all want to be our very best for her /

Bass Clarinet   all the time.

2nd Clarinet   When she's disappointed /

3rd Clarinet   or angry /

Bass Clarinet   it's awful /

3rd Clarinet   really awful.

1st Clarinet   We'd all die for her, I swear.

Percussion   Angela is not just a conductor. This is not *just* an orchestra. This is an opportunity for spiritual growth.

1st Trumpet   What?

Percussion   This is communion. This is providing an education in character and purpose. This orchestra is helping to grow socially focused, purpose-orientated musicians. We are redefining excellence. We are achieving our dreams. We are playing with a Winning Mindset.

1st Trumpet   Erm. What the hell?

Tuba   Ha! Yeah! Think you might have over-thought that a bit, mate?

1st Trumpet   It's just a band! We're just playing music. In a band. It's not a big deal.

Percussion   Nah, man, you're missing the bigger picture. Angela is, she's making *magic* here, man, she's /. . She's /. .

1st Flute   She is pretty amazing.

2nd Clarinet   It's true.

Bassoon   We all love her.

They take a big sigh of admiration for Angela.

3rd Clarinet   And we're all a bit scared of her.

They all nod and shudder. They shift in space.

Bassoon   Day two is more of the same.

Tuba   Arrive achy and bleary eyed from yesterday.

1st Trumpet   Morning /

Tenor Sax   morning /

2nd Alto Sax   morning /

1st Flute   oh my God! Alyssa beats me here every day!

Oboe   She's *always* early.

2nd Alto Sax   So dedicated.

2nd Flute   So professional.

1st Clarinet   She's my hero. Honestly. If I could just be a bit more like Alyssa /

1st Trombone   if we could all be a bit more like Alyssa /

1st Trumpet (*sarcastic*)   the world would be a greater place!

1st Clarinet   Shuttup!

They shift in space.

Bass Clarinet   We rehearse in this big old hall.

Tenor Sax   Boiling in the summer.

3rd Trumpet   Freezing in the winter.

Percussion   We set our music on the stands.

3rd Clarinet   Warm up our fingers.

2nd Flute   Do scales.

1st Trumpet   Read over the music from yesterday.

Tuba   Sip water.

Bassoon   Stretch.

1st Alto Sax   Cork grease.

3rd Trumpet   Valve oil.

Oboe   Reeds.

Bass Clarinet   Mouthpiece.

Percussion   Sticks

1st Clarinet   Posture.

3rd Flute   Breathing.

2nd Flute   Articulation.

1st Flute   Timing.

1st Trumpet   Volume.

2nd Trumpet   Pace.

3rd Trumpet   Detail.

3rd Clarinet   Nuance.

3rd Alto Sax   Feeling.

1st Alto Sax   Emotion.

Tuba   Power.

Bassoon   Flat.

2nd Flute   Sharp.

2nd Alto Sax   Staccato.

1st Flute   Legato.

2nd Trombone   Diminuendo.

2nd Clarinet   Crescendo.

Tuba   Count.

2nd Alto Sax   Two-four /

1st Trombone   Six-eight /

Tenor Sax   one two three four /

3rd Trumpet   two two three four /

Percussion   three two three four /

Oboe   four two three /

3rd Alto Sax   I'm lost.

1st Alto Sax   Listen!

2nd Flute   Eye contact.

1st Trumpet   Listening.

1st Clarinet   Tuning.

Bassoon   Playing.

Percussion   Listening.

1st Clarinet   Feeling.

Bass Clarinet   Listening.

1st Alto Sax   Listening.

Everyone   Listening.

They play intensely for a moment. It's silent but powerful in its frenzy.

1st Trumpet   Angela says /

Everyone   *good*!

1st Clarinet   And we all smile.

1st Flute   Happy we made her happy.

1st Alto Sax   Then she calls for us to do it again.

1st Trombone   And we groan.

Bass Clarinet   The music is never easy /

1st Clarinet   because we are the best players in the country.

1st Flute   So the selection of music should of course reflect that.

1st Trumpet   Like we said, this ain't no school band, bro!

3rd Trumpet   You sound stupid talking like that.

1st Trumpet   No I don't!

1st Flute   This music is never easy, but this year?

Tuba   This year? Wow!

Tenor Sax   This year it's, yeah, it's challenging.

2nd Clarinet   Really challenging!

Bass Clarinet   One piece in particular /

Everyone   *Cosmic Concerto*!

Percussion   It's been written especially for us /

Tenor Sax   by this mad composer /

2nd Alto Sax   Jeremy Jones.

2nd Clarinet   Who is rumoured to be coming to the concert on Saturday!

Oboe   He's coming to watch us play his piece!

Tuba   So, no pressure!

1st Trombone   Jeremy Jones /

1st Trumpet   composer extraordinaire /

Percussion   who blatantly takes acid.

1st Trumpet   Oh for sure!

Bass Clarinet   I mean, have you *seen* this?

2nd Flute   This first page?

2nd Alto Sax   The second phrase /

3rd Trumpet   after the coda?

Bassoon   Bar twenty-two?!

They all shudder.

Tuba   We all *hate* bar twenty-two.

1st Alto Sax   I will master it. I will.

1st Flute   It's challenging.

1st Clarinet & Oboe & Bassoon   *Really* challenging.

2nd Alto Sax   But Angela did say she wanted to challenge us.

Percussion   'Again', she says, 'let's try that again!'

Tenor Sax   And she taps her stick on her stand /

3rd Clarinet   and counts us all in.

2nd Trombone   We take a breath.

Oboe   A deep breath /

2nd Clarinet   and we're away!

2nd Flute   Swept up in it!

1st Trombone   And this time, somehow we play it better.

1st Trumpet   It's still not great.

Percussion   Because it's still really hard.

3rd Trumpet   Really hard!

2nd Clarinet   But somehow we muddle through.

Tuba   And there's this moment where we're all playing and it's fast and loud and /

Tenor Sax   suddenly the magic happens! Suddenly my ears are huge! I swear they must grow enormous, like giant ears like the BFG. Because I'm capable of hearing way more than normal. I can hear what I'm doing, the sound my instrument makes, my breathing, the turn of the pages, the pad of my keys. I can hear the instruments around me, and I realize it sounds different from the audience. It must sound so different to them than what I can hear. Because I'm *inside* the sound. In the centre of it. I'm *inside* the sound, inside the blend of it.

Everyone suddenly stands and grabs their chair. They run around **Tenor Sax**, *swirling around them in a big spiral.* **Tenor Sax** *dances alone in the centre, floating inside the sound. They all suddenly stop and stare at the front.*

2nd Alto Sax Then Angela calls for a coffee break.

3rd Alto Sax And we all breathe a sigh of relief.

They all breathe in and out together. They replace their chairs to their positions, stretch and shuffle about.

Tuba Cue for the toilets.

Trombone Cue for the microwave.

Bassoon Cue for the kettles /

2nd Clarinet and the big urn /

Oboe that makes everything taste a bit metallic.

Percussion And we're music geeks, so we talk about music /

Everyone a lot.

Tenor Sax Stuff we've heard /

Bass Clarinet or stuff we played.

1st Clarinet Who's got the best instrument /

1st Alto Sax the best tutor /

Oboe the best grades.

2nd Trombone Music music music /

Tenor Sax music music music /

2nd Trumpet music /

2nd Clarinet music /

2nd Trombone music /

3rd Alto Sax but also we're teenagers /

2nd Alto Sax so some of the chat in coffee breaks is, you know /

1st Trombone normal teenage stuff.

1st Clarinet Boys.

Bass Clarinet Gals.

Bassoon Non-binary pals.

2nd Flute Who's friends with who.

1st Alto Sax Who fancies who.

3rd Alto Sax Yeah, there's some pretty awful attempts at flirting!

They all turn to watch **1st Trumpet** *and* **1st Flute** *who blush.*

1st Trumpet   Hey!

1st Flute   Hey!

1st Trumpet   I like your, pencil, thing.

1st Flute   Thanks.

1st Trumpet   .

1st Flute   .

1st Trumpet   .

1st Flute   This piece is really challenging!

1st Trumpet   Nah. It's easy.

1st Flute   Oh. Well, I'm finding it hard /

1st Trumpet   I'm pretty hard /

1st Flute   what /

1st Trumpet   nothing! Nothing.

2nd Trumpet   Angela calls us back into rehearsals.

1st Trumpet   Oh thank God!

They all laugh and shift in space.

2nd Trumpet   And we start playing again, and, like, this might sound dumb but, I really love this!
Me too. It feels really good to be inside of it /

2nd Trumpet   inside the sound!

Percussion   Yeah!

2nd Trombone   Yeah. It's like /

2nd Trumpet   it's really cool. To be *inside* of a piece of music like that?! Your heart does this swelling thing, a bit like being on a rollercoaster, you can't help it thump and get bigger in your chest.

3rd Clarinet   Yeah! And like, I dunno, I just I guess I really like being, like a *small* part of, a bigger whole?

2nd Trumpet   Yeah!

3rd Clarinet   Like, I've got a job to do. And I can hear how it contributes to this bigger sound.

2nd Trumpet   Yeah, like we are this big wall of sound.

3rd Clarinet   We *are* music.

2nd Trumpet   Yeah!

3rd Clarinet Like, we are making this big sound *together*, and I've got a part to play in that.

2nd Trumpet Everyone has.

3rd Clarinet Exactly!

2nd Trumpet Every single one of us has got something vital that we have to do. It wouldn't sound the same without me, without any of us. We are all tiny little cogs in this big machine. I really like that.

3rd Alto Sax That's cool.

2nd Flute Yeah it is.

1st Trumpet Whatever. You lot take this way too seriously, I swear!

They all suddenly snap their heads to the front, sitting up straight, holding their breath.

Oboe (*loud whisper*) Angela gets grumpy when she's tired.

Bassoon (*loud whisper*) It's her blood sugar levels dropping.

Bass Clarinet (*loud whisper*) It's because she's hungover.

Oboe (*loud whisper*) Whatever it is we can tell she'll call for lunch soon.

2nd Clarinet (*loud whisper*) I hope so! I'm starving!

They all slowly lean forwards in their seats until their almost falling forwards.

Tenor Sax 'OK let's pause there!'

They all sit back and breathe a sigh of relief.

Bassoon Finally!

Tuba We all get up /

1st Alto Sax and unclick our neck straps /

3rd Clarinet and leave our instruments on the chairs.

Percussion We go to the pub /

1st Flute if we're old enough.

Tenor Sax Or fight over the microwave and the kettles.

Everyone Lunch!

They all get up and shuffle about. **3rd Alto Sax** *stays still. They speak to us.*

3rd Alto Sax No one talks to me at lunchtime. I'm poor and they're all posh. And I talk different from them. And they all know where I'm from. And yeah, I'm /

1st Alto Sax playing on a saxophone that school lent you?

3rd Alto Sax Yeah. and it's /

2nd Alto Sax   a bit shit /

3rd Alto Sax   but I'm still making it sound good. And I haven't /

1st Trumpet   even done my grades yet?

3rd Alto Sax   but I *am* actually good enough to do them /

1st Trumpet   sure.

3rd Alto Sax   I just haven't yet /

1st Trumpet   sure!

3rd Alto Sax   And they're amazed at who my teacher is, because he has /

1st Alto Sax   such a long waiting list!

2nd Clarinet   And he personally /

1st Clarinet   selects his students!

3rd Alto Sax   And so they all gossip about how /

Oboe   he must do lessons a bit cheaper than he does everyone else /

3rd Alto Sax   which he does. But not cos I'm a charity case or nothin'! It's cus he thinks I've got potential. And they all think /

Oboe   that's unfair!

3rd Alto Sax   And they're all /

2nd Trumpet   a bit jealous!

3rd Alto Sax   And they all /

1st Flute   don't think I should be here!

1st Trombone   No offence!

3rd Alto Sax   Their parents pick them up in their /

Everyone   big posh cars!

3rd Alto Sax   And I have to /

Oboe   walk to the bus stop?

1st Flute   Gross!

3rd Alto Sax   Angela saw me once and gave me a lift home /

1st Flute   oh my God?!

1st Alto Sax   What was it like?!

3rd Alto Sax   She smoked out the window.

1st Clarinet   Oh my God!

1st Flute   Iconic!

1st Alto Sax   What did you listen to?

3rd Alto Sax   Erm, the radio?

2nd Alto Sax   Which station?

3rd Alto Sax   I dunno.

1st Flute   Think!

3rd Alto Sax   I dunno!

1st Clarinet   What was playing?

3rd Alto Sax   Pop music?

2nd Alto Sax   Wow!

3rd Alto Sax   It was, alright, a bit weird.

They all turn their backs on **3rd Alto Sax**.

2nd Trumpet   It's lunchtime so it's /

2nd Trombone   stilted conversation /

Bassoon   up on battered sofas.

1st Clarinet   Crunchy crisps /

Oboe   in soggy sarnies.

1st Trombone   Packed lunch disappointments.

3rd Trumpet   And polystyrene cups of sweet caffeine.

Everyone turns to watch **1st Flute** *and* **1st Trumpet**.

1st Flute   Hey!

1st Trumpet   Hey!

1st Flute   How's it going?

1st Trumpet   It's going!

1st Flute   Ha ha! Yeah!

1st Trumpet   .

1st Flute   .

1st Trumpet   How's erm /. .

1st Flute   Yeah. Fine.

1st Trumpet   Cool.

1st Flute   Cool.

1st Trumpet .

1st Flute .

1st Trumpet .

1st Flute I like your hair today.

1st Trumpet Thanks.

1st Flute Did you do, something different?

1st Trumpet No?

1st Flute Oh. Well. Looks good.

1st Trumpet Thanks.

1st Flute .

1st Trumpet .

1st Flute Cool. Well I should /

1st Trumpet yeah.

Everyone gets the giggles and tries to hide it.

Tuba Angela sways her way back from the pub /

Bassoon and calls us back in.

Oboe We tune up.

Percussion And Angela taps her conductor's stick.

1st Flute And away we go again!

1st Clarinet Swept up in the sound!

1st Trombone Until something goes horribly wrong!

2nd Clarinet Yeah and it all comes to a great big screeching stop.

2nd Trumpet Bits of metal flying off in all directions /

3rd Trumpet sparks and /

1st Trumpet smoke and /

Everyone disaster!

1st Flute And Angela screaming /

1st Alto Sax stop /

1st Clarinet stop /

Everyone stop!

Oboe And then she swears under her breath /

Percussion but loud enough for all of us to hear /

3rd Clarinet and we all giggle.

Tenor Sax Because yeah, that was bad, like /

2nd Alto Sax & Tuba really bad.

3rd Clarinet And she sighs and shakes her head.

3rd Trumpet And somehow she unpicks it /

3rd Alto Sax and pulls each bit apart /

2nd Flute and finds what the problem is /

2nd Alto Sax and reworks it over and over /

2nd Trumpet and over and over /

Tenor Sax until it's right.

Tuba And *then* she puts it all back together.

Percussion And we're a smooth moving and grooving music machine again!

2nd Trombone Well, I dunno about that.

Bass Clarinet And Angela shouts, 'Oh yes!'

Tuba 'Oh yes! That was bloomin' fantastic!'

Bassoon And we all giggle, because it's a bit over the top /

Oboe and it's a bit embarrassing /

Bass Clarinet but also it's nice.

1st Flute I love Angela /

2nd Alto Sax I love Angela /

1st Trombone we *all* love Angela.

They swim around in their heart swelling love for Angela. Then they suddenly bump back to earth.

2nd Alto Sax Day three is Wednesday /

Bass Clarinet and Angela is late.

3rd Clarinet Where is she?

2nd Clarinet I don't know.

1st Trumpet Don't panic!

3rd Clarinet I'm not!

1st Trombone She'll be here soon.

3rd Clarinet   I know!

Percussion   Yeah she'll swan in with her silk scarf flowing /

Tenor Sax   and her perfume all wafting /

Tuba   all full apologies /

2nd Flute   and funny stories about the traffic /

1st Flute   or the boiler breaking /

2nd Trombone   or something that makes us all laugh /

2nd Trumpet   and instantly forgive her /

Oboe   because we love her!

1st Alto Sax   So we all just get ready /

3rd Alto Sax   and warm up /

Bassoon   whilst we wait.

They warm up. They check the clock. They try not to be worried, or annoyed.

3rd Trumpet   So, once, a while ago. I had this moment, this amazing moment with Angela.

1st Trumpet   Oi oi!

3rd Trumpet   No not like that, idiot! Like a teacher moment, a really cool teacher–student moment /

1st Trumpet   oi oi!

1st Clarinet   Shut up!

3rd Trumpet   Thank you.

1st Clarinet   No problem. Please continue.

3rd Trumpet   Haha, OK, well, it was about music.

1st Trumpet   Obviously

3rd Trumpet   Will you be me?

1st Clarinet   Me?

3rd Trumpet   Yeah. And I'll be Angela

1st Clarinet   OK.

3rd Trumpet   Cool. Thanks. OK so. Angela had asked me to stay behind one day, after rehearsals. Because she'd noticed that I didn't look very happy or, she thought I looked a bit, off, so she asked me if everything was OK. And I said yeah everything's fine I just. And then, I dunno why, she just has that way of getting things out of you /

1st Flute & 1st Clarinet   yes!

1st Flute She really does.

3rd Trumpet So suddenly I'm like, being really honest, about feeling stressed that I'm not good enough and even though I'm practising all the time it's like. I keep making these stupid mistakes and. I know, somehow I know I'm good. I don't mean to sound cocky or arrogant or whatever I just /

1st Flute it doesn't /

3rd Trumpet I just know I'm good. Like, I've got talent. And I could be *really* good. And something's holding me back. Like, I've been playing in this band for three years now, and I'm still on *third* position?! Is that just some patriarchy bullshit? Or like, is it because I'm really not showing what I can do? And if that's true then why am I holding myself back and what am I doing wrong and oh my God it's stressing me out! And suddenly Angela asks me, 'What does music feel like?'

1st Clarinet (*as 3rd Trumpet*) Feel like?

3rd Trumpet (*as Angela*) Yes.

1st Clarinet (*as 3rd Trumpet*) I, I dunno.

3rd Trumpet (*as Angela*) Yes you do . . . go on.

1st Clarinet (*as 3rd Trumpet*) I dunno /

3rd Trumpet (*as Angela*) yes you *do*!

1st Clarinet (*as 3rd Trumpet*) No, miss, I don't /

3rd Trumpet (*as Angela*) yes you do! Stop saying you don't because you're embarrassed just, take a breath, and answer the question. Because you *do* know and life is very short and I really don't have the time for this shit.

1st Clarinet (*as 3rd Trumpet*) Miss?!

1st Flute Did she really swear?

3rd Trumpet Yeah /

1st Trumpet she swears all the time /

3rd Trumpet she does. Anyway she just keeps asking me, what does music feel like? And I'm like, erm. /. . I dunno I, kind of *hear* it more than feel it? And Angela just stares so, I try again like, erm, well, I guess, I guess my mouth feels it? Like, like the vibration? I dunno /

1st Clarinet (*as Angela*) YES YOU *DO*!

1st Trumpet Wow?!

3rd Trumpet Yes! That's what she was like. Shouting at me like that. And then she goes, *confidence*!

1st Clarinet (*as Angela*) *Confidence*!

3rd Trumpet   And I'm, like, OK?! OK, my mouth feels it! And, and my fingers, I guess, yeah my fingers feel it, the, pressure? On the valves as I press them down. And I guess my ears feel it too? Like, the pitch? And the tone, of a good note or a bad note or /. . Like, actually, my whole body feels it! Like, there's *space* in my back? Like my ribs, they like *expand* out, and *open*, like wings? Yeah like wings and it's cool!

Everyone stands on their chairs and flaps their wings.

3rd Trumpet   And my stomach rises, and falls, as I breathe. It rises /

1st Trumpet   rises /

1st Trombone   rises /

Bassoon   rises /

Tuba   and /

Percussion   falls /

2nd Flute   rises /

2nd Clarinet   and /

1st Alto Sax   falls /

Bassoon   rises /

Tenor Sax   and /

2nd Alto Sax   falls /

2nd Trumpet   As /

Bass Clarinet   I /

Oboe   breathe.

3rd Trumpet   And my arms ache /

Percussion   oh God yeah /

3rd Clarinet   cus they're like, engaged?

3rd Alto Sax   Yeah.

3rd Trumpet   And my legs too maybe? Yeah, like the *whole* of me is working to keep a good posture. And it's hard work!

Tenor Sax   Yeah /

3rd Trumpet   and it gets *hot* in here so sometimes I can feel sweat running down my back /

1st Flute   nice /

3rd Trumpet   my shirt must be sticking to me and I feel blushy about that which obviously makes it worse, but mainly I'm focused on the music and feeling my /

2nd Clarinet   whole /

2nd Trombone   body /

Oboe   vibrate /

3rd Trumpet   with it and it's like I can feel the floor? The resonance of the whole orchestra buzzing through my feet on the floor? It rises up my legs up my back up my neck and through my skull this buzzing like this golden like this buzzing golden sound that flies up and out of me.

1st Clarinet (*as Angela*)   So, does music get made by you or the trumpet? Don't say you don't know.

3rd Trumpet   Both. Made by us both? It comes through me, but it needs me to start it. And when I'm open it flows. Oh my God! I just have to focus on being open? My job is to stay open.

1st Flute   Shit!

1st Clarinet (*as Angela*)   Don't swear.

1st Flute   But miss!

3rd Trumpet   And *that's* when I realize, I've been so worried about playing a rubbish note. About messing up, and ruining it all for everyone and. And instead I could be focusing on having fun? Don't hold on so tight that I squeeze the life out of it?! . . . And she just smiles, she smiles and is like /

1st Clarinet (*as Angela*)   there you go.

3rd Trumpet   And I smile. Thanks, miss.

1st Clarinet (*as Angela*)   Now /

Everyone   'don't fuck it up!'

They all laugh.

1st Trumpet   That's cool.

3rd Trumpet   Yeah.

1st Trumpet   I don't think you don't get First because you're a girl. I don't think it's got anything to do with gender.

1st Flute   You would say that though. Because you're a boy.

1st Clarinet   Yeah. Because you're privileged, in patriarchy you've got the privilege, so /

1st Trumpet   yeah OK yeah. I see that, I do, I'm just /. . Would you like to do a solo? Do you want one of the solos?

3rd Trumpet   You're giving me a solo?

1st Trumpet   Yeah. That OK?

3rd Trumpet   Yeah!

1st Trumpet   Cool. I've got like five to do this year so, I'm sure you could do one of them. I've heard you play. You're good.

3rd Trumpet   Thanks.

1st Trumpet   No problem.

Tuba   Angela!

3rd Clarinet   Oh thank God!

2nd Flute   She does swan in /

3rd Alto Sax   all silk scarf /

2nd Clarinet   and perfume /

2nd Trombone   and funny story /

Tenor Sax   and we forgive her /

1st Flute   and love her /

1st Alto Sax   and *finally* get started!

They prepare their instruments. They all turn a page at the same time. They take a deep breath.

Tuba   And all afternoon we focus on The Beast.

1st Trombone   The Beast?

Tuba   That's what I'm calling it. The Beast. The Big One. The Bloody Hard One.

Everyone   *Cosmic Concerto*!

Everyone shudders.

1st Alto Sax   I will master it. I will. I should be able to do this. I'm First Alto. Section Leader. It's my responsibility to be able to play the music, and play it well. I'm a Leader, I'm supposed to be an inspiration.

3rd Alto Sax   Hey! Everyone is struggling with it.

1st Alto Sax   I can't, I have to master it.

2nd Alto Sax   It's really hard.

1st Clarinet   I'm not sure I actually even like it /

1st Flute   oh I *hate* it!

Tuba   It's a Beast!

Percussion   Bar twenty-two?

1st Flute   Oh God, *don't*!

1st Clarinet   Bar twenty-two is keeping me up at night.

Oboe Bar twenty-two is giving me cold sweats.

Tenor Sax Bar twenty-two is all your worst fears combined and squished into the music stave like hell exploited onto manuscript paper.

1st Trumpet Very poetic.

Tenor Sax Thanks.

3rd Alto Sax I'm trying. I'm really trying.

3rd Clarinet My fingers just won't go fast enough!

3rd Trumpet I'm trying, I'm really trying!

3rd Clarinet I hate my fingers!

1st Clarinet You're making mistakes!

3rd Clarinet I know!

They all play really hard, frowning with concentration. Then they stop, look up to Angela exhausted, and slump in their chairs. **1st Alto Sax** *does not slump.*

1st Alto Sax We need to work harder! We need to work really hard.

2nd Alto Sax We *are* working hard. Aren't we?

3rd Alto Sax Yes.

1st Alto Sax No. Harder. We need to work harder! It needs to be *better*! We're not even barely trying!

3rd Alto Sax I think we're trying pretty /

1st Alto Sax they deserve excellence! I need to be better. I need to be better!

2nd Alto Sax But, you're amazing?!

3rd Alto Sax Yeah, Alyssa, you're amazing!

1st Alto Sax (*in her own world*) I *have* to be better. I *have* to be. I've got people expecting me to be Excellent! They've invested Time and Energy and *Thousands* of pounds into me. I've been provided with the Very Best Opportunities and Support and so there's *no excuses*!

3rd Alto Sax Alyssa? Are you /

1st Alto Sax (*in her own world*) I *have* to be better! It's up to *me* now! I *have* to be better, there's no room for error, I *have* to be better, I *have* to be better, I *need*, to be *excellent*!

1st Flute This year is really hard!

1st Trumpet Yeah. The music is mad!

Oboe It's Wednesday. The concert is Saturday night!

Bass Clarinet We only have *three* more days of rehearsal.

Bassoon Two and a half.

1st Flute What?

Bassoon Approximately eighteen and a half more hours.

1st Flute Stop! You're stressing me out!

Bassoon Sorry.

3rd Clarinet It's so stressful!

3rd Trumpet So stressful!

Tenor Sax I'm so stressed out!

3rd Clarinet I'm not having a great time, at school.

Everyone stops and looks at them.

3rd Clarinet Or at home, if I'm honest. Everything's a bit, of a mess right now. There's, there's A Lot going on! And the last thing I wanted to do was come here every day for the holiday and play music all day long. I'm actually really glad I came. Because sometimes, right in the middle of the piece, especially if it's hard and I'm having to really concentrate. And especially if we're playing well, and Angela hasn't stopped us to go back over something. If it's all going OK and I'm *really* focused then I just, get swept up in it! And I just forget everything else! It's like /. . I dunno, it's like /. . Like we're playing, and the music starts swirling and soaring around us, and we're playing, and playing and playing and then woosh!

They get lifted high up into the air. They soar. It's beautiful.

And suddenly I'm soaring! I'm soaring way above everything! I'm up there, in the place daydreams are, or where ideas come from, or where memories live. Up there in the floating space, above everything! I'm there, floating *inside* the music!

They float in the air, supported by the rest of the orchestra. Suddenly there's a loud bum note and they drop.

1st Flute The boys laugh.

1st Alto Sax But it's not funny.

1st Trombone Because today is *Wednesday*.

1st Clarinet And the concert is *Saturday*!

1st Alto Sax And the audience expects *excellence*!

Oboe And *some* people seem to forget that.

1st Alto Sax Angela is not happy.

Bassoon She's *really* not happy.

1st Alto Sax We are sent home, two minutes early, because she has /

Everyone 'just had enough!'

1st Alto Sax So we go home.

They all shuffle around their seats as one night passes.

Oboe And *none* of us sleep!

1st Trumpet I do.

1st Clarinet & Oboe How?!

1st Trumpet I dunno, I just, like, fall asleep?

Oboe Well, good for you!

3rd Alto Sax The next day is Thursday, and the tension is palpable.

1st Alto Sax Angela is not happy. Says she's /

1st Alto Sax & 1st Clarinet & 1st Flute 'very disappointed'.

1st Alto Sax And though she doesn't actually say it, I know it's *me* she's disappointed in.

The orchestra warm up.

Bassoon Angela tells us to tune up.

Oboe And she looks at me. As I'm First Oboe. I play the tuning note.

1st Trumpet And you get it wrong.

Oboe And I want to die.

Bass Clarinet And Angela grabs her coat /

2nd Trombone grabs her handbag /

2nd Trumpet says she's /

2nd Clarinet 'going for some fresh air!'

1st Trumpet And when she gets back we /

Percussion 'better be ready to play like professionals!'

Tuba Or we should /

1st Trombone 'get our stuff and /'

Everyone 'get out!'

1st Flute I try to give you a look /

1st Clarinet give you some comfort but /

Bassoon it's too late /

Oboe I already hate myself.

3rd Alto Sax Hey. Everyone makes mistakes.

Oboe Not me. I can't. I'm First Oboe! I tune the entire orchestra. I don't make mistakes.

3rd Alto Sax Yeah but /

Oboe no, no, you don't understand! You couldn't *possibly* understand!

3rd Alto Sax Why does everyone put so much pressure on themselves?

No one knows the answer.

3rd Trumpet She's coming!

Everyone sits up straight and watches Angela re-enter.

1st Flute She doesn't look at us.

2nd Clarinet Doesn't say a word.

2nd Flute Picks up her conductor stick, and taps it, says /

Bass Clarinet 'Bar twenty-two!'

2nd Trumpet And we all try our very best.

They strain to get it right.

Oboe 'Again!' she says.

They strain to get it right.

Tuba 'Again!'

They strain to get it right.

Bassoon 'Again!'

They strain to get it right.

3rd Alto Sax 'Again!'

They strain to get it right.

Tenor Sax 'Coffee!'

They all exhale relieved.

2nd Alto Sax Sugar and caffeine.

3rd Trumpet Staring into polystyrene.

2nd Trombone Hoping the liquid will transform us into better players.

Percussion Musical elixir?!

1st Trombone Sure. Any kind of miracle will do.

They all watch **1st Trumpet** *and* **1st Flute**.

1st Trumpet So, erm, is your boyfriend gonna come? To the concert?

1st Flute   No.

1st Trumpet   Oh.

1st Flute   I don't have a boyfriend.

1st Trumpet   Oh!

1st Flute   Yeah.

1st Trumpet   Oh, right.

1st Flute   Why?

1st Trumpet   No reason. Was just, wondering.

1st Flute   Is your girlfriend coming?

1st Trumpet   No I, I don't have a girlfriend, anymore I, I *did* have, and er. Yeah. That, didn't work out.

1st Flute   Oh I'm sorry.

1st Trumpet   That's OK. It's OK, she's, she's gone! Long gone. Good riddance! Crazy bitch!

Everyone stops.

1st Trumpet   I mean. I don't say that about her, I, *some* people do, some people talk like that, *I don't*. I, I respect women so I /. .

1st Flute   .

1st Trumpet   .

1st Flute   .

Basson   According to Maslow's 'Hierarchy of Human Needs' art is a means to self-actualization.

1st Trumpet   What?

Bassoon   At the bottom of the pyramid is the basic 'Physiological Needs', like food, water, sleep /

Percussion   sex.

Basson   Sex too yeah. Then we move up to 'Belonging Needs', like friends, family community. Then it's 'Esteem Needs', that feeling of accomplishment and purpose. Then at the top of the pyramid, the height of human experience, is 'Self-Actualization Needs'. This is where you're achieving your full potential.

1st Trumpet   Right?!

Bassoon   Well look, I'm fourteen, so I have all my basic needs met.

1st Trombone   You're fourteen?

Bassoon Yeah. And so I'm provided for by my parents and school and hobbies.

2nd Trumpet So?

1st Trumpet Yeah so what?

Bassoon So the only thing we have to focus on is 'Self-Actualization'! And Maslow said that *art* is a means to that, creativity plays a significant role.

2nd Trumpet And, what's that /

Bassoon so all we have to focus on is art?! How cool is that?! We're so privileged, all our basic human needs are completely taken care of, and the only thing left for us to do is *make art*?! Which opens us up to enjoying the Peak Experience of Humanity! Is that *incredible*?!

1st Trombone You're fourteen?

Bassoon Yeah.

1st Trumpet You are so weird.

Bassoon Yeah, yeah I know.

1st Trumpet (*laughing*) Like, so weird!

Bassoon Yeah /

1st Trumpet (*laughing*) like what is up with you?!

Percussion Hey, leave them alone yeah /

1st Trumpet (*laughing*) so weird?! So weird!

Percussion Hey! Shut up!

1st Flute Yeah stop it /

1st Trumpet (*laughing*) what?

1st Flute Why are you always such a dick?

1st Trumpet .

Everyone turns away from **1st Trumpet**, *who tries to laugh it off but is upset. They turn to us.*

1st Trumpet My parents got divorced last summer. Two weeks before my birthday. And like obviously they didn't mean to time it like that, obviously, but yeah, it was pretty shit. I know it's like, not a big deal for your parents to be divorced, it's like *really* common. And I'm lucky that my dad's still around when lots of people don't know their dads or, don't see them that often or whatever. So yeah, I *know* it's like, obviously not that big a deal and whatever but, yeah, it still felt shit. Because to be honest I thought everything was fine, at home. It was the four of us. And suddenly it's not? And it's like, I dunno like, someone knocked the walls down or, or ripped the roof off, like *there! There! Try and live like that!* /. . I guess that's what they mean by 'broken home'. Because yeah, it feels like that, like something broke. /. . Anyway, so I dunno if they'll both come to the concert. Guess it'll be weird for them to sit together. Be weird if they don't too. Either way it's, yeah it's weird.

1st Alto Sax Back in rehearsals and Angela focuses on the Saxophone section.

Tenor Sax Because someone's playing something wrong.

3rd Alto Sax And for once it's actually not me.

2nd Alto Sax Or me.

1st Alto Sax It's me!

Everyone stares at **1st Alto Sax**.

1st Alto Sax I play it wrong again and again and /. . I don't know what's wrong with me?!

Tenor Sax Angela singles you out /

2nd Alto Sax and make you play it /

3rd Alto Sax again and again!

1st Alto Sax And I can't do it. I can't do it! I don't know why but /

2nd Alto Sax every time you do it wrong she shouts /

3rd Alto Sax wrong!

Tenor Sax Wrong!

2nd Alto Sax Wrong!

1st Flute She keeps making you do it!

1st Clarinet And keeps shouting /

2nd Alto Sax wrong!

1st Trumpet Wrong!

2nd Clarinet Wrong!

Oboe 'Alyssa? What is going on with you?'

1st Alto Sax .

1st Trumpet It's humiliating.

1st Flute It's horrible.

1st Clarinet It's really, really horrible.

2nd Flute & 2nd Trumpet Wrong!

Bass Clarinet & Tenor Sax Wrong!

Percussion & 3rd Alto Sax Wrong!

1st Flute & 2nd Flute   Wrong!

1st Trombone & Tuba   Wrong!

Bassoon & Oboe   Wrong!

Everyone   Wrong! Wrong! Wrong!

They all leave the stage, one by one, as they shout 'wrong!'. Eventually **1st Alto Sax** *is on stage alone.*

1st Alto Sax   The problem with being good is then people expect you to be that, *all* the time. The problem with being good is you can *always* be better. The problem with being good is the bar is *so high*, that it's actually *impossible* to ever feel satisfied. The problem, with being good, is you never really feel that good. The problem with being good, is *everyone*, says you're good, and that's all they ever say about you, ever, like it's actually the only interesting thing about you so you *have* to be good at *all* times or else you're just a nothing-person. The problem with being good is you know you're nothing without it and you know you could be better so you never ever actually feel that great whenever someone is like oh-my-God-you're-so-good. The problem with being good is you think it'll solve things, like this heavy hole feeling in your chest, or like your parents' marriage, or like your sense of safety about the future like it'll all be OK, everything will *all* be OK because I'm really good at this thing so I'm gonna be good it's all gonna be /. . The problem with being good is you're not even sure you actually like it anymore. The problem with being good is /. . The problem with being good /. . The problem, the, the problem /. . The problem, the problem, the problem, the problem, the problem, the problem, problem, problem, problem, problem, problem problem problem problem problem problem problem problem problem problem problem problem /. .

1st Alto Sax *trashes the room, kicking and throwing the chairs away, in a fit of rage and panic. It's scary and also kind of awesome. When finished she stands centre stage, in the middle of all the mess, and looks at us. She pants, out of breath, until her breathing calms. She slowly bows, and stays bent double. Everyone else enters and stands in position, ignoring the smashed-up room. They speak to us.*

3rd Alto Sax   It's Thursday /

Oboe   the concert is *Saturday*!

1st Clarinet   Oh my God /

1st Flute   don't!

1st Clarinet   Oh, my, God!

1st Flute   Don't! Oh my God you're stressing me out!

1st Trumpet   We're actually in pretty good shape.

1st Trombone   Three out of the four pieces we're playing are sounding pretty good.

Tuba   But the fourth one. This /

Percussion *Cosmic Concerto!*

2nd Trumpet Cosmic Nightmare!

Oboe Angela makes us do it again.

1st Flute And again.

1st Clarinet And again.

Bass Clarinet And again.

Bassoon And we're trying!

3rd Alto Sax We're really trying!

2nd Clarinet But it's bar twenty-two!

1st Flute Oh my God bar twenty-two!

1st Alto Sax *slowly unbends from her bow, looks at us, and walks off stage, ignored by everyone else.*

3rd Clarinet That whole phrase!

2nd Trumpet The whole page!

2nd Trombone The whole piece!

1st Clarinet We're about /

1st Trumpet half-way through /

Bassoon when /

Oboe suddenly /

Tenor Sax Alyssa explodes with sick!

They all stare at the space where **1st Alto Sax** *should be.*

Tenor Sax It goes all over her music stand and all down her sax and all on her jeans. And it's this weird medical smell and she's foaming at the mouth and it's all looking really scary. And the Flutes /

Flutes scream!

Tenor Sax And Angela /

2nd Clarinet is *brilliant*!

Tenor Sax Like she somehow knows *exactly* what to do?

2nd Trumpet Like she's done it before?!

Tenor Sax Angela shouts at someone /

1st Trombone me, it was me /

Tenor Sax to call an ambulance.

Tuba   And everyone goes quiet /

Oboe   and really still.

Tenor Sax   And Angela is holding Alyssa and she keeps saying /

Bassoon   'it's OK, sweetheart, I've got you it's OK I've got you!'

Tenor Sax   And Alyssa is spitting up sick and foam and blood /

1st Flute   and Angela is covered in it /

Tenor Sax   but she doesn't seem to notice, she keeps stroking Alyssa's face.

Bassoon   'It's OK, sweetheart, I've got you!'

Tenor Sax   And Alyssa is crying and the sick is all in her hair, strawberry blonde mixed with chemical white /

1st Clarinet   and suddenly there's paramedics there?!

They all suddenly see the smashed-up room. It's shocking.

Tenor Sax   We're all told to get out!

2nd Trombone   To leave our instruments /

Tuba   and go outside /

Tenor Sax   immediately!

Percussion   So we do.

Tenor Sax   Our instruments sat on chairs, surrounding the paramedics, as they work on Alyssa, and they /

3rd Clarinet   take her away in an ambulance.

They all slowly collect a chair each. They hold it by the bottom of the chair legs. They dance with it, soft and slow, and strangely beautiful.

2nd Flute   And Mum tells me later it was an overdose. And I don't know what that is. And she explains. And she tells me that if I ever feel sad and lonely and stuck like that, I've got to tell her, I've *got* to. And Mum cries and I hug her and it feels weird like this the wrong way round?!

They slowly place their chairs back in position. They hover nervously next to them, looking at the empty seat. They speak to us.

3rd Trumpet   The next day is so weird.

Bassoon   So weird!

1st Clarinet   No one knows what to say to each other /

1st Flute   there's just like, *such* sadness and /

1st Clarinet   confusion?

1st Flute Yeah!

Oboe Because Alyssa was our idol!

1st Trumpet She was the best!

1st Trombone And she worked *so hard* to be the best! And then it made her /. . ? So, what does that mean? That *we* shouldn't try hard? Because if we do it'll make us unwell and, sad and /. . ? So we shouldn't try /

2nd Flute no! That's not what /

1st Clarinet I think we can still *try*?!

1st Flute Yeah it's OK to want to be good, right?

Tuba Yeah! I mean. I hope so.

Tenor Sax She just, put herself under so much pressure.

Tuba Oh my God, so much!

2nd Trombone So much pressure and *so hard* on yourself that like, you just *snap*?!

2nd Clarinet Yeah.

1st Trombone Yeah, how do you be good, like really good /

1st Flute excellent!

1st Trombone Yeah, how do you try to be excellent, and not *snap*?!

Silence. No one knows.

Bass Clarinet Angela's here!

Tuba She's wearing black.

Oboe And the twinkly eyes are cold.

Bass Clarinet She's all bloodshot.

Percussion And everyone is trying not to look at Alyssa's empty chair that's been wiped clean by antibacterial wipes.

1st Flute And Angela speaks about how Alyssa will be in hospital for a while /

Bassoon and she's fine /

Percussion and it's nothing to worry about.

Bass Clarinet And about how we've got to /

2nd Clarinet carry on /

1st Flute and play our very best.

3rd Clarinet For Alyssa.

Tenor Sax Because she'd want us to.

Oboe   And she says that Nathan will now be playing First /

Tuba   and Nathan squeaks that he /

2nd Alto Sax   can't! I'm sorry! I'm so sorry but, I can't I just can't!

3rd Alto Sax   And Angela's eyes flash to me, panicked, and I nod. Before I've even thought about it, I nod yes. I can do it. And everyone claps.

Sudden abstract moment of manic clapping or deadpan clapping and everyone staring at **3rd Alto Sax**. *Snarling animals prowling and approaching them. Then sudden snap back to reality.*

3rd Alto Sax   Angela sends me off with Mr Roberts who takes me to this smelly little room that I didn't even know existed. He says /

Tuba (*as Mr Roberts*)   'it's impossible to try and achieve Alyssa's brilliance, impossible!'

3rd Alto Sax   And his moustache gets all twitchy as he says it. And I nod vigorously like, yeah I know. And he goes /

Tuba (*as Mr Roberts*)   'we'll just have to try our best to be good enough'.

3rd Alto Sax   And I nod. We just need to be good *enough*. So we go through the music, bit by bit. Then we go over it. And over it.

Brass Section & Percussion   And over it /

Flutes & Double Reeds   and over it /

Clarinets & Saxophones   and over it /

3rd Alto Sax   and I am so hot in this horrible little room but I keep going. I keep working. I work so hard. My fingers ache and my gums are bleeding and my eyes are blurry and I feel completely mental, but I keep going. Because I have to. I just, *have to*. And the next day I come back into the hall and /

Everyone   sit in Alyssa's chair?!

2nd Flute   So weird!

Tuba   And no one thinks this is going to work!

1st Flute   A Third playing First?

1st Clarinet   It's unheard of!

1st Trumpet   It's going to be a disaster!

3rd Alto Sax   No one will really look at me, but I can tell they're /

2nd Clarinet   all looking /

2nd Alto Sax   sneaking glances /

2nd Trumpet   though we know we shouldn't.

Percussion It feels like when you're trying not to look at a car crash.

1st Trumpet Yeah!

Tuba Oh my God yeah!

Percussion Like you drive past and in your brain you're like /

Tuba don't look /

Tuba & Percussion don't look don't look don't look!

1st Trumpet But then, last second /

1st Trumpet & Tuba & Percussion you look!

1st Trumpet Yeah! This feels like that!

3rd Alto Sax Great! So *everyone* thinks I'm a car crash? You all totally expect me to be shit?

Oboe We didn't say that!

3rd Alto Sax But I can *feel* it!

2nd Clarinet Even Angela looks like she's *totally* dreading it.

Oboe Well, yes! This is our *last* rehearsal!

2nd Flute The concert is *tomorrow*!

1st Clarinet We are missing our Lead Saxophone /

Oboe and we have *no time* to find a replacement.

1st Clarinet This is our only hope!

Everyone Our *only hope!*

3rd Saxophone .

1st Trumpet Angela taps her stick on her music stand.

Tuba We all turn to our music.

Percussion Prepare our instruments.

3rd Clarinet Take a breath.

3rd Trumpet A deep breath.

Oboe And we start.

3rd Alto Sax And I play. And I play. And I play. And actually /

Bass Clarinet actually /

Bassoon actually it's not *that* bad /

Percussion it's actually, alright?

1st Flute   Somehow, *somehow* it's /

Tenor Sax   actually OK? It's /

3rd Alto Sax   it's the *best* I've ever played, ever! And yeah there's a few mistakes but we get through it and at the end I'm tired, I am *so* exhausted, but also like, so wired?!

Tuba   And Angela points /

3rd Alto Sax   at me /

Bassoon   and applauds!

2nd Trombone   And everyone applauds!

3rd Alto Sax   And I can't believe it!

2nd Alto Sax   No one can believe it!

3rd Alto Sax   And at coffee break First Flute comes over and says /

1st Flute   well done.

3rd Alto Sax   And then First Clarinet /

1st Clarinet   well done.

3rd Alto Sax   They say they /

1st Clarinet   didn't think I'd be able to do it.

1st Flute   No offence.

1st Clarinet   No!

1st Flute   But no one /

1st Clarinet   no one /

1st Flute   has ever jumped from Third to First /

1st Clarinet   not *ever*!

1st Flute   And so actually you must /

1st Clarinet   be really good?!

1st Flute   Even if you have to get the *bus* here /

1st Flute   and everything /

1st Clarinet   and anyway /

1st Flute & Clarinet   well done.

3rd Alto Sax   And yeah, it's not really a compliment, but I guess that's the best they can do, so I just say thanks.

3rd Clarinet   And then I go over to say I think you're inspiring. Because I do. And I know that's a big thing to say but, I just have to.

3rd Alto Sax And I smile. Cus I know you mean it. And actually I really needed to hear it.

Oboe And that day we rehearse /

Percussion the *hardest* /

1st Trombone we have /

3rd Trumpet *ever* rehearsed!

2nd Trombone We play /

3rd Alto Sax and we play /

Tenor Sax and we play!

2nd Trumpet We try /

Percussion and we try /

Tuba and we try!

3rd Alto Sax But we *still* can't get it right!

Tenor Sax And we're running out of time!

1st Flute And we still haven't heard anything more about Alyssa.

1st Trumpet And Angela still doesn't have that twinkle in her eye.

Tenor Sax And we still can't get through bar twenty-two without at least one of us exploding into musical flames!

3rd Trumpet But suddenly it's six o'clock?!

3rd Clarinet Nearly ten past!

Bass Clarinet And the car park is full /

Tuba of parents who are *very* patient /

Oboe but just really want to get home.

Percussion And though Angela would blatantly make us stay here all night if she could /

2nd Flute she can't.

2nd Alto Sax So we have to stop.

2nd Clarinet And we're sort of expecting some kind of rallying speech.

2nd Trumpet But really? There's nothing she could say.

Tuba We've failed.

1st Clarinet And tomorrow everyone will know it.

Bassoon We are sent home.

They shuffle about in a restless state.

1st Trombone   And no one sleeps that night.

1st Flute   Not a wink!

1st Trumpet   Not even me.

Bassoon   *Cosmic Concerto* spins round and round my head all night long!

1st Clarinet   Me too!

2nd Flute   Me too!

3rd Alto Sax   Oh God, me too!

Bass Clarinet   And when we wake up on Saturday /

2nd Trombone   we feel sick.

Oboe   I can't eat any breakfast I, I just can't.

Percussion   I just pace at home all morning until it's time to leave.

They get in formation and pace nervously.

1st Clarinet   We arrive at the concert hall /

1st Flute   all in bright white shirts and our school trousers and shoes.

1st Trombone   And I feel a bit stupid in mine.

1st Trumpet   You look a bit stupid.

1st Trombone   Shuttup!

Tuba   We're all standing in this corridor and it's really cold /

2nd Trumpet   but I'm sweating!

2nd Clarinet   Me too!

2nd Trumpet   Cos I'm excited and nervous.

Bass Clarinet   Yeah.

1st Flute   Yeah I feel like my body is on fire! Like, I'm shivering, and I dunno if it's because I'm cold or excited?

1st Clarinet   Oh my God I know!

2nd Trombone   And none of us can stop talking

2nd Saxophone   And we keep getting shhhh'd!

2nd Flute   And suddenly the door opens /

Percussion   and Alyssa's dad is there?!

1st Flute   Oh my God!

Bass Clarinet Everyone goes silent!

Bassoon And just, stares!

2nd Clarinet And he hesitates /

1st Trombone cos we're all staring /

1st Clarinet but then walks in /

3rd Alto Sax walks right over to me. And goes /

Tuba 'Here, Alyssa said to give you this.'

2nd Trumpet And he walks out.

3rd Alto Sax And I look, and in my hand, is her saxophone case. I open it and /

1st Clarinet oh my God?! Has she?

Tuba She's given you hers?!

Oboe There's a note!

Tenor Sax Open it!

3rd Alto Sax Hey. Thought you could use this. Have fun. Kiss.

1st Flute Oh my God!

3rd Alto Sax But before I can even think /

Tenor Sax the doors open /

Tuba and Angela walks out to lights!

Oboe And she speaks to the audience and she says something about Alyssa /

Bass Clarinet and we all go silent /

3rd Alto Sax and I feel embarrassed and I dunno why.

Bass Clarinet And then everyone claps.

2nd Alto Sax And then we walk out /

Tuba in a long line /

3rd Clarinet one by one.

1st Trumpet And we take our seats.

2nd Trombone And try to breathe.

3rd Trumpet And blink in the lights.

1st Clarinet Yeah why's it so bright?

Bassoon And suddenly it's time to begin!

Oboe And I'm lead Oboe, so I have the responsibility. I take a big deep breath and play the tuning note.

2nd Flute   And it comes out a squeak at first and she's /

Oboe   humiliated! Absolutely humiliated! But this is important, it's *the* most important thing /

Tuba   so she tries again /

2nd Trumpet   and she gets it right /

2nd Trombone   and we all feel relieved /

1st Clarinet   cos it's like she's keeping us all safe.

1st Clarinet   And we all tune up to her note.

1st Flute   And it's a bit squawky at first /

Bassoon   but then suddenly we all slot into this place, where we sound good together.

3rd Clarinet   And Angela taps her stick on her music stand.

They all look at Angela, take a deep breath, and play.

Tuba   And we begin the first piece.

Tenor Saxophone   And I can see my mum smiling!

2nd Saxophone   And that makes me smile.

2nd Trumpet   And I can see my dad!

Trumpet One   My dad's here! He's sat next to my mum! Even though they are divorcing they came together and sat next to each other and smiled and waved. And my sister looks bored but that's OK.

Tuba   I just wanna make them proud /

Trumpet Two   make them proud /

Everyone   make them proud of me.

They play.

3rd Clarinet   We play the first piece and /

3rd Trumpet   it goes really well!

2nd Flute   And everyone claps!

2nd Trombone   And my mouth smiles!

2nd Clarinet   And my heart soars!

1st Flute   And we play the second piece.

1st Clarinet   And it's harder to play but /

2nd Trumpet   we're warmed up now and /

3rd Clarinet   feeling more confident.

1st Trumpet   So we play it well /

Percussion   *really* well /

Tuba   and everyone claps!

Tenor Sax   And then, it's the final piece.

Tuba   The Beast!

Everyone   *Cosmic Concerto*!

Percusion   And it all goes quiet.

Tenor Sax   And Angela looks at us all /

Percussion   and her face all serious.

Bassoon   This is the last big hurdle /

1st Trumpet   this is it!

1st Flute   This is *the* moment /

Bass Clarinet   we've all been waiting for!

3rd Alto Sax   And I hold Alyssa's saxophone in my hands. And I do not feel worthy, of even touching it at all! And I seriously consider running away, just leaving, but /

Oboe   Angela raises her stick!

3rd Clarinet   And she whispers /

3rd Trumpet   she actually whispers /

Everyone   'I believe in you!'

Percussion   And seeing her lips /

Bass Clarinet   whisper *those* words /

3rd Alto Sax   is all we need.

Bassoon   And we begin!

3rd Trumpet   And we play!

2nd Flute   And it's hard /

1st Trumpet   it's really hard /

2nd Trumpet   it takes every single bit of focus /

3rd Trumpet   from every single one of us.

1st Trombone   And as we approach it. The dreaded /

Everyone   Bar twenty-two!

1st Flute And I'm scared I can't do it!

1st Trumpet I can't do it!

1st Clarinet I can't!

3rd Alto Sax I'm scared I'm not good enough!

Tuba I *know* I'm not!

2nd Flute I'm not!

3rd Alto Sax But I look up at Angela, and she's looking at us, and she nods. And I know she thinks we can do it, she believes. So we all take a deep breath.

Everyone inhales together.

3rd Alto Sax We give it *everything* we've got.

Everyone exhales together.

3rd Alto Sax And something *incredible* happens?!

They all start to rise to their feet and get up onto their chairs as they play over the next bit.

3rd Alto Sax We play, like we've never played before! We play, hard! No! Not hard, we play, full? Yeah, full! We are *full*, of the music like *it's* playing *us*! And just like Alyssa said in her note, she said *have fun*! So we do! And it's not excellent, not in a technically musically excellent kind of way, it's actually a bit of a mess. But it's *so full* of, I dunno, heart? Yeah! It's full of heart and soul and fun, that it *is* excellent! I mean, *this* is the kind of excellence that I want. We play /

1st Flute we play /

1st Trombone we play!

Tuba And it's like the music takes over?!

1st Trumpet Like we *trusted* ourselves /

1st Clarinet trusted each other /

Tenor Sax to play our very best /

3rd Clarinet and let go of the outcome!

3rd Alto Sax To let go /

1st Clarinet let go /

2nd Trombone let go /

Oboe and let it /

Everyone play *through* us!

2nd Alto Sax And it pushes us on, on *through* the bar /

Bass Clarinet *Through* bar twenty-two!

1st Trombone We're doing it /

Tenor Sax we're doing it /

1st Flute oh my God, we're doing it!

2nd Clarinet We've done it!

2nd Flute Oh my God!

Tuba But we're not done yet!

2nd Trombone The music pushes us through the bar /

Bassoon and on! Pushes us through /

2nd Flute the rest of the piece!

3rd Alto Sax And when my solo comes? I just, *play*! This mad messy solo that's totally unexpected! And there's some smirks around mouthpieces and yes! We're smiling, we're almost laughing, we're having fun! And we look up at Angela, unsure if she'll be cross, really angry with us for doing it wrong but, she's smiling! And there! There in her eyes /

Everyone her sparkle is back!

3rd Alto Sax And we play, and it's messy /

Tuba it's really messy /

Percussion but actually /

1st Trombone it sounds kind of good!

Bass Clarinet It sounds *great*!

Tenor Sax The music pours through us /

3rd Alto Sax and it *feels* /

Everyone incredible!

Everyone *is stood on their chairs, arms high up into the air, open like wings, head tipped back to the heavens. Then* **Tuba** *looks at us.*

Tuba And at the end, there's this pause.

Percussion *looks to us.*

Percussion Silence.

3rd Trumpet *sneaks a look at us.*

3rd Trumpet For ages.

Silence.

Basson Then, thunderous applause!

Everyone *jumps off their chairs and celebrates.*

2nd Flute   And everyone is on their feet!

3rd Clarinet   All the mums and dads /

2nd Trombone   and everyone else /

1st Trombone   everyone who's ever loved us /

3rd Clarinet   who's driven us to lessons /

Tuba   and rehearsals /

1st Clarinet   and music shops /

2nd Clarinet   and paid for everything /

1st Flute   and listened to us /

2nd Flute   when we got it wrong /

2nd Alto Sax   over and over /

2nd Trumpet   and over and /

1st Trombone   over and over /

2nd Alto Sax   and over!

Tuba   And right now we're here /

Bass Clarinet   all together /

Bassoon   and we did it /

2nd Flute   we did it!

3rd Alto Sax   We *all* did it!

Oboe   And everyone is so proud!

They dance. Joyful and bright. Community and celebration. We can't help but smile.

Orchestra

BY CHARLIE JOSEPHINE

Notes on rehearsal and staging, drawn from a workshop with the writer, held at the National Theatre, October 2023

How the writer came to write the play

Writer Charlie Josephine was in an orchestra as a young person; they spoke about how much they enjoyed it. Josephine spoke about how they stayed away from home when they took part in the national orchestra, and it was that experience that inspired the writing of the play.

Josephine spoke about how they were in a Connections play at Watford Palace Theatre and how much of a nourishing experience it was for them.

> 'I want the young people to have fun as they make the work, what it ends up being I'm less interested in. I want the young people to have fun with it and make it theirs.'

Welcome and intentions

Lead director Rob Watt set up some intentions for the room:

Openness

– The idea to explore new things, even if you've tried the activities before, Watt offered that the group should try to find something new and engage with the activities in the present.

Radical kindness

– Listening is an act of radical kindness.

Presentness

– An offer to try and remain present where possible.

Boldness

– There will be opportunities to something new. There are no right or wrong answers. Be bold in your thinking.

Warm-up

Exercise: Fingers and Palm

An exercise to wake up both parts of your brain.

The group stood in a circle, all facing inwards. Watt asked each person to stand with the left palm open flat with the palm facing upwards and with their right hand to point downwards with their index finger. When Watt said go, the group tried to catch the finger of the person next to them with their left hand, whilst trying to keep their right hand from being caught.

Exercise: Four Square

Using tape on the floor, Watt created a large square, then divided the square into four smaller squares.

The first four people stood in one square each, with Watt showcasing the starting square and the winning square. As the game goes on, each time a player is out, the group move up a square. The aim is to stay in the top square for as long as possible. Each time a player is out, and the group move up towards the winning square, a new player steps into the starting square. The starting square always serves first.

Play begins when the server drop bounces the ball and serves. The ball can only bounce once in any square before it has to be hit by a player. Each player should hit the ball with their hand into opposing squares with the aim to catch a player out.

Exercise: Line Up

Throughout this exercise, Watt offered new challenges to encourage a variation of communication styles. He asked the group to reflect on how they approached each task.

- Watt asked the group to line up in height order (without any limitations to their voices or gestures)
- He then asked the group to line up in order of their house numbers from lowest to highest (without using their voices)
- The group were asked to line up in order of the time they woke up, with the offer to be as specific as possible (without voice and without using their fingers)
- Lastly the group were asked to line up in order of their birthday (without the use of any gesture or voice)

Watt mentioned that parameters can sometimes make us feel constrained, but when you have to get creative, you have to embrace it. Encourage other ways of communicating and see restrictions as liberations.

Approaching the play

Exercise: Becoming a Detective

Watt opened up the idea of new beginnings. Meander through the play like the audience would.

Unpack the play with an evidence wall and instil curiosity in your young people.

Josephine added that this exercise encourages critical thinking and gives young people a sense of ownership over their choices.

The following headings were written on different pieces of paper and put up on the wall:

Questions, Assumptions, Facts, Locations, Times, Themes, Characters.

Questions

Something you don't know. Watt asked the group to try and keep the questions open.
Example: Where are we? How old are they?

Assumptions

When the character has done something, but you can't prove it in the text.
Example: The 1st Trumpet thinks they are the best.

Facts

Something that is true and can be proven by the text. Through the process, the questions and assumptions can become facts. Conversations about truth will come up, and it's up to you and the company to agree on what you decide are facts.
Example: The concert is on Saturday night.

Locations and time

Any locations or times that are mentioned in stage directions or in the play.
These can be used to draw a map.
Example: A church hall

Themes

Here are some of the themes spoken about in the session.
Success vs joy
Class
Suicide/self-harm
Community
Ego
Reputation

Pride
Status

Characters

Anything that is said or offered about character.
Example: It's said that they are 'the best in the country'.

This exercise is important in encouraging companies to not lock themselves away from possibility.

The following phrases can be helpful to introduce to the room: I assume, I believe, I think, I know.

Offering this kind of language allows an opportunity for openness, which then leads to a level of ownership within the actors.

Exercise: Reading Sections of the Play

Section one: Full stops.
   Watt asked the group to read one line at a time, but instead of reading as specific characters, he asked the group to switch readers every time there is a full stop. The readers didn't need to work in a specific order, and there was also the freedom to say lines in unison. This exercise can be used to introduce your company to the script and put the engagement onto the dialogue. It also helps with active listening.
   Josephine added that it allows the script to be messy from the start.

Section two: Punctuation.
   Josephine noted that they use punctuation very specifically to find the flow and it allows them to share their musicality through the script. The group were asked to read the section again, but this time switching the reader whenever there is punctuation.
   This exercise can help find the rhythm and be able to notice when there are longer beats and shorter beats.

Exercise: Script up on the Wall

Watt attached all the pages of the script across a wall so it could be seen in full. The script on the wall was sectioned (using a line across the page to signify the end of a section) every time something changed for the characters.

This exercise allows the group to notice the moments in the text that have more density. From this, you can consider the flow of the script. It offers space to realize when there is repetition, to notice the musicality and to see the script's internal rhythm.

Using this method, you can then add a timeline to the script with your group, so you can see it visually.

152 Charlie Josephine

Watt suggested you could title each section, with a heading that sums up that particular section. For example: Section One could be named 'Welcome to the Orchestra'.

Understanding the script

Exercise: Pointing

Using a section of the script, the group were asked to read one line at a time. Each time they read aloud; they should point towards what they are speaking about. The director's role in this is to ask live questions to the readers, asking them to be specific with their choices.

For example: If a reader is talking about the whole group, how can they include the whole group physically?

Watt explained how this activity automatically gets the group thinking more physically. It encourages actors to be specific and to understand what they are speaking about. Be careful of actors always choosing to point down. It's useful with this exercise to encourage your groups to open upwards.

Exercise: Repeating Lines

Using a section of the script, a character delivers their line, then the next character to speak repeats the previous line back as a question before saying their own line. This continues throughout the section.

This exercise is good for actors to listen and acknowledge what is being said before they speak. It can help when actors are disconnected from their onstage peers. It's important to note that this exercise would take too long if you were to do this for the whole script, but if actors aren't listening in certain sections, you can use it to help guide that.

Exercise: Take the Baton

Using a section of the script, every time a character speaks, they must be holding the baton. The baton can be any object (for example, a water bottle), or it could be made of paper. It needs to be something physical that can be taken by each reader every time they speak. The actors can take the baton in a variety of different ways; for example, think about whether characters want the baton or not.

For characters that aren't onstage, they should still be sat on the edge of the exercise. Each time someone is spoken about who isn't on stage, they should be tapped with the baton.

As a further layer, Watt asked for there to be no gaps in the script and to make the baton swaps clearer.

This exercise offers blocking ideas and brings it into the space. It also helps with the quality of intention, pace and who holds the power. It highlights who wants to speak and who doesn't. It is a useful exercise when actors are off book.

Exercise: Exploring Character

Ask actors to write a one-page biography, with the phrasing 'they are . . .', 'she is . . .', 'he will . . .', etc. Then you can rewrite it a few weeks later, and the group can see the developments they've been making on their characters.

Movement

Exercise: Physical Warm-up – Curiosity and Gratitude

Music was playing throughout this activity (see references at the end of the notes for music inspiration).

Josephine asked everyone to find a space in the room and asked them to think about their feet and to take a moment to be more curious with their movements. Allowing feet to move and guide them through the space. Slowly making their way up the body in the following order: from feet, then including the knees, hips, ribs, shoulders, elbows, wrists, head.

Guiding thoughts and questions as the group moved through the space:

- What pace do you have?
- How small can you make your movements?
- Try spelling your name with your body.
- Exploring through each body part.
- Being mindful of your neck, giving it some softness.
- Connecting the movements between the body parts.
- Maybe you are noticing your habits.
- Noticing what is happening around you.
- Sharing some love and openness to others in the room through your movements.

Then the instruction was given to allow the body to travel and be open to be inspired by other movements around you.

The exercise ended with some breathing. Josephine demonstrated how to breathe in a **backwards circle movement**. Breathing as you bring your hands up, back towards your chest and back to the ground in a circle motion. A good exercise for nerves and a grounding technique.

Exercise: Partner to Group Dance

Standing opposite your partner, each person offers a new movement into the space and the other copies, then the next person offers another new movement, and the cycle continues, becoming a dialogue between the two actors.

Participants were encouraged not to get too stuck on one type of movement and to keep exploring.

After a few minutes, Watt offered that the pairs could begin to form bigger groups, eventually with the group becoming one. Watt then led the group between two states, dancing small and dancing big, guiding the group through the dance. Creating different shapes and dynamics.

Josephine offered that there will be different abilities within a company and that these exercises exploring movement hopefully allow for a celebration of those human bodies, so that the young people have gratitude for their differences. Sometimes working with words isn't that accessible, so including movement is an important layer.

Exercise: Tempo

Watt led the group around the space, asking them to balance the space and offering that the group doesn't always need to move forwards. He offered changes in tempo by using a scale of one to ten, with one being the slowest tempo, five being the average tempo and ten being the fastest tempo.

Watt then asked the group to try this in freeform, so each person gets to rotate through the tempos at their own pace.

Josephine split the group, so that some people were moving at the tempo Watt offered, whilst the others continued to move around the space through walking.

It was observed that you didn't need instruments at all, or even pretend to play them – you are able to see all the different dynamics and choose where the focus is by putting a spotlight on certain characters.

This exercise can take actors out of their heads, invites a sense of freedom and gives people permission to be silly.

As a director, you don't need to be complicated. This exercise uses numbers and tempo, but it offers exploration. Setting up the parameters, and then being able to guide your group within those, could lead to a shared language about the movement in the play.

Exercise: Start, Stop, In, Out, Up

Watt set up the following words, and instructions on what to do each time one of the below words is said.

Start – to move around the space.
Stop – to stop with energy, so you are ready to move again.
In – to move to the centre of the room looking towards the audience.
Out – to move to the extremities of the space.
Up – to jump with the noise 'oooo'.
Down – to tap the floor with your hand, pushing all the energy down to the floor with the noise 'oooooff'.
Leader – everyone in the group kneels down and one person stays standing. Everyone should look up at the leader that is stood. The leader then starts off the movement again.
Follower – similar to leader, one person goes down and the others stay standing. Everyone in the room looks down to the follower.
Tempo – the rules of the previous exercise still apply, a tempo scale was offered into the space (one being the slowest tempo, five being the average tempo and ten being the fastest tempo).

Josephine spoke about how their writing is very fast paced, so they'd like groups to embrace the slow moments and allow the movement to take up some space in moments of silence and stillness.

Exercise: Instruments

The room was split into eight groups:

- Trumpet
- Saxophone
- Tuba
- Drums
- Flute
- Piano
- Clarinet
- Bassoon

Groups were asked to come up with as many words as they could to describe their given instrument.

Next, the groups were asked to find three movements that gave a sense of their instrument. The groups then shared back to the room.

Watt then asked individuals to showcase their movements one by one. Switching between instruments and conducting the movements like a physical orchestra.

This is an exercise that could help build character, try new things and find out new things about the character. There is a sense of conductor, tone and pace with this exercise and a way of bringing that language into the room.

Orchestra research

Watt shared an example of an orchestra seating plan. This example maps out the roles and placements of an orchestra, which could be useful to bring to a rehearsal room. Watt explained that research like this can help companies to explore new ideas. Think about what inspires you from this research, but also what can you lose from this research rather than simply replicating.

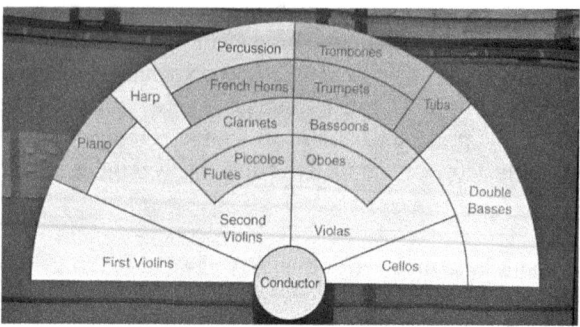

Watt split the room into small groups and asked them to look through the musical language reference sheet (find it online on here https://www.classicfm.com/discover-music/musical-italian-terms/) and to see whether any of the already existing language in the classical music world can relate to their production. Perhaps it can help with building the world, style, design, approach, etc.

Casting

Josephine is happy for characters to be split further for bigger casts. However, they said to make sure you read the writer's notes at the beginning and to look closely at how you split the roles. Some roles could be ensemble and non-speaking if that works for your group. Watt encouraged us to introduce movement as a language for non-speaking roles, so they add to the rhythm of the performance and feel part of the company and ensemble.

Auditions and casting: This is a preference depending on how you and your company work. If you were to hold auditions, you could run a workshop that includes some movement and some text work to see where the company are at with their confidence, etc. However, auditions can sometimes cause anxiety, so go with what is best for your group.

Josephine offered that it's nice when young people can use their own accents, and groups shouldn't feel pressured to use different accents. There are other ways to distinguish character, power and status.

Question and answer with Charlie Josephine

Some of these questions came from the 'question wall' from the earlier exercise.

Q: What are the differences between 1st, 2nd and 3rd in an orchestra?
A: 1st traditionally plays the more intricate parts. It's common that musicians will make their way up the orchestra starting in 3rd heading towards the 1st spot. There can be a lot of pressure and nervousness about being a 1st.

Q: Do you have any advice on developing the character of Angela?
A: Work through some character exercises, so that everyone has a shared idea of who Angela is. A wall of shared characteristics. A list of traits. There could be a physical manifestation of Angela. A scarf could appear when Angela speaks. Although no one is playing her, she should still feel very present.

Q: Do you have any exercises that can help young people with learning their lines?
A: Speed runs with a specific focus on lines, activities that look at punctuation and playing games with the text.

Q: How closely should we stick to the stage directions?
A: I tried to be really specific about the stage directions. But I hope it inspires you to do what you want with the work. But try and figure out why I've put that stage direction there and then how you do it I don't really mind. I just want you to know why, before deciding to do something else.

Q: There is some religious imagery with them rehearsing in a church – was this intentional?
A: It was an easy decision because that was where I rehearsed when I was in a national orchestra. But I am interested in the spirituality of art, and the divinity of poetry and theatre that it isn't associated with any religious beliefs but leaning into the magic of musicality. It's up to you whether you want to turn up the volume on those things or not.

Q: What advice would you give when working with the heavier themes of the play?
A: I'd encourage that you make it clear that you are always talking about the play. Make sure to know the signposting and have that available in your rehearsals. Check in with what your safeguarding policies are and follow those. Leaning on the principles of working, so that there is a safety to the work especially when there are bigger themes.

Q: With it written in your dialect, would you be OK for there to be any changes made by young people to suit their own dialect?
A: Yes, I am happy for young people to make it theirs. If they wouldn't use a word and want to replace it with something else, they can.

Q: What is the use of music in this play?
A: You'll need to experiment with that. There is no real right or wrong answer.

Suggested references

Oona Doherty – 'Sugar Army' and 'A Concrete Song'
Hofesh Shechter

158 Charlie Josephine

Pina Bausch
Elderbrook and Rudimental: 'Something about You' video
https://www.youtube.com/watch?v=N1EhXF1lskA

From a workshop led by Rob Watt
With notes by Grace Duggan

There are both Welsh-language and English-language versions of ***Dy Enw Marw/Your Name Is Dead***. If you would like a version without explicit language, please contact connections@nationaltheatre.org.uk

Elgan Rhys is a writer and collaborator working in theatre, TV and literature. His work advocates for the empowerment of young people, everyone in the LGBTQ+ umbrella and Welsh-speaking communities. Elgan Rhys has been an Associate Artist for two leading Welsh children's and young people's theatre companies, Frân Wen and Theatr Iolo, and produced *Y Pump*, a series of co-created YA novels which won two Wales Book of the Year awards in 2022.
elganrhys.net

Your Name Is Dead
by Elgan Rhys
in collaboration with Leo Drayton

Author's Note (Elgan Rhys)
Your Name Is Dead is a play written for audiences aged 14 and older. It has five core roles, eight additional speaking roles and numerous group scenes. The role of M/Max should be played by a performer who identifies as trans masculine. See character list for specific characteristics of the other core characters.

As a gay, cis male writer, I have found it important to use my privilege to centre voices that are underheard or misrepresented in mainstream culture. I have created this play in collaboration with the brilliant Welsh trans writer Leo Drayton (see Collaborator's Note for insight on the nature of our collaboration). The creation of the play also invited input from a group of Cardiff-based queer and trans people, facilitated by The Queer Emporium and Paned o Gê.

This play is set in a town in north-west Wales, and the characters' accents are associated with this area. Performers are welcome to attempt the accents, avoiding stereotypes. If not entirely comfortable, the performers should adapt the characters to their own accents. See page 166 for more on dialect.

The play has many culturally specific Welsh references, which should be retained even if accents are being adapted. Each production should decide how to feature the chorus of the Welsh-language song 'Yma o Hyd', e.g. to play as a soundtrack or to learn as a chorus, as long as cultural sensitivity is ensured.

Some other cultural references in the play can be adapted where each production sees fit; these references are noted with a * in the script.

Jigsaw is a strong metaphor in this play, with a few characters sometimes playing jigsaw. I encourage all productions to enjoy interpreting this metaphor in their staging, be it in a literal way or not.

In a time when trans and gender-non-conforming people are facing increasingly extreme hostility from ignorant and bigoted people with power, and hard-won LGBTQIA+ rights are under threat, there is an urgent need to form radical solidarities. See page 201 for a list of organizations doing valuable work around the themes of the play.

This play is an act of solidarity with all trans people.

Collaborator's Note (Leo Drayton)

My involvement in this project began when Elgan, a friend and someone I admire greatly, asked for input on his initial ideas for an National Theatre Connections play. We had a brainstorming session to discuss what it's like to be 16 and trans in Wales today, which sparked interesting ideas about freedom, choice and the act of changing your name. As a trans man, my experience of this at 16 was an important milestone in my journey, and I felt that this would be an interesting story to tell. After that session, Elgan asked me to collaborate with him on the development of the play and I immediately said yes. My role in the process was to read the latest draft of the play and give feedback on the authenticity of the character and story as well as the overall flow of the play. This was a very similar process to *Y Pump*, a previous project we had worked on together, a series of five books about five diverse characters, each written with a young co-writer to ensure authenticity. I was fortunate enough to be a co-writer on one of those novels, which introduced me to the writing world and some incredible people.

An element of this process that I am incredibly proud to have been a part of was a focus group session we had with other trans people who read the play and shared their opinion. It was a blessing to be able to have an open conversation about these experiences and hear their thoughts. I felt seen in a way I never had before; a group of people who shared common experiences, talking about a play that discusses those experiences. In a time where the trans community is facing a lot of negativity it was heart-warming to have an empowering and positive conversation about the community. And for that I am extremely grateful to Elgan, the National Theatre and to the inspiring people who came.

Growing up, I was part of a youth theatre group where we took part in the National Theatre Connections festival, and so I was honoured that through this process I was able to give input on something that would have meant a lot to me when I was that age. Theatre is immensely valuable, not only as a creative outlet and to build confidence, but also as a tool for exploring your own identity. This play offers a new perspective to those performers who can relate to Max and gives young people a chance to learn about the trans experience and to show support on a stage. I have never worked on a professional play before, and I am so grateful for all I've learned. To not only have an insight into the writing process but to also be a part of a radical play about something so important.

Having worked with Elgan before, I had total faith and trust that he would do this in a respectful way, shedding light on trans issues with the help of trans people, and that he would do the work that was necessary to understand the nuance in our experiences. I am so honoured and proud to have worked on this project and sincerely hope that this play will be a platform for trans and queer youth as well as young Welsh performers to explore and express themselves freely.

Your Name Is Dead is a story that needs to be shared.

Acknowledgements

Diolch o galon to Ola Animashawun for the invitation and his dramaturgy, to Leo Drayton for his insight and rigour, to Sera Moore Williams for her provocations, to Al Parr and Gareth Evans-Jones for their kindness, to Dylan Huw for his patience, to Timothy Howe and the members of Sherman Youth Theatre for kick starting the idea for this piece, to all of the NT Connections staff, and to Joey Madaffari, Rudy Harries, Kay R. Dennis, Vidhy Chaudhary, Branwen Neverwere and everyone at The Queer Emporium and Paned o Gê for your generosity and invaluable feedback.

Elgan Rhys

Characters

M/Max – *16 years old, trans masculine, he/him*
Bobby – *15 years old, male, he/they*
James – *18 years old, cis male, he/him*
Student – *any age, any gender*
Ceridwen – *17 years old, cis female, she/her*
Barista – *any age, any gender*
Customer/s – *any age, any gender*
Jano – *any age, any gender*
Resident – *late 80s, any gender*
Friend/s – *any age, any gender*
Nick – *any age, cis male, he/him*
Young Mam – *early 20s, cis female, she/her*
Young Dad – *early 20s, cis male, he/him*
Intercom (Voiceover) – *middle-aged, cis male, he/him*

Key

/ – point of interruption

... – character unable to finish thought or searching for thought/word

' ' – quoting something or someone

Dialect

(word – pronunciation – meaning)

'De*– *deh* – Innit

'Sti* – *sdee* – Y'know

* if performers have decided to adapt the characters to their own accents, they should cut these words.

Del – *dell* – Love

Yma o Hyd – *UM-ah awe HEED* – 'Still Here' (song title)

Ceridwen – *Keh-RID-when* – A character's name

Jano – *JAN-oh* – A character's name

Elin – *ELLE-in* – A character's name

Dafis – *DAV-iss* – A character's surname

Taid – *tied* – Grandad

Cariad – *CAR-yad* – Love

Caru ti – *CAR-ee Tea* – Love you

1. my jigsaw

M *enters, holding a letter with a real sense of pride. It's a certificate with his new name. We stay here for a moment. Then, snap into scene:*

M *and* **Bobby** *are queuing for a coffee.* **M** *is still holding on to the letter.*

M   I look different?

Bobby   Yes, you look different.

M   How do I *look* different?!

Bobby   You just, you just do?

M   I do *feel* different, 'de.

Bobby   Ooh . . . ?

M   Yeh-yeh, like, it feels *so* good! Feels like . . . (*Exclaims.*) I'm finally here!

Bobby *jumps at* **M**'s *excitement.*

Bobby   What do you mean?

M   The real me.

Bobby   Oh, yeah?

M   Yeh, real me finally here.

Beat.

Bobby (*laughing*)   Well, hello you!

M   HELLOWWW, *MEEE*!

The queue of people turn their heads. **M** *and* **Bobby** *laugh quietly.*

Bobby   Are you grieving though?

M   What?! No way, no! I've done enough of that 'de!

Bobby   I know I know, it's just, it's big, a big day for /

M   For *me*!

Bobby   Course. For you.

M (*an awkward laugh*)   You're not 'grieving', no?

Bobby   No, course not, no no no!

M   This 'de, it's like . . . complete opposite of grieving, 'sti.

Beat.

M   Like, you ever done jigsaw?

Bobby   What's jigsaw got to do with /

M   Just answer me! Done jigsaw?!

Bobby   Course I do jigsaws /

M (*laughing*)   You *still* do jigsaw?

Bobby   No. Maybe.

M *cackles.* **Bobby** *smiles.*

Barista   Next!

M *and* **Bobby** *move closer to* **Barista***.*

M   I *hated* jigsaw as a kid, I was good 'de, but hated it, cause thing is yeh, my mam always bought our jigsaws, like she bought most of our toys and clothes yeh, she bought 'em from charity shops, like Scope*? /

Bobby   I bought a Burberry* shirt from Scope* once /

M   Yeh, and you *chose* to do that. You ever bought jigsaw from a charity shop?

Bobby *shakes their head.*

M   Thing is 'de, when you buy jigsaw from a charity shop even though it says on the box 'sixty-piece jigsaw set' /

Bobby   Sixty? Easy!

M (*laughing*)   . . . even though it says 'sixty' on the box, it's never sixty /

Bobby   Right . . .

M   And my brother 'de . . . We used to do jigsaw together when we were little, And he wasn't bothered 'sti, he was *fine* when we got to the end of the jigsaw, but I, I was *raging* every time 'de, cause we'd never reach the end, no? There was always a piece or two *missing*.

And the worse 'de, this only happened once, but the worse was when there *was* sixty pieces, and I was *so* excited yeh, but when we got to the last piece . . . That last piece was a piece from *another* jigsaw set! And my brother tried to force that wrong piece on the jigsaw, but I kept shouting 'doesn't fit!'

And he just said, 'make it fit 'de.'

Hated that. Really hated it. So I screamed at him, 'sti. Like almost *roared*. And my brother just stood there with his face, like, ugh, just not bothered 'sti, and then . . . then . . . he started laughing!

So I went for it, I smashed the jigsaw and he just started shouting at me 'it's just a fucking jigsaw, it's just a fucking jigsaw' so I threw the box in his face, grabbed Mam's cricket bat and said I was gonna smash his head in . . . (*Beat.*) but I didn't obviously! /

M *laughing.*

Bobby   How old were you?

M   Eight. But, that rage 'de . . . (*refers to his body*) that's been here . . .

Beat.

M (*referring to certificate*)   When I got this today yeh, I felt this weird feeling, like good weird. This rage that's been inside me, I think it's left my body, 'sti. I know it sounds weird, and maybe that's why I look different. But it has, it's left me! Thanks to this free little piece of paper!

Bobby   It was free?!

M   My missing piece was free! And like, (*refers to his body*) I can't fix everything right now no, obviously got other pieces to change too (*refers to certificate*) but fixing *this* today . . . It's a start yeh. And I feel powerful. I'm a powerful jigsaw.

Bobby *looks at* **M** *a little confused.*

Bobby   So, you're a jigsaw now?

M *laughs.*

M   We're all jigsaws, yeh? Like one per cent of us are born with like a perfect set, and there's no need to change or find new pieces, and then the rest of us . . . born with a set that has missing pieces, or wrong pieces 'de.

Beat.

Bobby   You love an analogy don't you? And that's a *really* wanky analogy.

They both laugh. The queue of people turn their heads again. **M** *and* **Bobby** *quieten.*

Bobby   But seriously, I'm happy for you. And happy that it's . . . it's gone now.

M   No one's dead, Bobby /

Bobby   I know, what I mean is, you've *done* it /

M   Yes, but I'm still here /

Bobby   Yes, and you've reclaimed / something *big.*

M   I like that word / reclaim

Bobby   And now you can move on /

Barista   Next!

M *and* **Bobby** *move closer.*

Bobby   *We* can move on, as Bobby and. . .? /

M   You should do it.

Bobby   Huh?

M   I mean, everyone should. If you can, then you should. So, maybe . . . You should do it too? When do you turn sixteen again?

Bobby   Tomorrow . . .

M   Oh shit yeh, course, knew it. (*Beat.*) I can help you. We could do a list, like we did for me /

Bobby   A long list then a short list, then a *short* short list cause the short list you had was long yeah? /

M   I know, just have a go, do a list /

Bobby Dunno, not sure if I /

M Imagine, both of us reclaiming what our parents gave us. Right?

Beat – **Bobby** *is unsure, but gives in to* **M***'s fixation/idea.*

Bobby Yeah, OK, fuck our parents /

M *laughs.*

Barista Next!

M *and* **Bobby** *move closer.*

M You like both your parents though, no? And they like you? /

Bobby (*a lie*) Not really.

M *is surprized.*

Bobby Yeah, they can be, um . . .

Bobby *struggling to think (because he is lying).*

Bobby Like . . . dicks.

M What!? Both of them, dicks?

Bobby Sometimes.

M Really?!

Bobby Yeh-yeh . . .

M Only my dad that's a dick, 'sti. I'd rather Trump* as my dad.

Bobby *laughs.*

Bobby Yeh, and I'd rather Putin* as mine.

M That's not funny.

Beat – They laugh.

M Wouldn't be holding this now if it wasn't for my mam though, 'sti.

Bobby *shakes his head in agreement.*

M On my birthday 'de, she woke me up early, just poked me and didn't say a word no, and then did this weird nod . . . And I looked to where she nodded . . . Next to my bed, a piece of toast in a weird sixteen shape, but also 'de, next to the toast was a folded piece of paper, and I knew what it was . . . And she knew that I knew yeh . . . She'd already bought me the form to make this happen, 'sti. And she'd already signed it, and funny yeh, she put a kiss next to her signature! I was howling, and crying a bit.

Bobby Softie.

M I'm not.

Bobby *winks at* **M***,* **M** *nudges* **Bobby***.*

Bobby So tell me . . . what is it?

M What do I look like?

Bobby What d'you mean?

M Guess.

Bobby Guess? Just tell me, we're next!

M Guess!

Bobby Fine! Nick?

M Nick?! Nick! I don't look like a Nick. I'm not a, a twat, who loves money, like I want money, but I don't love it no, and Nick, Nick is the straightest cis white man who's been on like, *The Apprentice** or something, and got fired on the first episode, for being a, a selfish dick!

Barista Next!

M *and* **Bobby** *are the next to order.*

Barista What do you want, boys?

Bobby Vanilla latte, please.

Barista Name.

Bobby Bobby.

Barista (*writes name on cup*) Bobby. Anything else?

Bobby Pumpkin spiced latte, please.

Barista Name.

Bobby *looks to* **M**.

Bobby You're holding us back . . .

M *hands* **Bobby** *the letter.* **Bobby** *opens.* **Bobby** *looks at* **M**.

M Do you like it?

Bobby If you like it, I like it.

M Mam thinks it could've been more Welsh 'de, but you know what? I don't care. It's not hers, and *definitely* not my dad's! It's *mine*!

Bobby Yup, definitely *yours*! (*To* **Barista**.) Sorry, he's just having a moment.

M (*to* **Barista**) Today is all about *me*!

Barista No offence, del, just need a name so I can make you coffee.

Bobby *laughs,* **M** *smacks him playfully.* **Bobby** *leaves.*

M *is on his own. He turns, takes a deep breath – excited to share the news with his* **Mam**.

II. drive

M *arrives home.*

James *is in the living room, playing a car racing game on his Xbox*.*

M *enters the living room, and hasn't seen his brother yet.*

M   Mam! Mam, it's here! It's official!

M *waits to hear from his mam. Nothing.*

M   Mam?

James   What's official?

M *jumps, when he notices* **James** *is here.*

M   What you doing here, James?

James   What's official?

M   Does Mam know you're here?

James   Course she does, yeh.

M   Where is she?

James   I'll tell you, if you tell me what's official.

M   You *know* what's official.

James   Do I?

M   Yeh you do /

James   You're right, I do /

M   Not wasting my time talking to *you* about it, no.

James   Scared I'll go back and tell Dad, yeh?

Beat.

He deserves to know, 'sti.

M   He doesn't.

James   He's your dad, yeh.

M   You know what he's like.

James   He's changed, 'sti. (*Beat.*) Took me to the Wales match the other week. Just me and him. And we won we did, and you know what he did, when we won, he hugged me, 'sti. Hugged me really tight, not like tight-tight, like nice tight. And then he started singing 'Yma o Hyd', and I joined him, even though I can't sing for shit no, and then yeh, out of nowhere the rest of the stadium was singing with us too 'sti. The match was done, the players were gone, but we were still singing.

Beat.

M (*sarcastic*)   Sounds nice.

James   He *can* be nice.

M   Where's Mam?

James   And he gives me money.

M   Keeping you wrapped round his finger, yeh.

James   No, been giving me money to pay for my driving lessons 'de, and he paid for my theory. I passed that obviously, and he's just paid for my test too, 'sti.

M   Has he /

James   Can't wait to pass.

M   How do you know you'll pass?

James   I will. And when I do . . . I'm gonna drive, like all of the time 'de, gonna drive everywhere /

M   Haven't got a car.

James   Not yet, no.

M   Dad won't let you touch his car, 'sti /

James   I know, that's why I'm gonna buy one /

M   They're not cheap 'sti.

James   I know, you sound like Mam /

M   Where is she?

James   Dad said he'd help me buy one /

M   Did he?

James   Said he wants 'the best for his son'. Oh no. Said he wants the best for his *only* son.

M *begins to leave.*

James   You should start driving, 'sti.

M *stops.*

M   I'm not seventeen, no.

James   I could teach you.

M   No, don't trust you.

James   You could drive to work then. Heard the pay is shit at Allports*.

M   S'alright.

James   And you get to keep it all?

M Yeh. Buy Mam and me chips on Fridays, but otherwise.

James Get a discount?

M *nods.*

James Cool. I wouldn't buy her chips though. I'd save all my money, for my Porsche*.

M (*laughs*) A Porsche*? You wish.

Beat.

James Gonna be the best driver.

M *laughs, but* **James** *is serious. Over the next piece of dialogue,* **James** *is intensely engrossed with his race car game on the Xbox*.*

James Cause the thing is 'de, when you drive . . . *you* drive. No one else, no. And you know how it makes me feel?

M Powerful?

James More than that. I feel in charge. In *control*. When I drive, *I* make the decisions /

M Well, you *don't* /

James I do, *I* decide which way we're going /

M No, the roads do /

James *I* decide how fast we're going /

M Again, no, the speed limit does /

James And *I* decide where we end up.

M Yeh, OK, but roads are actually built by other people, so actually, *they* kind of decide where we end up yeh, and *they* decide on the speed limits, and they decide /

James *crashes his car on the Xbox.*

James Fuck's sake! Why'd you do that?!

M Didn't do anything /

James Yeh, you did. Distracted me, I could hear you, ready to go on about how (*mocking*) 'all decisions we make are, are' what's the word (*continues mocking*) 'the only decision that isn't . . .' *influenced*, yeh that's it, 'only decision that's *not* influenced is our decision about our name, *that* decision is *our* decision, only decision that isn't fucking influenced' /

M Informed.

James Informed, influenced, whatever 'de, don't give a fuck. Anyway, all names (*further mocking*) were 'built by other people' yeh.

Beat.

James (*laughing*)   Unless you've created a totally new, original name.

Beat.

What is it?

M *doesn't answer.*

James   Gonna have to tell me, 'sti.

M   Don't *have* to do / anything

James   You can't hide /

M   I'm not / hiding

James   Changed it on socials?

M   Not yet, / no.

James   Just tell me. I'm your brother.

M   Wanna let Mam know, first.

James   Well, she's not here 'de, so.

M   Where is she, James?

James *doesn't answer.* **M** *begins to leave again.*

James   Might never get the chance to tell her, no. Cause she's left.

M   What?

James   She left.

M   For work, probs.

James   No, she said she'd be a while, 'sti. Like a long while. Not sure when she'll be back, no. She had a suitcase too.

M   You're lying.

James   She said something about things being too much.

M   She says that all the time, about everything /

James   Oh no, different this time. She meant you. *You're* too much. With your new fucking name.

Beat.

M   That's something Dad would say, not Mam.

James   Well, they've been talking again, 'sti.

M *doesn't know what to say.*

James   Maybe she's with him /

M   She's not. She hates his guts. Me too /

James   And he hates your guts, too!

M *is enraged now . . . heavy breathing.*

James   Go on, smash something. Throw something. Punch me.

M *composes himself.*

James   But now that it's *official.* That you have a little *boy's* name. I'll punch back, harder.

M *leaves.*

James   Byeeeee.

III. where is Mam?

M *arrives at work – Allports* (Chippy).* **M** *serves customers throughout the scene.* **Bobby** *has come to visit.*

Bobby   Thought of some names.

M *doesn't respond.*

Bobby   Harder than you think, isn't it?

M   Mhm.

Bobby   Lots to think about.

M (*to customer*)   Two fifty.

Bobby   Wanna hear my list?

M *doesn't respond; gives the customer some change.* **Bobby** *annoyed at* **M** *now.*

Bobby   Oi!

M *jumps.*

M   I'm working! What?

Bobby   Talking to you.

M   Yeh, I know, sorry, but I'm /

Bobby   Got a list.

M   A list?

Bobby   Yes, a long list.

M   Cool, well done.

Bobby *unamused.* **M** *turns to* **Customer**.

Customer   A battered sausage, please.

Bobby   I'm seriously thinking about it now. Thanks to *you*. Said you'd help me?

M *yet again not responding.*

Bobby   But, there's no point . . . Cause my parents won't sign the form.

This grabs **M**'s *attention.*

M   What?

M *moves away from* **Customer**, *holding on to the bag with the sausage.*

Bobby   I told you, they're proper dicks.

M   What do you mean?

Bobby   Like, full-on saying . . . It's only trans people who get to change their names.

M   Whaaaaat . . .

Bobby   I know, they're so backwards.

M   That's so weird, cause they're like, OK with you being gay yeh? /

Bobby   Well . . . are they?

M   Really?

Bobby *shrugs.*

M   But you said they were OK with you wanting to change your pronouns, no?

Bobby   I never told them.

M *looks at* **Bobby**, *confused* . . .

Bobby   Cause I was scared.

M   Scared? Shit.

Customer   Excuse me, I'm waiting for my sausage /

M (*to* **Customer**)   Hang on!

Customer *unamused.* **M** *turns back to* **Bobby**.

M   Sorry, didn't realize it was that bad?

Bobby   It's OK, just glad I have you.

M   Course you do.

M *takes his apron off, and cwtches* **Bobby**.

Customer   Hello? (*Turns to another customer.*) I can't believe this, can you believe this? This is ridiculous! Where's the manager?

Customer *leaves; the remaining customers wait impatiently.*

Bobby *pulls away from the cwtch.*

Bobby Wanna hear my long list?

M I do, I really do, but later, OK?

Bobby Got some good names /

M Bet they're not as good as my new name. Later, though, OK.

Bobby Fine.

M (*offering the sausage*) You hungry? (*Putting apron back on.*) Now, why'd you come in, you needed to tell me something. Quick though /

M *turns to another customer.*

Bobby Your mam.

M *turns back to* **Bobby***; the other customer sighs.*

M My mam?

Bobby She didn't turn up for work today. Mam had to get someone in last minute. She was angry. Cause they're short-staffed, she said. But said it was out of character for your mam?

M *doesn't respond. All he can hear is his brother's words, 'You are too much.'*

Bobby Know where she is?

M's *apron is off once again; customers exclaim their impatience.* **M** *begins to leave.*

Bobby Where you going?

Customer *returns, and bumps into* **M**.

Customer (*furious, to* **M**) When I get hold of a manager I'm reporting you, what's your name?

M Move.

Customer You can't talk to a customer like that?!

M Move, *please*?!

Customer Let me see that!

Customer *looks at* **M**'s *work badge.* **Customer** *begins to laugh.*

Customer You're not fooling me. What's your *real* name?

M Battered Sausage.

M *smirks at* **Customer***, then leaves.*

Bobby (*shouting after* **M**) Remember about tonight!

Customer *looks to* **Bobby**. **Bobby** *bites into the sausage.*

Bobby (*mouth full*) Why you looking at me? I don't work here.

Bobby *leaves.*

Two customers step out from the queue, with some chips.

*

The two customers enter the space, apart from each other. They are **Young Mam** *and* **Young Dad** *from now on.*

As soon as they've entered, they clock each other.

They make their way towards each other.

They meet for the first time.

They share some chips.

They hold hands.

They leave.

M *returns, breathing heavily.* **Bobby** *enters in the opposite direction.*

Bobby (*direct address*)   At Christmas, after Mam's turkey dinner and then some M&S spotted dick, I told my parents that I'm going to change my pronouns: to he/they. I told them that I'm not trans, but if I was, that I'm lucky cause my name is kind of fluid. The name on my birth certificate is Robert. That's my dad's name, and my taid's too. It's a tradition. To pass on the name. But we've always called me Bobby. If I wanted to change it, maybe they'd be a little disappointed, cause I'd be breaking a tradition. But they'd definitely support me. They just want me to be happy. They're even happy for me to move to a city when I'm older, like Cardiff. That's where Mam studied. That would be like a tradition too yeah? Yeah, we're quite traditional. And we're super-close.

IV. looking for Mam

M *takes a deep breath, then enters the care home.*

A **Student** *nurse is at the front desk.*

Student   Ayaaaa.

M   Hi, here to check if /

Student   Visiting hours are between two and /

M   No no, not here to visit /

Student   Oh . . .

M   Here to see if /

Student   Are you a student too?

M   No, I'm in school / doesn't matter.

Student Oh, work experience is it?

M No-no /

Student To be honest, I'm not sure who you'd talk to /

M I'm not /

Student Don't know who's managing me, real poor management here /

M OK /

Student . . . and everyone's so busy, a virus going round I think, people are dropping like flies: dead /

M Shame /

Student *She*'s dead, *he*'s dead, *that* one's dead. Supposed to be learning how to be a nurse, but I'm just watching nameless old folk dying and dealing with check-ins. Oh, sorry, are you tonight's entertainment?

M No /

Student Are you the harpist? What's your name again, seen your name here somewhere /

M I'm not the harpist, I'm here to see if my mam's here.

Student Jesus, your mam's old.

M She works here.

Beat.

Student Ohhhhh!

M But, think she might've come in late or something, maybe, dunno /

Student I see, should've said.

M (*under his breath*) Tried to.

Student Let me have a look . . . What's her name?

M Um . . .

Student (*laughing*) Don't know your mam's name?

M What? Yes. (*Remembers.*) Elin!

Student Ellen?

M Elin.

Student (*a slight laugh*) OK.

M Elin Jones.

Student *looks at the sign-in sheet.*

Student Hm, one sec . . . (*Shouts.*) Jano! Jano?!

*A **Resident** from the care home enters with a box of jigsaw.*

Student   She's not Jano.

Resident *begins doing the jigsaw.* **M** *is fixated, staring.*

Student   Jano!

Janice (*offstage*)   Yeeeees?

Student   There she is. Has Ell . . . in (*winks to* **M**), has Ellen Jones come in today?

Janice (*offstage*)   Who's asking?

Student *looks at* **M**. **M** *stops staring.*

M   Oh, um, I'm her son.

Student (*shouts*)   . . . her son.

M (*snaps*)   I *am* her fucking son.

Student (*knee-jerk reaction, shouts again*)   He *is* her fucking son!

M's *blood starts to boil. They both wait for a response.*

Janice (*offstage*)   Oh, James, is it?

Student *looks at* **M** . . .

Student (*nervous*)   Is it?

M *biting tongue.*

M   Yes. (*Under breath, frustrated.*) Why not.

Student (*shouts*)   Yes, it's James.

Janice (*offstage*)   Oh, what a lovely bloke. But no, she's not here, she hasn't turned up today, not like her, but tell him to wait, gotta say 'ello to that handsome fella.

M *leaves and slams the door.*

Student   Jano? (*Beat.*) Jano?

Janice (*offstage*)   Yes?

Student   Save your feet. He's gone.

Student *begins to leave.*

*

As **Student** *is leaving they meet* **Young Mam** *in the space, with some news.* **Resident** *continues to do jigsaw.*

Student   You're pregnant.

Beat – **Young Mam** *doesn't know how to respond.*

Student   You're gonna be a mam.

Beat.

Student (*laughing*)   Forget Elin. From now on, *Mam*!

Young Mam *isn't laughing, her identity is about to change . . . As she leaves . . .*

Student (*direct address*)   Oh don't ask me about names. I'm rubbish with names. And *here*, we don't have the time to remember names. I'm joking. We do. But honestly, sometimes we don't. Always got stuff to do, some of the nurses are doing nearly sixty hours a week now, cause we're so short-staffed, you know. But, when I *do* have time, I'll make the effort to remind some of the residents who they are. (*To* **Resident**.) Some of us here need reminding of our name . . . Am I right, *Nerys*? Nerys?! (*Back to the audience.*) Too busy with her Garden of Eden jigsaw. Honestly though, when it's your time, your name won't even matter. Been here ages doing jigsaw, and needs no help. (*To* **Resident**.) Never stop doing jigsaws, no Nerys? Oh shit, that's Margaret.

Student *leaves with* **Resident**.

V. her second job

M *enters . . . There's a fancy doorbell. He rings the doorbell. The doorbell sound is long and ridiculous.* **M** *rolls his eyes. No answer.* **M** *rings again This time;*

Intercom   Name.

M   I'm looking for Elin Jones.

Intercom   Is that your name?

M   No, course not, it's my mams, she cleans here /

Intercom   Name. *Your* name /

M   Why do you need my name?

Intercom   Name.

M   My name is /

Ceridwen   I've seen you before.

Ceridwen *has entered, with a tennis racket.* **M** *turns to her.*

Ceridwen (*into intercom*)   Don't worry, Daddy, I know him.

Beat.

You go to the same school as me. But you're younger, aren't you? Year eleven?

M   Yeh.

Ceridwen   Knew it. I'm in sixth form. Warning, it's tough. Got to decide what course I wanna do at uni, and like, I just don't know, like events management, or like cosmetic science or something, in London obviously. Ahh, I hate making *big* decisions, know what I mean?

M   Mhm.

Ceridwen   But, to be honest I leave it all to my Mam, she can decide, she's good at that, and she's the one paying for it all, so. Anyway, sorry, rambling, but yeah you don't usually notice pupils that are younger than you. But I've noticed you. Seen you, around them corridors.

M   Cool.

Ceridwen   Yeah. You're interesting . . .

M   Am I?

Beat.

Ceridwen   How did you know?

M   Sorry?

Ceridwen   How did you know . . . You know . . . That you weren't . . .?

M   Oh. (*Beat.*) Just, always known.

Ceridwen   Wow . . . People like you are so . . . brave.

M *begins clenching fists.*

Ceridwen   Yes, you're so *so* brave and so . . . young.

M   You're literally a year older than me.

Ceridwen (*surprized he's in the area*)   What are you doing *here*? *You* don't live here.

M   No I know /

Ceridwen   Oh wait! You're Bobby's boyfriend, who works at the chippy?

M   Yeh . . .

Ceridwen   Cute! Love Bobby, don't love the chips at Allports* no offence, ha!

M   You know Bobby?

Ceridwen   Know him so, so well, we go way back, like family friends.

M   Really?

Ceridwen   His parents are legit, *the best.*

M   Not sure they are /

Ceridwen   Have you met them?

M   No . . .

Ceridwen Well, wait until you do, cause they are seriously . . . incredible. They've been, so, so . . . accepting of Bobby, with him being gay and all that you know. He's so lucky. Oh my God, they will *love* you. I think his dad, like, recently had a Twitter* row with J. K. Rowling*, like he really went for her, and then she, (*begins to laugh*) she blocked him. J. K. Rowling* blocked Bobby's dad on Twitter*?! How ridic and amazing is that?! He went viral. Bobby's dad, viral! Bobby and I lolled so much on Snapchat*.

M Really?

Ceridwen Gutted, though. Cause I do love the Potter*.

M *looks at her confused.*

Ceridwen Harry Potter*?

M Is my mam here?

Ceridwen Why would your mam be here?

M Cleans for you.

Ceridwen Elin's your mam?!

M *nods.*

Ceridwen Ohhhh cute! But no. She cleans on weekends, / can't wait for the weekend.

M I know that, but have you, or your parents, dunno, have they heard from her?

Ceridwen Caren* might have, she'll be back soon. Gone to hot yoga.

M Sorry, who's Caren*?

Ceridwen My mam. She hates it when I call her her real name. I bet your mam would hate that too?

M If she was called Caren*.

Ceridwen What?

M Her name's not Caren* /

Ceridwen No, I know . . .

M *has a little giggle to himself at the name Caren*.

Ceridwen You're weird . . . But come inside and wait if you want? Can make you a hot choccie?

M No, don't worry.

Ceridwen *approaches* **M**.

Ceridwen Is everything OK?

M Yeh /

Ceridwen You seem worried?

M No, well . . . no, I'm fine.

Ceridwen She talks about you a lot.

M Oh, yeh?

Ceridwen She mentioned you're changing your name? That's fun.

M She told you?

Ceridwen Yes.

M Actually, already changed it. Today.

Ceridwen Oh wow, OK. Congrats.

M Thanks . . .

Beat.

Ceridwen Don't know how you do it.

M Easy actually.

Ceridwen But it must be hard to, suddenly just *become* someone else /

M You don't become someone else. I'm still me. I'm *more* me.

Ceridwen But how did you decide on a new name? I understand why, but how? Did you chat with your brother or your mam? Cause you must care what they think. I know about your dad, so I know you wouldn't . . . Do you think the name reflects you? I just couldn't take the name my parents gave me away from them. Yeah, no, I couldn't put them through that.

M *begins to laugh.*

Ceridwen It must be hard for your parents.

M *begins to leave.*

Ceridwen Oh no, sorry, did I say something . . .?

M *stops, and turns to* **Ceridwen**.

M Must be hard for *them*?!

Ceridwen Well, yeah, must be, especially today /

M It's got nothing to do with them! I'm not a kid anymore no, and neither are you, I'm finally *being* me, the real me, I belong to me OK, my name belongs to *me*!

M *leaves.*

Ceridwen *buzzes the intercom.*

Intercom Name.

Ceridwen (*laughing*) It's Ceridwen, Daddy.

As **Ceridwen** *leaves, a crying baby sound emerges in the background.*

*

The crying baby continues; there's a football match on the TV in the background too with Dafydd Iwan's voice singing the anthem 'Yma o Hyd'.

Young Mam *rushes in; vomits into a bucket.* **Young Dad** *comes in with the baby, clearly frustrated with the crying.* **Young Mam** *wipes her mouth, exhausted.* **Young Dad** *hands her the baby, before returning to the football.*

Student *nurse enters.*

Snap: **Young Mam** *and* **Young Dad** *turn.*

Student   Well, you're gonna be Mam and Dad *again.*

Beat.

Wanna know the sex?

Before **Young Mam** *gets a word in:*

Dad   Yes.

Beat – a clear tension between **Young Mam** *and* **Young Dad**.

Young Mam *nods to* **Student**.

Student   This time . . . A baby girl!

Young Dad *celebrates.* **Young Mam** *watches him, no emotion.*

Student   I bet you have a lot of girlie names. You could give her *your* name.

Young Mam *looks at the nurse confused.*

Student   You could name her 'Mam'.

Student *laughs at her own joke.* **Young Mam** *doesn't laugh:*

Mam   My name is Elin!

Young Dad *pops too many pink party poppers.*

They all leave. **M** *and* **Ceridwen** *re-enter. Over* **Ceridwen***'s speech,* **M** *is waiting to meet* **Bobby**. **M** *is clearly uncomfortable; his body shows us this.*

Ceridwen (*direct address*)   I'm a proper daddy's girl, and sometimes he calls me his 'little goddess'. He's not Welsh, but he said that he chose my name. He liked what it meant. Ceridwen: 'Welsh goddess of rebirth, transformation and inspiration.' Nice, right? So there's a lot of thought that's gone into it. I couldn't change it. But if I had to, if I *had* to, I'd have to make sure it, like, *really* reflected me. It would *have* to be Welsh. Ooh, but maybe Frida? I just love Frida Kahlo, and she's a goddess? So I'd still be a goddess. (*Laughs.*) Maybe not. Love her though. Sad that she didn't like her body. Yes, really sad. (*Beat.*) I like my body.

Ceridwen *leaves.*

VI. Bobby's jigsaw

M *sits down, still clearly uncomfortable.* **Bobby** *enters pacing back and forth, with different shirts for* **M**.

Bobby   Sorry that tonight's not a surprize. I just thought I'd tell you cause, well, wasn't sure if you'd be up for it, with your mam . . .

Silence – **Bobby** *grabs a shirt.*

Bobby   What about this?

M *shrugs.* **Bobby** *grabs another.*

Bobby   This one?

M (*snaps*)   Doesn't fit me, yet.

Tense.

Bobby   Is everything OK?

M   No, Bobby, I feel like shit yeh.

Bobby   I know /

M   Don't know where she is /

Bobby   I know, I know /

M   And don't know why, no, why she's . . . today too like, don't know if she's changed her mind or . . . but I know she wouldn't lie to me 'de, but like, people *do* lie, people do surprize you yeh /

Bobby   I know, yeah, I know /

Beat.

M   Do your parents lie?

Bobby   What?

M   Do they lie? Would your mam lie to you?

Bobby   Um . . .

M   Or would *you* lie?

Bobby   Have I done something?

M   You know Ceridwen?

Beat.

Bobby   Ceridwen?

M   Yeh.

Bobby   Ceridwen who?

M   Not a lot of Ceridwens around here.

Bobby *thinks for a second.*

Bobby Oh, Ceridwen from (*rolls eyes*) 'Cheshire-by-Sea'?

M I was there today.

Bobby Why were you *there*?

M Mam cleans Ceridwen's house, yeh.

Bobby But your mam works for my mam at the care home, no?

M Yeh, two jobs 'de. She has to. For money.

Beat.

Ceridwen says she knows you 'sti, like you and her are family friends? Her family has a lot of money, 'de. Like, super-rich . . .

I know you don't live in Cheshire-by-Sea, but is your family rich too? Is that why you haven't invited me over to yours yet? Are you embarrassed by me?

Bobby Where's all of this . . . ?

M Answer me please.

Bobby You know why /

M Cause they're 'dicks'?

Bobby Yes.

M *Are* they?

Bobby What?

Beat.

M *Are* they?

Bobby *doesn't answer.*

M Why are you lying? Today was meant to be about me. And now, it's not. Like, I know I sound selfish 'de, but I've waited *years* for today. I wanted today to be about me . . . (*Close to tears.*) But *you*, you and my *mam*, the two of *you* . . . You're not letting me have my day. Cause you've both been lying to me. Do you even like my name? Cause I feel like you lied about that too, 'I like it if you like it' that's what you said, what does that even mean . . .

I want you to *love* it, yeh. It's my *name*. And I want my mam to love it too. But she's clearly having second thoughts . . .

I'll love *your* new name when you change it . . .

Beat.

M Why you not saying anything?

Bobby This is . . . it's just a *lot*.

Beat.

Yeah. It's a lot.

M   A lot.

Bobby   Maybe not a lot, just . . .

Beat.

It's no wonder you think your mam's disowned you because you changed your name, cause you're not . . . you're not *seeing* anything else right now /

M *laughs – can't believe what he's hearing.*

Bobby   I feel like you're fixated on your own . . . jigsaw, and no one else's . . . like, your mam, she's got her own shit happening, got her own jigsaw. And like *I* have a jigsaw too but it's felt like you haven't been *that* interested in *my* jigsaw, so yes, sorry, my parents aren't that bad . . .

And I probably won't change my name.

I've just been desperate for you to *see* me, you know? So, the only way to get through to you /

M   By *pretending* that . . .

Fuck.

That's fucked-up, 'sti!

Bobby   I just . . . things *are* different. But, I *do* really like you.

M *begins to leave.*

Bobby   Wait.

M *stops.*

M   What?

Beat.

Bobby   My mam asked me not to say anything, cause she'll look bad I guess.

M   What you talking about?

Bobby   Your mam booked today off work, ages ago.

Beat.

Know that doesn't help much, but.

M *continues to leave.*

Bobby   Where are you going?

M   I'm going to celebrate my new name. (*Beat.*) And you're not coming.

M *leaves.*

*

James *enters, and begins doing a jigsaw.*

In another area of the space **Young Mam** *and* **Young Dad** *enter. Over* **James***'s speech, they have an inaudible argument.*

James (*direct address*)   The only time I remember being called something else was when we were little 'de. Wasn't a nickname or nothing, it was pretty funny. And it was her. She hadn't grasped words yet. We were like four and two. And she went through a phase of shouting: 'Jam, Jam, Jam!' Remember me and Mam would be so confused yeh, cause she loved jam, like strawberry jam, she'd smother it all over her face sometimes. But anyway, we were always like, 'What do you want? James or jam?' and she'd just shout 'Jam, Jam!' with a massive grin and pointing towards me and the jam. She wanted both. And even though she'd smother jam all over herself, she *did* like me more, yeh. Cause I'd play with her. Jigsaw and stuff. And I'd call her . . .

James *pauses: almost notices the argument behind him.* **Young Dad** *leaves.* **Young Mam** *alone.*

James   Then we grew up, I guess. (*Choked-up.*) I liked her name. But yeah, with me, happy with just James.

He leaves abruptly. As **Young Mam** *leaves,* **M** *re-enters.*

VII. name party

M *has arrived at a surprise name reveal party. (But we don't reveal the name yet.)*

All   Surprize!

Blue party poppers; and the blaring music begins.

M *opens a can of Carling, and necks it. He begins to dance, celebrating . . .*

Over the following uptempo sequence, friends/family members come to question, congratulate and unintentionally offend **M** *– but he continues to dance. The celebration increasingly becomes more difficult for his body to sustain.*

Friend   Congratulations!

M   Thanks!

Friend   So brave!

M   Thanks . . .

Friend   Changed your socials, yet?!

A notable social media ping.

M   Yes! It's official!

M *opens another can, and necks it – remains to dance.*

Friend   It *actually* suits you!

M   I know, yeh!

Friend How do you choose a new name?!

M Easy!

Friend Are you a different person now?

M I'm still me, *more* me!

M *opens another can – necks it.* **M** *begins to struggle with the dancing – he's drunk, and reality begins to merge with memories and imagination. Becomes increasingly more surreal.*

Friend Gonna change my name too!

M You *should*. We *all* should!

Ceridwen I couldn't.

Friend You're an inspiration.

Ceridwen Ceridwen: 'Welsh goddess of rebirth, transformation and inspiration.'

Bobby Are you grieving though?

M Bobby?

Bobby's *disappeared.*

M I'm still here!

Another can open. **M**'s *dancing even more difficult.* **Resident** *enters, does their jigsaw throughout the rest of the scene.*

Ceridwen Sad that she didn't like her body. I like my body.

Customer You're not fooling me. What's your *real* name?

Barista Next!

James *You* are too much.

M No!

Ceridwen It must be hard.

M No!

Ceridwen For your parents!

M Fuck my parents!

Student *She*'s dead, *he*'s dead, *that* one's dead. I'm just watching nameless old folk dying.

Beat – The music stops for a second.

Student Are you the harpist?

The music and dancing resumes.

Intercom Name.

M My name is /

Customer Battered Sausage.

M FUCK YOU!

Barista Next!

Intercom Name!

Nick Nick. I'm a cis straight white man from *The Apprentice**. I was fired for being a selfish dick.

Barista Next.

Bobby Are you grieving though? /

M No! No! No!

Ceridwen It must be hard for your parents.

M/James FUCK OUR PARENTS! LEAVING!

James She meant you. *You* are too much. *You.*

M No, *you*!

Barista No offence, cyw, I just need a name so I can make you coffee.

James Maybe she's with him

Friend What was your birth name again?

M I wasn't born with a name! None of us were!

Everyone NONE OF US WERE!

M THIS PARTY'S SHIT!

As **M** *leaves the party,* **Young Mam** *enters. Pregnant with* **M**.

M Mam?

Intercom Name.

Mam Mam.

Intercom Your *real* name.

M Mam!

Young Mam *doesn't see* **M**.

James She's with him.

Student Name.

M Mam! I'm here!

Student You could name her 'Mam'.

Mam My name is Elin!

M/Mam I'm here! I'm still here!

Young Mam *begins to leave.*

M Mam!

James She's with him.

M I'm here! Mam! I'm still here! I'm still here. I'm still here. I'm still here. I'm still here. I'm still fucking here. Mam!

Silence – everyone has left, apart from **M** *and* **Young Mam**, *still here.*

Young Mam *sees* **M** *for the first time.*

In her hand, the cricket bat.

Young Mam *offers* **M** *the cricket bat.*

M *wants to resist the rage.*

But he grabs the cricket bat and leaves.

VIII. crash

M *enters his father's house cautiously – with a cricket bat in his hand. It's dark.* **M** *tries to switch on the lights. They're not working.*

M Dad?

No response.

Dad?

James He's not here.

M *jumps – cricket bat in the air.* **James** *is in the corner, facing away.*

M Why are you sat in the dark?

James Why are you here? He'll be back soon 'sti /

M Where is he?

James You know he doesn't want you here.

M Is Mam with him?

James You think she is?

M *shrugs.*

James Believe me now then?

M I've been looking for her. And like, she won't answer my calls or nothing, no. I've looked everywhere, everywhere but here, and I think maybe, me changing my name *was* too much for her /

James Oh, you and your fucking name, 'de.

He turns to face **M**. *His face is bruised.*

James How was your party?

M Did Dad . . . ? /

James No.

M James . . .

James I . . . (*a lie*) I crashed.

M Crashed? Crashed what?

James The car, obviously.

M Dad's car?

James Dad's car. Yeh. I took his car. Cause I was bored, always bored, nothing to do in this town and *we*, you and me, are stuck here 'sti, so I wanted to drive, and I took his spare keys, got in, put the keys in yeh . . . and started driving . . . I drove so fast 'de, so so fast, I drove faster than the speed limit, and no one could stop me, not even. . . /

M Dad?

James In control, a hundred miles per hour, but you know what? Being in control, feeling powerful, it never lasts . . . Cause *we* CRASH!

M *jumps, frightened.*

James We're weak. Look at us. Here, in the dark.

M You're scaring me.

James Barely no money for these lights.

M You said dad has lots of money, now? Paying for your driving lessons and that?

James You should go, he'll be back any minute.

M James . . .

James He's just down the road, gone to pay for 'lectric.

M Did Dad do this to you?

James I CRASHED HIS CAR!

Beat.

M I don't believe you, no. You lie. That's your thing. To get yourself out of Dad's fists. He hates you too. And you hate that. So you lie, and lie, lie some more to make yourself fit. Fit into what he wants you to be /

James Because it's easier!

M Did he do this to you?

James Know what your new name is, by the way. You *do* know your name is in Dad's favourite song?

M What?

James Ruined that song for him now. And for me. Ruined the Welsh football team for us.

He grabs his phone, and plays 'Yma o Hyd' (this plays over the rest of the scene). They wait to hear the first line of the song. Then the dialogue continues.

James This *is* all your fault, 'sti. Course it was too much for her, it's too much for all of us. One tiny decision, (*mocking*) that's not *informed* by everyone around you, one decision that's all about *you* /

M You sound like him again /

James You changing your name might've fixed things for you, but it's *finished* things, fucking final nail in the coffin for everyone else, for us /

M Stop it /

James Today, it's official. Today, you officially killed their daughter /

M Stop stop stop /

James She's dead now /

M No no no /

James Yes, yes, yes, just SHUT UP and let me be sad, and, and . . .! I just wanna go back, go back and, and do jigsaw with my little sister! But, you killed her! You killed my sister!

He snatches the cricket bat from **M**.

  James (*almost roaring*) You killed her!

  He unleashes a rage from inside him, and begins to smash things.

    You killed her!

    He continues to smash things.

      You killed her!

      . . . continues to smash things.

        You killed . . .!

        . . . continues to smash things.

          You killed [old name]!

> *He stops, approaches* **M** *with the bat.*
> *We don't hear the old name.*
> *The old name is covered by white noize.*
> **M** *clenching their fists. Eyes closed.*
> *Ears closed.*

A moment of suspension – is **James** *going to hit* **M**?

James *drops the cricket bat.*

M   Don't call me that name again.

James   Well, I can't, no. Your name is dead.

James *drops to the floor, begins sobbing.*

M *begins to leave.*

James   There's a letter.

M *stops.*

James   From Mam.

He grabs the letter from his pocket.

I'm sorry.

M *grabs the letter and leaves.*

IX. still here

M *is alone, holding a letter from his mam.*
A parallel of the opening image, but no sense of pride now.
'Yma o Hyd' chorus playing.

M *finds it difficult hearing this song to begin with – with it being associated with his* **Dad**.

Ry'n ni yma o hyd, x2	*We are still here x2*
Er gwaetha pawb a phopeth, x3	*In spite of everyone and everything x3*
Ry'n ni yma o hyd, x2	*We are still here x2*
Er gwaetha pawb a phopeth, x3	*In spite of everyone and everything x3*
Ry'n ni yma o hyd.	*We are still here.*

But the more he hears the words in the chorus, the more he feels a sense of empowerment.

M *is still here. Despite everyone and everything. He will face the world alone, if it means holding on to his new name. He is going to claim this protest song as his own, and start his new era as* **Max**.

X. our jigsaw

Max *is sat with the letter and a bag of chips. He hasn't read the letter yet.*

Bobby *enters with a bag and some ketchup sachets.*

Max *looks up.* **Bobby** *waves the ketchup sachets.*

Max (*laughing*)   Where d'you get those?

Bobby   Allports*.

They both laugh.

Max   Thanks . . . For coming here.

Bobby   Wasn't gonna let you be alone, no.

Beat.

And it looks really sad you eating chips on your own.

Max *smiles.* **Bobby** *sits next to* **Max**. *They begin to share the chips.*

Bobby   You look . . . tired.

Max   I am.

Beat – **Bobby** *notices a letter in* **Max**'*s hand.*

Bobby   What's that? (*Teasing.*) Changed your name again?

Max *laughs.*

Silence.

Bobby   I *might* change mine. One day. Just not ready yet.

Max   Course. (*Beat.*) Not sure many people are ready, 'sti.

Bobby   What d'you mean?

Max   My family, my mam . . . Weren't ready for me to change, no. To be honest, don't think any of them are over the fact that I'm trans /

Bobby   Jigsaw, you mean.

They laugh.

Max   But, seriously, think they still think it's a phase /

Bobby (*rolls eyes*)   A fucking phase.

Max   I know. (*Beat.*) When I wrote down my name, and finally held that tiny piece of paper . . . Honestly yeh, I breathed properly for the first time in, fuck it I'm gonna say it, I breathed *properly* for the first time in sixteen years.

Bobby   So, what's wrong?

Max   I *get* that it must be hard for them. I get it 'de. But I don't think they *really* get that I'm still here. Sometimes, think it would've been easier for them if she died, was dead 'sti /

Bobby   Don't say that /

Max   No, seriously, like *dead*-dead, rather than having to accept me, for me today. Accept that I've just . . . changed.

Bobby   For the better, 'de?

Max   Yeh, and this is just the beginning . . .

Silence.

Bobby   *I'm* proud of you, 'sti.

Max   I know.

Bobby   Just need good people around you now. (*Referring to himself.*) People who don't lie . . .

Beat.

I'm really sorry for lying, OK?

Max *smiles.*

Bobby   And I seriously like you. Like, *like*-like you.

Max   I like you too. *Like*-like you. And I'm sorry too.

Beat.

I *did* lose sight of you, of your /

Bobby   If you say jigsaw /

They both laugh.

Bobby *looks at the letter in* **Max**'s *hand again.*

Max   It's a letter.

Bobby *leans in closer to* **Max**.

Max   Can't bring myself to read it.

Bobby   Who's it from?

Max   Mam. Will you read it for me?

Bobby   Course.

Max *hands the letter to* **Bobby**. *He opens the letter. He reads.*

Bobby   Don't know if I'd call this a letter, no.

Max   What?

Bobby   More like a note. (*Reads.*) 'You know I'm proud of you. You're an inspiration, cariad. Wish I had someone like you, when I was your age. Back later tonight.'

In another area of the space, **Young Mam** *enters with a newborn in her arms.*

Bobby   'Caru ti . . .'

Mam (*to the baby*)   Caru ti, *Max*.

This is the first time we hear **Max**'s *name.*

Bobby & Mam (*signature*)   'Mam.'

Max *and* **Young Mam** *catch eye contact for a moment, then she leaves.* **Max** *begins to laugh. All seeds of doubt about his* **Mam** *leaves his mind.* **Max**'s *laughter grows, and grows, and then turns into a cry.*

Bobby   Come here.

He cradles **Max**.

Max's *crying slowly stops. Then:*

Max   You think we're all, just one big jigsaw?

Bobby   Oh no, here we go!

Max (*almost direct address, almost breaking the fourth wall*)   Maybe we are. And we're all made up of lots of pieces that make up one big giant jigsaw 'sti. And when things change, the jigsaw moves . . . some pieces, and some *people* move closer to you, some don't move, and then some, well, some might leave you . . .

And you know what's annoying? The rage that's been inside me, *that* rage piece that I have . . . it hasn't fully left me. Think it's gonna take me some more time. And like, my mam, she might have a little piece of, of grieving inside her, that's also gonna need some time.

A jigsaw's never complete, no.

We never stop doing jigsaw.

Bobby *begins to clap and applaud* **Max**'s *analogy.* **Max** *laughs.*

Max   Think I wanna tweak it.

Bobby   Tweak it? Tweak, what?

Max   I love my new name 'de, and it *is* mine . . . But . . . I *do* want a bit of Elin in it.

Bobby   A bit of who?!

Max   Elin. My mam. She said it could be more Welsh. So, maybe . . . one day . . . Macsen?

Bobby   Love it.

Max   Me too. And maybe, one day, Macsen *Dafis*.

Bobby   But Dafis is my surname . . . (*Realizes.*) Oh! Maybe!

Max   Maybe.

Bobby   Your mam would love that.

Max   She would, Elin likes you, likes us 'sti.

Beat.

Max   Gonna call her Elin from now on.

Silence – **Bobby** *looks at his watch/phone.*

Bobby   So . . . It's almost midnight, nearly my birthday . . .

Max   Oh shit! Sorry!

Bobby   No, no, it's OK! You've just been a selfish dick like Nick!

Max *hands on face, embarrassed.*

Bobby   I'm joking!

Max   Happy birthday.

Beat – **Max** *moves closer to* **Bobby**.

Max   Didn't get you anything though.

Bobby   It's OK.

Max   Shit boyfriend!

Bobby   So we *are* boyfriends again?

Max   Yeh . . . If you . . .?

Bobby *leans in to kiss* **M**.

They kiss.

They pull away.

Bobby *grabs his bag; in it there's a jigsaw.*

Bobby   Don't worry about getting me a present though. Bought something, well, bought both of us. . . /

Max   A jigsaw!

Max *looks closely at the jigsaw.*

Max   A jigsaw of . . . *here*?

Bobby   Yeah, our town, every corner of it.

Max   A *thousand* pieces?!

Bobby   I know it's a biggie, and I've not counted the pieces so don't know if /

Max (*laughs*)   Doesn't matter.

Beat.

So, for your sixteenth birthday, you wanna do jigsaw?

Bobby   I love jigsaw.

Beat.

Max   Me too.

The End.

Support

Trans Aid Cymru: transaid.cymru

Trans Aid Cymru is a mutual aid organization operating mainly in South Wales. They are a diverse group of trans, intersex and non-binary people who are trying to prevent poverty and isolation in the trans community through providing grants, support, signposting, advocacy and social space provision. They support anyone trans, intersex, non-binary, or anyone questioning their gender identity who is based in Wales.

Donate: opencollective.com/transaidcymru

Some more support:

North Wales TINN: instagram.com/northwalestinn
Meddwl: meddwl.org
Mind: mind.org.uk
Meic Cymru: meiccymru.org
Shout: giveusashout.org
The Mix: themix.org.uk
YoungMinds: youngminds.org.uk
Diverse Cymru: diversecymru.org.uk
Mermaids: mermaidsuk.org.uk
Paned o Ge: paned-o-ge.wales
Stonewall Cymru: stonewallcymru.org.uk
Aubergine Cafe Cymru: auberginecafe.co.uk

Dy Enw Marw
gan Elgan Rhys
mewn cyd-weithrediad â Leo Drayton

Nodyn gan yr Awdur (Elgan Rhys)

Mae *Dy Enw Marw* yn ddrama i gynulleidfaoedd pedair ar ddeg oed a hŷn. Mae ganddi 5 rôl graidd, 8 rôl siarad ychwanegol a nifer o olygfeydd grŵp. Dylai rôl Max gael ei chwarae gan berfformiwr sy'n hunaniaethu yn draws-wrywaidd. Gweler y rhestr gymeriadau am nodweddion penodol y cymeriadau craidd eraill.

Fel awdur hoyw, cis gwrywaidd, mae wedi teimlo'n bwysig imi ddefnyddio fy mraint i ganoli lleisiau sy'n cael eu tanglywed neu eu camgynrychioli mewn diwylliant prif ffrwd. Rwyf wedi creu'r ddrama hon ar y cyd â'r awdur traws Cymreig arbennig, Leo Drayton; gweler y 'Nodyn gan y Cydweithredwr' i gael cipolwg ar natur ein cydweithrediad. Yn rhan o broses creu'r ddrama hefyd cafwyd mewnbwn gan grŵp o bobl ifanc traws a cwiar o Gaerdydd, wedi'i hwyluso gan y Queer Emporium a Paned o Gê.

Mae'r ddrama hon wedi'i lleoli mewn tref yng ngogledd-orllewin Cymru, ac mae acenion y cymeriadau yn gysylltiedig â'r ardal hon. Mae croeso i berfformwyr roi cynnig ar yr acenion, gan osgoi ystrydebau. Os nad ydyn nhw'n gwbl gyfforddus, dylai'r perfformwyr addasu'r cymeriadau i'w hacenion eu hunain. Gweler tudalen 207 am ragor o wybodaeth am dafodiaith.

Mae'r ddrama yn cynnwys llawer o gyfeiriadau Cymreig diwylliannol-benodol, y dylid eu cadw hyd yn oed os yw'r acenion yn cael eu haddasu. Dylai pob cynhyrchiad benderfynu sut i gynnwys cytgan 'Yma o Hyd', e.e. i'w chwarae fel trac sain neu i'w ddysgu fel corws, cyn belled â bod sensitifrwydd diwylliannol yn cael ei sicrhau.

Gellir addasu rhai cyfeiriadau diwylliannol eraill yn y ddrama fel y mae pob cynhyrchiad yn ei weld yn addas; nodir y cyfeiriadau hyn gyda * yn y sgript.

Mae jig-so yn drosiad cryf yn y ddrama hon, gydag ambell gymeriad yn gwneud jig-so weithiau. Rwyf yn annog pob cynhyrchiad i fwynhau dehongli'r trosiad hwn yn eu llwyfaniad, boed hynny mewn ffordd lythrennol neu beidio.

Mewn cyfnod pan mae pobl draws a *gender-non-coforming* yn wynebu gelyniaeth gynyddol eithafol gan bobl â grym sydd yn anwybodus a rhagfarnllyd, a hawliau LGBTQIA+ y brwydrwyd yn galed i'w hennill dan fygythiad, mae ffurfio undod radical yn anghenrheidiol. Gweler tudalen 243 am restr o sefydliadau sy'n gwneud gwaith gwerthfawr ynghylch themâu'r ddrama.

Mae'r ddrama hon yn weithred o solidariaeth gyda phob person traws.

Nodyn gan y Cydweithredwr (Leo Drayton)

Dechreuodd fy nghyfraniad i at y prosiect hwn pan ofynnodd Elgan, ffrind a rhywun dwi'n ei edmygu'n fawr, am fewnbwn ar ei syniadau cychwynnol ar gyfer drama NT Connections. Cawsom sesiwn trafod syniadau i drafod sut beth yw bod yn un ar bymtheg ac yn draws yng Nghymru heddiw, a ysgogodd syniadau diddorol am ryddid, dewis a'r weithred o newid eich enw. Fel dyn traws roedd fy mhrofiad i o hyn yn un ar bymtheg oed yn garreg filltir bwysig ar fy nhaith, a theimlwn y byddai hon yn stori ddiddorol i'w hadrodd. Ar ôl y sesiwn gychwynnol honno, gofynnodd Elgan i mi gydweithio ag ef ar ddatblygiad y ddrama a dywedais 'ie' yn syth. Fy rôl yn y broses oedd darllen drafft diweddaraf y ddrama a rhoi adborth ar ba mor awthentig oedd y cymeriad a'r stori, yn ogystal â llif cyffredinol y ddrama. Roedd hon yn broses debyg iawn i gyfres *Y Pump*, prosiect blaenorol yr oeddem wedi gweithio arno gyda'n gilydd, sef cyfres o bum llyfr am bum cymeriad amrywiol, pob un wedi'i ysgrifennu gyda chyd-awdur ifanc i sicrhau dilysrwydd. Roeddwn i'n ddigon ffodus i fod yn gyd-awdur ar un o'r nofelau hynny, profiad a'm cyflwynodd i'r byd ysgrifennu ac i rai pobl anhygoel.

Elfen o'r broses dwi'n hynod falch o fod wedi bod yn rhan ohoni oedd sesiwn grŵp ffocws a gawsom gyda phobl draws eraill a ddarllenodd y ddrama a rhannu eu barn. Roedd yn fendith gallu cael sgwrs agored am y profiadau hyn a chlywed eu meddyliau. Teimlwn i mi gael fy ngweld mewn ffordd na chefais erioed o'r blaen; gyda grŵp o bobl sy'n rhannu profiadau cyffredin, wrth siarad am ddrama sy'n trafod y profiadau hynny. Mewn cyfnod lle mae'r gymuned draws yn wynebu llawer o negyddiaeth, roedd yn galonogol cael sgwrs rymusol a chadarnhaol am y gymuned. Ac oherwydd hynny dwi'n hynod ddiolchgar i Elgan, y National Theatre ac i'r bobl ysbrydoledig a ymunodd yn y sesiwn.

Wrth dyfu i fyny, roeddwn i'n rhan o grŵp theatr ieuenctid a buom yn cymryd rhan yng ngŵyl NT Connections, ac felly roedd yn anrhydedd i mi fy mod, drwy'r broses hon, wedi gallu rhoi mewnbwn ar rywbeth a fyddai wedi golygu llawer i mi pan oeddwn i'r oed hwnnw. Mae theatr yn hynod werthfawr, nid yn unig fel cyfrwng creadigol ac i fagu hyder ond hefyd fel arf i archwilio eich hunaniaeth eich hun. Mae'r ddrama hon yn cynnig safbwynt newydd i'r perfformwyr sy'n gallu uniaethu â Max, ac yn rhoi cyfle i bobl ifanc ddysgu am y profiad traws a rhannu cefnogaeth ar lwyfan. Dwi erioed wedi gweithio ar ddrama broffesiynol o'r blaen, a dwi mor ddiolchgar am bopeth dwi wedi'i ddysgu. Nid yn unig am gael cipolwg ar y broses ysgrifennu ond hefyd am gael bod yn rhan o ddrama radical am rywbeth mor bwysig.

Gan fy mod wedi gweithio gydag Elgan o'r blaen, roeddwn i'n ymddiried yn llwyr ynddo ac roedd gen i ffydd y byddai'n gwneud hyn mewn ffordd barchus, gan daro goleuni ar faterion traws gyda chymorth pobl draws, ac y byddai'n gwneud y gwaith oedd yn anghenrheidiol i ddeall naws ein profiadau. Mae'n anrhydedd a dwi'n falch iawn o fod wedi gweithio ar y prosiect hwn, ac yn mawr obeithio y bydd y ddrama yma yn blatfform i bobl ifanc traws a cwiar yn ogystal â pherfformwyr ifanc Cymreig archwilio a mynegi eu hunain yn rhydd.

Mae *Dy Enw Marw* yn stori sydd angen ei rhannu.

Diolchiadau

Diolch o galon i Ola Animashawun am y gwahoddiad a'r ddramatwrgiaeth, i Leo Drayton am ei fewnwelediad a'i drylwyredd, i Sera Moore Williams am ei hanogaeth, i Al Parr a Gareth Evans-Jones am eu caredigrwydd, i Dylan Huw am ei amynedd, i Timothy Howe ac aelodau Theatr Ieuenctid y Sherman am ysbrydoli syniadau cychwynnol y darn, i Gwmni Ifanc Frân Wen am y darlleniad cyntaf o'r ddrama, i holl staff NT Connections, ac i Joey Madaffari, Rudy Harries, Kay R. Dennis, Vidhy Chaudhary, Branwen Neverwere a phawb yn y Queer Emporium a Paned o Gê am eu haelioni a'u hadborth amhrisiadwy.

Elgan Rhys

Cymeriadau

M/Max – *un-ar-bymtheg, traws-wrywaidd, fo*
Bobi – *pymtheg, gwrywaidd, fo/nhw*
James – *deunaw, cis gwrywaidd, fo*
Myfyriwr – *unrhyw oed, unrhyw ryw*
Ceridwen – *dwy-ar-bymtheg, cis female, hi*
Barista – *unrhyw oed, unrhyw ryw*
Cwsmer/Iaid – *unrhyw oed, unrhyw ryw*
Jano – *unrhyw oed, unrhyw ryw*
Preswylydd – *wythdegau hwyr, unrhyw ryw*
Ffrind/Iau – *unrhyw oed, unrhyw ryw*
Nick – *unrhyw oed, cis gwrywaidd, fo*
Mam Ifanc – *ugeiniau cynnar, cis benywaidd, hi*
Dad Ifanc – *ugeiniau cynnar, cis gwrywaidd, fo*
Intercom (Troslais) – *canol-oed, cis gwrywaidd, fo*

Allwedd

/ – torri ar draws cymeriad

... – cymeriad yn methu mynegi mwy neu'n meddwl/chwilio am eiriau

' ' – dyfynnu rhywun neu rywbeth

Tafodiaith

(*gair – ystyr*)

'De* – *Ynde*

'Sti* – *Wyddost ti*

* *os yw'r perfformwyr wedi penderfynu addasu'r cymeriadau i'w hacenion eu hunain, dylid torri'r geiriau hyn.*

Chdi** – *Ti*

Gelan** – *Chwerthin*

Dwmbo** – *Dwn i'm/Wn i ddim/Sai'n gwbod*

Yndi** – *Ydi*

Rŵan** – *Nawr*

Efo** – *Gyda*

** *os yw'r perfformwyr wedi penderfynu addasu'r cymeriadau i'w hacenion eu hunain, gall newid i'r geiriau mewn italics neu eiriau cyfatebol yn eu tafodiaith eu hunain.*

I. fy jig-so

Daw **M** *i mewn, mae'n dal llythyr yn ei law gyda balchder. Dyma tystysgrif gyda'i enw newydd. Rydym yn aros yma am ennyd. Yna, snap mewn i olygfa:*

Mae **M** *a* **Bobi** *mewn ciw am goffi. Mae* **M** *yn dal gafael yn ei lythyr.*

M Edrach yn wahanol?

Bobi Ia, wyt, ti'n edrych yn wahanol.

M Sut dwi *edrach* yn wahanol?

Bobi Ti jyst, ti jyst yn?

M Dwi *teimlo* wahanol, 'de.

Bobi O. . .?

M Yndw-yndw, fel, ma'n teimlo *mor* dda! Teimlo fel . . . (*Ebychu.*) Finally, dwi yma!

Bobi *yn neidio ar gyffro* **M**.

Bobi Be ti meddwl?

M Fi go iawn.

Bobi O, ia?

M Ia, finally ma'r fi go iawn, *yma*.

Curiad.

Bobi (*chwerthin*) Wel, helo chdi!

M HELOOOOO *FIII!*

Mae'r ciw o bobl yn troi eu pennau. **M** *a* **Bobi** *'n chwerthin yn dawel.*

Bobi Ti'm yn fel grievio, ddo?

M Be?! No wê, na! Di neud digon o hynna do!

Bobi Gwbo, gwbo, jyst ma'n fawr yndi, dwrnod mawr i /

M I *fi*!

Bobi Th'gwrs. I chdi.

M (*chwerthin lletchwith*) *Ti'm* yn 'grievio' nagwt?

Bobi Na, th'gwrs ddim, na na na!

M Hyn 'de, ma fel . . . hollol opposite i grievio, 'sti.

Curiad

M Fel, ti di neud jig-so blaen?

Bobi Be sgen jig-so neud fo /

M Jyst atab fi! Ti di neud jig-so?!

Bobi Do, yndw, dwi neud jig-sos /

M (*chwerthin*) Ti *dal* neud jig-so?

Bobi Na. Ella.

M *yn chwerthin.* **Bobi** *'n gwenu.*

Barista Nesa!

M *a* **Bobi** *'n symud yn agosach i'r* **Barista**.

M O'n i casau jig-so pan o'n i fach, o'n i dda 'de, ond casau o, cos peth ydi 'de, o'dd Mam fi bob tro prynu jig-sos, wel o'dd hi prynu rhan fwya toys a dillad ni o charity shops 'de, fel *Scope /

Bobi Neshi brynu crys *Burberry o *Scope unwaith /

M Ia, a nes di *ddewis* neud hynna. Ti rioed di prynu jig-so o charity shop?

Bobi *yn ysgwyd pen.*

M Peth ydi 'de, pan ti prynu jig-so o charity shop 'de even ddo ma'n deud 'sixty-piece jigsaw set'/

Bobi Chwe-deg? Hawdd!

M (*chwerthin*) . . . even ddo ma'n deud 'sixty', dio byth *yn* sixty /

Bobi Reit . . .

M A brawd fi 'de . . . o'dd ni arfar neud jig-so fo'n gilydd pan o'dd ni fach. Ac o'dd o'm yn bothered 'sti, o'dd o'n fine pan o ni'n dod i diwadd y jig-so, ond o'n i, o'n i'n *flin* bob tro 'de, cos sa ni byth yn cyrradd y diwadd, na? Cos o'dd na bob tro darn neu ddau *ar goll*.

A'r gwaetha, nath hyn m'ond digwydd unwaith, ond y gwaetha o'dd pan *oedd*na sixty-pieces, ac o'n i *mor* excited 'de, ond pan nath ni gyrradd y darn ola . . . O'dd y darn ola na o set jig-so *arall*! A nath brawd fi trio fforsho'r darn wrong na ar y jig-so, ond o'n i cadw gweiddi 'dio'm yn ffitio!'

A nath o jyst ddeud, 'neud o ffitio 'de'

O'n i casau hynna. Rili casau hynna. So neshi gweiddi ar fo, 'sti. Fel bron *sgrechian*. Ac o'dd brawd fi jyst yn sefyll yna efo gwynab, fel, ych, jyst ddim yn bothered 'sti, a wedyn . . . *wedyn*. . . na'th o ddechra chwerthin!

So eshi am fo, neshi chwalu'r jig-so a nath o jyst dechra gweiddi 'jyst jig-so dio, jyst blydi jig-so' so neshi taflu'r bocs at gwynab o, grabio cricket bat Mam a deud bo fi am smasho pen fo mewn . . . (*Curiad.*) Ond neshi ddim obviously! /

M *yn chwerthin.*

Bobi Faint oed o chdi?

M   Wyth. Ond, y teimlad *blin* na 'de . . . (*cyfeirio at ei gorff*) sy di bod yn fa'ma . . .

Curiad.

M (*cyfeirio at tystysgrif*)   Pan geshi hwn heddiw 'de, neshi teimlo weird teimlad, fel weird da. Ma'r teimlad *blin* ma sy di bod tu fewn fi, dwi meddwl bod o di gadal corff fi, 'sti. Gwbo ma'n swnio weird, ac ella dyna pam dwi edrach wahanol. Ond ma wedi, ma di gadal fi! Diolch i'r free darn o papur ma!

Bobi   O'dd o am ddim?!

M   O'dd darn coll fi am ddim! A fel, (*cyfeirio at ei gorff*) dwi methu fficsho bob dim rwan na, obviously ma genai darna erill i newid fyd (*cyfeirio at tystysfrif*) ond ma fficsho *hwn* heddiw . . . Ma'n ddechra yndi. A dwi teimlo'n bwerus. Dwi'n jig-so pwerus.

Bobi *'n edrych ar* **M** *yn ddryslyd.*

Bobi   So, ti'n jig-so rwan?

M *yn chwerthin.*

M   Da ni gyd yn jig-sos, yndan? Fel ma one percent o ni di geni efo fel y set perffaith, a ddim angan newid neu ffindio darna newydd, a wedyn ma pawb arall o ni . . . di geni efo set sy efo darna ar goll, neu darna wrong 'de.

Curiad.

Bobi   Ti yn lylio analogy wyt?! A ma hwnna'n proper cringy analogy.

Y ddau'n chwerthin. Y ciw o bobl o'u blaenau'n troi eu pennau eto. **M** *a* **Bobi** *'n tawelu.*

Bobi   Ond seriously, dwi'n hapus i chdi. A hapus achos . . . ma di mynd rwan do!

M   Sa neb di marw, Bobi /

Bobi   Gwbo, be dwi meddwl di, ti di *neud* o /

M   Ia, ond dwi dal yma /

Bobi   Ia, a ti di reclaimio / rwbath *mawr*.

M   Licio'r gair yna / reclaimio

Bobi   A rwan, ti gallu symud mlaen /

Barista   Nesa!

M *a* **Bobi** *yn symud yn agosach.*

Bobi   Da *ni* gallu symud mlaen, fel Bobi a. . .? /

M   Dylsa chdi neud.

Bobi   E?

M   Fel, dylsa pawb neud. Os ti gallu, dylsa chdi. So, ella . . . Dylsa chdi neud o fyd? Pryd ti'n troi'n sixteen eto?

Bobi Fory . . .

M O crap ia, obviously, oni gwbo hynna. (*Curiad*) Fedrai helpu chdi. Sa ni gallu neud list, fel nath ni i fi /

Bobi Long-list wedyn short-list, wedyn *short*-short list achos o'dd y short-list o'dd gen ti yn hir oedd? /

M Gwbo, jyst cal go, gna list /

Bobi Dwnim, dwi'm yn siwr os /

M Dychmyga, y ddau o ni di reclaimio be nath rhieni ni rhoi i ni. Ynde?

Curiad – **Bobi** *yn ansicr, ond yn rhoi mewn i obsesiwn/syniad* **M**.

Bobi Ia, ocê, stwffia rhieni ni /

Y ddau'n chwerthin.

Barista Nesa!

M *a* **Bobi** *yn symud yn agosach.*

M Ti licio rhieni chdi ddo, na? A ma nhw licio chdi? /

Bobi (*celwydd*) Dim rili.

M *yn synnu.*

Bobi Go iawn, ma nhw gallu bod yn, ym . . .

Bobi *yn stryglo i feddwl (achos ei fod yn dweud celwydd).*

Bobi Fel . . . pricks.

M Be?! Y ddau o nhw, pricks?!

Bobi Weithia.

M Rili?

Bobi Yndi-yndi . . .

M M'ond dad fi sy prick, 'sti. Sa well gen fi *Trump fel Dad fi.

Bobi *yn chwerthin.*

Bobi Ia, a sa well gen fi *Putin fel un fi.

M Hwnna'm yn funny.

Curiad – y ddau'n chwerthin.

M Swni'm yn dal hwn heblaw Mam fi ddo, 'sti.

Bobi *'n ysgwyd ei ben yn gytun.*

M Ar penblwydd fi 'de, nath hi ddeffro fi fuan, jyst pokeio fi a ddim deud dim byd na, a wedyn neud y nod weird ma efo pen hi . . . A neshi edrych i lle o'dd hi'n nodio

. . . Drws nesa i gwely fi, darn o tôst mewn siâp weird sixteen, ond hefyd 'de, drws nesa i'r tôst o'dd darn o papur di plygu, ac o'n i gwbo be o'dd o . . . Ac o'dd hi gwbo bo fi gwbo 'de . . . O'dd hi'n barod di prynu y fform i neud hwn digwydd, 'sti. Ac o'dd hi di signio fo, a ffyni 'de, o'dd hi di roi sws drws nesa i signature hi! O'n i gelan, a crio bach.

Bobi Softie.

M Nadw.

Bobi *yn rhoi winc i* **M**, **M** *yn rhoi nudge i* **Bobi**.

Bobi So deutha fi . . . be dio?

M Be dwi edrach fel?

Bobi Be ti meddwl?

M Gesha.

Bobi Gesho? Jyst deutha fi, ni sy nesa!

M Gesha!

Bobi Ocê! Nick?

M Nick?! Nick?! Nick!!! Dwi'm yn edrach fel Nick. Dwi'm yn, yn loser sy lyfio pres, fel dwisho pres, ond dwi'm yn lyfio fo na, a ma Nick, Nick ydi'r straightest cis white man sy di bod ar fel, *The Apprentice* ne wbath, a wedi cal 'you're fired' ar episode cynta, am fod yn, yn selfish prick!

Barista Nesa!

M *a* **Bobi** *yw'r nesa i archebu.*

Barista Be da chisho, bois?

Bobi Vanilla latte, plis.

Barista Enw.

Bobi Bobi.

Barista (*sgwennu enw ar gwpan*) Bobi. Wbath arall?

Bobi Pumpkin spiced latte, plis.

Barista Enw.

Bobi *'n edrych draw at* **M**.

Bobi Ti'n dal ni nôl . . .

M *yn rhoi'r llythyr i* **Bobi**. **Bobi** *yn ei agor.* **Bobi** *yn edrych ar* **M**.

M Ti licio?

Bobi Os ti licio, dwi licio.

M Mam fi meddwl sa gallu bod mwy Cymraeg 'de, ond ti gwbo be? Dwi'm yn careio. Dim hi bia fo, a *definitely* ddim Dad fi bia fo! *Fi* bia fo!

Bobi Ia, definitely *chdi*! (*i'r* **Barista**) Sori, ma'n cal moment bach.

M (*i'r* **Barista**)   Ma heddiw i gyd am *fi*!

Barista No offence del, jyst angan enw so fedrai neud chdi coffi.

Bobi *'n chwerthin,* **M** *yn rhoi smac charweus iddo.* **Bobi** *yn gadael.*

Mae **M** *ar ei ben ei hun. Mae'n troi, cymryd anadl fawr – yn gyffrous i rannu'r newyddion gyda'i* **Fam***.*

II. dreifio

Mae **M** *yn cyrraedd adra.*

Mae **James** *yn lolfa, yn chwarae gêm rasio ceir ar ei Xbox*.*

Mae **M** *yn cerdded i mewn i'r lolfa, heb weld ei frawd eto.*

M Mam! Mam, yli be dwi efo! Ma'n official!

M *yn aros i glywed gan ei fam. Dim byd.*

M Mam?

James Be sy official?

M *yn neidio, wrth sylwi bod* **James** *yma.*

M Be ti neud ma, James?

James Be sy official?

M Di Mam gwbo bo chdi yma?

James Obviously ma hi.

M Lle ma hi?

James Nai ddeutha chdi, os ti deutha fi be sy official.

M Ti *gwbo* be sy official.

James Ydwi?

M Ti yn /

James Ti'n iawn, dwi yn /

M M'yn wastio amsar fi siarad i *chdi* am y peth 'de.

James Ofn nai fynd nôl a deutha Dad, ia?

Curiad.

Ma haeddu gwbo, 'sti.

M Dio ddim.

James Dad chdi dio, 'de.

M Ti gwbo be mae o fel.

James Ma di newid 'sti. (*Curiad*) Nath o gymyd fi i gêm Cymru wsos o blaen. Jyst fi a fo. A nath ni ennill, a ti gwbo be nath o, pan nath ni ennill, nath o hygio fi 'sti. Hygio fi rili tynn, dim fel tynn-tynn, fel tynn neis. A wedyn nath o ddechra canu 'Yma o Hyd', a neshi joinio fo even ddo dwi methu canu gwbl na, a wedyn 'de, allan o nunlla o'dd pawb arall yn y stadiwm yn canu efo ni fyd 'sti. O'dd y gêm di gorffan, y players di mynd, ond o'dd ni dal i ganu.

Curiad.

M (*nawddoglyd*) Swnio neis.

James Ma gallu bod yn neis.

M Lle ma Mam?

James A ma'n rhoi pres i fi.

M Ma cadw chdi'n wrapped round his finger, yndi.

James Na, di bod yn rhoi pres i fi talu am driving lessons fi 'de, a nath o talu am theory fi. Neshi pasho hwnna obviously, a ma newydd talu am test fi fyd.

M Ydio /

James Methu aros i pasho.

M Sut ti gwbo, ti am pasho?

James Dwi mynd i. A pan dwi yn . . . Dwi am ddreifio fel trw'r amsar 'de, dreifio i bob man /

M Sgen ti'm car.

James Dim eto, na.

M Neith Dad no way gadal chdi twtshad car fo, 'sti /

James Gwbo, dyna pam dwi am brynu un /

M Di nhw'm yn cheap 'sti.

James Gwbo, ti swnio fel Mam /

M Lle ma hi?

James Dad di deud neith o helpu fi prynu un /

M Go iawn?

James Deud ma isho'r 'gora i mab fo.' O na. Deud bod o isho gora i *unig* mab fo.

M *yn dechrau gadael.*

James Dylsa chdi ddechra dreifio, 'sti.

M *stops.*

M Dwi'm yn un-deg saith, na.

James Swni gallu dysgu chdi.

M Na, dwi'm trystio chdi.

James Sa chdi gallu dreifio i gwaith wedyn. Clwad bod tâl yn crap yn *Allports.

M Ma'n iawn.

James A ti ca'l cadw fo gyd?

M Yndw. Prynu chips i Mam a fi ar ddydd Gwenars, ond fel arall.

James Ti cal discount?

M *yn nodio.*

James Cŵl. Swni'm yn prynu chips i hi ddo. Swni safio pres fi gyd, gyfar *porsche.

M (*chwerthin*) *Porsche? You wish.

Curiad.

James Dwi am fod y dreifar gora.

M *yn chwerthin, ond mae* **James** *o ddifri. Dros y pwt nesaf o ddeialog, mae* **James** *yn ymgolli yn ei gêm rasio ceir ar yr Xbox*.*

James Cos peth ydi 'de, pan ti dreifio . . . *chdi* sy dreifio. Neb arall, na. A ti gwbo sut ma neud fi teimlo?

M Pwerus?

James Mwy na hynna. Teimlo in charge. *In control.* Pan dwi dreifio, *fi* sy neud decisions /

M Wel, ti *ddim* /

James Dwi yn, *fi* sy dewis pa ffordd da ni mynd /

M Na, y lonydd sy /

James *Fi* sy dewis pa mor ffast da ni mynd /

M Eto, na, y speed limit sy /

James A *fi* sy dewis lle da ni endio fynu.

M Iawn, ocê, ond ma lonydd i gyd di cal creu gan pobl arall, so actually, *nhw* sy kind of dewis lle da ni endio fynu, a *nhw* sy dewis be di speed limits, a *nhw* sy dewis /

James *yn crasho'i car yr ar Xbox.*

James God's sake! Pam nes di hynna?!

M Neshi'm byd /

James Do, nes di. Distractio fi, gallu clwad chdi, barod i fynd on am sut (*dynwared*) 'ma holl decisions da ni neud yn, yn' be di'r gair (*parhau i ddynwared*) 'yr unig decision sy *ddim* yn. . .' *influenced,* ia, dyna fo, 'yr unig decision sy ddim yn influenced ydi decision ni am enw ni, y decision *yna* ydi decision *ni,* yr unig decision sy ddim yn blydi influenced.' /

M   Informed.

James   Informed, influenced, whatever 'de, dwi'm careio. Eniwe, ma bob enw (*mwy o ddynwared*) wedi 'creu gan bobl arall' yndi.

Curiad.

(*Chwerthin.*) Unless bo chdi di creu enw hollol orginial, newydd.

Curiad.

Be dio?

M *ddim yn ateb.*

James   Ti goro deutha fi rwbryd, 'sti.

M   M'yn *goro* neud / dim

James   Ti methu cuddiad /

M   Dwi'm / cuddiad

James   Di newid ar socials chdi?

M   Dim eto, / na

James   Jyst deutha fi. Brawd chdi dwi.

M   Dwisho deuth Mam gynta.

James   Wel di hi'm yma 'de, so.

M   Lle ma hi, James?

James *ddim yn ateb.* **M** *yn dechrau gadael eto.*

James   Ella gei di byth chance i ddeutha hi. Cos ma'i di mynd.

M   Be?

James   Ma'i di gadal.

M   Gyfar gwaith, probs.

James   Na, nath hi ddeud bo hi am fod dipyn 'sti. Fel di mynd am hir. Ddim yn gwbo pryd fydd hi nôl, na. O'dd hi efo suitcase fyd.

M   Ti deud clwydda.

James   Nath hi ddeud wbath, am petha'n bod too much.

M   Ma'i deud hynna trw amsar, am bob dim /

James   O na, gwahanol tro ma. O'dd hi meddwl chdi. *Ti'n* too much. Efo sodding enw newydd chdi.

Curiad.

M Hwnna wbath sa Dad yn ddeud, dim Mam.

James Wel ma nhw di bod yn siarad eto, 'sti.

M *ddim yn gwbo beth i ddweud.*

James Ella bo hi efo fo /

M Di ddim. Ma hi casau guts fo. A fi fyd /

James A mae o casau guts chdi, fyd!

M *yn flin rwan . . . anadlu trwm.*

James Go on, chwala wbath. Tafla wbath. Pynsha fi.

M *yn llonyddu ei hun.*

James Ond wan bod o'n *official*. Bo chdi efo enw *hogyn* bach. Na'i pwnsho nôl, *yn galetach.*

M *yn gadael.*

James Traaaaa.

III. ble mae mam?

Mae **M** *yn cyrraedd ei waith;* *Allports (Chippy).* **M** *yn gweini cwsmeriaid drwy'r olygfa. Mae* **Bobi** *wedi dod i ymweld ag ef.*

Bobi Di meddwl am rhei enwa.

M *ddim yn ymateb.*

Bobi Anoddach na ti'n meddwl, yndi?

M Mhm.

Bobi Lot i feddwl am, lot.

M (*i gwsmer*)   Two fifty.

Bobi Tisho clwad list fi?

M *ddim yn ymateb; rhoi newid i'r cwsmer.* **Bobi** *yn annoyed efo* **M** *rwan.*

Bobi Oi!

M *yn neidio.*

M Dwi gweithio! Be?

Bobi Siarad i chdi.

M Ia, gwbo, sori, ond dwi /

Bobi Gen i list.

M List?

Bobi Ia, long-list.

M Cŵl, da iawn.

Bobi *yn unamused.* **M** *yn troi at* **Cwsmer**.

Cwsmer Battered sosij, plis.

Bobi Dwi'n seriously meddwl am y peth rwan. Diolch i *chdi*. Nes di ddeud sa chdi helpu fi?

M *eto, ddim yn ymateb.*

Bobi Ond, dim pwynt . . . Achos neith rhieni fi ddim arwyddo'r ffurflen.

Mae hyn yn denu sylw **M**.

M Be?

M *yn symud i ffwrdd o* **Cwsmer**, *yn dal gafael yn y bag gyda'r sosij.*

Bobi Neshi ddeutha chdi, ma nhw'n proper pricks.

M Be ti meddwl?

Bobi Fel, full on deud . . . M'ond pobol trans sy cal newid enwa nhw.

M Beeeee . . .

Bobi Gwbo, ma nhw mor backwards.

M Hwnna mor weird, cos ma nhw'n fel, ocê efo chdi'n bod yn gay yndi? /

Bobi Wel . . . ydi nhw?

M Rili?

Bobi *yn codi'i ysgwyddau.*

M Ond nes di ddeud bo nhw'n ocê efo chdi isho newid pronouns chdi, na?

Bobi Neshi byth deutha nhw.

M *yn edrych ar* **Bobi**, *wedi drysu* . . .

Bobi Achos o'n i ofn.

M Ofn? God.

Cwsmer Sgiwshwch fi, dwi'n aros am fy sosij /

M (*i* **Cwsmer**) Hang on!

Cwsmer *yn synnu.* **M** *troi nôl at* **Bobi**.

M Sori, neshi'm sylwi bod o mor ddrwg a hynna?

Bobi Ma'n iawn, jyst falch bo genai chdi.

M Obviously.

M *cymryd ei ffedog gwaith i ffwrdd, a rhoi cwtsh i* **Bobi**.

Cwsmer Helo? (*Troi at gwsmer arall.*) Dwi methu coelio'r peth, ti'n gallu coelio'r peth? Ma hyn yn ridiculous! Lle ma'r manager?

Cwsmer *yn gadael, y cwsmeriaid sy'n weddill yn aros, yn ddiamynedd.*

Mae **Bobi** *yn tynnu i ffwrdd o'r cwtsh.*

Bobi Tisho clwad long-list fi?

M Yndw, rili isho, ond wedyn, iawn?

Bobi Genai rhei enwa da /

M Bet bo nhw ddim mor dda a enw newydd fi. Wedyn ddo, iawn.

Bobi Iawn.

M (*cynnig y sosij*) Ti llwgu? (*Rhoi'r ffedog nôl ar.*) Wan, pam ddes di mewn, nes di ddeud bo gena chdi wbath i ddeutha fi. Quick ddo /

M *yn troi at gwsmer arall.*

Bobi Mam chdi.

M *yn troi nôl at* **Bobi**, *y cwsmer arall yn rhoi ochenaid.*

M Mam fi?

Bobi Nath hi'm troi fynu i gwaith heddiw. O'dd rhaid i Mam gal rhywun mewn munud ola. O'dd hi flin. Achos ma nhw short-staffed, dyna udodd hi. Ond deud bod o'm fel Mam chdi?

M ddim yn ymateb. Yr oll mae'n gallu ei glywed yw geiriau ei frawd 'Ti'n too much'.

Bobi Ti gwbo lle ma hi?

Mae ffedog **M** *i ffwrdd eto, cwsmeriaid yn ebychu eu diffyg amynedd.* **M** *yn dechrau gadael.*

Bobi Lle ti mynd?

Cwsmer *yn dychwelyd, ac yn bympio mewn i* **M**.

Cwsmer (*yn gandryll*) Pan dwi'n cael gafael ar manager, dwi'n reportio chdi, be di enw chdi?

M Symud.

Cwsmer Ti methu siarad i cwsmar felna?!

M Symud, *plis*?!

Cwsmer *yn edrych ar bathodyn gwaith* **M**. **Cwsmer** *yn dechrau chwerthin.*

Cwsmer You don't fool me 'de. Be di enw *go iawn* chdi?

M Battered Sosij.

M *yn smircio ar* **Cwsmer**, *cyn gadael.*

Bobi (*gweiddi ar ôl* **M**)   Cofia am heno!

Cwsmer *yn troi at* **Bobi**. **Bobi** *yn cymryd brathiad o'r sosij.*

Bobi (*ceg llawn*)   Pam ti'n edrych ar fi? Dwi'm yn gweithio ma.

Bobi *yn gadael.*

Mae dau gwsmer yn camu o'r ciw, gyda tships.

*

Mae'r ddau gwsmer yn cyrraedd y gofod, ar wahan i'w gilydd. Nhw yw **Mam Ifanc** *a* **Dad Ifanc** *o hyn ymlaen.*

Fel mae nhw'n cyrraedd, mae nhw'n gweld eu gilydd.

Mae nhw'n gwneud eu ffordd tuag at ei gilydd.

Mae nhw'n cwrdd am y tro cyntaf.

Mae nhw'n rhannu'r chips.

Mae nhw'n dal dwylo.

Mae nhw'n gadael.

Mae **M** *yn dychwelyd, yn anadlu'n drwm.* **Bobi** *yn cyrraedd o'r cyfeiriad gyferbyn.*

Bobi (*cyfeiriad uniongyrchol*)   Dwrnod dolig, ar ôl cinio dolig Mam a bach o spotted dick M&S, neshi ddeud wrth rhieni fi, bo fi am newid pronouns fi: i fo / nhw. Neshi ddeud bo fi ddim yn trans, ond os byswn i, bo fi lwcus achos ma enw fi'n kind of fluid. Enw ar tystysgrif geni fi di Robert. Dyna di enw Dad fi, a Taid fi fyd. Mae o'n traddodiad. I pasho'r enw mlaen. Ond da ni wastad di galw fi'n Bobi. Os swni isho newid o, ella sa nhw bach yn siomedig, achos swni torri traddodiad byswn. Ond sa nhw definitely cefnogi fi. Ma nhw jyst isho fi fod yn hapus. Ma nhw even yn hapus i fi symud i ddinas pan dwi'n hŷn, fel Caerdydd. Fana ath Mam i astudio. Sa hwnna bron fel traddodiad fyd bysa? Ia, da ni'n eitha traddodiadol. A da ni'n rili agos.

*

IV. chwilio am mam

Mae **M** *yn cymryd anadl ddofn, cyn cyrraedd y cartref gofal.*

Mae **Myfyriwr** *nyrsio wrth y desg.*

Myfyriwr   Aiaaaaa.

M   Hai, yma i jecio os di /

Myfyriwr   Ma visiting hours rhwng dau a /

M Na na, dwi'm yn visitor /

Myfyriwr O . . .

M Yma i weld os di /

Myfyriwr Ti'n stiwdant fyd?

M Na, dwi'n ysgol / m'otch.

Myfyriwr O, profiad gwaith ia?

M Na-na /

Myfyriwr Bod yn onast, dwnim pwy ti fod siarad efo /

M Dwi'm yn /

Myfyriwr Dwnim pwy sy manijo fi, management gwael yma di mynd /

M Ocê /

Myfyriwr . . . a ma pawb mor brysur, virus gwmpas y lle dwi meddwl, pobol *dropping like flies*: marw /

M Siom /

Myfyriwr Ma *hi* di marw, mae *o* di marw, r'un *yna* di marw. Dwi fod i ddysgu sut i fod yn nyrs, ond dwi jyst watshad hen bobol di-enw yn marw a delio efo check-ins. O, sori, chdi di entertainment heno?

M Na /

Myfyriwr Chdi di'r harpist? Be di enw chdi eto, di gweld enw chdi fa'ma rwla /

M Dwi'm yn chwara telyn, yma i weld os di Mam yma.

Myfyriwr Jesus, mam chdi'n hen.

M Mai *gweithio* ma.

Curiad.

Myfyriwr Ooooo!

M Ond, meddwl bo hi di dod mewn yn hwyr ne wbath, ella, dwmbo /

Myfyriwr Dwi'n gweld, pam nes di'm deud.

M (*dan ei wynt*) Neshi trio.

Myfyriwr Gad fi gal lwc . . . Be di enw hi?

M Ym . . .

Myfyriwr (*chwerthin*) Ti'm yn gwbo enw Mam chdi?

M Be? Yndw. (*Cofio.*) Elin!

Myfyriwr Elin?

M Elin

Myfyriwr (*yn herio, tynnu tafod*) Ti shŵr?

M Elin Jones.

Myfyriwr *yn edrych ar ffurflen arwyddo mewn.*

Myfyriwr Hm, un eiliad . . . (*Gweiddi.*) Jano! Jano?!

Mae **Preswylydd** *cartref gofal yn ymddangos gyda bocs jig-so.*

Myfyriwr Dim Jano di hi.

Preswylydd *yn dechrau'r jig-so.* **M** *yn syllu.*

Myfyriwr Jano!!!

Jano (*off llwyfan*) Ieeeee?

Myfyriwr Dyna hi. Ydi Elin, Elin Jones di dod mewn heddiw?

Jano (*off llwyfan*) Pwy sy gofyn?

Myfyriwr *yn edrych ar* **M**. *Sylw* **M** *nôl at* **Myfyriwr**.

M O, ym, mab hi.

Myfyriwr (*gweiddi*) . . . mab hi.

M (*snapio*) Fi *ydi* blydi mab hi.

Myfyriwr (*knee-jerk ymateb, gweiddi eto*) Fo *ydi* blydi mab hi!

Gwaed **M** *yn berwi. Y ddau'n aros am ymateb.*

Jano (*off llwyfan*) O, James, ia?

Myfyriwr *yn edrych ar* **M** . . .

Myfyriwr (*nerfus*) Ia?

M *brathu ei dafod.*

M Ia. (*Dan ei wynt, rhwystredig.*) Why not.

Myfyriwr (*gweiddi*) Ia, James dio.

Jano (*off llwyfan*) O, am ogyn lyfli. Ond na, di'm yma, di'm di troi fynu heddiw, ddim fel hi, ond deutha'r ogyn aros, rhaid fi ddeud helo i'r ogyn bach del.

M *yn gadael a slamio'r drws.*

Myfyriwr Jano? (*Curiad.*) Jano?

Jano (*off llwyfan*) Ia?

Myfyriwr Safia dy draed. Ma di mynd.

Myfyriwr *yn dechrau gadael.*

*

Fel mae **Myfyriwr** *yn gadael mae nhw'n cwrdd â* **Mam Ifanc** *yn y gofod, gyda newyddion. Mae'r* **Preswylydd** *yn parhau i wneud jig-so.*

Myfyriwr   Ti'n disgwl.

Curiad – **Mam Ifanc** *ddim yn gwbod sut i ymateb.*

Myfyriwr   Ti mynd i fod yn Fam.

Curiad.

(*Chwerthin.*) Anghofia Elin. O hyn 'mlaen, *Mam!*

Mam Ifanc *ddim yn chwerthin, ei hunaniaeth ar fin newid . . . Fel mae hi'n gadael . . .*

Myfyriwr (*cyfeiriad uniongyrchol*)   O paid a gofyn i fi am enwa. Dwi'n rybish efo enwa. A *fa'ma,* sgena ni'm amsar i gofio enwa. Dwi'n jocian. Ma gena ni. Ond o ddifri, weithia sgena ni ddim. Wastad stwff i neud yma, rhei o'r nyrsys yn neud bron i sixty hours a week rwan, chos da ni'n short-staffed, ti gwbo. Ond, pan dwi *efo* amsar, nai ymdrech i atgoffa rhai o'r residents pwy di nhw. (*i* **Preswylydd**) Rhai ohona ni angen cal ein atgoffa o'n enw . . . Yn does, *Nerys*? Nerys!? (*nôl at gynulleidfa*) Rhy brysur efo'i jig-so Garden of Eden. O ddifri ddo, pan ma amsar chdi dwad, fydd dim bwys am enw chdi. Di bod yma oria yn neud jig-so, a di'm angan help. (*i* **Preswylydd**) Nei di'm stopio neud jig-sos, na nei Nerys? O balls, Margaret di hon.

Myfyriwr *yn gadael gyda'r* **Preswylydd**.

*

V. ei hail swydd

M *yn cyrraedd cloch drws ffansi. Mae'n canu'r gloch. Mae sŵn y gloch yn hir, ac yn ridiculous. Mae* **M** *yn rolio'i llygaid. Dim ateb.* **M** *yn canu'r gloch eto. Tro yma:*

Intercom   Name.

M   I'm looking for Elin Jones.

Intercom   Is that your name?

M   Na, course not, it's my Mam's, she cleans here /

Intercom   Name. *Your* name /

M   Why do you need my name?

Intercom   Name.

M   My name is /

Ceridwen   Dwi di gweld ti o'r blaen.

Ceridwen *wedi cyrraedd, gyda raced tennis.* **M** *yn troi ati.*

Ceridwen (*mewn i'r intercom*) Don't worry, Daddy, I know him.

Curiad.

Ti'n mynd i'r un ysgol a fi. Ond ti'n fengach, dwyt? Blwyddyn un-ar-ddeg?

M Ia.

Ceridwen Knew it. Dwi'n chweched. Warning, mae'n rili anodd. Gorfod dewis pa gwrs dwi isio neud yn Brifysgol, a fel, dwi jyst ddim yn gwbo, fel events managements, neu cosmetic science neu rwbath, yn Llundain obviously. Aa, casau gorfod neud dewisiada *mawr*, ti gwbo be dwi feddwl?

M Mhm.

Ceridwen Ond, i fod yn hollol onast dwi'n gadael o gyd i Mam fi, geith hi ddewis, ma hi'n dda neud hynna, a hi sy'n talu am fo gyd, so. Anyway, sori, rambling, ond ia ti'm yn sylwi ar disgyblion sy'n fengach na ti. Ond dwi di sylwi ar ti. Dwi di gweld ti, gwmpas coridors.

M Cŵl.

Ceridwen Ie. Ti'n ddiddorol . . .

M Ydwi?

Curiad.

Ceridwen Sut o ti'n gwbo?

M Sori?

Ceridwen Sut o ti'n gwbo . . . Ti'n gwbo . . . Bo ti ddim yn. . .?

M O. (*Curiad.*) Jyst, wastad di gwbo.

Ceridwen Waw . . . Ma' pobol fel ti mor . . . ddewr.

Mae dwrn yn ffurfio yn nwylo **M**.

Ceridwen Ie, ti mor *mor* ddewr a mor . . . ifanc.

M Ti literally blwyddyn yn hŷn na fi.

Ceridwen (*synnu bod* **M** *yn yr ardal*) Be ti'n neud *fa'ma*? Ti'm yn byw fa'ma.

M Na gwbo /

Ceridwen Oh wait!!! Ti di boyfriend Bobi, sy'n gweithio'n chippy?

M Ia . . .

Ceridwen Ciwt! Caru Bobi, ddim yn caru chips *Allports no offence, ha!

M Ti'n nabod Bobi?

Ceridwen Nabod o mor, mor dda, da ni mynd way back, fel family friends.

M Rili?

Ceridwen Ma rhieni fo legit, *the best.*

M M'yn siŵr os ydi nhw /

Ceridwen Ti di cyfarfod nhw?

M Na . . .

Ceridwen Wel aros nes ti yn, achos ma nhw'n seriously . . . incredible. Ma nhw di bod mor, mor . . . accepting o Bobi, efo fo'n bod yn gay and all that ti'n gwbo. Mae o mor lwcus. Oh my god, neith nhw *caru* ti. Dwi'n meddwl nath Dad o, fel, cael Twitter* row efo *J. K. Rowling yn ddiweddar, fel *he really went for her*, a wedyn nath hi, (*dechrau chwerthin*) nath hi blocio fo. *J. K. Rowling yn blocio Dad Bobi ar Twitter*!? Pa mor ridic o amazing di hynna?! Ath o'n viral. Dad Bobi, viral! Nath Bobi a fi lolio loads ar Snapchat*.

M Rili?

Ceridwen Gutted, ddo. Achos dwi yn caru bach o *Potter.

M *yn edrych arni'n ddryslyd.*

Ceridwen *Harry Potter?

M Ydi Mam fi ma?

Ceridwen Pam sa Mam ti ma?

M Ma'i llnau i chi.

Ceridwen Elin di Mam ti?!

M *yn nodio.*

Ceridwen Ooo ciwt! Ond na. Ma hi'n llnau ar weekends, / methu aros nes weekend.

M Gwbo hynna, ond wyt ti, neu rhieni chdi, dwmbo, di nhw di clwad gen hi?

Ceridwen Ella bydd *Caren wedi, fydd hi nôl yn fuan. Di mynd i hot yoga.

M Sori, pwy di *Caren?

Ceridwen Mam fi. Ma hi'n casau pan dwi'n galw hi'n enw go iawn hi. Dwi'n siŵr sa Mam ti'n casau hynna fyd?

M Os na enw hi sa *Caren.

Ceridwen Be?

M Dim enw hi di *Caren /

Ceridwen Na, dwi'n gwbo . . .

M *yn chwerthin i'w hun ar yr enw *Caren.*

Ceridwen Ti'n weird . . . Ond tyd mewn i aros os tisho ddo? Fedra i neud hot choccie i ti?

M   Na, paid poeni.

Ceridwen *yn agosau at* **M**.

Ceridwen   Ydi bob dim yn OK?

M   Yndi /

Ceridwen   Seemio tha bo chdi'n poeni? /

M   Na, wel . . . na, dwi fine.

Ceridwen   Mai'n siarad am ti lot.

M   O, yndi?

Ceridwen   Nath hi sôn bo ti am newid enw? Hwnna'n fun.

M   Nath hi ddeutha chdi?

Ceridwen   Ie.

M   Di newid o'n barod actually. Heddiw.

Ceridwen   O waw, OK. Congrats.

M   Diolch . . .

Curiad.

Ceridwen   Don't know how you do it.

M   Hawdd actually.

Ceridwen   Ond mashwr bod o'n anodd i, jyst *troi'n* rhywun arall felna /

M   Ti'm yn troi'n rhywun arall. Dwi dal yn fi. Dwi'n mwy fi.

Ceridwen   Ond, sut ti'n dewis enw newydd? Dwi'n dallt pam, ond sut? Nes di siarad efo brawd ti neu mam ti? Achos mashwr ti'n careio be ma nhw meddwl. Dwi'n gwbo am Dad ti, so dwi'n gwbo bysa ti ddim . . . Ti meddwl bod yr enw'n reflectio ti? Swni jyst methu cymryd yr enw nath rhieni fi rhoi i fi, i ffwrdd o nhw. Ie, na, swni methu rhoi nhw drwy hynna.

M *yn dechrau chwerthin.*

Ceridwen   Ma rhaid bod o'n anodd i rhieni ti.

M *yn dechrau gadael.*

Ceridwen   O na, sori, neshi ddeud wbath . . . ?

M *yn stopio, cyn troi at* **Ceridwen**.

M   Anodd i *nhw*?!

Ceridwen   Wel, ie, rhaid bod o, enwedig heddiw /

M   Dio'm byd i neud efo nhw! Dwi'm yn blentyn ddim mwy na, a ti ddim chwaith. Dwi finally dechrau bod yn fi, y fi go iawn, fi sy bia fi ocê, fi sy' bia enw *fi*!

M *yn gadael.*

Ceridwen *yn canu'r intercom.*

Intercom Name.

Ceridwen (*chwerthin*) It's Ceridwen, Daddy.

Fel mae **Ceridwen** *yn gadael, mae sŵn babi yn crio yn y cefndir yn ymddangos.*

*

Mae sŵn y babi yn crio yn parhau: mae yna gêm bel-droed ymlaen ar y teledu yn y cefndir hefyd gyda llais Dafydd Iwan yn canu'r anthem 'Yma o Hyd'.

Mam Ifanc *yn rhuthro mewn i'r gofod; yn chwydu mewn i fwced.*

Daw **Dad Ifanc** *i mewn gyda'r babi, yn amlwg yn rhwystredig gyda crio.* **Mam Ifanc** *yn sychu ei cheg, blinder llwyr.* **Dad Ifanc** *yn rhoi'r babi iddi, cyn troi nôl at y pel-droed.*

Myfyriwr *nyrsio yn cyrraedd.*

Snap: **Mam Ifanc** *a* **Dad Ifanc** *yn troi.*

Myfyriwr Wel, da chi mynd i fod yn Mam a Dad *eto.*

Curiad.

Da chisho gwbo y rhyw?

Cyn i **Mam Ifanc** *cael gair mewn:*

Dad Ydyn.

Curiad – tensiwn amlwg rhwng **Mam Ifanc** *a* **Dad Ifanc***.*

Mam Ifanc *yn rhoi nod i* **Myfyriwr***.*

Myfyriwr Tro ma . . . Merch fach!

Dad Ifanc *yn dathlu.* **Mam Ifanc** *yn ei wylio, yn ddi-emosiwn.*

Myfyriwr Dwi shwr gena chi lot o girlie names. Sa ti gallu rhoi dy enw *di* iddi.

Mam Ifanc *yn edrych ar y nyrs yn ddryslyd.*

Myfyriwr Sa ti gallu enwi hi'n 'Mam'.

Myfyriwr *yn rhoi chwerth ar ei jôc.* **Mam Ifanc** *ddim yn chwerthin:*

Mam Enw fi di Elin!

Dad Ifanc *yn popio gormod o pink party poppers.*

Pawb yn gadael. **M** *a* **Ceridwen** *yn dychwelyd. Dros araith* **Ceridwen***, mae* **M** *yn aros i gwrdd â* **Bobi***.* **M** *yn amlwg yn anghyfforddus; ei gorff yn dangos hyn ini.*

Ceridwen (*cyfeiriad uniongyrchol*) Dwi'n proper Daddy's girl, a weithia mae o'n galw fi'n 'his little goddess'. Dio'm yn siarad Cymraeg, ond ma'n deud na fo nath ddewis enw fi. O'dd o licio'r ystyr. Ceridwen: 'Welsh goddess of rebirth, transformation and inspiration' Nice, right? So ma na lot o feddwl di mynd mewn i'r peth. Swni methu newid o. Ond, os swni gorfod, os swni *gorfod,* sa rhaid i fi neud yn shŵr bod o'n fel *rili* reflectio fi. Sa fo'n *gorfod* bod yn Gymraeg. Ww, ond ella Frida? Dwi jyst yn caru Frida Kahlo, a ma hi'n dduwies? So swni dal yn dduwies. (*chwerthin*) Falla ddim. Caru hi ddo. Trist do'dd hi'm yn licio corff hi. Ie, rili trist. (*Curiad*) Dwi licio corff fi.

Ceridwen *yn gadael.*

*

VI. jig-so Bobi

Mae **M** *yn eistedd, dal yn anghyfforddus. Mae* **Bobi** *yn cyrraedd yn camu yn ôl ag ymlaen ar gyflymdra, gyda wahanol crysau ar gyfer* **M**.

Bobi Sori bo heno ddim yn sypreis. O'n i jyst meddwl swni deutha chdi achos, wel, o'n i'm yn siŵr sa chdi up for it, efo Mam chdi . . .

TAWELWCH – **Bobi** *yn dangos crys.*

Bobi Be am hwn?

M *yn shruggio.* **Bobi** *yn nôl crys arall.*

Bobi Hwn?

M (*snapio*) Dio'm yn ffitio fi, eto.

Tyndra.

Bobi Di bob dim yn iawn?

M Na Bobi, dwi teimlo fel crap yndw.

Bobi Gwbo /

M M'yn gwbo lle ma hi /

Bobi Gwbo, gwbo /

M A m'yn gwbo pam, na, pam bo hi . . . heddiw fyd fel, m'yn gwbo os ma hi di newid meddwl hi neu . . . ond dwi gwbo sa hi'm yn deu clwydda i fi de, ond fel, ma pobl *yn* deu clwydda, ma pobl yn sypreisio chdi yndi /

Bobi Gwbo, yndi, gwbo /

Curiad.

M Di rhieni chdi deu clwydda?

Bobi Be?

M Di nhw deu clwydda? Sa Mam chdi deu clwydda i chdi?

Bobi Ym . . .

M Neu, sa *ti* deu clwydda?

Bobi Ydw i di neud wbath?

M Ti nabod Ceridwen?

Curiad.

Bobi Ceridwen?

M Ia.

Bobi Pa Ceridwen?

M Dim lot o Ceridwens rownd fa'ma.

Bobi *'n meddwl am eiliad.*

Bobi O, Ceridwen sy byw yn (*rolio'i llygad*) 'Cheshire-by-Sea'?

M O'n i yna heddiw.

Bobi Pam o chdi *fa'na*?

M Mam yn llnau tŷ Ceridwen, yndi.

Bobi Ond ma Mam chdi gweithio i Mam fi yn y care home, na?

M Yndi, dau job 'de. Rhaid i hi. Am pres.

Curiad.

Ceridwen yn deu bo hi nabod chdi 'sti, fel bo hi a chdi family friends? Ma teulu hi efo lot o bres, 'de. Fel, super rich . . . Gwbo bo chdi ddim yn byw yn Cheshire-by-Sea, ond, ydi teulu chdi rich fyd? Dyna pam bo chdi heb invitio fi i lle chdi eto? Ti'n embarrassed o fi?

Bobi Lle ma hyn i gyd di. . .?

M Plis atab fi.

Bobi Ti gwbo pam /

M Cos ma nhw'n 'pricks'?

Bobi Ia.

M Di nhw yn?

Bobi Be?

Curiad.

M Di nhw *yn*?

Bobi *ddim yn ateb.*

M Pam ti deu clwydda? O'dd heddiw fod am fi. A wan, dio ddim. Fel, gwbo bo fi swnio selfish 'de, ond dwi di witchad blynyddoedd am heddiw. O'n i isho heddiw fod am fi . . . (*Agos i ddagra.*) Ond *ti,* ti a *Mam* fi, y ddau o *chi*... Da chi'm yn gadal fi gal dwrnod fi. Cos da chi'ch dau di bod yn deu clwydda i fi. Ti even yn licio enw fi? Cos dwi teimlo fel nes di ddeu clwydda am hynna fyd, 'licio fo os ti licio fo' dyna udis di, be ma hynna even meddwl . . .

Dwisho chdi *lyfio* fo, 'de. *Enw* fi dio. A dwisho Mam fi lyfio fo fyd. Ond ma hi obviously cal second thoughts . . .

Nai lyfio enw *chdi* pan ti newid o . . .

Curiad.

M   Pam ti'm yn deud dim?

Bobi   Ma hyn yn . . . ma jyst yn *lot*.

Curiad.

Ia. Ma'n lot.

M   Ma'n lot.

Bobi   Ella ddim yn lot, jyst . . .

Curiad.

Fel no wonder ti meddwl ma Mam chdi di disownio chdi achos ti di newid enw, achos ti'm yn . . . ti'm yn *gweld* dim byd arall ar funud /

M *yn chwerthin – methu credu beth mae'n glywed.*

Bobi   Dwi teimlo tha bo chdi'n fixated ar . . . ar jig-so chdi dy hun, a neb arall . . . fel, Mam chdi, ma hi efo stwff ei hun yn mynd mlaen, efo jig-so ei hun. A fel ma gena *fi* jig-so fyd ond ma teimlo fel ti ddim di bod hynna mewn i jig-so *fi,* so ia, sori, di thieni fi ddim mor ddrwg n hynna , , ,

A dwi probably ddim am newid enw fi.

Dwi jyst di bod yn desperate i chdi *weld* fi, ti gwbo? So, r'unig ffordd i neud hynna, i gal chdi i weld fi /

M   Trw cogio bod . . .

God.

Ma hwnna messed up, 'sti!

Bobi   Dwi jyst . . . ma petha *yn* wahanol. Ond, dwi *yn* rili licio chdi.

M *yn dechrau gadael.*

Bobi   Aros.

M *yn stopio.*

M   Be?

Curiad.

Bobi   Nath Mam fi deutha fi beidio deud dim, achos neith hi edrych yn ddrwg I guess.

M   Be ti son am?

Bobi   Nath Mam chdi bwcio heddiw off gwaith, ages yn ôl.

Curiad.

Bobi   Gwbo bo hynna ddim yn helpu chdi lot, ond.

M *yn parhau i adael.*

Bobi   Lle ti mynd?

M   Mynd i ddathlu enw newydd fi. (*Curiad*) A ti'm yn dwad.

M *yn gadael.*

*

Daw **James** *i mewn, a dechrau gwneud jig-so.*

Mewn rhan arall o'r gofod daw **Mam Ifanc** *a* **Dad Ifanc** *i mewn. Dros araith* **James**, *mae nhw'n cael ffrae anghlywadwy.*

James (*cyfeiriad uniongyrchol*)   Yr unig amsar lle dwi cofio rhywun yn galw fi rwbath arall, o'dd pan o'dda ni fach 'de. Dim nickname na'm byd felna, o'dd o eitha funny. A hi o'dd o. O'dd hi'm di graspio geiria eto. O'dda ni tua pedwar a dau. Ac o'dd hi mynd drw phase o gweiddi: 'Jam, Jam, Jam!' Cofio fi a Mam mor confused 'de, cos o'dd hi'n caru jam, fel strawberry jam, sa hi'n cyfro gwynab hi gyd yn jam weithia. Ond eniwe, o'dd ni wastad fel 'be tisho? James neu Jam?' a sa hi gweiddi 'Jam, Jam!' efo gŵen massive a pwyntio ata fi a'r jam. O'dd hi isho'r ddau. Ac even ddo o'dd hi'n cyfro gwynab hi efo jam, o'dd hi *yn* licio fi mwy, 'de. Cos swni chwara efo hi. Jig-so a stwff. A swni galw hi . . .

James *yn seibio: bron a sylwi ar y ffrae tu ôl iddo.* **Dad Ifanc** *yn gadael.* **Mam Ifanc** *ar ei phen ei hun.*

James   Nath ni tyfu fynu wedyn, I guess. (*Llwnc.*) O'n i licio enw hi. Ond ia, efo fi, hapus efo jyst James.

James *yn gadael yn swrth. Fel mae* **Mam Ifanc** *yn gadael, mae* **M** *yn dychwelyd.*

*

VII. parti enw

M *wedi cyrraedd parti datgelu enw sypreis. (Ond dydyn ni ddim yn datgelu'r enw, eto)*

Pawb   Sypreis!

Daw party poppers glas; a cherddoriaeth ffyniannus yn cynnau.

Mae **M** *yn agor can o Carling, a'i llowcio. Mae'n dechrau dawnsio, dathlu . . .*

Dros yr olygfa byrlymus canlynol, mae ffrindiau / aelodau teulu yn dod i gwestiynu, llongyfarch a'n anfwriadol pechu **M** *– ond mae'n parhau i ddawnsio. Mae'r dathlu yn mynd yn fwyfwy anodd i'w gorff ei gynnal.*

Ffrind   Llongyfarchiada!

M   Diolch!

Ffrind Mor ddewr!

M Diolch . . .

Ffrind Di newid socials chdi, eto?!

Sain ping cyfryngau cymdeithasol nodedig.

M Do!!! Ma'n official!

M *yn agor can arall, a'i llowcio – parhau i ddawnsio.*

Ffrind Ma *actually* siwtio chdi!

M Yndi, gwbo!

Ffrind Sut ti'n dewis enw newydd?!

M Hawdd!

Ffrind Ti'n berson gwahanol rwan?

M Dwi dal yn fi, yn *mwy* fi!

M *yn agor can arall – llowcio.* **M** *yn dechrau stryffaglu wrth ddawnsio – mae'n feddw, a realiti yn dechrau uno gyda atgofion a'r dychymyg. Daw pethau'n fwyfwy swreal.*

Ffrind Dwi am newid enw fi fyd!

M *Dylsa* chdi. Dylsa *ni gyd*!

Ceridwen Swni methu.

Ffrind Ti'n inspiration.

Ceridwen Ceridwen: 'Welsh goddess of rebirth, transformation and inspiration'

Bobi Ti'm yn grievio ddo?

M Bobi?

Bobi *'n diflannu.*

M Dwi dal yma!

Carling arall yn agor. **M** *yn dawnsio, yn anoddach.* **Preswylydd** *yn cyrraedd, yn gwneud jig-so drwy weddill yr olygfa.*

Ceridwen Trist do'dd hi'm yn licio corff hi. Dwi licio corff fi.

Cwsmer You don't fool me 'de.

Barista Nesa!

Cwsmer Be di enw *go iawn c*hdi?

James *Ti'n* too much.

M Na!

Ceridwen Ma rhaid bod o'n anodd.

M Na!

Ceridwen I rhieni ti!

M Stwffia rhieni fi!

Myfyriwr Ma *hi* di marw, mae *o* di marw, r'un *yna* di marw. Jyst watshad hen bobol di-enw yn marw.

Curiad – y gerddoriaeth yn seibio am eiliad.

Myfyriwr Chdi di'r harpist?

Cerddoriaeth a'r dawnsio'n ail-gydied.

Intercom Name.

M Enw fi di /

Cwsmer Battered Sosij.

M STWFFIA CHDI!

Barista Nesa!

Intercom Enw!

Nick Nick. I'm a cis straight white man from *The Apprentice**. I was fired for being a selfish prick.

Barista Nesa.

Bobi Ti'm yn grievio ddo? /

M Na! Na! Na!

Ceridwen Ma rhaid bod o'n anodd i rhieni ti.

M / James STWFFIA RHIENI NI!

James O'dd hi meddwl chdi. *Ti'n* too much. *Ti*.

M Na, *chdi*!

Barista No offence cyw, jyst angan enw so fedrai neud chdi coffi.

James Ella bo hi efo fo.

Ffrind Be o'dd enw geni chdi eto?

M Cheshi'm fy ngeni fo enw! Nath neb o ni!

Pawb NEB O NI!

M PARTI MA'N CRAP! GADAL!

Fel mae **M** *yn gadael y parti, daw* **Mam Ifanc** *i mewn. Yn feichiog gyda* **M**.

M   Mam?

Intercom   Name.

Mam   Mam.

Intercom   Your *real* name.

M   Mam!

Mam Ifanc *ddim yn gweld* **M**.

James   Ma hi efo fo.

Myfyriwr   Enw.

M   Mam! Dwi fa'ma!

Myfyriwr   Sa ti gallu enwi hi'n 'Mam'.

Mam   Enw fi di Elin!

M / Mam   Dwi fa'ma! Dwi dal yma!

Mam Ifanc *yn dechrau gadael.*

M   Mam!

James   Ma hi efo fo.

M   Dwi fa'ma! Mam! Dwi dal yma! Dwi dal yma. Dwi dal yma. Dwi dal yma. Dwi dal yma. Dwi dal yma. For god's sake, dwi dal yma. Mam!

TAWELWCH – pawb wedi gadael, ond **M** *ac* **Mam Ifanc**, *dal yma.*

Mam Ifanc *yn troi ac yn gweld* **M** *am y tro cyntaf.*

Yn ei dwylo, mae bat criced.

Mae **Mam Ifanc** *yn cynnig y bat criced i* **M**.

M *yn ceisio gwrthsefyll y cynddaredd.*

Ond mae'n cymryd y bat criced ac yn gadael.

VIII. crasho

Mae **M** *yn cyrraedd cartref ei dad, yn ofalus – gyda'r bat criced, yn ei ddwylo. Mae'n dywyll. Mae* **M** *yn ceisio rhoi'r golau ymlaen. Dydyn nhw ddim yn gweithio.*

M   Dad?

Dim ateb.

Dad?

James   Dio'm yma.

Mae **M** *yn dychryn – y bat criced yn yr aer. Mae* **James** *yn y cornel, yn wynebu i ffwrdd.*

M   Pam ti isda yn y twllwch?

James   Pam ti fa'ma? Fydd o nôl fuan 'sti /

M   Lle mae o?

James   Ti gwbo dio'm isho chdi yma.

M   Di Mam efo fo?

James   Ti meddwl bo hi?

M *yn shruggio.*

James   Coelio fi wan 'lly?

M   Di bod yn chwilio am hi. A fel, di hi'm yn atab ffôn hi na dim, na. Dwi di chwilio bob man, bob man ond fa'ma, a dwi meddwl ella, o'dd fi'n newid enw fi *yn* too much i hi /

James   O, chdi a sodding enw chdi, 'de.

James *yn troi i wynebu* **M**. *Ei wyneb wedi cleisio.*

James   Sut o'dd parti chdi?

M   Dad nath. . .? /

James   Naci.

M   James . . .

James   Neshi . . . (*celwydd*) neshi crasho.

M   Crasho? Crasho be?

James   Y car, obviously.

M   Car Dad?

James   Car Dad. Ia. Neshi cymyd car fo. Cos o'n i bored, mor bored, dim byd i neud yn dre ma a da *ni*, chdi a fi yn stuck yma 'sti, so o'n isho dreifio, a neshi cymyd goriada sbâr fo, eshi mewn, rhoi'r goriada mewn 'de . . . a dechra dreifio . . . neshi ddreifio mor ffast 'de, mor mor ffast, neshi ddreifio yn ffastach na'r speed limit, a neb yn gallu stopio fi, dim even. . . /

M   Dad?

James   *In control*, a hundred miles per hour, ond ti gwbo be? Ma bod *in control*, teimlo'n pwerus, byth yn para . . . Chos da *ni* CRASHO!

M *yn neidio, gyda ofn.*

James   Da ni'n weak. Edrych ar ni. Fa'ma, yn twllwch.

M   Ti dychryn fi.

James   Bron dim pres i dalu am gola.

M   Udis di bo Dad efo lot o pres, wan? Talu am driving lessons chdi a ballu?

James Dylsa chdi mynd, fydd o nôl munud.

M James . . .

James Ma jyst lawr y lôn, di mynd i talu am letrig.

M Dad nath hyn i chdi?

James NESHI CRASHO CAR FO!

Curiad.

M M'yn coelio chdi, na. Ti deu clwydda. Dyna thing chdi. I gal chdi dy hun allan o ffists Dad. Ma'n casau chdi fyd. A ti casau hynna. So ti'n deu clwydda, deu clwydda, a mwy o clwydda i neud dy hun ffitio. Ffitio mewn i be mae o isho chdi fod /

James Chos ma'n haws!!!

M Fo nath hyn i chdi?

James Gwbo be di enw newydd chdi, by the way. Ti *yn* gwbo bo enw chdi yn favourite cân Dad?

M Be?

James Ti di ruinio cân fo rwan. Ac i fi. Ruinio tîm football Cymru i ni.

James *yn estyn ei ffôn, ac yn chwarae 'Yma o Hyd' (mae hwn yn chwarae dros weddill yr olygfa). Mae nhw'n aros i glywed llinell cyntaf y gân. Yna mae'r ddeialog yn parhau.*

James Bai chdi *ydi* hyn i gyd, 'sti. Obviously o'dd o'n too much i hi, ma'n too much i ni gyd. Un decision bach, (*yn wawdlyd*) sy ddim yn *informed* gan pobl o gwmpas chdi, un decision sy gyd amdan *chdi* /

M Ti swnio fel fo eto /

James Ella bo newid enw chdi di fficsho petha i chdi, ond ma di gorffan petha, final nail in the coffin i pawb arall, i ni /

M Stopia /

James Heddiw, ma'n official. Heddiw, ti officially di lladd merch nhw /

M Stop stop stop /

James Ma'i di marw wan /

M Na na na /

James Do, do, do, jyst CAU HI a gad fi fod yn drist, a, a. . .! Jyst isho mynd nôl, mynd nôl a, a, neud jig-so efo chwaer bach fi! Ond, ti di lladd hi! Ti di lladd chwaer fi!

Mae **James** *yn snatshio'r bat criced o ddwylo* **M**.

James (*bron yn sgrechian*) Ti di lladd hi!

James *yn rhyddhau cynddaredd o tu fewn iddo, ac yn dechrau chwalu pethau.*

James Di lladd hi!

James *yn parhau i chwalu pethau.*

Di lladd hi!

. . . parhau i chwalu pethau.

Di lladd. . .!

. . . parhau i chwalu pethau.

Di lladd [hen enw]!

James *yn stopio, agosau at* **M** *gyda'r bat. 'Da ni ddim yn clywed yr hen enw. Mae'r hen enw wedi'i orchuddio gan 'white noize'. Mae* **M** *yn clensian ei ddyrnau. Ei lygaid ar gau. Ei glustiau ar gau.*

Ennyd o dyndra – ydi **James** *am daro* **M***?*

Mae **James** *yn gollwng y bat criced.*

M Paid byth galw fi enw yna, eto.

James Wel dwi methu, na. Enw chdi di marw.

James *yn disgyn i'r llawr, yn beichio crio.*

M *yn dechrau gadael.*

James Ma na llythyr.

M *yn stopio.*

James Gan Mam.

James *yn estyn y llythyr o'i boced.*

James Dwi sori.

M *yn cymryd y llythyr a gadael.*

IX. yma o hyd

Mae **M** *ar ei ben ei hun, yn dal llythyr gan ei fam.*

Y ddelwedd hon fel y ddelwedd agoriadol, ond dim balchder rwan.

Cytgan 'Yma o Hyd' yn chwarae.

Mae **M** *yn ffeindio hi'n anodd clywed geiriau'r gân, i ddechrau – gan ei fod yn gysylltiedig â'i* **Dad**.

Ry'n ni yma o hyd, x2

Er gwaetha pawb a phopeth, x3

Ry'n ni yma o hyd, x2

Er gwaetha pawb a phopeth, x3

Ry'n ni yma o hyd.

Ond, y mwyaf mae'n clywed geiriau'r cytgan, y mwyaf mae'n teimlo'r synnwyr o rymuso.

Mae **M** *dal yma. Er gwaethaf pawb a phopeth. Mi wnaiff wynebu'r byd ar ei ben ei hun, os mae'n golygu dal ymlaen i'w enw newydd. Mae'n mynd i hawlio'r gân brotest hon fel ei gân ei hun, a dechrau ei gyfnod newydd fel* **Max**.

X. ein jig-so

Mae **Max** *yn eistedd gyda'i lythyr a bag o chips. Dydy o heb ddarllen y llythyr eto.*

Daw **Bobi** *i mewn gyda bag, a ketchup sachets yn ei ddwylo.*

Mae **Max** *yn edrych i fynu.* **Bobi** *yn chwifio'r ketchup sachets.*

Max (*chwerthin*)   Lle ges di rheinia?

Bobi   *Allports.

Y ddau'n chwerthin.

Max   Diolch , , , am ddod yma.

Bobi   O'n i'm am gadal chdi fod ben dy hun, na.

Curiad.

A ma'n edrych rili trist chdi'n buta chips ben dy hun.

Max *yn gwenu.* **Bobi** *yn eistedd drws nesa i* **Max**. *Mae'n nhw'n dechrau rhannu'r chips.*

Bobi   Ti edrych . . . di blino.

Max   Dwi wedi.

Curiad – **Bobi** *yn sylwi ar y llythyr yn nwylo* **Max**.

Bobi   Be di hwnna? (*herio*) Di newid enw chdi eto?

Max *yn chwerthin.*

TAWELWCH.

Bobi   *Ella* na'i newid un fi. Un dwrnod. Jyst ddim yn barod eto.

Max   Th'gwrs. (*Curiad.*) M'yn shŵr os ma lot pobl yn barod, 'sti.

Bobi   Be ti meddwl?

Max   Teulu fi, Mam fi . . . O nhw'm yn barod i fi newid, na. Bod yn onast, dwi'm yn meddwl bo nhw dros y ffact bo fi'n trans /

Bobi Jig-so, ti meddwl.

Mae nhw'n chwerthin.

Max Ond, seriously, meddwl bo nhw meddwl bod o'n phase /

Bobi (*rolio'i lygaid*) Blydi phase.

Max Gwbo. (*Curiad.*) Pan neshi sgwennu enw fi lawr, a dal y darn bach o papur na yn dwylo fi . . . Onast 'de, neshi fel anadlu am tro cynta ers, stwffia fo dwi am ddeud o, neshi anadlu am tro cynta *go iawn* ers sixteen years.

Bobi So, be sy bod?

Max Dwi *getio* rhaid bod anodd i nhw. Dwi getio fo 'de. Ond dwi'm yn meddwl bo nhw *rili* getio bo fi dal yma . . . Weithia, dwi meddwl sa di bod yn haws i nhw sa hi di marw 'sti, sa hi'n farw /

Bobi Paid deud hynna /

Max Na, seriously, fel *marw*-marw, yn lle bo nhw goro derbyn fi, fel fi heddiw. Derbyn bo fi jyst . . .

. . . di newid.

Bobi For the better, 'de?

Max Ia, a jyst y dechra 'di hyn . . .

TAWELWCH.

Bobi Dwi prowd o chdi, 'sti.

Max Gwbo.

Bobi Jyst angan pobl da o gwmpas chdi rwan. (*cyfeirio at ei hun*) Pobl sy ddim yn deud clwydda . . .

Curiad.

Dwi rili sori am ddeud clwydda, ocê?

Max *yn gwenu.*

Bobi A dwi seriously licio chdi. Fel, *licio*-licio chdi.

Max Dwi licio chdi fyd. *Licio*-licio chdi. A dwi sori fyd.

Curiad.

Neshi stopio 'gweld' chdi, chdi a /

Bobi Os ti deud jig-so /

Y ddau'n chwerthin.

Mae **Bobi** *'n edrych ar y llythyr yn nwylo* **Max** *eto.*

Max Llythyr dio.

Bobi *yn agosau at* **Max**.

Max Dwi ofn agor o.

Bobi Gan pwy mae o?

Max Mam. Nei di ddarllan o i fi?

Bobi Th'gwrs.

Max *yn rhoi'r llythyr i* **Bobi**. *Mae'n agor y llythyr. Mae'n ei ddarllen.*

Bobi Swni'm yn galw hwn yn llythyr, 'de.

Max Be?

Bobi Mwy fel nodyn. (*yn darllen*) 'Ti gwbo dwi prowd o chdi. Ti'n inspiration, cariad. Wish swni efo rhywun fel chdi, pan o'n i oed chdi. Nôl hwyr heno.'

Mewn man arall o'r gofod, mae **Mam Ifanc** *yn cyrraedd gyda babi newydd yn ei dwylo.*

Bobi 'Caru chdi . . .'

Mam (*i'r babi*) Caru chdi *Max*.

Dyma'r tro cyntaf ini glywed enw **Max**.

Bobi & Mam (*llofnod*) 'Mam.'

Mae **Mam Ifanc** *a* **Max** *yn dal cyswllt llygaid am ennyd, yna mae hi'n gadael. Mae* **Max** *yn dechrau chwerthin. Pob amheuaeth oedd ganddo am ei* **Fam** *yn gadael ei feddwl. Chwerthin* **Max** *yn tyfu a thyfu, nes mae'n troi mewn i grio.*

Bobi Ty'd yma.

Bobi *yn gafael yn* **Max**.

Mae crio **Max** *yn araf, yn stopio. Yna:*

Max Ti meddwl da ni gyd, jyst yn un jig-so mawr?

James O na, *here we go!*

Max (*bron yn gyfeiriad uniongyrchol, bron yn torri'r pedwerydd wal*) Ella bo ni. A bo ni gyd di neud allan o lot o ddarna sy neud un jig-so massive 'sti. A pan ma petha newid, ma'r jig-so'n symud . . . rhei darna, a rhei *pobl* yn symud yn agosach ata chdi, rhei ddim yn symud, a wedyn rhei, wel, rhei yn gadal chdi . . .

A ti gwbo be sy annoying? Y teimlad *blin* na sy di bod tu fewn fi, y darn blin na sy gen fi . . . dio ddim di rili gadal fi. Dwi meddwl ma hwnna am cymyd bach mwy o amsar. A fel, Mam fi, ella bo gen hi darn bach o, o grievio tu fewn hi, a ella ma hwnna angan bach o amsar fyd.

Di jig-so byth yn gorffan, na.

Da ni'm yn stopio neud jig-so.

Mae **Bobi** *yn rhoi'r clap fwyaf i gymeradwyo analogy* **Max**. **Max** *yn chwerthin.*

Max Dwisho tweakio fo dwi meddwl.

Bobi Tweakio? Tweakio, be?

Max Dwi lyfio enw newydd fi 'de, a fi *sy* bia fo . . . Ond . . . dwisho bach o Elin yn fo.

Bobi Bach o pwy?

Max Elin. Mam fi. Nath hi ddeu sa fo gallu bod mwy Cymraeg. So, ella . . . un dwrnod . . . Macsen?

Bobi Lyfio.

Max Fi fyd. Ac ella, un dwrnod, Macsen *Dafis*.

Bobi Ond Dafis di surname . . . (*Sylweddoli.*) O!!! Ella!

Max Ella.

Bobi Sa Mam chdi lyfio hynna.

Max Bysa, ma Elin yn licio chdi, licio ni 'sti.

Curiad.

Am galw hi'n Elin o hyn mlaen.

TAWELWCH – **Bobi** *yn edrych ar ei watsh / ffôn.*

Bobi So . . . mai bron yn hannar nos, bron yn penblwydd fi . . .

Max O crap! Sori!

Bobi Na, na, ma'n iawn! Ti jyst di bod yn selfish prick fel Nick!

Max *dwylo ar ei wyneb, embarrassed.*

Bobi Dwi jocian!

Max Penblwydd Hapus.

Curiad – **Max** *yn symud yn agosach at* **Bobby**.

Max Dwi'm di cal dim byd i chdi ddo.

Bobi Ma'n iawn.

Max Crap boyfriend.

Bobi So da ni *yn* boyfriends eto?

Max Yndan . . . Os ti. . .?

Bobi *yn rhoi cusan i* **M**.

Mae nhw'n cusanu.

Mae'n nhw'n tynnu i ffwrdd o'r gusan.

Mae **Bobi** *yn estyn ei fag, mae jig-so yn y bag.*

Bobi Paid poeni am gal presant i fi ddo. Di prynu wbath, wel, prynu wbath i ni. . . /

Max Jig-so!

Max *yn edrych yn agos ar y jig-so.*

Max Jig-so, o . . . *fa'ma*?

Bobi Ia, dre ni, bob cornal.

Max *Mil* o ddarna?!

Bobi Gwbo ma'n lot, a dwi heb gyfri'r darna so dwi'm yn gwbo os /

Max (*chwerthin*)   M'otsh.

Curiad.

So, gyfar penblwydd chdi'n sixteen, tisho neud jig-so?

Bobi Dwi lyfio jig-so.

Curiad.

Max A fi.

Y diwedd

Cefnogaeth

Trans Aid Cymru: transaid.cymru

Mae Trans Aid Cymru yn sefydliad cydgymorth sy'n gweithredu'n bennaf yn Ne Cymru. Maent yn grŵp amrywiol o bobl drawsryweddol, rhyngrywiol ac anneuaidd sy'n ceisio atal tlodi ac unigedd yn y gymuned draws trwy ddarparu grantiau, cefnogaeth, gwybodaeth, gofodau cymdeithasol ac ymgyrchu. Maent yn cefnogi unrhyw un trawsryweddol, rhyngrywiol, anneuaidd, neu unrhyw un sy'n cwestiynu eu hunaniaeth rhywedd yng Nghymru.

       Cyfrannu: opencollective.com/transaidcymru

Mwy o gefnogaeth
North Wales TINN: instagram.com/northwalestinn
Meddwl: meddwl.org
Mind: mind.org.uk
Meic Cymru: meiccymru.org
Shout: giveusashout.org
The Mix: themix.org.uk
YoungMinds: youngminds.org.uk
Diverse Cymru: diversecymru.org.uk
Mermaids: mermaidsuk.org.uk
Paned o Ge: paned-o-ge.wales
Stonewall Cymru: stonewallcymru.org.uk
Aubergine Cafe Cymru: auberginecafe.co.uk

Dy Enw Marw/Your Name Is Dead

BY ELGAN RHYS IN COLLABORATION WITH LEO DRAYTON

Notes on rehearsal and staging, drawn from a workshop with the writer, held at the National Theatre, October 2023

How the writer came to write the play

As a queer playwright, Elgan Rhys finds it important to centre queer and marginalized voices. It was important to him that young people connected to and felt seen in the play and so wanted to collaborate with a young person during the writing of it. Rhys picked the age of 16 as a transitional age, and the theme of agency as a starting point. Rhys met with a group of young people in Cardiff and asked them what was on their minds. From this workshop, Rhys decided to collaborate with a young person who wanted to develop as a writer; Leo Drayton. The idea of agency stuck, and led to the idea of exploring our relationships with our names and how a name can give agency, especially in the case of people who are trans.

Drayton talked about his trans experience as a 16-year-old, an experience that was challenging and sometimes lonely, and one that felt very different to the cis experience. Having to answer so many questions and deciding how you want to be labelled was an additional challenge to that of cis 16-year-olds. He talked about how when he changed his name, he expected things to slot into place, but, although it felt empowering, it brought up new challenges. Drayton wanted the play to explore the complexity involved when you question why you are called what you are called and the links to nationality, family history and more.

As Welsh people, nationality felt particularly important to both Rhys and Drayton due to the Welsh identity often feeling marginalized within the United Kingdom. This was partly why it was so exciting for Rhys to write a play in both Welsh and English for National Theatre Connections.

Rhys and Drayton connected with a queer and trans group in Cardiff at The Queer Emporium, who were invited to give their thoughts. The group raized the importance of educating the companies of young people working on this, as there are some big subjects that might be raized which feel highly politicized by the current political climate. These subjects include: terminology trans people prefer, the lived experience of trans people, and how it affects their interactions and their navigation of spaces.

Approaching the play

Lead director Gethin Evans invited the group to collect ideas under four headings:

- Key Questions (Questions the play asks)
- Key Challenges (Challenges that the play gives you)
- Gestures (What is the play's gesture to the world?)
- Images (Any images that spring to mind)

Here are some of the gestures the group saw in the play:

- The gesture of naming ourselves/others
- A gesture of a facade: how we present ourselves, our truth, and how we fulfil expectations of others
- The gesture of labelling
- A gesture of community
- A gesture of rejecting fitting in
- A gesture of truth
- A gesture of lies
- A gesture of grieving
- A gesture of celebration
- A gesture of connection and community to young trans people

Rhys saw the play as a gesture of agency and one of connection. M reaches a place of trying to take his agency through naming, but also realizing it is important to share agency with others.

Key Questions
- How does it feel to be a young trans person in North Wales?
- How does it feel to be supported by a parent as a trans/queer young person?
- How does it feel to be rejected by a parent as a trans/queer young person?
- How does it feel to be the partner of someone trans?
- How does it feel to a young queer person questioning their identity?
- How do we share agency?
- What's in a name?
- How do parents of young trans people feel about name changing?
- How can grief and celebration coincide for trans young people and their parents?
- How does it feel to become a parent?
- How does it feel to support a trans partner or friend?
- How does class affect this?
- You might find different questions. If so, what questions did you find and how might they inform your version of the production?

Here are some of the images offered by the group:

- The cricket bat
- The coffee shop conversation – stillness amongst the chaos of mundane things
- Puppetry of the jigsaw

- Books/schoolwork
- Grabbing/physical owning of something
- Local place and identity
- Chip shop
- Paperwork and forms
- Duos and pair work, within an ensemble
- Anger
- Barista
- Props
- Colour vs black and white
- Party hats and party rings vs a funeral vibe that's being forced on M
- Birth/rebirth and death
- Smoke
- Gender reveal parties
- Confetti
- Party chaos vs solo moments

Here are some of the challenges the group identified:

- The physicality of the play
- Transitions – this play has many transitions
- Clash of the ensemble and movement meeting the naturalistic – how can a concept support this?
- Sensitivity – to the subject, as well as to the act of educating a company and an audience; to the act of creating empathy for this marginalized group for company and audience; to the act of creating complexity, and to the relationships between students and parents
- Naturalism of dialogue with characters of many different ages all being played by young performers

Approaching the subject matter of the trans experience was something the group talked about. They agreed it is important to have some education and consultation from the trans community for the production.

Some of the participants had already begun organizing conversations with a trans representative from a charity, or got members of the trans community in their institution or local community involved in helping to educate themselves and preparing to run workshops with their cast. Including different voices and embracing the complexity of how people navigate the experience seems important, and making sure any trans young people don't bear the burden of educating their company.

You may also want to think about how the play will feel in the context of your performance venue and the people who will attend. What is the community response to trans people, and how can you position your audience in the right place before they arrive? Can there be a pre-show discussion or statement? Is it a post-show discussion? It is a gallery with an exhibition? Is it a programme note? And how does your company want to do it?

It is of the utmost importance that the trans young people in your school, theatre company or youth group feel held and respected in this process, just as much as the rest of the company.

There are some resources at the end of these if you are looking to connect with charities or organizations who might have resources to help young trans people.

Themes

Themes identified by participants included:

- Agency
- Gender
- Identity
- Language
- Love
- Parenting
- Motherhood
- Institutions
- Solidarity
- Community
- Body
- Masculinity/Toxic masculinity
- Trust
- Abuse

Structure, style and transitions

Rhys writes in a very naturalistic style, but there is freedom for everything around it to be non-naturalistic. Evans noted that on previous productions with Rhys, naturalistic dialogue has been accompanied with ensemble movement to great effect.

The play contains a lot of transitions (both literally and with regards to the subject matter), so Evans suggested these could become a significant element in terms of the style of the production. What story can you tell for M and his mother in the transitions? How can they lose or pass each other? How might the jigsaw feature? What metaphor do you want to build for M's and Mam's experiences? How can the transitions echo M's gender transition, or his transition to adulthood, or his mam's transition.

Language

The language in this play is very much tied to nationality and setting. If you are doing this play outside of Wales then do not change the nationality of the characters or the setting in North Wales. However, it is more important to be truthful to the story than to get the accents right. Better to allow your actors to focus on the story, subject matter and the character, than be faced with the big challenge of accents, and it is important to avoid stereotypes.

It feels important that some Welsh words or phrases remain, but if you are not doing a Welsh accent then feel free to remove the words marked with an asterisk. There are more guidelines on this in the note from the playwright with the text.

Characters and characterization

Evans talked about identifying the overarching want and need of each of your characters, then giving them a hobby, and bringing in that hobby for people. For example, some soil for a character who likes gardening.

Rhys said that the idea of a young mum started to present itself in his writing, and it made Rhys think about how someone's name and identity changes when they become a mother. So, it seemed interesting to look at these journeys alongside each other. Mam/Elin has a full journey through two babies, a failed marriage and then gets her name back. She's been aware since becoming a mother that she's lost her identity, and perhaps M's journey has sparked something in her to think back through that journey of loss and regaining. This renaming and M being old enough to do that is also part of evaluating her situation as a parent when her child is becoming an adult with agency. M is turning 16 and gaining power. Her journey is also one of grieving for the name she gave and perhaps a little for the daughter she thought she had, before M was out. Mam is very much supportive, but it is important not to deny the complexity of those feelings.

Rhys had originally meant for the play to only feature young people as the characters, but as he was writing, older characters entered into the story (Mam, the employees at the care home and the elderly resident). It is important to make sure these characters don't feel like stereotypes.

Approaching the text

Here's an approach for looking more closely at the script. You may want to do this yourself and then do it together with your cast to explore your characters and their objectives.

Read the scene and stop every time there is a fact. The workshop looked at Scene Six.

Some of the facts the group noted:

- Bobby is helping M try on clothes.
- M doesn't fit the clothes yet. (Presumably this feels attached to their gender identity.)
- M's mum is still missing.

Then read it again and note all of the events. The events are moments when something changes.

The group found these events in the first part of Scene Six.

- M snapping 'it doesn't fit me'
- 'Or would you lie?'
- 'I was there today'
- 'For money'
- 'Are you embarrassed by me?'
- Bobby doesn't answer
- Bobby doesn't answer after 'I'll love your new name when you change it'
- 'It's just a lot'
- 'And I probably won't change my name'

After you've done this, think about what the characters want in this scene. In Scene Six, the group initially thought they want to be noticed and to be understood, and M wants clarity.

Look to find the juiciest conflicting wants for every character. After deeper discussion, they then decided that M wants Bobby to say they love their new name, but Bobby does not want to.

Exercise: Forward and Back

Once you've looked over the script with your cast or your individual cast member for that scene, ask the actors to stand opposite each other. If you do this exercise, it's useful to have explored the motions of towards and away in your warm-up so that your cast has that in their movement vocabulary and is tuned in.

Get the actors to read their character lines without much intention, and take steps towards or away from the other person. Get them to do it slowly. Break each line down into each thought, use the punctuation to help you see where a thought ends. Explore every action as towards or away. Then keep trying it and make different decisions – what does it reveal? Discuss how it felt, where it felt right or wrong, or where you discovered something unexpected.

This exercise is useful to strip exploration back to simple intentions. It can help to build the foundation of intention. It's not about being perfect, it's about finding what resonates.

There is another level to this exercise where two people might explore Bobby and M further. Two other people feed the lines to the actors, and the Bobby actor and M actor repeat their line while either pushing or pulling the actor. This is an interesting way to further explore the intentions in the scene. If your cast aren't confident with contact, then you could use bamboo sticks balanced between one finger of each person.

A further level of exploration is to include the events in these exercises. You can click every time there is an event (which you will have identified previously.) Each time there is a click, actors should acknowledge the event that has just happened and how it might affect the movements they are doing or about to do.

Casting

The casting for this production needs to be handled carefully, as the writers want it to be respectful of the trans community. Therefore, it is a balance between what is best for your process and your company, alongside what feels supportive of the trans community in a time when it is still very difficult to be trans.

There are lots of things to consider when asking a trans person to play this role:

- Are they comfortably out in the environment and community you are working in? Do their parents know? Are they too close to any of the issues at this moment? Will it feel empowering? If it doesn't, is there someone there to support them?
- Do they have the support they need within and outside of the cast to support them through the process?
- Do you have the resources to get other trans people involved, so that they don't have to carry the educational burden of the play?
- Does the person cast have the resources to handle a potentially complex audience response from the production?

The writers would strongly encourage casting a performer who identifies as trans-masc. If this proves difficult, here are the best next alternatives (in preferred order):

- a performer who identifies as trans-femme, and switch M/Max's gender identity to trans female too (see below for changes to script)
- a performer who identifies as cis male, and keep M/Max as is

Please do not cast cis female for this role.

If you do cast a trans-femme performer, please change the following in the script:

- M's pronouns from he/him to she/her
- change M to A

- change Max to Angie
- change Macsen to Angharad (pronounced ang-HA-rad)
- any reference to M as a boy in present day, change to girl
- any reference to M as a girl in the past, change to boy

Another suggestion from the workshop was the possibility of casting collectively, and having a group of young people all play M. Drayton observed that that would reflect the complexity of gender, and it would be important to make sure there were slightly more male/trans masc. actors than cis female.

What is vital is that trans people are involved in making this show in some way. They may be backstage roles, they may be people who come in to have conversations with the young people, or they may be not 'out' and still find discreet ways to be involved.

With regards to the gender of other roles in the cast, it feels important to have people playing roles where they identify with the gender. But saying that, you might want to heighten the absurdity by having no matching genders between actors and characters – it is your production. Rhys observed that it did feel important for James to feel real in his toxic masculinity, so it would be preferred for his role to be played by a cis male. What is clear is that gender and how people are read with regards to their gender does really matter in this play, and it needs to be thought about carefully.

Production, staging and design

Rhys suggested finding a concept which helps you bring out the central question of the production. Some of the ideas around chip shop papers and other paperwork came up from one group.

Participants explored how they might approach the party scene. They were asked to consider how they would describe the experience M is having. What words would they use? Words from participants included: lonely, chaos, sensory, overwhelming.

Other images/moments discussed included the bat and the fact the mother gives it to him. What does the bat represent? Why is it given? What action comes with it? Does the mother give him the bat because she has made him angry? Or does she give him the bat because he has her bold energy too? Or is it a complex mix of both?

Think about what actually happens in the reality behind the stylized energy scene. What is the actual real time of the sequence? A few hours? A whole night? Look at the facts in the scenes either side and find what makes sense to you. Freewrite what you see in that sequence then go back to what can be teased out. What sensory elements could help you heighten the tone? Keep testing different ideas to see which ones resonate with you and your company.

It could be that M got drunk and memories blur with reality. And the cricket bat was something he had found himself to take to his dad's.

The group then took their write-up of ideas and wrote down how they would make is in no more than seven steps. What are the seven steps that would get you to the finished project?

Top tip: You could build the choreographic sequence out of a warm-up every week.

Some of the ideas the group came up with:

- Throw a party in a school hall, then choreograph a party from the results.
- Play around with movement languages as warm-ups. For example: playing around with limited space, then big space.
- Explore soundscapes – what can you use to make them vocally or otherwise? What recorded sound might you want to use?

Exercises for use in rehearsals

An introduction exercise

Give the group ten seconds to introduce their name to everyone in the circle. Then get them to do the same again but they must also receive the other person's name. Then, same again, but four seconds instead of ten.

Warm-up games

Evans pointed out the importance of finding a game the group loves and using it to build skills.

Dance circle

Start a move and then see what someone brings to change the dance. Add noises. You can pass it round the circle or send it to the next person, or if your group is more confident you can just start and see what changes and develops within the group.

Partner warm-up game 'Hey'

Start by tapping your knees to a rhythm, then every second go you point either left, right or up. Keep doing that sequence of knee tap, then point in one of the three directions, then knee tap, then point in one of the three directions and so on. Now turn to a partner and do the sequence together, keep pointing in whatever direction (left, right or up) you as an individual want to point. If you both point in the same direction then after the next knee tap you point at each other and say hey. And then go back to the game after the next knee tap. All this should be in rhythm. Keep going and you can gradually speed up until someone makes a mistake. When someone makes a mistake, the other person wins.

Hand-slapping routine for groups

Stand in a circle with your palms raized to the people either side of you. You say the following words rhythmically: *double double this, double double that, double this, double that, double double this that.* On *double* tap your hands against the people either side of you, on *this* tap your hands palm to the people on either side, on *that* the same but back of hands. This is a good routine to enable people to connect in or connect out at the end of a rehearsal.

Wah

Standing in a circle, someone puts their hands up and brings them down together, palms together to point at someone while saying 'wah'. The person receiving puts their hands together above their head and says wah, and the people either side of the receiver in the circle put their hands together near the receiving person's stomach with a wah. Then the person who received brings their hands down to point at someone else with another wah and the game continues. The wah's should feel rhythmic, and if someone makes a mistake or hesitates they sit on the floor but stay in the circle. This makes it more challenging as the game goes on, as you have to be aware of who you are next to and who is still in.

Crabs

A slightly more physical way to decide between two winners at the end of a game. Ask your two winners to stand with their palms to each other. They should be close enough that their arms are slightly bent. They then crouch down so they are balanced on their toes with their palms still touching. When you say go, they have to try and knock each other over. They are not allowed to move or adjust their feet, and they can only push on the other person's palms. The last to fall over and touch the floor or move their feet wins.

Original Zip Zap Boing

The moves are:

- 'Zip' – Send a zip to the next person either clockwise or anticlockwise. The 'zip' is accompanied by the player holding both hands together and pointing at their target.
- 'Zap' – Send a zap across the circle to someone the player makes eye contact with.
- 'Boing' – Rebounds a zip or a zap back to the last player. The 'boing' is accompanied by holding both hands up in front of you.

Yeehaw Zip Zap Boing

The moves are:

- 'Yeehaw!' – Sending zip becomes a yeehaw with a knee slap in the direction you are sending it.

- 'Hoedown' – 'Yeehaw' can only change direction with a person saying hoedown and moving their arm as if pulling on a lever, like a train driver honking their horn. This bounces the 'Yeehaw' back the way it came.
- 'Ride 'em Cowboy' – If someone gallops into the circle saying 'Ride them cowboy' then everyone has to gallop to a new space in the circle.

You can make your own version using well-known phrases from TV shows like *EastEnders*, or other topics relevant to your group.

Developing your ensemble

Evans ran a physical exploration and advized it was something you could build up over weeks, and was useful to warm up your actors to playfulness, intention, movement and ensemble. You might want to use part of it to start an exploration of character.

Take your time going through them so individuals can explore each layer you build. This exercise in the workshop took around 25 minutes.

Evans gave the following instructions:

'Stand in a large circle and shut your eyes. Find a neutral place, feet flat on floor, knees relaxed, relax your jaw and breath.

Take a breath and feel air coming from your feet up to your knees, then a breath from your feet up to your waist, then a breath from your feet all the way up to your bellybutton. Then all the way up to your shoulders. Then up to your shoulders and down to the tips of your fingers. Then all the way up to the top of the head. Another filling the whole body and out.

Open your eyes. Cross the circle and find somewhere new to stand in the circle.

Do the same thing but you're going to all arrive back into a circle at the same time. Make sure the circle stays roughly the same size. Keep going until you all reach the edge at the same time.

Take a walk around the room finding all the little details.

Then you're all going to collectively arrive at the sides of the space, then all start walking at the same time without saying anything.

Then take focus from the room to the absolute unique geniuses you are walking past. See each other.

Then take your gaze from the individuals, to a sense of awareness of everyone in the room. You should feel like you know where even those behind you are.

Then without saying anything, all go to the centre of the room and pause together, and without saying anything, start walking again.

Now play with changing direction.

Next, explore how your journey can be affected by those around you; maybe there is a moment of gently following or finding a flow with a person, then breaking away and keeping walking. Start to really notice the pathways you cross and think how those airflows affect you. What else can you find? Can you disrupt a pathway of someone else? How can you work in more than just twos? Just keep being influenced by the patterns of movement in relationship with each other.

Without talking, all together you are going to work out how and where you stop together, and then start again.

By now you should have: patterns of movement, a sense of relationship to each other, space.

Next explore a sense of pace. One is stillness, seven is utter chaos. What would you name the current pace?'

(For the workshop leader: It can be useful to set an intention, for example, 'this feels like the pace you would have if you need a wee', 'you've just arrived at the beach', etc. Move the participants through the paces up to seven and then down to still. Then start testing them.)

'Collectively as a company you are going to travel from a zero then work your way through the paces up to seven, and then back down to stillness. All without talking. Be specific and move together.

Enjoy the change in breath as you slow down.

Walk around the room and find journeys towards things that you notice. Once you reach the thing, find a new thing to journey towards. Do you take direct journeys or longer journeys?

Then play with the journey of moving away from things. Play with the idea of how quickly or intensely you move away from things.

Now play with both the speed and intensity of moving away and towards, so you might go from zero per cent to 100 per cent.

Now instead of objects, take that exploration to the people around you in the room. Explore different speeds, and the slowest and fastest moves away and towards.

Then relax and travel at the speed of three. You now have zero to seven speed, space, patterns, towards and away with the levels of intensity from zero to 100. Play with all these things. Find the limits.'

You can take people out and give them moments to observe, before sending them back in.

If at any point individuals look like they are tense, encourage them to loosen their jaws and connect with their breathing.

At the end of the exercise, invite participants to return to a circle collectively, take a moment, then sit and take a moment to reflect on the exercise.

This is a way to create a language that everyone can tap into. It can be the beginning of an improvisation for your cast and, because they know it, they can be playful routes into creating images, like the party image for example.

Get to know your groups and see when to introduce each element; you might want to introduce these bit by bit rather than all at the same time. Evans would also add the skill of repetition, physical levels, balance – how does it start to tip and where does that take you? You can add character into this as well and can explore character intention, as well as images from the play or props.

Question and answer with Elgan Rhys

Q: Where is the play set?
A: Elgan has set the play in his hometown of Pwllheli, though it is never stated. It could be imagined in another northern Welsh town.

Q: Is Ceridwen's sadness about Frida Kahlo because of her naivety?
A: Absolutely!

Q: What is the relationship between Bobby and M? Are they tactile? At what stage is their relationship?
A: They are in the early days of their relationship and just getting comfortable with each other. They have probably kissed, but not done a huge amount more.

Q: Did James crash Dad's car?
A: No, the bruises are a result of abuse.

Q: Where's Mam?
A: She's gone for some space, potentially for a drink with a friend to process the big day – she is grieving for the name she gave and perhaps a little for the daughter she thought she had, before M was out. Mam is very much supportive, but it is important not to deny the complexity of those feelings.

Q: How did Bobby and M meet?
A: School, but this relationship is relatively new and not at the 'I love you' stage yet. M was presenting female when they met; this is opening up complexities to Bobby and may have him questioning his identity.

Q; Where's Dad?
A: He's always near, but in one scene he has gone to pay the electric bill.

Q: Why does Mam not want to know the gender of her baby?
A: Because she doesn't care, as long as they're healthy.

Q: What's M's birth/previous name?
A: Elgan Rhys and Leo Drayton agree that it doesn't need to be known.

Suggested references

Gendered Intelligence (Charity)
TV shows: *Sex Education*, *Heartstopper* (please check age appropriateness for your group)
Leo Drayton recommended some poems by transgender poets about their relationship to the body:
    Anna Akana – 'How Trans Men Expose Female Privilege'
    Drew Anderson – 'A Self-Made Man, Coming Out Transgender' (KCET)
    Atlanta Team – 'Public Trans' (Brave New Voices (Finals): Youth Speaks)
    Cameron Awkward-Rich – 'Break-Up Letters' (Button Poetry)
    Cameron Awkward-Rich – 'Obligatory' (Button Poetry)
    Max Binder and Mo Crist – 'Real Boy/Real Girl' (Button Poetry)
    Edwin Bodney – 'The Night My Father Accompanies Me to a Gay Bar' (All Def Poetry x Da Poetry Lounge: All Def Poetry)
    rafael casal – 'Barbie & Ken 101' (Def Poetry)
    rafael casal – 'first week of a break-up' (def poetry | Brad Conover)
    Jacie Cloutier – 'The Trans Poem' (Raw Word)
    Dia Davina – 'In Between' (Vancouver Poetry House)
    Dia Davina – 'A Boy Called Everything' (Vancouver Poetry House)
    Daughters – 'Transgender Poem' (skylarkeleven)
    Leo Drayton – 'The Welsh me, spoken word poem' (Roundhouse Poetry Slam 2022)
    Ian Drewery – 'Dear anonymous', a slam poem
    Darling Fitch – 'War of Attrition' (Spoken Word Poem) Transgender Poetry
    Justice Gaines – 'Letter from Xem' (Button Poetry)
    Andrea Gibson – 'Queer Youth Are Five Times More Likely to Die by Suicide' (Button Poetry)
    Golden – 'To the Transphobic Cis White Gay Men at Pride' (Button Poetry)
    Alysia Harris and Aysha El Shamayleh – 'Hir' Poem about trangsgendered youth (ARDIOUS NEVENTREN)
    James Hartzer – 'Trans Boy's Broken Toe' (Button Poetry)
    Him Within – 'Transgender' (spoken word, Nathan Lux Fortune)
    'I didn't mean to' – an LGBTQ spoken word poem (Max Keane Poetry)
    '#IStandWithTrans' Transgender Awareness Week (spoken word poem, bp)
    Leyla Josephine – 'I Think She Was a She' (spoken word, guardianwitness)
    Kay Kassirer – 'Angry Trans Poem' (Vancouver Poetry House)
    Adrian Kljucec – 'Mirrors' (Brave New Voices 2012: Get Lit – Words Ignite)
    Maya – 'Straight People' (Queeriosity: Youth Speaks)
    Lee Mokobe – A powerful poem about what it feels like to be transgender (TED)
    Emory Oakley – 'How to Be Transgender' (Vancouver Poetry House)
    Sam(ira) Obeid – 'Pigtails' (Button Poetry)
    Charlie Petch – 'how to tell if a poem is trans or not' (Vancouver Poetry House)

Quaint – 'Transparency' (Vancouver Poetry House)
Rat the King – 'This is a Transgender Poem' (spoken word by Rat G)
Sam Rush – 'Neverland' (Button Poetry)
'Save Me I'm Gay' // ABQ Slams (Da Poetry Lounge)
Ollie Schminkey – 'How to Love Your Body in 10 Easy Steps' (Button Poetry)
EJ Schoenborn – 'What Gender Are You?' (Button Poetry)
EJ Schoenborn – 'A Series of Responses to Transphobic People Answered by Sharks on the SyFy Channel' (Button Poetry)
Shihan – 'This type love' (Def Poetry Jam: Kenyan Poets Lounge)
Ethan Smith – 'A Letter to the Girl I Used to Be' (Button Poetry)
Sonder – 'What It Is to Be Trans' (Vancouver Poetry House)
Sonder – 'To the Girl I Never Was But Killed in the Process of Realizing That' (Vancouver Poetry House)
Mojdeh Stoakley – 'Trans Prayer' (Button Poetry)
Ray Stoeve – 'Dysphoria Days' (Ray Stove)
Alok Vaid-Menon – 'Trans/Generation' (UnErase Poetry)
Floyd VB – 'I Have a Body' (Vancouver Poetry House)
Ashe Vernon – 'For Anyone Who's Listening' (Button Poetry)
Miles Walser – 'T'rans Health Clinic' (KilometersW)
Miles Walser – 'On Vanity' (SlamFind)
Miles Walser – 'Hierarchy' (Button Poetry)
'We Are Transgender | A Poem by Gray Crosbie' (BBC The Social)

Trans YouTubers who make trans-specific content:

Jammidodger – @Jammidodger

Samantha Lux – @_samanthalux

Songs with trans vibes:

'Why Am I Like This?' – Orla Garland

'Second Puberty' – Jake Edwards

'This Is Home' – Cavetown

'Boys Will Be Bugs' – Cavetown

'A Better Son/Daughter' – Rilo Kiley

'The King' – Ethan Jewell

From a workshop led by Gethin Evans
With notes by Stephanie Kempson

KISS MARRY PUSH OFF CLIFF

by Josh Azouz

Josh Azouz is an award-winning writer working across stage, screen and radio. His work has been shown in the UK and across the US. Recent plays include *The Get* for BBC Radio 3; *Once Upon a Time in Nazi Occupied Tunisia* at the Almeida; *The Night After* for Headlong and BBC 4; *The Mikvah Project* at the Orange Tree, The Yard and for BBC Radio 4; *Buggy Baby* at The Yard; and *10,000 Smarties* at the Old Fire Station.

Josh Azouz won a Channel 4 playwright award for *Buggy Baby*. The LA Theatre Works production of *Once Upon a Time in Nazi Occupied Tunisia* is nominated for best audio drama at The Audies. In addition to writing, Azouz works as a theatre director, teacher and has been an associate artist at The Yard and MUJU (a Muslim-Jewish theatre company).

Josh Azouz lives in London with his wife and two young children.

Characters

Marco
Ricky
Kiara
Jess
Tamer
Carl
Franky the Dog
Noush
Giant Moth

Writer's Note

Marco, **Ricky**, **Kiara**, **Jess**, **Tamer** *and* **Noush** *have all just finished their A-Levels.* **Carl** *is a year older. The character's names are suggestions for genders, but if unachievable, companies may cast differently and change pronouns to suit their needs. The part of* **Giant Moth** *might be realized by a chorus of actors/dancers/puppet/single performer or imagined in an entirely different way.*

The play takes place on the cliffs in Eastbourne over two days and nights in June. Perhaps avoid tents or large pieces of set that close down the playing space/minimize the vastness of the environment.

On the whole the characters speak fast and think on the line, not before the line.

To counterpoint this speed there are beats, pauses and blank spaces on the page. These are silences of varying lengths which should be filled with thought action.

( ) = words in brackets should be played by the actor, but not voiced.

. . . = a hesitation, an unspoken thought, a trailing off, an easing in.

One

Marco *is asleep in his sleeping bag.*

Ricky, **Kiara**, **Jess**, **Tamer** *and* **Carl** *sit on a log in silence.*

Franky the Dog *is with them, panting.*

It's the moment after a decision has been made.

Pause.

Ricky *walks over to* **Marco**.

Ricky Wake up.

Marco Mm.

Ricky Wake up.

Marco Mm-mm.

Ricky I'm serious get up.

Marco In a bit.

Kiara Marco wake up!

Marco *remains asleep.*

Beat.

Ricky *drags* **Marco** *around in his sleeping bag.*

Marco OK OK OK! (I'm awake.) Head . . . my head . . .

Tamer *gives* **Marco** *a drink of water.*

Marco What was that stuff last night?

Jess Tequila.

Marco The Mexicans know how to party.

Carl The bottle said it was from Ipswich.

Marco Yeah but who knows what Aztec day of the dead shit is in that recipe – what's that smell? Is that cow . . .? Oh my God I've rolled in cow shit. (**Marco** *kicks off his sleeping bag.*) I can't deal with that at the moment. Get me home. Gimme bus fumes any day. Why is everyone up?

Carl It's camping, you always get up early.

Jess The sun has got his hat on hasn't he Carl?

Carl I suppose he does Jess.

Tamer Should have brought an eye mask Carl.

Ricky (*as if reminding the group*) Last night was mad wasn't it.

Marco Just a bit. That sausage fight, and then the hedge diving, who knew Jess was next level at hedge diving, I'd never have made that bet. Why am I outside?

Kiara You must have been sleepwalking.

Marco That could have ended badly. (*Gesturing cliffs*.)

Ricky Yeah you'd be washed out to sea before anyone knew you'd gone missing.

Jess To be fair the fall would kill you first.

Marco It's all coming back to me – the tent was a sauna and Tam kept farting. That's why I slept outside.

Ricky Look, Marco, we've got something to tell you.

Marco . . . Who's we?

Kiara All of us.

Marco . . . You've *all* got something to tell me.

Jess Yes.

Marco Been snaking on me while I was in the land of nod.

Tamer It's not like that.

Marco Go on then.

Ricky Tell him.

Tamer Me?

Ricky Said you would.

Tamer I mean it doesn't really matter who tells –

Ricky You've been close since primary.

Tamer And what?

Jess I swear to God will somebody just tell –

Ricky Be my guest, Jess

Marco TELL ME WHAT?!

Kiara We'd like you to camp somewhere else tonight.

Marco What?

Kiara We'd like you leave this place and camp somewhere else.

Marco What?!

Jess Or do whatever. You don't need to camp. But yeah. Leave.

Marco Is this a joke?

Jess/Carl/Ricky/Kiara No.

Beat.

Marco Tam?

Tamer Yeah this isn't easy cos, I do, really, respect you and –

Marco Respect me?!

Tamer Let me finish, Marco – so what it is yeah, is, some of the things you say and in particular last night, are just sort of . . . *not on.*

Kiara You make me feel sick.

Marco Wow what did I say?

Ricky It isn't just about the words, it's the intention –

Jess The trouble with words is you don't know whose mouths they've been in.

Kiara Right, yep, um what happened last night crossed a line.

Marco What exactly did I say?

Carl It definitely doesn't need repeating.

Marco Hold on is this a prank?

Ricky No.

Marco Yes it is.

Ricky This is not a prank, we're asking you to leave.

Kiara Telling you, it's not a question

Carl Alright, K, that's not nice.

Kiara None of this is *nice*, we're asking someone we've been friends with for time to *go.*

Tamer However bad it is for you, it's worse for Marco.

Marco HELLOOO!

Ricky Tam do you have a problem?

Tamer No!

Jess You out of all of us should be behind this.

Tamer And I am – hundred per cent!

Marco Tamer?!

Tamer You make me feel ashamed.

Marco That's how you feel about yourself.

Tamer This is what I'm talking about-

Marco Tam – no – this isn't – I don't care what you are –

Jess Sounded like you cared last night.

Marco This isn't happening – you know me – *you know me*!

Kiara We can't stand it anymore.

Marco Stand what?!

Ricky We've tolerated you for years, but now school is over we don't have to tolerate *shit*.

Marco What is this?!

Jess It's an intervention.

Marco That's when you save a drug addict – not this – I don't even know the word for this!

Ricky Excommunicate.

Marco Big word, Rick!

Jess Never heard of it.

Ricky It's like at my church, when you cast someone out.

Jess Someone like who?

Tamer Like infidels.

Kiara Can we please get back to the point –

Ricky We're excommunicating you Marco. Never contact us again.

Beat.

Marco I just say stuff to wind you up.

Kiara You're saying the past how many years – when did he start changing?

Jess Two, three years ago.

Kiara So the past three years have been one big wind-up?!

Marco Yes! I don't care about any of that stuff – just – (all of you)

Ricky Pack up Marco.

Marco Ricky you literally lived in my house last year.

Ricky And it was horrible.

Marco ?! Jess?

Jess This is painful now, but long term maybe it's for the best.

Marco For the best?! We talk! How has this never come up?!

Jess I did try and tell you.

Marco No you didn't, and you say every thought that comes into your head.

Tamer That's true, girl doesn't have a filter.

Jess Sorry I'm honest.

Kiara We're getting distracted again –

Marco Yeah let's get back to destroying a friend *that's a vibe*!

Ricky You're making this harder than it has to be.

Marco *I'm* making this harder?!

Kiara There's no need to get so emotional.

Ricky You must have seen this coming.

Marco How?!

Tamer Come on, man major side-eye.

Marco That's side-eye – that's not this – this – *this*?!

Carl Excommunication.

Kiara Look the longer you draw this out the more deep it is for everyone.

Marco How can you say that after last night?

Tamer Last night?

Kiara That was nothing.

Tamer Marco?

Marco Nothing happened.

Jess Carl saw.

Carl I did, yeah.

Marco Oh.

Tamer What happened last night?

Jess Marco kissed Kiara.

Marco I think you'll find Kiara kissed Marco.

Kiara For like four seconds.

Marco Yeah no drama.

Carl More like ten seconds. But it's cool. K and me aren't . . . like we're not . . . are we?

Tamer Wait you two actually kissed?

Ricky Yes! Keep up!

Kiara It was nothing, Marco kisses everyone.

Tamer Not everyone.

Marco Am I being chucked out for kissing you?

Kiara No.

Marco Carl?

Carl This is nothing to do with me.

Kiara Carl?!

Carl Babe, I'm behind you, but this is your crew's thing.

Ricky It's not about the kiss, the kiss was nothing.

Marco You're right the kiss *was* nothing, only a moment of *pure joy*. Cos we'd finished school and we were finally on this trip, and Carl's van didn't break down and Tam had made a banging playlist and Jess had brought a top selection of snacks. There was no traffic on the A23 – it was all so perfect – and then we found this incredible spot – and we made a fire an actual fire, and when Kiara started singing the little mermaid only half ironically, I was hyped, not gonna lie I was buzzing – but that kiss could have been with anyone – even you Carl – cos it was like a kiss of friendship –

Kiara Stop, Marco, stop –

Marco Seriously, I'd give my life for any of you, so you get why I'm finding all this a bit hard to WRAP MY FUCKING HEAD AROUND?!

Ricky It's very simple: we want you to leave.

Marco . . . You're scaring me.

Jess There's nothing to be scared of.

Marco . . . Tam?

Tamer I'm sorry, Marco.

Ricky Go take your tent, or we can bin it.

Marco What did I say? Just tell me – or don't – but whatever it is, I didn't mean it, I'm sorry.

Pause.

Die. Literally die all of you.

He leaves.

Franky the Dog *whimpers sadly.*

Two

Franky the Dog You faces, you nose, you banana, the sea – sniff sniff, wet – sniff wet woof – No Marco. Marco gone. Miss miss miss miss miss – tennis ball. Heart explodes. For tennis ball. Best friend. Love. Eternity. Bum scratch bum scratch bum scratch, alone, game. What game? Where game? I'm. I'm. Not. Nothing. Where's Ricky? Sniff sniff, no Ricky. Hungry – Yes! YES! Sniff sniff only cow – too big – big cow – moo woof – dreaming now . . . BISCUITS – tongue dry – sound – almost silence – ear drum – blood flow – BISCUITS – Where's Ricky? Ricky keeper of BISCUITS! God! Biscuit god! Lick bum – Marco. Sad. Happy. Sady haddy scary. Ahhhhh – Marco gone. Big ahhhhh – Marco gone. Me hungry. Where's Ricky? Eat. Eat you. Death. I'm twelve years old. Not long. Not long left. Bum scratch. Sniff sniff. You. Me. Lost.

Ricky *enters.*

Ricky Franky, look what've I got.

He is holding a biscuit. **Franky** *leaps at* **Ricky** *and devours the biscuit.*

Kiara *arrives with a mattress.*

Kiara All the others feel firm.

Ricky *sets up a foot pump and starts pumping up the mattress.*

Kiara Bet you wished you'd bought the electric pump.

Ricky (Are you joking.) Think about our quads. We'll be busting shorts all weathers.

Ricky pumps

You gonna finish with Carl then.

Kiara Why would you think that?

Ricky . . .

I just thought you'd split up when you started uni.

Kiara You thought wrong.

Ricky Will you see other people?

Kiara I'm not too sure.

Ricky Have you not had the talk?

Kiara We're gonna have a chat about it yeah.

Ricky And what d'you reckon? Going exclusive, or what happens in Glasgow stays in Glasgow, or like do bits but tell each other everything –

Kiara Yeah it's really none of your business.

Ricky Glasgow is missions.

Kiara Ricky.

Ricky Not exactly a vibe is it, getting a twenty-five-hour train.

Kiara Calm down twenty-five hours.

Ricky You might as well split up and just enjoy your summer.

KIARA *looks at* **RICKY** *curiously.*

Pause.

KIARA Should I take over?

Ricky I'm good.

Kiara It's painful watching you.

Ricky *sits.*

Kiara *pumps.*

Ricky D'you feel bad?

Kiara About what?

Ricky Marco.

Kiara It was always gonna happen.

Ricky He started to cry a bit.

Did you see that?

I felt bad then.

Kiara You can't just run your mouth and expect to get away with it.

Ricky What if he genuinely believes none of it?

Kiara Stuff was said. And I'm done tolerating stuff I hate. Like when people stand about and do nothing, genocides happen.

Ricky . . . Is this the same?

Kiara Whatever, there's a time and a place for jokes, but when your friend is going through a crisis, they need support.

Ricky You've got muscular legs.

Kiara Why are you looking?

Ricky Cos I'm looking.

Beat.

Kiara *Look* somewhere else.

Beat.

Ricky *lays back on the grass.*

Franky *licks* **Ricky**'s *face.*

Ricky Stop.

Franky *licks.*

Ricky FRANKY!

Kiara What's up with her?

Ricky   She wants a walk.

Kiara   Can't she run around here?

Ricky   She could, if I'd brought a tennis ball.

Franky The Dog   Woof woof!

Kiara   I've got a conker. (Does that work?)

Ricky   You carry around a conker?

Kiara   Long story.

Ricky   If I chuck it, it'll probably get lost.

Kiara   I've been meaning to get rid of it.

Ricky   Franky, smell this, not food OK, it's a tennis ball, this is a tennis ball. I'm going to throw it and then you'll fetch it back.

Kaira   Wait – what if she swallows it by accident?

Ricky   No she's too smart for that. Aren't you, Franky?

Franky the Dog   Woof woof.

Ricky *throws the conker.* **Franky** *runs off after it.*

Pause.

Kiara   I swear it looks *more* deflated.

Ricky   I told you we should have bought the electric pump.

Pause.

Kiara   When Marco got upset, it annoyed me. I think I lack basic levels of compassion.

Ricky   You'll probably make quite a good doctor.

Pause.

Kiara   I can't see Franky.

Ricky   She'll be ripping apart some bird.

Kiara   I thought that was a cat thing.

Ricky   Franky isn't like other dogs. Why d'you kiss Marco?

Kiara   . . .

To test Carl.

Ricky   . . . So you *are* into him.

Kiara   Yes.

Ricky   Only. I thought kissing Marco meant you *weren't* into Carl.

Kiara Yeah I can see how you might think that.

Ricky And I thought kissing Marco might actually mean you're into me.

Kiara . . . Now that's some weird logic.

Ricky Well, you're not into Marco, are you?

Kiara No.

Ricky So . . .

Kiara I'm with Carl. And the five of us –

Ricky The four of us now.

Kiara Okay the four of us are tight and we shouldn't mess with that.

Ricky God what must it be like to be you.

Kiara How d'you mean?

Ricky To be able to have anyone.

Kiara That's not true.

Ricky Be with me.

Kiara . . .

We don't get with friends.

Ricky Kissing Marco sorta violated that rule.

Kiara No it didn't, cos it wasn't a romantic kiss.

Ricky I thought I saw some tongue.

Kiara That's in your mind.

RICKY Come on K . . . don't make me . . . explode.

Kiara . . .

Jess, **Tamer** & **Carl** *enter with wicker baskets full of blackberries.*

Kiara Christ, it's like we're in an Enid Blyton novel.

Tamer Enid who?

Kiara Blyton – ask your parents.

Tamer Enid Blyton sounds haram.

Ricky Probably isn't. Probably should be.

Jess Thank you for the delicious blackberries Jess, oh no worries, how did you get them? Well, let me tell you. So we're walking across this field, and we come across this bramble with hundreds of blackberries. There we are, picking and plucking, plucking and picking when out of nowhere this crazy farmer comes charging towards us – the boys drop their baskets and dash – leaving me to face the crazy farmer alone. Course then I realize. It isn't a farmer. It's a scarecrow.

Ricky (*eating*)   So these are *fresh* fresh.

Carl   Are they bollocks, they're from Tesco's.

Tamer   Yeah we ended up going into Eastbourne.

Carl   Buying wicker baskets – Jess's idea.

Jess   Quite funny, no?

Kiaira   Seriously?

Jess   Yes babes.

Ricky   You should have just picked the fresh blackberries.

Tamer   Jess is superstitious about scarecrows.

Jess   I'm not superstitious, but the scarecrow meant we were on somebody's land and I'm not really into thieving.

Tamer   That didn't stop you in Tesco's.

Kiara   What's in the bag?

Carl   Oh yeah. Jess's bullshit distracted me. Look. (*He opens the bag.*)

Ricky   What is it?

Carl   A rabbit.

Kiara   Is that real?

Carl   Yes.

Ricky   Oh my God!?

Kiara   You killed a rabbit?

Carl   Technically Tamer killed it.

Tamer   Carl very much helped.

Carl   I did help yep.

Kiara   How?!

Tamer   You don't wanna know.

Ricky   Are you fucking mad?!

Jess   Why the surprise? We told you we were going hunting, and look, we've returned with an afternoon snack and dinner. What have you two achieved? That mattress looks flatter than paper.

Kiara   Am I supposed to be impressed?

Carl   I was thinking it might be tasty on the barbecue.

Kiara   I'm vegan.

Jess And Tam is going through a halal phase it's all gravy.

Carl I got you some cauliflower bites.

Ricky You'll kill it but you won't eat it. Interesting.

Tamer I killed it quickly and like humanely, so extra blessings and that.

Ricky Jesus, Tam – who are you?

Tamer At the minute, a really devout Muslim.

Kiara (*to the group*) You come back with blackberries and a dead rabbit. Why can't you be normal and just pick up some weed?

Jess We got something a lot stronger than weed. Funny story that actually –

Carl Here we go.

Jess So we're outside Café Nero, it gets to quarter past, Tam says he wants a mocha, Carl needs the toilet.

Carl I *did* – that wasn't an excuse.

Jess They leave me alone – *again*!

Tamer The guy arrived early.

Jess A Ford Fiesta playing, I wanna say… Eastbourne Drill, parks up on the corner. Flashes it's lights.

Ricky Not exactly subtle for a drug dealer.

Jess This guy doesn't give a shit. This guy's professional. Am I about to be gunned down in broad daylight?

Tamer You're the customer, why would you be gunned down?

Jess He might think I'm an informant. He was jumpy at first, thought he was meeting *a Carl*.

Kiara Why d'you leave her?

Carl Them sausages had gone right through me.

Jess All good though. His name was Gavin. More acne than I expected. Drove around the block and sold me enough hallucinogens to move these cliffs to Norway. His words.

Ricky When he said Norway did he actually mean France?

Jess No I think he meant Norway cos he's a drug dealer, not a geography teacher.

Carl Jess thinks she's Escobar cos she bought drugs from a child out of his mum's Fiesta.

Jess You can only play who's in front of you, *lad*.

Carl I'd have sucked back in the poo not to hear about it.

Kiara Roll us a spliff then?

Jess Alright babes steady on.

Kiara We're doing a lot of talking and I want to get high already.

Jess So we can forget the awful thing we've done.

Ricky What awful thing is that?

Jess I dunno. He had it coming. Let's get mashed.

Jess takes out a little bag.

Kiara That's not weed.

Jess Very observant, K. It's acid.

Ricky Whoa.

Kiara I'm not sure how I feel about acid.

Jess We only finish school the once.

Ricky I don't wanna mess up my brain.

Carl, *who has been inspecting the bag, eats one of the 'pills'.*

Tamer Did you just chew one?

Carl This isn't acid.

Jess Yes it is.

Carl Trust me it isn't.

Jess Are you like some acid expect?

Carl I just know a Mento when I taste one.

Kiara Mento, as in the sweets?

Jess There's an A on the front.

Carl What, 'A for acid'?'

Tamer Oh my days.

Ricky This is priceless. So Gavin the drug dealer bought a pack of Mentos, and drew an A on each of them?

Kiara *tries one, so does* **Ricky**.

Kiara Yep Mentos.

Ricky Nice, actually.

Carl You mug.

Jess Shutup why are you here? Shouldn't you be down the post office collecting your pension?

Kiara Don't be a cow, Jess.

Jess Sorry, K, it's just I felt like I was out with *grandad*.

Carl I'm in the year above.

Jess It was the sheer amount of time he took in the toilet.

Carl Well you try squeezing out fourteen pounds of nutty Armageddon.

Kiara ... That's something your dad would say.

Carl I'm OK with that. I like my dad.

Kiara Bit of a brute though, isn't he. And I don't mean in a sexy caveman type of way. I mean like a thug.

Carl Thought you liked thugs.

Kiara Not really, they're ... predictable.

Franky the Dog *enters, her mouth covered with blood. Drops the conker at* **Kiara***'s feet.*

Ricky Franky ... what have you eaten?

Franky the Dog *just whines, a little guilty.*

Ricky What have you eaten, girl?

Ricky *takes* **Franky***'s face in his hands.*

Ricky You'll make yourself sick if you keep eating everything you see.

Tamer Should we go look for Marco?

Everyone looks at **Tamer***.*

Kiara I'm surprised at you, Tam.

Tamer He likes attention, he doesn't mean any of it.

Ricky Tell yourself that or Marco's been hating you since day dot.

Tamer I still think we should look for him.

Jess It's getting dark, you can't just walk around the cliffs on your own.

Tamer So come with?

Kiara Chill, Tam. Have a Mento.

Ricky Yeah. Have a Mento.

Beat.

Jess *picks up the bag of Mentos and turns around to do something to the log.*

Beat.

Carl Should we go out for dinner?

Kiara What?

Carl I dunno. Just. We could have a meal.

Kiara Yes I know what dinner is.

Carl There's a lot of restaurants in Eastbourne. Something I noticed as we drove in. After we could go to a hotel.
Not like an Ibis or a Travelodge . . .
An inn. We could stay in an inn.

Kiara The five of us?

Carl No, Kiara. You and me.

Kiara *turns away from* **Carl**.

Kiara What are you doing babes?

Jess I'll show you when I'm done.

Ricky There's quite a lot of waiting around in camping isn't there. You just sit about and wait. What for? Sunset.

(*To* **Kiara**.) I s'pose we could go for a hike.

Beat.

Kiara Alright.

Beat.

Carl I first went camping with my dad. He's a massive *Doctor Who* fan and wanted us to go somewhere in Wales, the idea being, we'd do a day trip to the Doctor Who Experience in Cardiff. Dad had a two-man tent, but I got it into my head I'd sleep on my own. My mum said are you sure? I was only nine or something so it would have been legit to camp with Dad. The weekend before we went, I practiced putting up my tent in the garden. I didn't want my older cousins mugging me off and my dad pulling rank and forcing me to share. And then the day arrives, and my mum is fussing loads. She's trying to pack my owl teddy. But I put my foot down on that one. You can't take an owl teddy on a camping trip with men. Anyway, we get to the site. I set up my tent. It looks fab. The first night – no problem. I wake up feeling like a champion. But the second night is a different story. A panther had escaped from the local zoo, and mauled a man, to the point where this man was in hospital fighting for his life. My dad begged me to come and stay in his tent, but I was like nah, I can handle some cat. So there's nine-year-old me in the tent, my toes so cold I've stuck them in a beanie, holding myself in the foetus position, and the wind, I swear the wind is going to blow me away – then I realize I haven't locked the tent. I've zipped up the inside but not the outside, and the inside door is a sheer type of material – any passing panther will see a man cub on a plate. I start to pray. I think this is how I'm gonna die. What a fool. Why didn't I share with my dad? He's six foot four and sleeps with a hunting knife. I figure, if this is how I'm gonna go, I'd like to see my attacker coming. I turn over in my sleeping bag to face the door – I obviously don't consider that a panther won't necessarily enter via a door – but nine-year-old me has sussed it out that this was the direction he'd come. I'm shaking. This is the end. And then my knee scratches against something. I reach down and discover a pocket sewn into my sleeping bag. In the pocket is the little owl teddy. My mum had sewn a pocket into my sleeping bag and packed my owl.

Beat.

Kiara   What happened with the panther?

Carl   I dunno.

Kiara   OK, but what happened after you found the owl?

Carl   I gave it a cuddle didn't I.

Turns out that story isn't about a panther.

He stares at **Kiara**.

Beat.

Ricky   Wanna go for that hike then?

Beat.

Kiara   Maybe later.

Beat.

Jess   Finished!

She steps aside to reveal a lot of beer bottle caps stuck on the log using chewed-up Mentos as adhesives.

Before we leave, we'll hide this log in a bush. When we come back next year, we'll take out the log and add some more bottle caps. And the year after the same. The year after the same. In a few years it'll be the shiniest log in England. Be like a beacon to our crew.

They all stare at **Jess**.

Tamer   Yeh I'm gonna go look for Marco.

Three

Gale-force winds.

A shivering **Marco** *takes off his shirt. His boots. His trousers. He's about to take off his boxer shorts –*

Noush *runs to meet him.*

Noush   Stop!

Marco   I'm burning up!

Noush   Put your clothes back on!

Marco   I'm on fire!

Noush   You think you are – you're not!

Marco   How do you know!?

Noush   Paradoxical undressing.

Marco   What!?

Noush *wraps him up with clothes and blankets and pairs of socks and a sleeping bag.*

Noush   You're suffering from hypothermia, and bizarrely your body is instructing you to take your clothes off which is leading to more heat loss. The next thing you'll be doing is getting down on your hands and knees and digging a hole.

She hugs **Marco** *very tight.*

Noush   Don't get any ideas I'm saving your life.

Noush *lets go.*

How do you feel?

Marco   I'm not sure.

Noush   Hot or cold?

Marco   Warm.

Noush   Warm's good. Here – drink this.

Marco *drinks.*

Marco   Thanks. I should be getting off.

Noush   Maybe stay in the warm a bit longer, restabilize your body temperature.

Pause.

Marco   How do you power that? (*A strange-looking heater.*)

Noush   Solar.

Marco   Cool.

Beat.

Noush   Where were you going?

Marco   Eastbourne. My friends are camping near Birling Gap. I stupidly volunteered to go get some drink.

Noush   Is there a camp site in Birling Gap?

Marco   Not officially, we just set up wherever looked epic. My friends thought we should go nearer the cliff, like not the edge, but towards it, cos . . . I don't even know you know. My friends like to live dangerously. They're pretty wild.

280   Josh Azouz

Noush There's actually a pub in East Dean, which is like 2 kilometres away from Birling Gap. You'd have been better off going there for drink.

Marco I'll know for next time.

Noush Yeah.

Beat.

Marco What's your name?

Noush (Anoushka.) Noush. It's always been Noush.

Marco Hi, Noush. I'm Marco.

Noush I know.

Beat.

Marco How do you know?

Beat.

Noush I'm in your year at St Luke's.

Marco (Oh.) Yes you are. Sorry. I'm bad with faces.

Noush And names.

Marco And names.

Noush I'll try not to take it personally, but I can't promise anything, Marcus Jason De Souza.

Marco You're freaking me out a bit now.

Noush I'm not a stalker or anything.

Marco Yeah yeah yeah course not.

Noush I just know who's in my year. Probs cos we've been in the same year for the last seven.

Marco Yeah I think if I didn't have hypothermia, I would have recognized you straight away.

Beat.

Noush Do you want a Celebration?

Marco Huh?

Noush *gives* **Marco** *a chocolate.*

Marco *smiles and eats the chocolate.*

Marco How many nights are you camping?

Noush The foreseeable future.

Marco That's a long time.

Noush I'm gonna get bad results. So I need to not be at home when my parents find out. They'll go insane and drink themselves stupid.

Marco Right.

Noush I figured I'll stay out here until at least a month after the results. If I do need to return home, by that time they should be dead.

Marco Dead?

Noush From the drink.

Marco You're not close then.

Noush Too close. They have no boundaries.

Marco I wish my parents were more like that.

Noush You don't. They give my ten-year-old brother vodka.

Marco (*quietly*) Whoa.

Noush Yeah. I had to get away. I sold my grandfather's watch and came here.

Marco What d'you get for it? If you don't mind me asking –

Noush No it's cool. Forty-five quid.

Marco . . . so . . . how are you gonna survive?

Noush I'm gonna get a job in Eastbourne. Save up some money. Rescue my brother in the autumn. Get some sort of witness protection so my parents can't find us. They'll be devastated, but if my exam failure doesn't do the trick, the disappearance of their children *will* explode their liver. Why didn't you just get the bus to Eastbourne?

Marco I don't know.

Noush Mad you've been walking all day.

Marco What are the chances you'd be camping a few miles from a whole load of St Luke's lot?

Noush Yeah it's spooky. But that's the universe . . .

Marco Yeah.

Noush She always has a plan.

Beat.

Noush This is definitely not a chirps, but I've got a six-man tent. You can stay until the storm breaks.

Beat.

Marco (*moved*) Thank you.

Four

Ricky, **Jess**, **Kiara**, **Carl** *all huddled under an umbrella.*

Franky *sits, sniffing a newspaper.*

Pause.

Carl We could drive back tonight.

Ricky Not a fan of the rain?

Carl Come on, this is rubbish.

Ricky I thought you'd been camping with men.

Carl Yeah but now I've got a car, I don't hang about for stuff I don't like.

Ricky More of a van than a car. Quite dodgy when you think about it. Like why did you buy a van? What's your game – people trafficking?

Kiara Will you both shut up!

Beat.

Jess Tam's been gone nearly three hours.

Kiara Should we split up and look for him?

Carl No phone signal, we wouldn't know if the other person found him.

Ricky Forget Tam.

Jess Sorry, what?

Ricky He's eighteen years old. He chose to go searching for a racist homophobic terf.

Jess He went to look for his friend.

Ricky Yeah and it's a bit of rain, it's not a sandstorm in the Sahara Desert. He most definitely checked into a B&B.

Kiara So what are you saying?

Ricky I'm saying, we stop worrying about Tam, we certainly stop talking about Marco and we enjoy our last night. Let's play truth or dare.

Kiara Cool, I'm going to bed – are you coming?

Carl Yep.

Kiara Night babes.

Jess Night.

Carl & Kiara *walk off.*

Beat.

Ricky Got something to say Jess.

Beat.

Jess Come. Let's go look for Tam.

Ricky No. Out of principle no.

Jess What principle?

Ricky Searching for Marco is allying with Marco.

Jess So you're just gonna stand here?

Ricky I'm gonna go to bed.

Jess God this is terrible . . . this is so . . .

Ricky Are you crying?

Jess No . . . just . . . we've been dreaming of this trip . . . then we kick out Marco, and Tam goes off, and it's weird with Carl being here, it's just . . .

Ricky Things end Jess. And it's not deep, it's life. Are any of us actually going to keep in touch from September?

Jess What?

Ricky You'll be doing art stuff, I'll be in Bristol, Kiara will be in Glasgow, Tam will be boxing, Marco will be in Leeds. Maybe this is the end . . . and maybe this is a natural sort of thing that happens, like my brother isn't friends with anybody from school. All his friends are from uni or work and maybe that's the way it goes. You can't hold onto friends just coz of history. Did you see it all working out differently?

Jess Shut up.

Ricky Like we'd be in each other's lives forever? Like on stags, at weddings, christenings, circumcisions –

Jess I swear you don't even believe what you're saying.

Ricky All pitching up at the same cemetery, reserving plots side by side for when the time comes.

Jess As if you're not gonna try see Kiara after September.

Ricky I'm not. And you should wake up and realize that friendships die. It's natural.

Jess There was nothing natural about what we did to Marco.

Ricky Sort of was. Like his uncertainty, over, I dunno – *the holocaust*. That's morally weak. To survive you cut out the weak.

Jess We're not chimps.

Ricky Not just chimps, it's natural to cut out the weak, the diseased, Marco's views are sort of diseased.

Jess You afraid of catching something?

Ricky I'm just sick and tired of his filth.

Jess Would you have been so amped to cut him out if it weren't for the kiss?

Ricky That's got nothing to do with it.

Jess I saw your face. The life drained out of you, cos you always thought, if K was ever gonna get with someone in our year, it'd be you.

Ricky Is it jokes being the local busy bee?

Jess Better than some guy who took seven years to find his balls – I heard about your little *move* –

Ricky I don't need to listen to this.

Jess What a numpty.

Ricky You're lucky you're a girl.

Jess Sorry?

Ricky I said you're lucky you're a girl.

Jess Are you *actually* threatening me?

Ricky No, I'm just glad you're a girl.

Jess And I'm glad you haven't got a gun! I mean seven years of unrequited love, we're talking massacres. (**Ricky** *moves a step closer to* **Jess**.) – what you're gonna step to me now?! I will lay you out like butter!

Beat.

Tam *enters.*

Ricky Alright Tam nice stroll?

Tamer I'm soaked.

Jess (*faux seriousness*) We were very worried about you.

Ricky Jess actually was. Did you find him?

Tamer (*Dry*) Yeah I found him.

Jess Well, you tried, that's better than the rest of us. You're definitely the kindest.

Ricky Kindest or weakest?

Tamer We should have put Marco to bed, or told him to shut up, or *educated him.*

Ricky We literally tried to do all those things.

Tamer I just hope he's found shelter.

Ricky It's Eastbourne not Everest!

Tamer I'm gonna burn for this.

Jess Tam . . .?

Ricky That guilt – *dash it*. You took a stand. That's courage.

Tamer You got a funny definition of courage bro.

Ricky Whatever, I'm going to bed.

(*To* **Jess** *as a peace offering.*) Laterz margarine.

Jess What, like your threat is now just water under the bridge?

Ricky Hold up, that's a tune . . .

He sings the guitar riff from 'Under the Bridge' by the Red Hot Chili Peppers. Walks off.

Tamer Margarine?

Jess 'Lay you out like butter, spread you like margarine.'

Tamer Have you two been beefing again?

Jess Just some silliness.

Tamer What have we done.

Jess Stop Tam.

Tamer You don't let someone you care about –

Jess He shamed you, Kiara was crying, Ricky was biting his lip –

Tamer He was drunk –

Jess Marco says that stuff all the time!

Tamer But it's on us to look past that bit of him and overcome –

Jess Why should that fall on us?

Tamer Cos that's in our control. It isn't his fault that he believes what he believes.

Jess Yes it is – who else?

Tamer It's hard to believe the right things.

Jess You do a lot of defending of Marco.

Tamer Yeah . . . well . . . I . . .

He exhales.

Jess Oh . . .?

Tamer Yeah.

Beat.

Jess Since when?

Tamer Since . . . *I knew*.

Jess How? How can you though?

Tamer *shrugs*.

Jess You kept that candle burning on the d-low.

Tamer I know he doesn't like boys, so . . .

Jess Are you sure Marco doesn't like you? He likes Amir Khan.

Tamer I think there's only room in his life for one brown boxer.

Jess Our friendship group is very weird, everyone keeps falling in love.

Tamer After he left, I was almost relieved. (But now I miss him.)

Jess Don't stress Tam . . . there'll be so many boys out there.

Pause.

Tamer When I'm thirty-five, if I haven't found anyone, can we get married?

Jess (*flat*) My gosh. So romantic. Also – why are you assuming I'll be alone?!

Tamer . . . You're an artist . . . You'll be alone.

Jess . . .

With cats?

Tamer Not even.

Five

The next morning. Brilliant sunshine.

Marco That was the overall gist.

Beat.

Noush I thought they were your friends.

Marco They are.

Noush Don't you like them?

Marco I do.

Noush So why say those things?

Marco It just came out.

Noush Like a waterfall of hate.

Marco Yeah – *what*?

Noush Why did it just come out?

Beat.

Marco After Kiara kissed me, she turned to Jess and gipped.

Noush Gipped?

Marco Vomited.

Noush Was your breath bad?

Marco Pretended to vomit, not actual vomit. I just lost it. And it's not difficult for me to think of these things, because I'm around this stuff at home. Even the gestures come very easy.

Noush There were gestures?

Marco Yes.

How is this funny?

Noush It's definitely not, it's . . . it's just at school . . . (No.)

Marco What?

Noush I always thought . . .

Marco Go on.

Noush I always thought you were quite, boring.

Marco I am. I'm very boring.

Noush (*smiling*) Stop –

Marco I am properly boring – my favourite ice-cream is vanilla, I like playing *FIFA*, if it's a sunny day I'll go sit in the park.

Noush And you've got all these problematic views.

Marco I obviously don't believe these problematic views.

Noush That's almost worse. You're just hurting people for what, a laugh?

Marco I didn't mean to hurt anybody.

I'm gonna go back and say sorry again.

Noush What, beg?

Marco If that's what it takes.

Noush I dunno you know. Like those things you said . . . they're not exactly forgettable.

Marco For thirty seconds I lashed out, but then it passed, it passed. And the nice boring Marco came back. Ninety five per cent of the time that's me.

Noush Has this sort of thing happened before?

Marco . . . Yeh.

Beat.

Noush Why does it keep happening if you don't believe it?

Marco I don't know.

Beat.

Noush There was a day in April which was really hot. I sat in my bedroom for thirteen hours . . . doing London Heathrow to Singapore Changi on Microsoft flight simulator.

Marco Do you wanna be a pilot or something?

Noush No.

Marco Wow.

Noush What I'm saying is we all do stuff we regret.

Marco (*sadly*) I guess.

Noush And I don't wanna bitch about your mates, but none of that group are great. Like Ricky is smug. Kiara is a cynic. Tam is weak. Jess doesn't know who she is, so can't be counted on for loyalty. They're all sort of terrible people.

Marco Yeah I just really miss them.

Noush So go do conversion therapy for all your weird views – if that doesn't work ask them to do a lobotomy and remove all the problematic bits of your brain. Hey, what if your left with only being able to eat and poo?

Marco Noush, seriously, what should I do?

Noush You're asking the wrong person.

Marco Why?

Noush Cos we wouldn't be friends in the first place.

Marco Got too many friends have you?

Noush Chris and Alysha are gonna visit once I'm set up.

Marco Just visit?

Noush They're friends, not soul mates.

Marco Whatever.

Noush You don't even know who Chris and Alysha are do you.

Marco Yes I do.

Beat.

Noush Apologize then. Say it was all a wind-up and obviously not what you believe or actually think.

Marco What if I believe a bit of it?

Noush *flinches.*

Pause.

Marco Your six-man tent is immense, it's like a small house.

Noush Mm.

Marco Do you think I could stay one more night?

Noush I've got stuff to do tonight.

Marco Oh.

Noush Yep.

Marco Sorry I didn't know who you were yesterday.

Noush No worries.

Marco Why did you decide to come here of all places?

Noush I'd heard about Beachy Head and wanted to check it out.

Marco Wait, this is Beachy Head?

Noush Yeah.

Marco This is Beachy Head.

Noush Yes!

Beat.

Marco (Oh no.)

Beat.

Marco (*casual*) What you up to tonight then?

Noush Nothing special.

Marco Are you sure?

Noush Am I sure?

Marco Don't do it!

Noush Don't do what?

Marco Like don't – I get that your life isn't easy – but people will miss you – your brother – parents – there are counsellors who can help – medication – just please don't do what I think you're going to do tonight.

Noush What are you talking about?

Marco *You know.*

Noush I don't?!

Marco You're alone, depressed, metres from a cliff edge.

Noush   I'm not depressed.

Marco   We're at Beachy Head, it's famous for that sort of thing!?

Noush   For what sort of thing?!

Marco   I've heard about this. When people have decided to do it, they're very chilled, you'd think they'd be nervous or crying, but no, when people decide *to do it*, their anxiety disappears – cos they've finally made a decision.

Noush   What are you talking about?!

Marco   Don't kill yourself, please don't kill yourself!

Noush   Why would I do that?!

Marco   I don't know!

Noush   *Should* I kill myself?

Marco   Obviously not!

Noush   What, cos I've got shit parents, you assume that I'd wanna kill –

Marco   No no, I just assumed, cos you're *here*, and you said you had stuff to be getting on with tonight – *alone*.

Beat.

Noush   I was just going to read my book.

Beat.

Marco   I have completely misjudged this situation. That happens, I get an idea into my head, I'm like a dog with a bone. You try rip it from my jaws, I won't let go. Stubborn. Stupid. Dumbo wasn't just a Disney elephant, he was reincarnated as *me*!

Noush   Nah, you're spot on, I was thinking of killing myself.

Marco   Oh my God I dunno if you're joking or not?!

Noush *smiles.*

Beat.

Alright.

Stay tonight.

At your peril. (*Fake evil laugh.*) Mwhah-hahahahaha.

Six

Franky the Dog *is tied up.*

Franky the Dog   Woof woof woof woof woof – no listen – saving – me saving – woof woof woof woof – sniff sniff – rabbit – Franky eat – tongue flap flap – ouch – ouchy ouchy – pinecone – sniff sniff – fire, warm, cooking, cooking smells – dread

– terrible dread – Marco sappy – must save – save who? Bum lick – undecided – miss miss miss miss miss – tennis ball. Heart explodes. For ball. Best friend. Love. Eternity. DREAD. Sniff sniff woof. Nothing. Signs? Save Ricky. Game. What game? Games over. Lost energy. Dying young. DREAD – WHERE? Wet bum sniff woof tongue flap – FRANKY EAT – FRANKY HUNGRY – why dread? Not psychic. Not *not* psychic. Save Ricky. Future. Woof. Save Ricky – woof woof woof WOOF WOOF WOOF WOOF WOOF WOOF WOOF WOOF WOOF WOOF WOOF WOOF!

Seven

The sounds of howler monkeys and other animals not native to Eastbourne. It's more like a Central American rainforest.

Noush *is staring at something out at sea.*

Marco *is trying to focus on the same point but keeps checking* **Noush**.

Marco   I can't stop the thoughts.

Noush   The thoughts are just passengers.

You're the driver.

Driving a car the size of the universe.

Marco   OK.

Noush   The thoughts sit in the back. They don't tell you where to go.

Marco *slurps his tea. It breaks* **Noush**'*s concentration.* **Marco** *whispers 'sorry'.*

Marco *starts falling asleep.*

Suddenly wakes.

Marco   Something is happening.

Noush   Good.

Marco   Something is rushing around me.

Noush   Let it rush

Marco   Noush!

Noush   I'm here.

Marco   It's rushing, rushing, am I moving?!

Noush   Yes! (*But he isn't.*)

Marco   I'm moving!

I'm so fast, look how fast I'm going, I'm on an avalanche, I'm on top of an avalanche, riding it, surfing it, WHAAAAAAAAAAAAAAAAAAAAAAAAAAA AAAAAAAAAAAAAAAAAAAAAAA Look at the sky! Look at the sky, Noush!

Noush I'm looking!

Marco We're flying! We're flying!

Noush Keep going!

Marco There's something in my stomach!

Noush Let it out!

Marco I'm scared!

Noush Don't be scared, let it rip!

Marco What is happening!?

Noush Explanations are for later! Be a snake and swallow the experience whole! Let it rip! Let it rip! LET IT RIP!

Marco *opens his mouth as wide as it can go.*

Something leaves his body.

Marco *smiles, it is deeply pleasurable.*

From the edge of the cliff a **Giant Moth** *approaches.*

It is beautiful and inviting.

Marco *and* **Noush** *are spellbound.*

The beat of the **Moth**'s *wings turn musical.*

The **Giant Moth** *starts to dance. It's wonderful.*

The **Giant Moth** *leaves.*

Noush *switches off a speaker. The sounds of the rainforest, etc . . . stop.*

Beat.

Marco What the fuck did you put in that tea?

Noush Just mint.

Marco Bollocks just mint!

Noush What you *saw* was your mind.

Marco In my mind?

Noush I didn't say that.

Marco OK what's going on?!

---

1 Or substitute 'hell'.

Noush You saw something for the first time, it's a surprise, I mean I wasn't expecting the moth to visit tonight.

Marco You've seen that before?!

Noush Yes. The fact it came tonight, during your first training – the moth must sense potential.

Marco Potential?

Noush To be a warrior.

Marco Riiiiiight.

Noush There are things the world won't immediately show us, we have to peer beneath the surface of things and truly *look*.

Beat.

Marco How d'you get into all this?

Noush I was working in McDonald's . . . and one day, in the dairy freezer, I found my manager screaming at the milk, holding a clump of her own hair. We got talking. Turns out the manager used to have warrior visons, but the visions had recently abandoned her. She started training me to use my mind, teaching me lots of shamanic practices. I think she hoped that by training me, she might rediscover her own powers.

Beat.

Marco I didn't see a moth.

Noush . . . OK.

Marco I didn't see anything.

Noush OK.

Marco Whatever *you* saw, wasn't real.

Noush Are things only real if we agree on their realness?

Marco . . .

This is nuts, you're nuts, I just wanted to go camping with my mates.

Noush And you can get back to that tomorrow.

Marco I have to go home tomorrow. I've got a shift in Sainsbury's. Kiara is at Greggs. Ricky is on a building site. Tamer is in training – and Jess . . . does Jess. The plan was – do our jobs, and then meet up at night and weekends and . . . (**Marco***'s voice cracks slightly*) that was the plan . . .

Noush Plans change.

Marco I bet they're all laughing at me now.

Noush They might not be thinking about you at all.

Marco *swallows; that thought is unbearable.*

Noush *puts her arm on* **Marco**'s *shoulder to support him.*

Pause.

Marco   What d'you mean . . . warrior?

Noush   I mean facing the world on your own.

Marco   That sounds . . . *shit*.

Noush   Sometimes, but you do get surprises.

Marco   (That doesn't make sense.) We saw that thing, *together*.

Noush   Imagine what you might experience alone.

Marco *wants to know and doesn't want to know.*

Marco   I'm so lost, Noush.

Noush   Try making one decision at a time.

Pause.

Marco   Might I see you after tonight?

Beat.

Noush   Make another decision

Marco *crumples.*

Pause.

Marco *stands.*

Marco   I'm gonna go back and see them.

Beat.

Noush   Be careful.

Eight

Midnight.

The group sit on blankets, perhaps surrounded by candles.

Ricky *might play the guitar.*

Jess, Tamer & Kiara *listen or sing.*

Carl *is asleep in* **Kiara**'s *lap.*

Franky *is chewing a book.*

The song finishes.

Tamer Mega stars.

Kiara Less light pollution.

Jess Say that five times.

Kiara Huh?

Jess It's a tongue twister.

Kiara Less light pollution less light pollution less light pollution less light pollution.

Jess Oh it's not.

Ricky Is there any rabbit left?

Tamer Just the carcass.

Ricky Not about that. How were the cauliflower bites?

Kiara Yellow.

Jess Mega stars mega stars mega stars mega stars mega stars mega stars – also not.

Ricky When is your next fight?

Tamer August the seventh.

Ricky You ready?

Tamer I gotta lose a couple of pounds.

Jess Carl is a bit of a lightweight.

Kiara Jacket potatoes makes him sleepy.

Jess I take the piss, but I actually think he's a top guy. Really happy for you, K.

Kiara Cheers, babes.

Ricky (*to* **Tamer**) Do you think you'll end up with a Muslim?

Jess & Kiara Whoooooaaaaaaaaaaaaaaaaaa.

Ricky It's just a question.

Tamer I'd like to. It'd make everything easier.

Ricky For who?

Tamer For me.

Kiara I can see that.

Ricky Wish you luck.

Jess What?! You'd be so sad.

Kiara How d'you know what'll make Tam sad?

Jess He'll be denying himself, admit you'll be sad?

Tamer If it was down to Marco, he'd frogmarch me into a mosque draped in a rainbow flag.

Ricky Good thing it ain't.

Tamer I dunno . . . maybe I am a coward.

Jess You literally step into a ring and get punched.

Tamer Nah that's me hiding being a one-two and an uppercut.

Jess So? What's wrong with hiding bits of your life? Monday morning you want a Muslim wifey, Monday night you want dick. Have both. Have everything. Accept no compromizes.

Kiara And the award to the most naïve goes to . . .

Jess *playfully pushes* **Kiara** *over.*

Beat.

Tamer Who's going to drop off Marco's tent?

Rick If he wanted it, he'd have taken it with him.

Jess I can.

Kiara Don't bother.

Jess I live nearest his house.

Kiara And?

Jess For karma, I wanna go back and make peace.

Kiara Hey look if you wanna prioritize doing that, then you prioritize doing that.

Jess *and* **Kiara** *stare at each other.*

Beat.

Jess Have you ever heard of the Dyatlov mystery?

Kiara No.

Jess A group of Russian students go camping in the mountains.

Ricky (*flat*) Wow you're actually telling a ghost story.

Jess It isn't a ghost story, it happened in like the 1950s. A group of Russian students go camping in the mountains, and they all die.

Kiara What a story.

Jess To this day we don't really know *how* they died.

Tamer Ooooooooo.

Jess Seriously. The rescuers found a tent covered in snow, but it had been slashed from the inside. As if someone was trapped in the tent and slashed their way to freedom. Two of the students were frozen in their underwear. Another student had her tongue and eyeballs missing. No one had died in the same way. Which is why nobody could work out what had actually happened. There's a load of theories. Had the students interrupted some military experiment and been killed in a cover-up? Had they stumbled onto an indigenous tribe and been attacked? Radiation fall-out was one theory. The abominable snowman another. Some locals said they saw balloons of light in the sky which meant it could be aliens. Or maybe it was just good old-fashioned bears. In the end they put the cause of death down as an avalanche. That never explained the eyeballs or the nakedness.

Kiara They have to write a cause of death, even if the autopsy was inconclusive.

Jess I reckon one student just lost it and killed everyone.

She stares at **Kiara** *for a moment.*

Carl Morning . . .

Kiara Hey.

Carl What time is it?

Kiara Just after midnight.

Carl I ate too many jacket potatoes.

Tamer Can we drive home?

Ricky What?

Tamer The tent is gonna be a furnace.

Ricky We're not driving back tonight.

Tamer We could be home in less than two hours.

Ricky What is wrong with you?

Jess Tam, it's the last night.

Tamer I just really need to sleep in my own bed.

Ricky I'm sleeping out here.

Kiara You'll get bitten.

Ricky I've got a lot of repellent.

Carl To be fair I feel alright, we *could* drive back.

Ricky Absolutely not – yo why don't we all sleep out here? That'll be something for the old memory box.

Beat.

Carl Let's drive home.

Beat.

Kiara OK.

Nine

Later that evening.

Ricky *and* **Tamer** *and* **Jess** *are asleep outside.*

Franky the Dog *keeps watch.*

Franky the Dog I've always fancied being a doorman.

I'm not really one for authority, so working for the police as a sniffer, or the army as a scout would never have fit. But working the door at a disco, I'd be good at that. I'd be nice and pettable at the beginning of the evening, but if someone had *had* one too many or was making fruity remarks to the ladies, I'd have had no qualms about clamping my jaws around the scruff of their collar and dragging them out. Now if you were to ask me on a scale of one to ten what my level of dread is, with ten being maximum dread – 'the apocalypse is nigh', and one being 'I'm a Barbie girl in a Barbie world' I'd say . . . four.

Marco *enters.*

Marco Hello Franky.

Franky the Dog Now it's eight.

Marco *and* **Franky** *stare at each other.*

Marco *takes a step forward.*

Franky the Dog Woof woof –

Marco I've just come back for my tent.

Franky *doesn't budge.*

Marco *takes out a tennis ball.*

Franky the Dog *eyes it up drooling.*

Beat.

Marco *throws it.*

Marco Go on fetch.

Franky No.

Marco Go on Frank.

Franky Definitely not.

Marco All good Frank, all good.

Franky You won't tempt me!

Marco Go get that ball! We can play all night!

Franky No no no! I will suppress my desire!

Pause.

Franky *runs to get the ball and disappears.*

Marco *runs over to* **Ricky**, *and delicately drags his sleeping bag away from* **Tamer** *and* **Jess**.

Beat.

Tamer (*eyes closed, half asleep*)   Marco?

Is that you?

Marco   Yeah.

Tamer   You came back.

Marco   Go to sleep, Tam.

Tamer   OK. In the morning yeah?

Marco   Yeah.

Tamer   Forget about the other night.

Marco   Yeah.

Tamer   You be you . . .

Marco (*sadly*)   Yeah.

He kneels down by the sleeping **Ricky**.

A horribly tense pause.

Marco *zips up the sleeping bag and locks the zip with a padlock.*

Ricky *wakes and starts kicking.*

Jess (*half-asleep*) Hey?

Marco Jess!

Jess . . . what's going on . . .?

Ricky *has managed to stand himself up and is jumping around shouting.*

Marco *panics, pushes* **Ricky** *to the ground, which starts him rolling towards the cliff-edge.*

Franky *returns with the tennis ball.*

Time might slow down.

Franky *starts barking and chasing the rolling* **Ricky**.

Jess *and* **Tamer** *are now fully awake and join the chase.*

Will they reach the rolling **Ricky** *in time?*

End.

Kiss/Marry/Push Off Cliff

BY JOSH AZOUZ

Notes on rehearsal and staging, drawn from a workshop with the writer, held at the National Theatre, October 2023

How the writer came to write the play?

Azouz wanted to write about unrequited love having felt it keenly as a teenager. He also recalled a camping trip being the first time he left the bubble of his family. A camping trip is an environment where conventions and rituals can differ from the norm. This makes it fertile territory for drama. The first draft was inspired by living in a remote area of Costa Rica as well as drawing on people's voices from his own school days, a workshop with LAMDA students, and young people he currently teaches in Kilburn.

Marco finds himself on a pilgrimage of sorts around the cliffs of Eastbourne. This is lonely and painful, and yet perhaps there are wonderous things you can see and experience that you miss in a group. Azouz wanted to capture the transient, glorious, terrifying fever pitch of this time in these young people's lives. They are on the cusp of leaving one world and entering another.

Approaching the play

During the workshop, participants wrote down questions and concerns about their productions. These included:

- How to deliver clarity of space
- How to stage Marco's encounter with the moth effectively
- Casting within a big company and getting representation right
- Conveying the diversity of the characters
- How to keep cast members in character when they are not engaged in the dialogue
- How to create risk for the ending moment
- How to make the dog feel playful
- How to encourage confidence in the non-naturalistic moments
- How to incorporate movement

Lead director Hannah Hauer King recommended storyboarding the play before rehearsals begin, as it can help to frame moments and imagine it spatially.

There isn't one way to storyboard, but one method could involve drawing out the set or performance space on several index cards or A4 paper, and sketching how the set/

actors might move or shift from each given scene to another. The drawings don't need to be accomplished, but can just give the director a sense of how they might stage a scene or create a different sense of location. It can be useful to problem solve staging before rehearsing, and get a sense of what the space might need or look like from a design perspective. For example, you might storyboard the final scene of the play to see how it might look, and facilitate Ricky falling off a cliff.

Sectioning the play

Hauer King recommended sectioning the play as a useful activity to work out what is happening in each scene so that every moment counts. This can be done alone as preparation, and/or with actors.

1. Start with Scene One. What happens in that scene, what time of day does it occur and where? Sometimes that information is provided by the writer, sometimes you have to infer. Go through all the scenes.
2. Write down a list of locations. Doing this with the young people will help them conceptualize the play.
3. Write down the situation of each scene, and the most important beats.

Important beats can be understood as gear shifts, changes in topic – a significant dramatic or emotional shift in a scene. Sometimes the writer might specify important beats clearly, other times important beats can be found during text work between actors and a director. Usually it's a combination of both.

Hauer King noted that she doesn't use the acting technique of actioning, but she does identify characters' super-objectives, i.e. what does Carl want from the camping trip?

It is important the characters know what they want from moment to moment. The characters tend to know why they're saying things, and Azouz wrote the play with units in mind. Supporting the performers to identify wants and intentions will support with clarity.

Themes

In a discussion with the group, the theme of ritual was touched upon. The ritual of burning coursework after exams was mentioned, as was the drinking game 'Ring of Fire'. Finding games or rituals to do in the space with your company could be a good exercise to get them engaging with the environment, and could foreshadow the shamanistic moments in the play. It was noted that the theme of separation will resonate with lots of the performers, as will the theme of relationships fracturing as they are at a transitional moment in their lives.

Characters and characterization

Hauer King reinforced the importance of character work. During a discussion with participants, some exercises for building character were suggested:

- Character hot-seating
- Visualization; closing eyes and picturing the environment
- Inventing a character's morning routine
- Creating a character backstory
- Improvisations in character
- Improvising the night before the play starts
- Reading out statements, and inviting actors to decide how much their character agrees by moving to a space in the room
- Character lists:
  - What I say about myself
  - What other characters say about me
  - What the writer says about me
- Facts, beliefs and questions
  - Facts provided by the text, inference about the characters, any questions that remain
- Character webs: give actors an A4 piece of paper, and invite them to draw lines to show how they relate to certain people. This might start to generate thoughts around physical proximity and staging.
- Do you like your neighbour?
- Augusto Boal's mirror exercise
- Laban

Full details of some of these practices and guidance on how to incorporate them into a rehearsal process are easy to find online.

Animal Work

Hauer King noted that animal work can be very helpful for loosening people up, particularly in relation to how they use touch to interact with each other and objects. This work is about instinct, and also status. It allows the performers to bounce off each other, which is very exciting theatrically. It is also a useful way to get people to emote in a safe space. If everyone goes through the animal work, it might make the person playing Franky feel less inhibited.

To set up this work, invite the performers to imagine what animal their character would be, and choose a line that feels like the essence of that character. Don't worry about what the animal looks like, but consider their nature. If you are playing Franky, what is their human version? The following instructions can be used to guide actors through the exercise:

Warm-up

- Breathe, stretch to the ceiling. Flop over and let your neck relax. Bend and straighten one leg at a time. Come back up vertebrae by vertebrae. Look up, let your jaw go and go 'ahhhh'.
- Chin to chest, hands on the back of your head, stretch your neck and back. Swing your arms side to side. Bring your shoulders up and release them. Shake your right hand, shake your left hand, shake your left foot, shake your right foot.

Approaching the character

- Go for a walk around the room, Notice how you are in the space. Notice how you move; are you tired, are you energized, do you have any aches or pains?
- Start making eye contact with people. Notice what it's like for you – is it strange, or easy? Without changing anything, start to think about your character, how are they different from you? Do they walk slower, quicker, are they more shy or more confident?
- Invite the young people to change into that character when you have counted from 10 to 1.
- Start muttering the line. Think about voice. Do they sound like you, are they louder than you? Get louder, and even louder, then full force.
- Keep walking as your character. Think about that line and how it resonated with you. What is it like to be them? What is their inner tempo? What is it like saying it? Counting from ten to one, go back to being yourself.

Introducing the animal work

- Count down from ten to one to bring the performers into character. Ask them to notice what it's like to be back with them, keeping their animal in mind.
- Count from ten to one again, and actors should start to mutter their line.
- Introduce the scale: ten is fully human, and one is full animal. As actors move through the scale, keep saying the line. This should transform into animal noises. Bring the performers to one.
- Start noticing other animals, who might get in your way. Consider how you might interact with animals in the space.
- Next go where your animal feels most safe. Then go to where your animal feels most powerful.
- Bring the performers out of this work by moving back up the scale from one to ten.
- Invite the performers to reflect on their discoveries.

Character exercise

The following exercise is aimed at exploring allegiances in the play. It may also start to create the dynamics onstage.

- Walk around the room, find a space and stop. Close your eyes and think about the line you have chosen. At random, start saying lines into the space.
- Come into the perimeter of the space. One at a time, come into the middle and say the line in character.
- If your character agrees, come forward and you say your line in response. If you're playing the same character you will agree.
- Notice how it feels when people agree, and how it feels when no one agrees.

A week before the end of the rehearsal process, you could repeat this exercise and get them to say a line that they are struggling to get to grips with.

Casting

When casting in a non-diverse school, Azouz recommended changing the word 'brown' on p. 286 for 'Muslim', and then you have greater flexibility.

With a big cast, you could split characters so that they are played by multiple actors. This gives you an opportunity to find a theatrical way of handing the part over, as well as providing an opportunity to explore character collaboratively. Azouz's preference would be for human characters to be played by individual actors rather than split, to enable the audience to make a strong connection and go on a deeper journey with each character. However, for larger groups, there might be potential for Franky the Dog to be split or played by a chorus.

Consider the skillset of those you are trying to find a role for. Could you use them for movement work? In terms of casting Franky, consider whether there's an actors who could challenge their energy into playing the dog? With a big cast, Franky's voice could be split between multiple performers.

Production, staging and design

Azouz recommended following your instinct when it comes to design. It could be an empty space with just a log and your actors. Azouz reflected that it can be exciting for a writer when directors pick up on missed opportunities and add additional layers to the play in their productions. You should feel free to follow those impulses.

There is also the opportunity to make the production environmentally intense. Your production could lean into magical realism; is it set in the British countryside, or the rainforest, or somewhere in between? Could you create characters out of the elements of the natural world? If you are going to explore elements of magical realism, it's important to do this work first so that the company buys into the theatricality of it.

Locations in the play:

- The campsite at Birling Gap. (Near the cliff at Birling Gap)
- Noush's campsite near Beachy Head. (Near the cliff at Beachy Head)
- The place where Marco is found by Noush. (This might be the above)

Is it a 'campsite' or just a patch of grass where they've pitched their tents?

The campsite

The campsite is the most predominant location, and Hauer King recommended that if there's one setting to invest in, it's this one. You can then layer additional locations on top of your 'holding world' by finding fun, clever ways to evoke them.

The campsite is a big space near a cliff. Azouz wrote the play imagining the journey from a school in London to Eastbourne. Beachy Head was chosen as it is a place famous for suicides. There is something interesting about a group of teenagers thinking 'let's go there', which might not be driven by suicidal intent, but could be morbid curiosity.

Ideally this location would not be changed, as it is evocative of danger. These themes of peril and taking risks resonate with this stage of life. There is also something evocative about it being an elevated space; the characters are suspended, and there is a sense of the depths beneath.

The group discussed the importance of layering in the edge of the cliff early in the production. Make a clear choice about what you want the audience to feel. Could a motif of the lighthouse at Beachy Head be used?

Consider what the characters have brought with them. Have they brought water, or alcohol? Hauer King recommended making early decisions about whether you will have consumables, or whether it's going to be prop-free.

Questions to consider include: How long have they been there? How much detritus have they accumulated before we meet them? Do you want your audience to immediately understand they're at a campsite, or do you want to reveal it gradually? The length of the journey the students have been on will impact on the initial scenes; what has happened on the journey? How exhausted or fed up with each other are they?

In the workshop, participants created the campsite using objects available in the room, considering what felt important to have in the space. This could include something that evokes the tents, a fire pit and a sense of elevation.

When doing this exercise with your cast, you could put some music on to create a playful atmosphere. Hauer King reflected that even if what you glean from this exercise is 'I want nothing', that is useful.

Hauer King noted that having objects in the space is really fun for a sense of play. Toys can be useful to play with, and objects can lead to a physical language; do they use them to hide, or push people around? How do they entertain each other and move around in the space? For example, a tepee could provide space for Marco to hide in. Perhaps Noush could be at the back of the space, and her first entry to the play is when she pops out of the tent. Maybe they are throwing all their rubbish into a big bonfire in the middle.

The moth

Azouz stated that the moth should feel real for the people who are viewing it. However, the staging is open for you and your company to decide.

The moth is a metaphor for change and could be used to ask questions about how Marco transforms. He is not a violent character at the start of the play, but by the end he does something unspeakably violent. Is that because of how he's been treated by the group, and/or does his encounter with the moth unlock something? The theatrical language of the moth should be different from the language of the dog.

Hauer King said that you could argue that his transformation is the decision to go back. You could say that the moth comes, which enables Marco to face his fears, face the pack, the people who excluded them. Hauer King doesn't think he goes there to hurt Ricky. He's expecting to see everyone there, but they're not there and he panics.

Staging ideas summarized from a discussion

- The moth could be lots of small objects that form a big object
- Could humming be used?
- Productions could use a sound or visual motif thread through the production, which culminates in the appearance of the moth
- Something could appear out of an existing prop, e.g. a spider web coming out of a backpack
- Could you create the moth with no actors? For example, a fan with fabric, or several lights coming together?

The following is a summary of questions asked by the directors about the moth:

Q: Is the moth a reference to **The Silence of the Lambs***?*
A: I love that film, and that scene, but the moth was not a conscious reference. There is something benign about this moth. However, this is not a regular clothes moth, it's something much more majestic.

Q: What is the significance of the moth?
A: A butterfly is pure and beautiful. Something about a moth is harder to contain. There is something resonant with Marco's journey. The moth is the potential; he could go either way. Someone was chucked out of their family and they meet someone else who shows them something special. You could even not attempt to represent a moth, but ask; how do I represent 'a hidden world', arousal, beauty and wonder? It's completely fine for the audience to not know what it is, because the characters name it.

Q: How much of the moth stays with Marco after this experience?
A: I'm not sure! It absolutely has an impact. He is transformed but he doesn't have an outlet for his transformation.

Q: Does the moth show him the potential paths?
A: The moth could be visions of potential futures.

The dog

The animal work could be used to make choices about the dog. Where is the dog on the scale of zero to ten? Does this change from scene to scene? Azouz reflected that the dog goes on a journey; at the beginning of the play Franky's impulses are baser and more dog-like. The dog's text at the start can be seen like music, and the actor playing Franky just has to respond to the text. As the play goes on, Franky eats a book and newspapers and gains more vocabulary. Azouz stated that the choice to make the dog really human is an option. You can also play with how literal the dog is through costume.

Costume

The entire play takes place over two days during British summertime. Consider the weather and the temperature, and the fact that some of them probably have better gear than others. There's a mixture of wanting to look good and wanting to be practical.

Costume can feel very personal. You could invite the young people to draw their costumes, and put them up on the wall. One participant suggested talking about semiotics in a really simple manner. What signal is your costume sending to the audience? If this character wants to look cool, how do you communicate that clearly to an audience?

Speak to the actor playing Marco early on about the moment he is found with his trousers down, and ensure that they are central to decisions about how to stage this and are comfortable with it.

Warm-ups

- In a circle, one person at a time holds a ball and says (for example) their name, pronouns and favourite morning beverage. Then, throw or roll the ball to someone else in the space, who must repeat the name and the favourite beverage of the person who threw the ball.
- HI YA! Send someone across the circle a slash with a 'HI!'. The recipient then raises their hands above their head with a 'YA!'. The two people either side of the recipient turn towards them and say 'HUH', moving their hands towards them in a slashing motion. The recipient then sends the slash to the next person with a 'HI'! And the game continues. If you are too slow or make a mistake, you have to either come into the middle and make animal noises to distract the players, or become adjudicators. When you're down to two, have a 'laugh-off'; whoever laughs first wins.

Soundscapes

In the workshop, Hauer King worked with the group to create a jazz circle. In a circle, choose an environment, e.g. 'the cliff top'. Then each person chooses a sound to illustrate that environment. It can be as literal or non-literal as you want, and you can do anything you want with your body to make a sound. It can be useful to start with a melodic sound. One person starts, and then as you go around the circle each person adds a new sound. Once you have created your soundscape, you can conduct the orchestra by building and reducing volume.

You could start with something not related to the play to get them started, like a sports match at a pub, or a jazz bar in 1980s New York. You can also put them in groups and get them to choose a location for their soundscape. In addition, you can play a song and then use it as inspiration for a jazz circle. Hauer King demonstrated this with the song 'Down' by Marian Hill.

This could also be used in a way which is less about location and more about mood. If you have a big ensemble, it's a great way to keep them active. Strong singers can keep a bit of melody going underneath.

In a discussion about the uses of soundscapes, the following suggestions were made:

- Campfire songs could be used as inspiration
- This work may be useful for the transitions
- Sound could be used to make the appearance of the moth euphoric
- Snatches of a song heard throughout the piece could all come together during the rolling off the cliff
- Each character could have a musical theme

Azouz noted that he is attached to 'Under the Bridge' as the song choice because it relates to Jess' previous line.

Building physical sequences

In the workshop, participants explored how to create narrative physical sequences. They stood in a group facing Hauer King, who told the story of a person who has woken up in a casino. Hauer King performed a sequence of physical actions to represent waking up, stretching, drinking from a big glass of whisky, which turns into a big dice, then rolling the dice across the floor, taking a big drag of a cigarette, throwing it, walking outside, it's raining, hailing a taxi and walking into the distance. The group practised this a couple of times and added vocalization. A participant then led the group to create a sequence about going into a supermarket and biting into a disgusting apple. Then text and vocalization was added.

The group then used these ideas to create the moth, thinking particularly about the stage direction 'the beat of the moth's wings turned musical'.

When the groups showed their work, Hauer King supported the groups to develop a beginning, middle and an end. The groups incorporated elements such as levels, rhythm, breath and travelling, sound without tone and sound with tone. Hauer King suggested layering in characters to these moments; what's their response to what's happening?

Improvisation

Improvisation was touched upon throughout the day as a good tool to help with actors not feeling involved when they're not part of the dialogue, and to build character. Hauer King recommended improvising being at the campsite when nothing is happening.

Kiss/Marry/Push Off Cliff

To facilitate an improvisation, Hauer King gave the following the tips:

- Be really clear on the story beats of the improvisation
- Do a five to ten minute exercise that brings actors into character
- If you feel the improvisation falling flat, you can whisper prompts into their ears
- It may be useful or interesting to get them to improvize other characters

The final scene

The final scene raises some questions, which were discussed in the workshop:

- Is pushing Ricky of the cliff premeditated?
- If it isn't, where does Marco get the padlock?
- Is Marco intending to scare Ricky, without intending to kill him?
- Maybe Marco wants to say his peace, and sees Ricky as his main rival
- Does Marco want to re-join the group?
- Is Ricky Marco's main obstacle?
- Is Marco just trying to silence Ricky?
- Is he testing the rest of the group to see if they'll rescue Ricky?
- Is Marco motivated by the humiliation of being found semi-naked, which is terrible for a teenage boy?
- At the start of the play, Ricky drags Marco in his sleeping bag; is this a tit for tat?

Azouz reflected that there is something comical about the moment when Ricky bounces up in his sleeping bag, and the audience should laugh at that moment. Before this, Ricky's been screaming and it's scary. It should be horrific for Ricky to be locked into his sleeping bag. An interesting challenge for directors is: How do you traverse between horror, comedy and back to horror again?

The following notes are a summary of the discussion about the final scene:

The final moment leaves the audience with a sense of 'to be continued', a literal cliff-hanger. Is there a way of Ricky falling down that isn't just falling to the ground? Could it be slow motion or assisted motion? Slow motion is the opposite of what's happening, which could be an interesting dynamic: slow chaos. The rolling could also not be literal; the person rolling could be standing up. With a company, you could do a tableau of each beat in a scene and then join them up. You could also underscore the final scene, or have performers reading out stage directions. You can create the horror of the edge of the cliff through performance. Leaning forward to look over it can give a sense of incline. Could the audience be the edge, and are they scared of them? Imagine a fish tank: Franky could put his nose on the edge of the fish tank and stare at the audience. Could you foreshadow the final moment of the play with falling motifs? Ricky can't see where he is, so he could just be rolling like a maniac. Consider ways to evoke the nearby sea: the peril of the ocean and the power of the water. Be aware of the final image being too conclusive.

Final questions

Q: Should the actors keep their native accents?
A: Yes! The actors should feel confident to just 'come at it', without worrying about getting their accents right.

Suggested references

The Dyatlov Pass Incident: https://en.wikipedia.org/wiki/Dyatlov_Pass_incident
Work by writer Carlos Castaneda

From a workshop led by Hannah Hauer King
With notes by Lucy Allan

The Periodicals

by Siân Owen

Siân Owen was born and raised in Newport, South Wales and is a graduate of the MA Writing for Performance Programme at Goldsmiths College. Her play *Restoration* won the Oxford Playhouse New Writing Competition. She has been part of the Sherman Cymru Advanced Writers Group, the Royal Court Studio Group and the BBC Writers Group – Welsh Voices.

She is currently on attachment at the National Theatre and under commission from Box of Tricks Theatre Company and Papertrail. Previous work includes additional material for *Under Milk Wood* at the National Theatre; *How to Be Brave* for Dirty Protest; *This Land* for Pentabus; *Another Place* and *Pieces* for BBC Cymru Wales and Radio 4; and *Pride and Prejudice* for Audible.

Characters

All the characters have taken names from the periodic table. Each character can be played by any gender.

Neon – *Chemical properties – used for lighting. Character properties – doesn't sleep at night; Neon isn't wired that way. Neon works best when it is dark. Hyper-vigilant.*

Lithium – *Chemical properties – lithium is very reactive and flammable. It can damage skin on contact. Character properties – there is a specific autistic diagnosis called pathological demand avoidance. Not all schools or institutions recognize it, and if it is not understood these young people are seen as trouble/aggressive/naughty. But what it actually means is these young people have a huge level of anxiety over any demands (small or big) and they can have physical, aggressive reactions to a demand. To help these young people you need to find ways to take the anxiety away – give control, choice, don't ask direct questions. Often typical schooling and systems do not allow these young people to function. NB: Demand avoidance is also very common in young people with trauma.*

Mercury – *Chemical properties – mercury is a rare element. Too much mercury can kill a person. Character properties – Mercury is the captain. Nobody knows why they are called Mercury – everyone else has a name that fits them. We find out why they are called this in the course of the play.*

Gold – *Chemical properties – a valued substance, important and reliable. Character properties – all of the above. Also they don't say a single word, ever.*

Silicon – *Chemical properties – silicon is a valuable element in electronics. Character properties – Silicon is a master of fixing electronics/computers/anything with a circuit board, etc. They also invent things. They are from somewhere else. They are from another place. They are from 1983 so speak a different kind of language to everyone else. NB: Silicon is a teenager like all the others. They are just from 1983. In my mind this was because I wanted to include a character who had no home they could get to any more – it doesn't exist anymore – it isn't safe to travel back there. But maybe there are other reasons they are from 1983 – feel free to explore.*

Magnesium (Mags) – *Chemical properties – magnesium burns with a very bright light. Character properties – their body does something involuntary when they least need it to. They glow bright when they are scared or fearful. Which makes it impossible for them to hide.*

Evian – *the new kid who has just arrived at the landfill. We don't know anything about them yet.*

The Methanes – *Chemical properties – a gas, methane is a product of certain human activities; it is also created at landfill sites and needs to be piped out as it is so explosive.*

Character properties – the chorus. Ethereal, omnipresent. The chorus will fill in the gaps and tell us backstory, etc. The characters cannot see The Methanes but The Methanes see everything and get everywhere. NB: Methane doesn't smell. It is odourless which is why is so dangerous on landfill sites. The Methanes can be played by one to 100 actors. Each line by The Methanes is to be said by a different actor.

Maude Hatchett – *Education Secretary, Head of the Attendance Alliance.*

Aide *to Maude Hatchett.*

Edward – *member of the press.*
John – *member of the press.*
Annabelle – *member of the press.*

Setting

Now
A landfill site on the edge of your nearest town or city. Unless you know it is there you would never know it is there

Notes

_____	When a character has this where they would usually talk it means they don't know what to say or don't want to say anything.
/	When this is shown after or before dialogue it means the characters interrupt or talk over each other.

Scene One

Maude Hatchett   Good evening,

As *proud* head of the Attendance Alliance, I met with the prime minister as a matter of urgency this afternoon.

I am speaking to you tonight to inform you all that, as of 7.25 tomorrow morning, emergency legislation will come into effect making it illegal for any children to be absent from school.

From this time, the Troop and Trace Force will have immediate powers of detention and imprisonment for all children absconding.

The Troop and Trace Force are now at record levels after refugees and all those under immigration law have been ordered to join their ranks. Training is taking place for these new recruits in detention centres across the country.
The initial measures we put in place have seen an uptake in compliance.
And I thank you, those who have listened.

But the fines and imprisonments for parents of repeat offenders is still not turning the tide completely.
Graph one please.
So we need to do more.

And I have a message for you, Ghost Children.
You will haunt us no longer.
Tearaways.
Terrors.
Truants.
Rest assured, myself and all of the Attendance Alliance will get you back where you belong.
Back into the system.
Back into line.
Don't Stay Home.
I think we have time for some questions.

Annabelle   What about if someone is ill?

Maude   Guidance will be available.

Edward   When?

Maude   7.24 tomorrow morning.

John   How many Ghost Children are there, Education Secretary?

Maude   Our data says we are down to the thousands.

Annabelle   How many exactly?

Maude   I have been charged by the Prime Minister to find these anomalies . . . these outliers.

And I will.

John But what about the parent marches?
Hundreds of thousands taking to the streets against this / policy

Maude Totally untrue.

Edward What about the rumours of teachers threatening to also stay away in solidarity?

Maude Absolute rubbish. RUBBISH.

Annabelle You don't know where these children are do you?

Maude _____

John Dame Hatchett?

Maude _____

Edward Education Secretary?

Maude I'm just waiting.

She takes out her phone and starts texting – speaking aloud what she's typing.

Why am I still waiting?
You've one job.
Don't mess up.

Annabelle Who are you messaging?
Maude?

Aide Thank you all. That's it for today. The minister is very busy. Thank you. Out. This way. OUT.

The **Aide** *pushes the press out.* **Maude** *texts furiously.*

Maude Text me. NOW.

Scene Two

Evian *walks in warily, holding a phone they are using as a map.*

Evian Here? Surely this can't be the right place. This place is a dump.

A flurry of text messages arrive all at once. **Evian** *panics and tries to get the phone to quieten down. But the noise has already alerted* **The Methanes** *who gather around them.*

The Methanes Oh a new arrival.
Welcome. Welcome to the Sandy Heads Landfill Site.

Evian *gags as they are overcome by the smell.*

Evian Oh my God. What's that smell?

The Methanes It's not us.
We don't smell.
That is not us.
We are *au natural*.
We are odourless.
It's all the rotten decaying melting mush that stinks.
Why are you doing that? You know they (*Evian*) can't hear us
Or see us.
I was talking to them (*the audience*).
Oh there's been another delivery. (*Looking into the audience.*)
Just arrived.
The latest detritus to land here.

Evian *starts rummaging through bits of the rubbish. They gag. They are looking for a good place to hide the phone they have.*

The Methanes (*to the audience*) Well, you are all welcome here.
The old,
the scraps,
the broken,
the cast-offs,
the exhausted,
the knackered
and the worn-out.
We are of this place,
a by-product,
We are everywhere in this place
hanging in the air
lurking under piles
in pockets and crevices.
In the right hands we are useful,
helpful,
a solution.
Filter us for good.
In the wrong hands?
Flammable
Explosive
Dangerous.

Evian *finds a good hiding spot for the phone. And then one for themselves.*

The Methanes We are The Methanes
Allow us to introduce you to the others . . .

The Methanes *move items, open things, move sheets to expose each character – all are still asleep apart from* **Neon**.

The Methanes Mercury.
It was their idea to come here.
Nobody else would dream of coming here.

At least that's what they thought.
Until Mercury found Silicon head deep in a pile of old electronics.
As usual.
Silicon was lost until the others arrived.
For Silicon is from another place.
Together they started on making this a place they could stay.
They got to work on making a base.
Old mattresses, steam cleaned with a broken steam cleaner that Silicon mended.
Bits of old fabric sewn together for blankets.
A cooker, elements replaced and hob working.
That's the thing with this place. You can find anything and everything you need.
If you look hard enough.
Use your skills.
Dig deep enough.
And you might find Gold.
Nobody knows anything about Gold.
Gold doesn't say a word.
Silence is Gold(en).
But Gold works hard, gathers, mends and protects.
Solid.
Neon never sleeps.

Evian *pulls back when they see* **Neon** *watching over everything.*

The Methanes Neon isn't wired that way.
Neon works best in the dark.
So Neon keeps watch.
It was Neon who found Magnesium.
Mags for short.
Glowing bright, actually glowing terrified.
Hiding in amongst the washing machines and tumble driers.
This is Lithium
A storm of a soul.
Swept here by the gale force winds of change out there.
And now they are all here seeking shelter.
Seeking sanctuary
Seeking security
Seeking peace.

Evian *has been lurking and skulking, trying to stay out of sight but they walk into an area that triggers a horrible – sounding alarm. It sounds like a school bell.*

Maybe like this: https://www.youtube.com/watch?v=TrJVgGnA7rw

They all wake/run/rush to see what is happening.

Silicon Security breach. Someone has triggered the alarm.
Someone else is here.

Mercury POSITIONS.

Mags *runs and hides in a wardrobe or a fridge. The others all rush to places. All apart from* **Lithium** *who stands and shouts.*

Lithium Turn it off turn it off turn it off . . .

Silicon I'm on it.

Silicon *runs to a piece of equipment to try and turn the noise off.*

Neon Gold come with me.

Silicon It's Sector Two.

The Methanes They're over there.
There.
Over there.

The Methanes *try and help expose* **Evian** *but they can't be seen or heard.* **Mercury** *is left with a screaming* **Lithium**. **Mercury** *tries to help* **Lithium** *but they can't calm them until the noise stops. Finally, it does.* **Mercury** *helps* **Lithium** *back up to their feet as they have been screaming in a ball position.*

Silicon Well, that was effective.

Lithium Could you not have picked any other noise?

Neon *and* **Gold** *have found* **Evian** *and escort them back to the others.*

Neon Hiding in a fridge.

Evian I was . . . I . . . I was just . . . looking.

Neon Watching. Snooping.

Evian I'm sorry.
I didn't mean to . . . I was just . . . scared.

Mags Are you on your own?

Evian Yes.

Lithium Were you followed?

Evian No.

Silicon Why are you here?

Evian Mole.

Neon So . . .?

Evian So?

Mercury Didn't Mole tell you to say something?

Evian Oh yes, er . . . Avocado.

Neon *makes the noise of a wrong answer in a game show.*

Evian   No Avogadro.
AVOGADRO. Sorry.
I always do that. Always mess it up.

Lithium   Do you always sweat so much too?

Mags *comes out of their hiding spot. Sees* **Evian** *struggling. Gives them a bottle of water.*

Mags   What's your name?

Evian   Evian. It's . . . French?

Mercury   I'm Mercury.

Lithium   Lithium.

Neon   I'm Neon.

Silicon   Silicon.

Mags   I'm Magnesium. Mags for short. And that's Gold.

Evian   Are those your real names?

Mercury   Is Evian yours?

Evian   _____

Neon   What should we do?

Mercury   Neon and Lithium you know what to do.

They go to **Evian**.

Mercury   Arms up.

Neon *and* **Lithium** *body-search* **Evian**. **Evian** *tries to resist but* **Gold** *steps forward.* **Evian** *complies.*

Neon   Nothing.

Evian   Mole said no phones, no personals, no nothing.

Neon   What do you want to do?

Mercury   Start the induction.

Lithium   Are you sure?

Mercury   It's what we do.
Two days.

Mags   Isn't it usually a week?

Gold *takes* **Mags**' *hand.* **Gold** *beams at* **Mags**. **Mags** *can't help but smile back.*

Mercury   You've got two days.

Evian   To what?

Mercury   To make sure.

Evian   And what if you aren't sure? What happens then?

Mercury *walks away.*

Evian   What would happen then? Why do I need an induction?

Neon   To see if you can be here.

Evian   But I have nowhere else to go.

The Methanes *get nearer* **Evian**. *Sniff them.* **Lithium** *looks really hard at* **Evian**.

Lithium   You messed up the password.
And why didn't you just shout it like you were supposed to when you got here?

Evian   I don't do so well under pressure.

Neon   Join the club.

Neon *and* **Lithium** *walk off.*

Evian   That's what I want to do.
I want to join.

The Methanes *form a guard of honour and* **Evian** *goes through it.*

The Methanes   And so it begins . . .

Scene Three

Mercury, **Gold**, **Neon** *are setting out bowls and cutlery for breakfast.*

Neon   Why's Mole sent them here *now*?

Mercury   It must have been an emergency. For them.

Neon   I think we should move it forward.

Mercury   No. We stick to the plan.

Lithium, **Mags** *and* **Evian** *walk into the base mid-conversation.*

Neon *and* **Mercury** *break up their conference quickly.*

Mags   . . . And we can help you gather some nice things to have around your bed.
People throw away the nicest things. I've got some gorgeous paintings.
Lithium has a lovely family photo album.

Evian   I thought you weren't allowed personal things?

Lithium   Oh it's not my actual family.

Mags   We'll add you to the rota for a shower.

Evian   A rota?

Mercury   We have to have a system as it takes a while to warm the water back up.

Evian   You have hot water here?

Neon   What do you think we are, savages?

Evian *laughs. For a little too long.*

Evian   But how?

Lithium   Science and engineering.

The stuff we use like the washing machine and the computers make heat right? So we channel that back to the water.

Evian   Wait, you have electricity too?

Mercury   Wait till you see the games area.
OH THAT IS GOING TO BLOW YOUR MIND.

Mags   You want some breakfast, Evian?
I hit the jackpot yesterday.
Found a whole box of beans, still in date.
They're the ones with the sausages.

Evian   Are those bowls and the cutlery . . . all from . . . in . . . here?

Mercury   This crockery is worth a fortune on eBay. (*Offering a bowl of beans.*)

Evian   No thanks. No.

Neon   We've got crisps. Prawn Cocktail or Roast Chicken.

Evian   No. I'm alright.

Lithium   It's not just junk food here you know.
Tell them . . . tell them what you've done, Mags.

Mags   Oh just a bit of growing is all.

Lithium   You've got a full-on allotment, Mags.
All from packets of seeds that have been thrown away.
Carrots.
Potatoes.
Cucumber.
Strawberries.
Making sure we get our vitamins.
We'll need to make some cuttings won't we?

Mags   Why?

Neon   Because um . . . because we . . . we'll need more?

Lithium   You could grow anything anywhere, Mags.

Silicon *comes into the base very excited, carrying something, interrupting them all.*

The Methanes *follow, equally delighted.*

Silicon   I've found one. Finally.

The Methanes   They have. They have found one.
At last.

It is a cassette player like this:

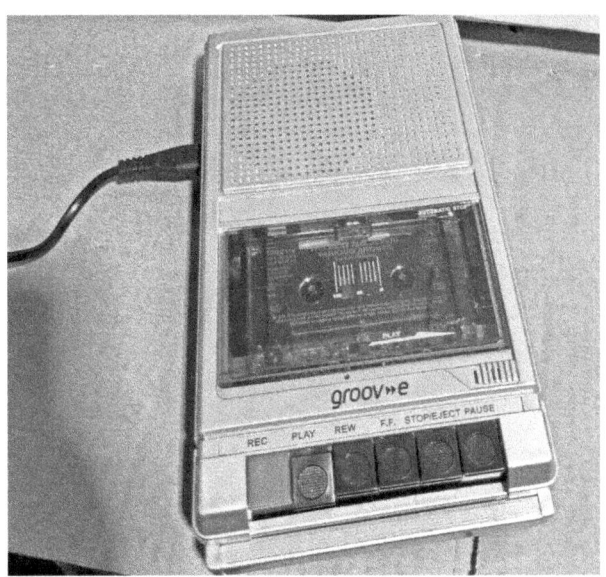

The Methanes   A Dixons TR17 Cassette Record Player
With Automatic Stop button.
BOXED.

Silicon *starts fiddling with a TV from the eighties that is pride of place somewhere in the camp. They attach the cassette player to the TV with wires.*

Silicon   If I just put this here and that there.
This wire into here . . .
Right. Now. On.
Load Prog 1
Aaaaannnnndd play.

Then there is this noise: https://www.youtube.com/watch?v=V0EfycbDhiw (25 seconds in is where it starts to get particularly horrible).

Mercury   Oh my God what is that?

Lithium   ARGH. Turn it off.

Silicon   I can't. The volume dial is broken on the telly.

Lithium TURN IT OFF.

Lithium *is starting to want to physically fight the noise . . . or the person making it. Sensory overload.*

Mags (*glowing faintly*) Please make it stop.

Gold *comes over and turns the TV off. Then helps* **Lithium** *calm. They're all super – stressed now.*

Mercury What was that?

Silicon A game loading.

Neon A what now?

Silicon *Manic Miner*. I always wanted that one. There was this whole case of them. Game cassettes. *Pac-Man. Jet Set Willy*. And *Manic Miner*.

Neon Manic. Miner?

Silicon A computer game.

Neon What computer?

Silicon A ZX Spectrum. State of the art. Skill city. I'll show you.

Mercury Not unless you can turn it down.

Silicon I told you: the volume is broken on this one.

Mercury So find one where it isn't?

Silicon But this is a Philips 1002 Colour TV 22-inch screen.

The Methanes Ooooooo.

Neon That's not a TV. That is a tank.

Silicon EIGHT pre-tuned channels which are selected by light action push buttons. It has provision for TV games and video recorder.

The Methanes *cheer.*

Mags Video recorder?

Silicon Automatic frequency control 4-inch forward facing loudspeaker.
Teak effect finish to cabinet.
Complete with stand.
Cat No 530/2325
Our Price: £315
Argos catalogue autumn/winter edition.

The Methanes *clap.*

It was top of my Christmas wish list before . . . before

Evian (*laughing, to* **Silicon**) Where are *you* from?

Silicon   1983.

Evian   Yeah right.

Silicon   Yeah. Right.

Evian   But why are you here? Where were you before?

They all let out an audible disapproval of that question. Including **The Methanes**.

Lithium   Wow. You don't ask them that. Don't answer that, Silicon.

Evian   OK. OK.

Mercury   We have a rule here. No-one asks about before.

Evian   Right. Sorry.

Mercury   Nobody would come to live in a place like this unless they had to. And that's all anyone needs to know.

Awkward pause.

Silicon   Anyone want to help me find a TV?

They all go apart from **Mercury** *and* **Evian**. *Awkward silence.*

Evian   Right. So.
Do you just game all day?

Mercury   NO. I mean. Yeah. They have found a load of old consoles and set them all up but . . . that's just necessity right?
We do arts and crafts too.

Evian   What are you making?

Mercury   We read. We do experiments. We grow. We mend. We fix.
But mainly we just are. We can just *be* here.
You know?

Mercury *starts to clean up the breakfast things.* **Evian** *helps.*

Mercury   Oh, thanks. I don't often get help to . . . I mean usually it's kind of my thing to clean up.

Evian   Sorry.

Mercury   No you're all right. It's nice.
To have some help.

Evian   You have to keep things clean right?
Shall I throw this away?

Mercury   Someone might want some in a bit.

Evian   I'll throw it away.
Do you have bleach or spray?

Mercury (*pointing*)   Over there.

Evian   This needs a wipe. One, two, three, four.
And this. One, two, three, four.

Evian *is totally focused on the cleaning. Obsessive wiping . . .* **Mercury** *watches them with interest and compassion.* **Mercury** *joins in and they clean together.*

Scene Four

Mercury *and* **Neon** *are moving boxes.* **The Methanes** *are gathered around.*

Neon   I really think we should just do it now.

Mercury   We're not ready. Silicon has done all the calculations. We need that last bit of fuel to ferment. Or we won't have enough.

The Methanes   You need enough.

Neon   But I can feel it. It's brewing. The news is horrible.

The Methanes   They're coming to get you.

Mercury   Then don't watch it.

Neon   But we need to know what's happening. We don't need surprises.

Mercury   Exactly. Did you see how all those noises going off worked for everyone earlier? Bedlam. No. No surprises. No shocks. No changes. We go as planned. We do things our way, Neon. Everybody knows what's what.

Neon   Not everyone. I think it's time to tell the others.

Mercury   Not yet. Any wrong moves now and it could all fall apart. They could fall apart. And I need to keep them safe.

Neon   *We* need to keep them safe.

The Methanes   You need to *go.*

The Methanes *make things rumble and shake. They are trying to make* **Mercury** *and* **Neon** *jump into action but instead they are just making them scared.*

Neon   Mercury. I don't like this at all.

Mercury   I know.

Neon   I can feel my legs starting to freeze. This is not good.

Mercury   What do you need?

Neon   To know I can fight back. To know we all can.
We don't have enough. If it came to it.

Mercury   Make more then. Rest now. Then make some tonight.

Neon I'll need some help.

Mercury No. This just needs to be between us.

Neon But what if they /

Mercury One more sleep.

Neon For you maybe.

Mercury Sorry.

Neon *walks off.*

Scene Five

It is night-time.

The Methanes Night.
All are asleep.
Apart from Neon.
Of course.
But they're not alone.
There's someone else.
Lurking.
Pacing.

Evian *is kind of hiding. Away from the base. They are rooting around in the rubble. Looking for something . . . then success! They pull out a mobile phone from its hiding place. They turn it on. No signal. They panic, hold the phone high, try to get higher but also try not to make a sound. They get a bar or two. They dial.* **The Methanes** *shake a rubbish pile.*

Evian (*whispering*) Hello? Can you hear me?

I can't . . . you're all broken up . . . there's no reception . . . no . . . I can't . . . hello? No no no. I'll text. I'll text now. Hello?

The rubbish pile crashes down and makes a noise.

Neon *comes to investigate.* **The Methanes** *scatter and* **Evian** *quickly hides the phone.*

Neon How did I know it would be you?

Evian How come you're up?

The Methanes Long ago. When humans lived off the land and hunted and were hunted someone always had to keep watch at night.

Neon I don't sleep at night.

The Methanes It is a fact that some humans are not wired for sleep.

Evian   Oh. Right. What never?

Neon   Nope. My brain just doesn't like switch off or whatever.

The Methanes   They keep different rhythms. And science believes that this is a throwback to those times.

Evian   Same. Actually I am the same. I can never sleep.
I can't relax.

The Methanes   Hyper. Vigilance.
And it can change your actual chemistry.
Make you shaky.
Make you freeze.

Neon   You hot?

Evian   No. Freezing.

Neon   You're sweating.

Evian   Always sweating on something.

Neon *watches* **Evian**.

Evian *starts to sort rubbish into piles – into some kind of order.*

Neon *has seen this kind of thing before.*

Neon   I'm not sure there's much point tidying that.

Evian   I'm not tidying. I'm making an order.
They're out of order.

Neon   Is it?

Neon *watches* **Evian**.

Neon   How bad is it out there at the moment?

Evian   It's bad. There's more and more riots starting all over.

Awkward pause.

It's scary.

Neon *sits.* **Evian** *joins him. They can't get comfortable on whatever they are sat on.*

Neon   You'll get used to it.

Evian   Even the smell?

Neon   It's better than other places I have spent time in.
Living like this . . . we have everything we need.

Evian   Really?

Neon   Yeah. Space. Time. We're off radar.
They think we're for the scrap heap anyway.

So we're just hiding in plain sight.
Stealthy.
Like those B2 Stealth Bomber planes.
Lithium told me a really cool fact about them.
To build them they had to invent all the components from scratch.
Like everything. New technology. New fuel. New weapons.
New ways. New order.
That's just what we're doing here.

Evian   But we aren't at war.

Neon   Aren't we?

Neon *walks away.* **Evian** *takes their phone as if going to text, then hides it away on themselves instead.*

Neon (*from off*)   You coming?

Scene Six

Maude Hatchett *is holding another press conference.*

Maude   First question please. Um . . . John. *The Times Chronicle*?

John   Any updates, Education Secretary? A source told me today that you had something big,

Maude   Yes. Thank you, John. The intelligence is that there are groups, bands, vagabonds, together, in hiding. But they won't be able to hide for much longer. Annabelle . . . *Cloud News* . . .

Annabelle   The riots have been increasing, Dame Hatchett. Parents visibly taking up arms to protect their children.

Maude   What you are talking about there, Annabelle, is one incident, captured and then spread all over social media, to incite violence . . . this will not be tolerated.

Annabelle   But, Education Secretary . . . our source tells us that there are more children missing this week from schools than ever before and /

Maude   EDWARD. *The Cablegram.*

Edward   Can you comment on the footage that has been shared by members of the public right across the country showing the armed trucks in convoy?

Maude   There are operations by the Troop and Trace in locations all over the country that we believe have been possessed by these Ghosts, these shadows, these devils /

Annabelle   They are children and young people

Maude   Quite right. So they need to do what they have been told. Thank you. (*Trying to leave.*)

John What about the footage of the Prime Minister saying you're, and I quote, 'finished'.

Maude I have already said to the Prime Minister that I am TOTALLY committed to this.

I am obsessed. Right now I have a military jeep waiting to take me to a site of very specific interest.

Edward And do you have anything to say to these children, Education Secretary?

Maude Yes I do.
How dare they?
How DARE they?

I always win.
100 per cent.
Don't test me.

Scene Seven

The next morning. **Gold** *is with* **Lithium** *and* **Silicon**. **Silicon** *is playing loud noises from some tech – maybe it's more computer sounds, maybe it's some eighties music. But* **Gold** *is helping* **Lithium** *try and stay calm when they hear the loud noises.* **Evian** *approaches* **Mercury,** **Neon** *and* **Mags**.

Mercury You want to help us today?

Evian With what?

Mags Finding gold.

Evian Isn't that Gold sat right there?

Mags Not that Gold. Real gold. Actual gold.

Mercury Actually, Mags, I had something else that maybe we could /

Mags (*panic*) But it's Thursday.

Mercury Of course it is. What was I thinking?
(*Quickly to calm* **Mags**.) Let's go find some gold.

Evian In the ground?

Mercury Mainly in old TVs.

Evian Why?

Neon It's a good conductor of electricity.

Evian No, I meant why do you need gold?

Neon For money.

Evian What do you need money for?

Mercury To buy stuff.

Evian You leave this place?

Mags Never. Why would we want to do that?

Neon We get it all delivered.

Mercury You have loads more questions don't you?

Evian Yeah tons. Like about internet and how do you pay for anything and what do you buy and /

Neon We set up a few PCs and laptops and hacked into some Wi-Fi. We set up an account with postgoldformoney.com There's a post-box just outside the entrance. Then they pay us via PayPal. We used an old locker we found to set up a drop-off box.

Evian PayPal is for eighteen-plus.

Mercury There's hundreds of wallets and purses in this place. And people's paperwork. IDs. We use them. And we only get stuff we need.

Mags Like salt and vinegar crisps.

Mercury And first-aid stuff, medicine.
We try and use most stuff form here but some stuff we just can't get.

Evian So your plan is to stay here, forever?

Mercury Time to go Gold digging.
You coming?

Scene Eight

Lithium and Silicon *are playing Xbox.* **Mercury**, **Mags** *and* **Gold** *are silently sorting out all the pieces of gold that they have found.* **Evian** *goes and sees what is going on in the game.*

Lithium Arrrrgggghhhhh.

Evian You've got to move over there.

Lithium _____

Evian You're never going to do it with that many coins.

Lithium (*raging*) I know.

Silicon Enough now, Evian.

Evian Go right. RIGHT.

Lithium *is starting to seethe.*

Evian You need to get over there.
THERE.
Press B.

Lithium I AM.

Evian You're pressing Y.
Now you're pressing X.
B. B. B. Beeeeeeeeeee.
PRESS B.

Evian *starts pressing B on the controller.* **Lithium** *explodes.*

Lithium (*exploding*)   AAAAARRRRRRGGGGGHHHHHHHHHH

Lithium *kicks the TV and it falls.* **Lithium** *then starts to pick things up and throws things, and one thing almost hits* **Mags**. **Mags** *glows brightly.*

Evian What is the *matter* with you?

Lithium *hasn't got the words but they make this frustrated, angry cry.* **Lithium** *runs at* **Evian**.

Lithium *holds* **Evian** *by the throat.* **Gold** *goes to help.* **Gold** *doesn't touch* **Lithium**. *The whole group know not to place hands on* **Lithium** *when they are dysregulated.*

Gold *starts to do some breathing exercises with* **Lithium**.

Neon You shouldn't talk to Lithium like that.

Evian I was just trying to tell them what they needed to do.

Neon Exactly. And you shouldn't talk at all when Lithium is trying to game.

Evian (*to* **Mags**)   Urgh (*repulsed/scared*) – you're a different colour.

Silicon Come on, Mags. Let's go and water some seeds, yeah?

Silicon *takes* **Mags** *off.*

Mercury What are you *doing*?

Evian Sorry. SORRY. I'm making a right mess of this.
I was trying to help.

Mercury Come with me. Now.

Scene Nine

Mercury *has taken* **Evian** *outside the camp.* **The Methanes** *have followed.*

Mercury I was in school with Lithium.

Evian I didn't think we were supposed to talk about before.

Mercury You're not supposed to ask anyone about before.

We were mates since nursery.
We knew how to talk to Lithium.
For Lithium not to . . . for Lithium to be OK.
We knew how to get a rise too.
Do what you just did.
But we were Lithium's mates.
We wanted to help.
But school never did.
They just used to lock Lithium in a room all the time.

Evian   Oh.

Mercury   For hours sometimes.

They'd give them too much to do, talk like that, give orders and demands and you don't have to, you know? They kept doing it and Lithium would blow and they'd grab them and force them into this cupboard room. And lock the door.

Evian   Oh.

Mercury   Don't ever talk to Lithium like that again.

Evian   I really am sorry. I always say the wrong thing.
Gets me into a lot of trouble.

Mercury   Evian, what is your social worker called?

Evian   Janet.

Mercury *smiles, relieved.*

Mercury   Mole.

Evian   Mole.
Why didn't you just ask me that before?

Mercury   I told you. We don't ask. None of the others know we've all got the same social worker.

Evian   To protect her.

Mercury   To protect us all.

Evian   I really am sorry.
I'll say that to Lithium too.
And Mags. I'll explain.
I don't say the right things.
When I'm under pressure.

Mercury   When you're scared.

Evian   Yeah. I am scared.
This is my only chance to . . . my mum she . . .
I can't talk about it.
Please don't kick me out.

Let me make it up to them. To you.
I can clean.
And sort.

Evian *tidies.* **The Methanes** *keep messing up what* **Evian** *has done. They don't like* **Evian**.
Evian *keeps going though, obsessively tidying.*

I can make things look like they were never there.
No surface left cluttered.
No sign of any mess.
Make like a ghost.

Mercury   Can I trust you?

Evian   Of course.

Mercury   I'm being deadly serious now. I shouldn't / . . . the group are entirely dependent on . . .

Evian   I want to help.

Pause.

Mercury   Come with me.

Scene Ten

Under a tarpaulin, an armoury. Weapons made out of bits of rubbish. And a vehicle made out of whatever you can think of.

Evian   What is this?

Mercury   This is Exodus.

Evian   What?

Mercury   Our escape route.
We can't stay here anymore.
Mole has found us a new site.

Evian   Where?

Mercury   Nowhere. It doesn't exist on a map. It's perfect.

Evian   But how?

Mercury   Lithium and Neon and Gold and Silicon.
They've MADE A CAR thing powered by fuel made out of rubbish.

Evian   Are those weapons?

Mercury   We know they're after us.
We might need to defend ourselves.
We've used whatever we could find here.

Evian   And this was your idea?

Mercury   The others had all the actual ideas. I plan. I look after.

Evian   Of course you do.
What did Mags do?

Mercury   Well and, we try not to worry Mags with how bad things are.
Mags has seen enough.

Evian   Wow.

Mercury   What?

Evian   I didn't expect such a . . . you guys really are something, aren't you? I mean that is a whole . . . you've made a whole . . . stealth bomb.

Mercury   But bombs leave a massive mess. A trail of destruction.
And you've said how good you are at making things . . . disappear.

Evian   So?

Mercury   We need to vanish.

Evian   When?

Mercury   We go tonight. And we need never to have been here.
I need the camp to vanish. (*Trying not to panic.*)

But we can't panic Mags because we can't go anywhere if Mags is frightened because Mags glows when they're scared and we need to move in the dark. Stealth. And so I need your help.

Gather everything we need to take with us. And then make the camp vanish. Like no one was ever here.
Without Mags noticing.
Do you understand?

Evian   It's all to go in this car thing right?
Everything you need?

Mercury   Yep. That's our only way out. OK?

Evian   I know what I need to do.

Mercury   Thank you. I knew I could trust you.
Let's go. I'll make you a list of what we need.

Evian   You go ahead. I just need to size everything up.

Mercury *goes.*

Evian *takes their phone out.*

They take a load of photos.

The Methanes *get in them and pose.*

Scene Eleven

Lithium *approaches* **Mags** *who is watering seeds.* **Mags** *glows.*

Lithium   I frightened you. I *am* frightening you.
I'm going to go, OK?
I'll find somewhere else.

Mags   No. Don't do that.

Lithium   I can't stay. I'm not . . .

Mags   Not what?

Lithium   Normal.

Mags   Join the club. That is what this club is isn't it? Why we're all here?

Lithium   I've tried so hard.
Been sent to so many counsellors or whatever.
It's just like this . . . whoosh . . .
That I can't control.
Can't even remember what I've done after.
There are all these gaps.
I thought it had gone. Here.
Just with you guys but then Evian . . .
I can't fix it, Mags. It's always going to be there isn't it?
I'm 'broken'.

Mags   I'm a 'freak'.

Lithium   'Out of control'.

Mags   'Damaged'.

Lithium   'I'm dangerous.'

Mags   'I'm defective.'

Lithium   I'm sorry.

Mags   So am I.

Lithium   You haven't done anything wrong.

Mags   I wasn't talking about that.

Lithium   I don't want to frighten you.

Mags   Oh I'm scared of everything. I'm so tired of it.

Lithium   What if I said . . . I would . . . you know . . . be there.
To protect you. But I can't.
I can't promise.

Mags   It's just part of you. Part of your chemistry. You don't do it on purpose.

Lithium I try and stop. I would never actually. To you.

Mags Don't go.
Please.
Stay here?

Lithium That's the first time anyone has ever asked me to do that.

Lithium *goes and hugs* **Mags**. **Mags** *glows but in a totally new colour.*

Mags Wow. That's never happened before either.

Scene Twelve

Back at the camp. **Gold**, **Silicon** *and* **Lithium** *are watching the news.* **Mercury** *arrives just in time to see a new press conference from* **Maude Hatchett**. *During which* **Evian** *also comes back and sees.*

Maude Hatchett *is in a military jacket. She looks very flustered and like she wants to be anywhere else but here.*

Annabelle Education Minister.
Are you still Education Minister?

Maude Very much so, Annabelle.

And if those are the kind of questions I am going to get this morning then I will leave now as I have far more pressing things to address.

Edward Before you go, Minister.
Many people may see you and forget that you are indeed a mother yourself.
If your child was one of these delinquents what would you say?

Maude Edward.
This is exactly what I would say.
Enough is enough
Where are you?
Turn your phone back on.
Don't forget all I have done for you.
The sacrifices
And this is how you repay me?

Edward Um . . . Minister?

Maude WHERE ARE YOU?

Maude *walks out.*

They all stay silent as **Gold** *turns off the TV.*

Mercury I think she's actually gone mad.

Neon *comes rushing in.*

Neon   Mercury, Mole has messaged.

Mercury   What? What did it say?

Neon   'Your dad will be picking you up tonight. I've been held up.'
I think maybe Mole pressed a wrong button.
It doesn't make sense does it?

Mercury   No no no no no.

Silicon   What?

Evian   What's happening?

Mercury   It's Mole. Mole's been captured.

Neon   How do you know?

Mercury   That message is a code.

Lithium   So what do we do?

Mercury   I'm thinking. Let me think.

Mags *arrives with a big box. They all try and hide what is happening and act normal.*

Mags (*excited*)   Del-iv-ery.

Lithium   You were quick.

Mags *opens the box.*

Mags   Salt and vinegar crisps.

Everyone cheers including **The Methanes**.

Toilet paper.

Louder cheers.

Yeezys size 12. (*Feel free to insert any popular brand of daps/trainers here.*)

Gold *takes them and smiles.*

Hype T-shirt – blue. (*Same as above with clothing.*)

Neon   Sweet.

Mags   M&Ms. Chocolate Brownie.

Mercury   Thank you very much.

Mags   Batteries.

Silicon   Woohoooo.

Mags   OK?

ALL   YEAH.

Evian   Why don't you just tell Mags?

Mercury   What?

Lithium   Mate. Seriously.

Mags   Tell me what?

Mags *starts to glow the scared colour.*

The Methanes *make the BBC News App go off on* **Evian**'s *hidden phone.*

https://www.youtube.com/watch?v=xavWxTsclDQ

Silicon   What was that?

Mags   That's the sound of bad news.

Evian   The TV. It's the news music.

Mercury   The TV isn't on.

The Methanes *clap. It goes off again.*

They do it again and again.

Everyone begins to search around for the noise but it keeps moving.

Eventually **Gold** *realizes the noise is coming from* **Evian** *and uncovers the phone.*

Silicon   What's going on, Evian?

Evian   _____

Lithium   Why have you got a phone?

Evian   Because I wanted to feel safe.

Mercury   Have you contacted anyone while you've been here?

Evian   It was off. I turned it off. Honestly.

The Methanes *smile and then clap.*

Loads of messages arrive all at once. Like when you walk back into a good connection spot after no signal.

Evian *goes to run but the others stop them.*

Evian *is restrained while the phone is wrestled off them.*

Mercury *takes it and reads the messages out loud.*

Neon   'Where are you?
Don't mess this up. Like you usually do.
After everything I have done for you, the sacrifices I have made.
Failure is not an option.
You're such a disappointment.'

And you've replied.
With pictures of us.

And Exodus.

Mags *glows scared.*

Gold *picks up one of the weapons they have been crafting and goes towards* **Evian**.

Mags Woah, Gold. What are you doing?
What is that?

Evian *That* is what they're hiding from you, Mags.
They're making weapons.

Mags Why?

Evian To hurt people.

Neon To defend ourselves.
They're coming for us, Mags.

Mags Who are?

Silicon The Attendance Alliance.
They have troops, Mags.

Mags You said they were nothing to worry about.

Lithium We didn't want to scare you.
But we have to go.

Evian They've been planning it for ages, Mags.
Not telling you.

Mags What? Why?

Mercury Just to keep everything OK for you.

Evian I'll show you, Mags.

Mercury What are you doing? (*To* **Evian**.)

Evian The right thing. Wait, I'll show you. I'll show you everything.

Evian *runs offstage.*

Mags (*to* **Lithium**) You promised.

Lithium And I haven't broken it.
This was to protect you.
We know you hate change and moving and being scared.

Silicon But we have to go. To a new place.
We've built a car. To get us there safely.

Evian *is pushing the car on and holding one of the weapons in the other hand.*

Evian Here you go, Mags.
This is what's really going on.

Silicon   How have you got our car?

Neon   How do you know about our car?

Mercury   I told. I needed help.

Mags   What is all this?

Evian   This is the end of the road.

Evian *smashes the vehicle. Absolutely rage smashes it. They can't get near them to make it stop either. The others scream and shout but* **Evian** *carries on.* **The Methanes** *stop it in the end – maybe by holding* **Evian**. *Maybe by throwing stuff at them. Maybe by creating a massive bang that shocks everyone so they all freeze.*

Mercury   What did you do? What have you done?
I asked for your help.

Evian   I *am* helping.
Just hand yourselves in. They won't hurt you.

Mags   How do you know?

Evian   I *know*.

Evian   They will not stop until they have you where they want you.

Mercury   I thought you were one of us.

Evian   One of you? You are ANARCHISTS.
No . . . that's too cool.
You are ANIMALS. Living like this.
It's not right.

Neon   Is that right?

Evian   You are upsetting the status quo. Everything that's going wrong out there. Is all your fault. It's . . . it's . . . it's . . .

Neon   About time?

Evian   It's CHAOS.

Neon   That's what most of us here live through all the time.

Evian   And it's spreading and dirty and not the way we do things.
Why couldn't you just all come back after lockdown?

Mags   Come back? To where? From where?

Evian   Just go home.

Mercury   I CAN'T.

Evian   You would if you really wanted to. Of course you can.

Mercury   Do you not think that is all I want?

Evian Then just do it. It's that simple.

Mercury Do you want to know why I am Mercury here? /

Mags You don't have to do this /

Mercury Mercury is poisonous to humans.
I am poisonous.
To one human.
My most important human.
Before I came here I cared.
My mum is very ill.
And I had to care so much that I missed school.
Then the virus came and kept us in and
just for a little bit EVERYONE got a taste of
what it's like to have to care ALL the time.
But then there was a race to get back to normal. Back to how it used to work. Back to school.

But I couldn't go back . . . not into that germ pit because if I did . . . I could kill her . . . and that would be the end of it. So I had to go, because if I'm not there they can't blame her and fine her and I can't take back tiny germs of doom.
So whatever you do, you will not make me go back.

Neon I'm never going back.

Mags *just glows terrified.*

Lithium I'm not being held again. NO.

Silicon I actually cannot go back.

Evian ENOUGH. You have to. You think *you* can change things.

Silicon It's not just us. I've heard things.

Neon How many did they say on the news?
Thousands?

Evian _____

Mercury Hundreds of thousands?

Evian They don't know, OK. That's the whole problem. There could be over a million. But she will not stop. She will do anything to get you all back. Whatever it takes. She hates losing. She won't lose. So you have to come back with me now. You have to.

Mercury Who won't stop?

Evian The head of the Attendance Alliance. Maude Hackett.

Mags Why do you care? She's a total /

Evian She's my mother.

Lithium   What?

Neon   And she sent you in here?

Evian   I had no choice.

Neon   Well, she's right. You are a disappointment.

The piercing noise of a ZX Spectrum game loading fills the air.

Lithium   What's that noise?

Silicon   I set up new alarms on the parameters.

Evian   They're here.

Mags   Who is?

Evian   Troop and Trace.

Mercury   You told them?

Alarm after alarm goes off. **Mags** *is glowing.*

Neon   There's so many.

Mercury   We just need to go. Come with us.

Evian   Oh so I've passed your little induction have I?
I thought you hated tests.
Hypocrites.

Neon   You've got it all wrong. The induction is to check we fit you.
To see if you think we can help you.

Mercury   And we can.

Lithium   There's still time, Evian. Call them off.
Go on. Just make the call.

Neon   We aren't wired so differently.
Come with us. Help us make a new order.

Silicon   You know us now.
We just want to be left to our own devices.

Mags   Where's the harm in that?

Mercury   We are both here because of our mums.
Seems like we all have a lot in common with you.

Evian   Give me my phone.

Neon   YES, Evian. You do understand. You do know.

Evian *is handed their phone and then after a beat they stamp on it and break it.*

Neon   NO.

Evian I am NOTHING like you.
LOOK AT YOU.
Garbage.
Eating trash.

You're right, Mercury.
You are germs. Making society ill.

You live in chaos.
You cause chaos.
YOU ARE CHAOS.
Disorder.
Dissent.
Defective.
Insubordinate.
Vagabonds.
Devils.

You just need to get in line and get back into the system.

Silicon I don't have anywhere to go back to.
My place doesn't exist anymore.

Evian Oh there's places for people like you.
IT WAS FINE. Until you lot all started /

Neon Started what?

Lithium Not doing what we were told?

Neon Started sticking up for ourselves?

Mercury Showing there may be another way?

Mags Started to shine a little bit?

Evian Started crawling out of the dark.
It worked before.

Mercury Not for us.

Evian But you don't count.

Silicon *goes over to a box and starts to take something out.* **The Methanes** *run to help them.*

Evian What is that thing?

Silicon This is a base unit for a CB radio.

Neon A radio what?

Silicon Citizen band radio. For people . . . anywhere.

You can talk to each other. They use it in war zones . . . truckers use it to tell others about the police or accidents or invasions.

Lithium   Silicon I don't think that is going to work here.

Silicon   It does work. I've been using it already.
And at night . . . I've been hearing things . . . just rumblings.

The Methanes *start a rumbling again . . . the earthquake from the start replicated.*

The Methanes   And on the wind and in the air there have been
murmurings
ruminations
voices in the dark

You can feel it.
The winds of change.

The sound of a coming storm.

Silicon *turns on the CB radio and it sounds like rain but it is crackle and static:*

Silicon   Are there any handles out there?
This is Silicon.

Mercury   Silicon, what are you doing?

Silicon   I am looking for help.
Like you use those little magic phone boxes in your hands to reach out and talk.

Mags   To others in the dark.

Neon   To others on watch.

Lithium   To others with no other way out.

Silicon   Are there any handles out there?
This is Silicon.
I am one of the Ghost Children
Are there any more out there?

Nothing. Static. Crackle.

This is Silicon.
I am one of the missing

Nothing. Silence. Crackle. The noise of the approaching Troop and Trace is terrifying.

Evian   If I fail she'll destroy me.

Mercury   So you destroyed us? How many are there?

Neon   I'll go look.

Neon *runs to see.*

Silicon *puts the radio down, but* **Gold** *walks over to* **Silicon** *and puts the talking device back in their hand.* **Gold** *wants* **Silicon** *to keep trying.*

Silicon   This is Silicon.
They're coming for us.
We need help.
Is there anyone else out there?
We are at the Sandy Heads Landfill site.
Coordinates 51 degrees
29 minutes
17 seconds north.

Neon *re-enters.*

Neon   They've got dogs, bulldozers and guns, we're surrounded.

Silicon (*to the talking device*)   Did you hear that?
Anyone? Please?

Mags   Lithium, what do we do?

Lithium   A promise is a promise. I won't let them harm you.

Evian   There's nothing you can do. I told you, resistance is futile. She will not stop until you are squashed. You're an embarrassment.

Lithium *grabs a weapon and is about to run offstage and confront the troops.*

Mercury   No. Wait. We have to stick together.

Gold *encourages everyone to link arms.*

Evian   You're totally outnumbered.
Who do you think will help you now?
Losers.

The group close their eyes. The sound of the approaching 'army' grows louder.

Then a voice from the dark.

Pegasus   This is Pegasus.
Calling Silicon.
Assistance call heard.

Then slowly all the tech on the site lights up – the TV, the radio, etc. – and voices light up the dark from all the equipment.

Aquarius   This is Aquarius calling.

Solar   This is Solar calling.

Tetris   This is Tetris calling . . . en route. With friends.

Name after name tell us they can hear/they're on their way/they aren't alone. **The Methanes** *can take the part of the voices . . . as many as needed . . . each one with* *their own bespoke and specific handle . . . you are invited to be creative and imaginative with these names and what they say to show support.*

The group look amazed. As the voices get louder the 'army' gets quieter until the threat is totally drowned out by the noise of the voices from the dark.

Evian *stares at* **Mercury** *and then runs away terrified. The group stand together and listen. The noise of the voices grows and grows and as it does, so do the smiles on the faces of* **Mercury**, **Mags**, **Lithium**, **Gold**, **Neon** *and* **Silicon**. *They are not alone. There is a hope. There is something worth fighting for.*

Blackout.

But **Mags** *glows the colour they did during the hug with* **Lithium**. *Bright and strong.*

End.

The Periodicals

BY SIÂN OWEN

Notes on rehearsal and staging, drawn from a workshop with the writer, held at the National Theatre, October 2023

Introductions and warm-ups

Warm-up: Sequences

In a circle create a repeatable sequence of names. Someone starts by saying the name of someone else in the group. Once named this person will name someone else. Continue this until everyone has said someone else's name (the last person to go will say the name of the person who started the sequence). Then repeat the same sequence. A tip to set up the sequence smoothly is to keep your hand in the air until your name has been said – that way people can see who is yet to go.

Once the name sequence is running smoothly set up a new sequence, with a different order of people, throwing a ball around the group. Repeat this until smooth and then layer this upon the name sequence.

Once these are smooth, add a new sequence where the group switch places with someone else in the circle, giving them a high-five when you get to them. Layer this on top of the ball and names sequence.

Once these are running smoothly add a sequence where members of the group come to the middle of the circle in turn and bang a drum (or chair) maintaining a constant rhythm. Then add the other sequences so there are now four sequences running simultaneously.

A key to the game is not worrying if it goes wrong – pick up the sequence again and keep going.

Why?

The group talked about the benefits of the exercise. It encourages being aware of others, links to other skills such as picking up lines, sharing breath and not panicking. It works brilliantly as a focus exercise that 'clears the mind' before moving onto rehearsing the play.

Lead director Ola Ince mentioned it can be a great exercise to run over a rehearsal process, adding a new sequence every so often as it creates a great sense of group achievement.

Exercises for use in rehearsals

Exercise: World of the Play

Ince introduced an exercise designed to help companies build a shared sense of the world of the play.

Stage one

The groups were given 15 minutes to go through a visual art book as a group (this could be photography, art, sculpture – any visual art). Without talking the groups needed to mark with post-it notes or scraps of paper any of the pieces of art that resonated with them in response to the play. The fact the exercise was done in silence meant it encouraged intuition rather than an academic response to the art.

Stage two

After selecting their art works the groups (now able to talk again) discussed what the images selected had in common. How did this now curated selection of images link to the world of the play?

Responses

Themes found by the group included:
- Dark images with blurred edges
- Images of people tended to be in silhouette and shadow, so this made the group think about the hidden identities of characters
- Lots of texture – because the world needs to feel real
- The duality of dark colours and brightness, which represented the dark world of the play but the colourful characters with hope living within it
- Structure and concrete. Brutalist architecture
- Earthiness, wet mud, damp coal
- Images of nature resurfacing through human-made environments
- Importance of objects symbolizing home
- Images of cages and de-humanization
- Images of authority and power
- Soldiers and conflict

Why?

The group discussed how this exercise was a great way to process initial reactions to the play and to build a shared sense of its world. The fact the first stage took place without speaking meant that it relied on intuition and an artistic response rather getting too academic. It also meant the later conversations were more focused. It was a great launching pad for more in depth discussions.

Exercise: Drawing Images

Splitting a piece of paper into six boxes, the groups drew an image in each box. These images could be any reaction to the play, but for example could be: a pivotal moment, how you want the audience to react, how the play should look, what it should make the audience think about, how the audience should feel, an energy, an aspect that's important to capture, audience configuration, how it would smell or taste.

On a second piece of paper the groups listed a series of cultural influences the play made them think about. These were three books, three songs, three films, three news stories.

Responses

Responses to the exercise of drawing six images included:

- Smells of the play. Dettol, petrichor (smell after rain), grease, damp, mustiness
- Six emojis of how the audience feel (shock, joy, confusion, fear, intrigue, despair)
- A brain with the characters' inner thoughts
- Explosions with clarity at the centre
- Technology (old school and nostalgic)
- Characters
- Audience feeling uncomfortable at the start. Feel hopeful and positive by the end
- Soundscapes
- The logo of the Conservative Party
- Periodic table
- Lithium exploding in water
- Outside forces watching an explosion and doing nothing
- Masks
- The cast exiting into the audience at the end of the play
- Scales (representing Evian's state of mind)
- Art made from rubbish. The work of Tim Noble and Sue Webster
- Image inspired by *Happy Days* (Beckett play)
- A mound of rubbish
- Image inspired by *The Lorax* (Dr Seuss book) of children saving the world
- Image of Maude delivering her speech. She has the ultimate status in the light and the others are out of the light. Is this how she sees herself?

- Mags glowing – an image of connection
- Evian's anger with people around them

Responses to the cultural influences exercise included:

Books

- *Station 11* (dystopian novel where the world has crumbled and a group of people need to build it back together)
- *Winnie-the-Pooh* (as many of its characters could be neuro-diverse or experiencing mental health issues)
- *The Drowned World* (a dystopian novel set after an environmental disaster)
- *Human Kindness*
- *Lord of the Flies*
- *Cosmic Comics*
- *Happy Days*
- *Holes*
- *1984*
- *The Lorax*

Music

- 'Song 2' (Blur)
- 'Another Brick in the Wall' (Pink Floyd)
- *Star Wars* 'Imperial March'
- *Oppenheimer* soundtrack
- 'Changes' (Bowie)
- 'Heroes' (Bowie)
- 'I Hate You So Much Right Now' (Kelis)
- 'Brutal' (Olivia Rodrigo)
- The work of Kae Tempest
- 'The Sound of Silence' (Simon and Garfunkel)
- 'Insomnia' (Prodigy)

Films

- *Hunger Games*
- *Mad Max*
- *Hook* (because of the children coming together at the end)
- *The Beach*
- *Peter Pan*

- *I Am Legend*
- *Wall-E*
- *Labyrinth*
- *The Outsiders*
- *Ready Player One*
- *Transformers*
- *Black Mirror*

News stories

- Theresa May running through a field of wheat
- Theresa May's 'Hostile environment for immigrants'
- Children with autism being more likely to commit suicide
- School attendance issues post-Covid
- A story of a local dump where nearby schools are having to close as the air quality is so poor
- The schools RAAC concrete scandal
- Gillian Keegan talking about the teachers' strikes
- A story that there will be 9,000 more young offenders by 2027 because of school absences
- Ken Robinson's lectures on creativity in schools (YouTube)
- Einstein's quote 'Everyone is a genius but if you judge a fish by its ability to climb a tree it will spend its life thinking it's a failure'
- Students striking over environmental disaster?
- A story about local bin strikes
- Children disappearing in refugee settings

Why?

Similar to exercise two, the group discussed how this is a great exercise for building a shared sense of the world of the play and is a jumping-off point for having a structured conversation about a group's initial reactions.

Approaching the text

Exercise: Facts and Questions

Ola Ince introduced an exercise that she explained is crucial to her process – Facts and Questions.

Divide a piece of paper in half. On one half you will collect 'Facts' and on the other 'Questions'. Read through the play and collect all the facts and questions, writing them on this paper as you go.

A fact is something you know in the play for certain – a concrete thing the writer has told you. An example in *The Periodicals* is that 'There is a rubbish dump' or 'Maude is the Education Secretary'.

A question is something that is up for debate. Examples in this play could include 'What is the rubbish dump like?' or 'How long has Maude been in this job?' Writer Siân Owen doesn't tell you this, so you need to make a decision yourself.

Facts tell you what Owen has already decided. Questions show you what decisions you need to make as part of your process. Some will be things you need to research and some will be where you can make creative decisions that will be unique to your production.

Why?

The group discussed the many benefits of the exercise including:

- It's a great exercise for making sure you aren't making assumptions or pre-conceived choices that don't actually work with the text.
- It helps you realize any things you have misunderstood.
- It helps make sure that all the members of the company are on the same page and have the same understanding of the world.
- It helps you realize where the director and actors can bring their own ideas in.
- It helps you establish a base level of characterization. You really consider what has happened to the character and what the script tells you about them.
- It helps you realize what you need to research.
- It helps young actors understand how important each of their lines are.
- It helps young actors understand the 'present tense' of the scenes. What the characters know when.
- It can help start conversations about the wider themes.

Exercise: Actioning

Ince introduced an exercise based on the rehearsal technique of 'Actioning'. This is a process where you ask actors to find the right verb to explain what they are attempting to do to the other actor on stage. It ensures that every line has a reason (an 'action') for saying it and makes sure the actors' performances are 'active' (they are always trying to impact on others on stage).

Ince shared an exercise that has the benefits of the 'Actioning' process but is much more physical and connected to an actor's impulse.

Stage one

With each sentence spoken in a script, a physical action to Push/Pull/Squash or Lift, another actor *must* be chosen. You have to physically do this action while saying the line. Ideally the action must involve two hands and be as intense as it can be safely (check in with partners to check where they are comfortable being touched and for any existing injuries). If the line is delivered to the group, be creative with how you physicalize this.

If running the exercise early in the process, before lines are learnt, a second groups of actors can feed in the lines, which should then be repeated by the actor performing the physical exercise.

Ince emphasized that it's great to be brave – wrong but strong. You will soon know if it's the right or wrong physical action. She encouraged the group to go with their impulse and not overthink it. Really connect to the line both physically and vocally.

Stage two

After using this exercise to go through a scene, use your findings to discover what a character's 'objective' is for the scene. An objective is what the character is trying to achieve from others in the scene.

Ince encouraged the group to use the following format to articulate these:

I want you **(who?)** to . . . . . **(what?)**

Some examples included:

I want **Maude** to **pay me attention.**
I want **Mercury** to **keep me safe.**
I want **everyone** to **be quiet.**

Why?

The group fed back the following reasons why the exercise was useful:

- Helps to establish relationships between characters that weren't always obvious on the page.
- Really useful for students who struggle to connect physically to language.
- Helps to find the various character relationships and different 'scenes within scenes'.
- Helps to find the specificity on who are you saying the line too.
- The smallest line became meaningful and important.
- Helps to focus on specificity and changes within long sections of language.
- Ensures something is being done with each line to help keep the dramatic action flowing.

Question and answer with Siân Owen

Q: Can we take out swear words?
A: Yes. Make it appropriate for your group.

Q: Can we edit a scene?
A: Have fun and empower your young people to tell the story. Be free to find the best way to do that as long as the story still makes sense.

Q: Are there any character visuals (design, costumes) you want us to re-create?
A: Again, be guided by what makes you feel comfortable and what comes out of your process.

Q: Can I put a series of projected news headlines or data at the end of the play to connect it with our world?
A: Yes! Sounds great.

Q: Why is Silicone from 1983?
A: I wanted someone who had no home to return to. I didn't want this to be about geography, politics or war so I chose somewhere I liked – 1983! The key thing is it's a way of having a character who can't go back home.

Q: Who are The Methanes?
A: Methane is a byproduct of waste. It came from my research on landfills. I learnt gas is explosive. But it can be channelled by landfills and become useful. This felt like there was a connection to our school system. Kids help each other but this has often been seen as a problem.

Q: Why are they there?
A: It's a handy way of getting lots of people on stage! I was also conscious that groups might have people who really want to be involved but might not want many or any lines, so it's a way for people to be involved in a way they feel comfortable with.

Q: Are there any others dumped at the landfill – anyone outside of the characters we meet?
A: Not in my mind – but it's a good question.

Q: How long have the main characters been there?
A: Longer than six months. Enough time to establish routines and systems.

Q: Is Scene Two straight after Scene One in the timeline?
A: Yes – it's the same time. Maude's texting Evian at the end of Scene One.

Q: The Methanes seem to pre-empt danger – how do they know it's coming?
A: They are magic!

Q: When creating Evian did you imagine them having OCD?
A: In my mind they do have OCD. It developed as I was writing the play, it wasn't always going to be the case but the more I wrote the more it seemed to work.

Q: Why does Maude take the situation so personally – using lots of personal language such as 'I want to win'?

A: I soaked up loads of press conferences from politicians including Gillian Keegan (Education Secretary at the time of writing) and others. A key influence was a Suella Braverman speech where she said 'it was *her* ambition' to move immigrants to Rwanda. Why *her* ambition? It was a really personal and bizarre way of referring to a situation.

Q: Why that specific tape recorder?
A: It was my dad's. He was a teacher and it's one he used to have!

Q: When creating Mags did you have a way to make them glow?
A: The joy of being a writer is to not have to work it out! I've grown in my bravery as a writer through the support of the National Theatre. I don't have to worry about that – over to you! She's magic.

Q: Are there any encroachments from the outside world into the dump. How does waste get there? Do they have to avoid workers on the waste dump for instance?
A: I watched documentaries about landfill for research – they are huge – miles and miles in size. The kids in the story have found the bit that's untouched. An area of the tip that's not active, it's being left alone to settle. You used to have people checking for dangerous methane levels but now it's done through sensors so often people wouldn't need to visit areas of the landfill for years and years.

Q: Is Silicone actually a child still or an adult from 1983?
A: They are physically and mentally a teenager. They are just from 1983 – like a time drop.

Q: Why do young people never leave the landfill site?
A: They don't want to. It's their safe space. The world is too horrible to leave.

Q: Is Mole really Evian's social worker?
A: No. But they are everyone else's. The authorities have got the information so have arrested Mole as a way in.

Q: What has Mags seen? Is there a pre-existing specific trauma? Or a trauma all have experienced?
A: It is open to interpretation, but I do think Mags has seen something no one else has, a specific trauma. But there is probably a shared trauma for the group (for instance the way Covid was for the current generation of young people). It's your decision to decide what they have experienced. Something for you to find in the rehearsal room.

Q: When does Mercury know that Evian isn't trustworthy. Or do they trust them?
A: They trust them because of the Mole cover story. They have no reason to doubt that story. The kids in general are wary of authority but there is no reason to think Mole has been compromised.

Q: Did they choose their own names? Why is Mags shortened?
A: It's easier to say Mags than Magnesium the whole time! I think it's what would happen in a group. Yes, they've given themselves their own names. They can be who they want to be.

Q: Why doesn't Gold speak?
A: Very practically I wanted to have a character that could be played by someone who might not want to speak. But lots of children choose not to speak for a variety of

reasons in life, neurodiversity, or trauma for instance. I wanted these kids represented. But there is a whole personality there – they just choose not to speak.

Q: How does Maude find out about the group?
A: The Attendance Alliance have lots of resources – think MI5 or MI6 level.

Q: Are the voices we hear at the end from a different place? Or nearby now?
A: All of it. There are so many kids missing or under the radar around the world. Until you look you don't see it. They are finding each other in this moment.

Q: Are the characters' backstories open to interpretation?
A: Absolutely!

Q: Is there anything you want Gold to be doing?
A: They are watchful, the reassuring presence in the space. Gold knows what they need to do. They might be gaming, making food. Be assured they know what they are doing.

Q: Is Gold called Gold because they are non-reactive, or a play on the phrase 'Silence is golden'?
A: Both!

Q: There are a number of awkward pauses in the play. What's happening in these moments?
A: Maybe the pause is symbolizing 'We don't want to go there' or 'We aren't prepared to talk about it'. Maybe you don't need it. Find it in rehearsals.

Q: You say all characters can be played by any gender. Does this include Maude? What about the mother/son relationship with Evian?
A: If you can embody a hateful, bigoted, cruel person then do that. That's the important thing to capture in the character. Maude is Evian's mum, so if you can keep the mother/son dynamic please do. But if not a father/son or father/daughter, or mother/daughter could work too. The most important thing is to capture the uncomfortable relationship between them and the sense of character. If you feel the best actors to play these characters are not the genders they currently are in the play I don't want to restrict you.

Q: If you could pick three key narrative moments, what would they be?
A: That's really hard! Mags and Lithium. Where someone asks you to stay after being asked to go. The feelings are the important thing. The group together working out their strengths that others view as weakness. The ending – they are not alone. The voices in the dark. It was inspired by a video I saw in Covid where people in a town would flash lights on and off in unison. The feeling that people weren't alone.

Q: Is Evian an only child?
A: Most definitely.

From a workshop led by Ola Ince
Notes by Tom Bellerby

National Theatre

REPLICA

by Titas Halder

Supported using public funding by
ARTS COUNCIL
ENGLAND

Titas Halder is a writer, director and musician. His first two plays, *Run the Beast Down* at the Marlowe and the Finborough and *Escape the Scaffold* at The Other Room and Theatre503, saw him nominated for Best New Writer at the Stage Debut Awards. His play *The Basement* was a finalist for the Verity Bargate Award. He trained on the Royal Court Theatre Young Writers' Programme and at the Donmar Warehouse as Resident Assistant Director. For the National Theatre he has been a director and playwriting tutor for New Views and was staff director on *Consent*.

Titas Halder has worked extensively on new writing and developing new plays. His work as director includes *The Lemon Table* (co-directed with Michael Grandage) on UK tour; *Sinners Club* at Soho Theatre, Theatr Clwyd and The Other Room; *A Boy and His Soul* at Kiln; and *The Dance of Death* at Donmar Trafalgar. He is currently writing his first feature film. He performs and records as Titas and the Fox.

Characters

Cora, **Sam**, **Alex**
Chris *and* **Jude**
Ash *and* **Mika**
Lewis
L J *and* **Tucker**
Auden
Morgan

Names

Most of the names are gender neutral.
Gender of characters/pronouns can be changed as desired.

Setting

One – various locations within a school
Two – the dig
Three – the school, and elsewhere, past and present

Les règles du jeu

Something always happens in a *Pause*.
A *Beat* is more for rhythm.
A / means the next line overlaps.
A (line in brackets) can either be said or unsaid.
The play is told out of chronological sequence.

One

1

School. **Alex** *and* **Cora**.

Alex He's been replaced.

Cora Replaced?

Alex Yeah.

Cora With what?

Alex With *something*.

Cora What do you mean replaced?

Alex He's different. He's not the same. Since the trip he's been different.

Cora Why do you care?

Alex I do care. Not about *him*. About you – I'm *concerned*, I'm saying I'm just saying – I do care, because something's happened and it is very wrong.

Cora You don't like him.

Alex No, it's not it's not it's not about that, it's not about you and me. I mean, we can at least be in the same room can't we?

Cora Do we have to be?

Alex It's not about us. It's about him. I'm not saying he's *being different*, I'm not saying oh he's depressed and behaving weirdly, I wouldn't care about that, if it was *that* he could just go around being depressed. What I'm saying is that he's been *replaced*. He is *not the same*, the same . . . I don't want to use the word *person* – because he's *not* – he has become someone, some*thing* else. He has become some other thing.

Pause.

Cora *What?*

Chris *and* **Jude** *arrive.*

Chris Can I have that fiver back?

Alex What fiver?

Chris The fiver you / owe me –

Alex Did you find him?

Chris He's hiding somewhere.

Jude Sometimes he goes to the art block.

Alex What does he do there?

Jude I don't know – art?

Alex By himself? On a break? That's weird. What's he doing up there? He could be doing anything.

Cora Drawing?

Alex Plotting.

Chris Plotting what? Plotting like plotting against us? Plotting an attack?

Alex I don't know. He could be. You have to admit, he's been different since the trip. Something's been off.

Jude That's true. Since the trip, something's been off with a lot of things.

Alex He's sinister. Odd, odder than ever. He's got *even more* . . .

Cora What?

Alex Whatever he is. He doesn't behave like everyone else, does he? There's something wrong with him. That's obvious.

Cora He hasn't been replaced.

Chris Do you think he's been replaced?

Cora No.

Alex I'm *being serious*. He isn't him. He is not him. He's like a casing. Like he's got a human shell.

Cora He's shy. He's quiet.

Jude I think he's funny.

Alex Are you – are you *mad*? He's not shy, he's not *funny*. He's not quiet, he's *silent*. He always does his homework, he never gets in trouble. It's weird. He is not to be trusted. What do we know about him? Nothing. Where did he come from? What school? Has he ever said? He just appeared. They brought him into class one day. Did he even go to a school? We don't even know.

Cora You could just ask? Have you ever thought about finding out first instead of opening your mouth?

Alex Why do you care so much?

Cora I don't care.

Jude Let's find out then.

Cora What?

Jude If you think something's happened to him, why don't we find out.

Cora I don't think anything's happened.

Alex I'm telling you. Something is wrong.

Jude I believe you.

2

Locker room. **Cora** *and* **Lewis**.

Cora I'm telling you the truth.

Lewis I don't believe you. I can see it in your eyes. You're excited. Since the trip there's a, you've been. You're changed. Chang*èd*. Your skin is rippling. Your skeleton has been shook. You think I can't tell? I can. SEE? I *knew* it. I know everything about you. There is something. What. Is it?

Pause.

Cora Since the trip. I've been experiencing time differently.

Lewis OK, that is not what I was expecting you to say.

Beat.

Different how? How, different?

Cora Just, different. Jumbled.

Lewis Jumbled.

Cora Confused. Sometimes I feel like everything is happening very slowly, sometimes it happens in an instant. Sometimes it feels like things have already happened, and other times it feels like it's now and everything's fine.

Lewis And what is it now?

Cora Now it's now.

Lewis It's now now?

Cora Yeah it's now.

Pause.

Lewis Am I – am I the only normal one left? Since the trip? Am I the only one being normal?

Cora No.

Lewis MAN ALIVE. I missed out.

Cora You didn't miss / out.

Lewis Are you (serious) – ?! I've clearly massively missed out. I've massively missed out on something, whatever it is – I have completely missed out. FOMO is real. FOMO is real. What did I miss?

Cora Nothing.

Lewis You went on the trip. You came back, and now you're *experiencing time differently* – UM. SOMETHING HAPPENED.

Cora Well . . . OK actually there's, there is . . .

Lewis Yeah?

Pause. **Cora** *thinks long and hard. She decides not to say.*

Cora Mr Sands.

Lewis I beg your pardon?

Cora You know, Mr Sands. When you're in a train station or something and they say 'Can Mr Sands report to the control room' – and you know it means there's a bomb or a fire or some kind of disaster. Mr Sands. Well, there was a proper Mr Sands on the trip.

Lewis Oh my God. You're LYING. Did something *happen*? Like *happen happen*? Oh my God something happened didn't it. Because people are talking.

Cora What.

Lewis People are saying that you / and –

Cora I don't care what people think.

Lewis Sam. The one who came here last term. People are saying things. Like he's hiding his identity. He's got a fake passport or something. Maybe he's *unstable* / or

Cora He's / not . . .

Lewis He could be one of those kids that grows up and murders his parents. You know. He could be insane. Because people are saying that on the dig you went off together. Down to the caves where you're not allowed to go.

Cora Who said that?

Lewis I dunno.

Beat.

Cora. What happened in that cave?

Pause.

Cora We've barely even talked. Never.

Lewis You've never talked?

Cora We have never talked.

3

A quiet place. **Ash** *and* **Mika**.

Ash Have you chosen?

Mika Are you joking? Have I chosen? This is. They're treating us like cattle. They want us to choose which gate to go through but they all end up going to the . . . you know, where they kill / all the –

Ash Abattoir

Mika Abattoir. They want us to go to the abattoir *voluntarily*. Choose this, decide this. It'll only determine the rest of your life, and you can only do it if it's useful to *me*, not *you*. Oh, and by the way, surprize, you owe us a lot of money. You need to pay us, forever. So now you're locked in. What if I don't want to decide? What if I don't want to choose now? What if I want to see what happens? What if I want to ask you a question?

Ash Me?

Mika No, *them* you – not *you* you. What if I want to *ask things*. Disobey. Question the rules. Why shouldn't I? We have to. We should be allowed to. I have my own experience. Why should it be denied? Why are you denying it?

Ash Me?

Mika NO. Not *you* you – *them* you. They deny it. They deny me. I don't have to do what they say just cos I'm young and they're old. They're wrong. We should be throwing old people into skips. For what they've done to us. They're vampires. Bloodsuckers. Feeding on your youth.

Ash Mine?

Mika YES, *yours*.

Pause.

Ash So you haven't chosen then.

Mika No. I'm stressed about it.

Beat.

I don't know what I wanna do. I just want to float. In the ocean.

Ash What, drowning?

Mika Drifting. Why can't we just drift about?

Ash We?

Mika Yeah. Drift.

Ash Float.

Pause.

Well, sometime, at some point, you gotta choose.

Mika I choose . . . to tear it down. I choose to tear it all down.

Pause.

Ash Mika, I don't want to fuck up my future.

Beat.

You don't think it's too far

Mika No

Ash What we did

Mika *No.*

Pause.

Ash Do you think we should come clean?

Mika No.

Ash You don't think we should come clean.

Mika No.

4

The IT room. **Alex** *and* **Auden**.

Auden A simulacra is like a copy. An imitation. It's sort of like. Replacing reality with a representation of it. – You're not gonna hit me are you?

Alex What are you on about? Why would I hit you?! – Carry on. What I'm saying is do you think it's *possible*?

Auden Well, they cloned a sheep in 1997.

Pause.

Alex So?

Auden So that was ages ago. They've probably done all sorts of things in secret since then. I mean what are you talking about like, AI?

Alex No like. An impostor. A *thing*, a bad *thing*. A threat.

Pause.

Auden Do you really think – Why do you think he's different?

Alex Just answer theoretically. Come on, you're a year ahead right? You're clever. What if it was true? And if it were, how would I persuade other people to believe me?

Auden Well, I suppose . . . it's not *impossible*. There are lots of things we can't explain. I like facts. But we can't know everything. Something can be true, and real, without you knowing anything about it. Like there are things we can't *see* but they're real.

Alex Like?

Auden Gravity. Why are you stuck down to the floor? You aren't / aware of it.

Alex Yeah yeah yeah, everyone knows about gravity.

Auden There are lots of extra-sensory phenomena / which –

Alex What do you mean, like ghosts?

Auden No, not like ghosts. Maybe ghosts. Well, no. *Light* – we don't see ultraviolet light, but it's there. For example, if we were in the dark, and we turned on a UV light, we'd see all the jizz stains on your trousers.

Alex Um. Did you just insult me?

Auden Yes, sorry. I couldn't help it.

Alex *laughs.*

Alex No it's good, it's good, I like it. But here's the problem yeah? If something seems like it's obviously not true, then no-one's going to believe it.

Auden What is obviously not true? What is true and not true?

Alex Well, if something's true, it's true, isn't it. You can't argue with that.

Auden No. Truth is not absolute. Truth is power. It's more like, if you control the room – you *decide* what's true and what's not.

Pause.

Alex You're actually genuinely a child genius aren't you. Right. But. I'm talking about *what's real and what's not real.*

Auden You mean. What people *perceive* to be real versus what is *actually* real. Like, we say the sun goes down, but it doesn't actually go down.

Alex What.

Auden *We* turn away from the sun. *We're moving.* The earth. It's not the sun going down, but that's what we say. It's not what happens. It's not what's real.

Alex The sun going down isn't real.

Auden Not really.

Alex My head is exploding. Now I don't know what's real. OK wait – so you can prove to people that what they *think* isn't necessarily true. You can get them to doubt the truth.

Auden Yes.

Alex OK, OK that's really good. And then. Flip it round. Can you take something which we know to be true, and make people think it's false?

Auden Yeah. Of course. Like, is the world flat. It isn't. But there are some dumbarses who think it is because they've been fed a bunch of shit from the internet. And the thing is – once they believe *that lie*, then *all of reality* is malleable. They'll believe anything.

Alex OK. And. How do you. How would you. See you're a genius, see? How do you apply this to a *person*? Like – what if you were looking at something real in front of you. Someone. But you wanted everyone to think they're looking at something else completely – how do you get people to think that, to *doubt* that?

Auden   Like a mirage

Alex   No, a *person*. A person.

Auden   What?

Alex   What I'm saying is. How do you prove that you're a person?

Pause.

Auden   You would do a test.

5

Art block. **Sam** *sits alone, drawing.* **Cora** *enters.*

Cora   Hey.

Startled, **Sam** *knocks over his pencil case. All manner of bits go flying. They get down and pick up all the pens and pencils.*

Cora   What are you drawing?

Sam   Nothing.

Sam *folds up his picture.*

Cora   You'll ruin it.

Sam *ignores her. After a pause.*

Cora   What did you tell people? About the beach? Sam. Did you say anything?

Pause. **Tucker** *enters. He stares at* **Sam**. *He has a pencil. He walks over to* **Sam** *quite carefully and then jabs him with it.*

Sam   Ow!

Cora   What are you doing?

Tucker   Is it true?

Cora   Is what true?

Tucker   Him. It. He.

Pause. **Sam** *is bewildered.* **Mika** *enters*

Mika   I saw you at the dig. On the beach, by the cliff. He walked all the way down to the sea. He went into the cave. And you followed him. You went in together. I saw him mutate. Like molten metal. I saw you both. I watched you melt.

Cora   That is obviously not true.

Mika   Which bit?

Pause. **Cora** *goes to leave with* **Sam**. **Mika** *blocks their path.* **Cora** *squares up to* **Mika**. **Alex, Jude, Chris, Lewis** *arrive.*

Cora Did you tell them we were here?

Lewis No.

Tucker You saw what he did at the dig. He flipped out at me. He went mad.

Cora You mean you got scared and had a nosebleed?

Tucker *No.* He *does* something to you. He *looks at you.*

Mika (*enjoying it*) What?!

Tucker There's something wrong with him. Everyone's saying.

Mika *laughs.* **Alex** *smiles.* **Auden** *arrives, out of breath.*

Auden I heard the same . . . thing . . . sorry . . . I ran up the stairs.

Jude There's a secret about you. That the school kept hidden.

Alex Go on. Make the argument.

Jude You don't talk to anyone, you spend your breaktimes alone. Most of the time you never speak in class. But when you do, you're the class clown. Both of those things are about hiding yourself. You don't want anyone to know who you are. And you *watch us.* How many of you have been in class and looked round to see him staring at you? He stares at you doesn't he? (*to* **Cora**) That's true isn't it? And you stare at me. Why? Do you not understand emotions? What happened on the trip? Did you malfunction? Everyone saw.

Sam I'm (sorry) . . . I got upset.

Alex The whole time he's been here. There's always been something wrong with him.

Jude You look like us. You act like us. But you're not the same as us, are you? Tell the truth.

Alex He's like a corrupted program. A copy.

Auden We should study him. Like a science experiment. A phenomenon.

Mika How do you want to do that? Cut him open? Do an autopsy?

Tucker Magnets.

Lewis Take a sample. A strand of hair.

Alex A blood sample.

Chris What's that thing, that thing – we did it in Philosophy, that test, to see whether you're human or a robot – named after that guy, the dead guy

Auden You mean the Turing test. To see whether you're talking to a computer or a human.

Tucker *Exactly.* We should do that.

Pause.

Alex We're taking him.

Cora Where?!

Alex C block basement.

Cora You're not.

Alex OK. Tell us then. Tell us where you came from. How you got here. What school you went to. Why you left. Tell us, and I'll leave you alone.

Sam I just . . . came here.

Jude What happened to you before?

Sam .

Alex I don't care what happened. I don't care how you got here or who you are. I know you're a *thing* – you're not a real person.

6

Somewhere secret. **Sam** *and* **Cora**.

Sam I dreamt I was eating an apple. One of the red ones, it looked crisp and delicious. But as I went to take a bite I could see it was soft, I could feel it going rotten. And as I held it in my hand I could see that around the bottom there was a ring of flies. Thin, brown, moth-like. Parasitic, vile. And I threw the apple across the room into the bin.

Pause.

The next day I woke up with an itch. And I looked down to see something crawling under my skin – an undulating ridge burrowing across my upper arm. But I wasn't panicked. I lay still as it started to bore a tiny hole through me to come out. I remember thinking – it's better that it's coming out, than staying in. Painless, it pierced through my skin, and out dropped a maggot. White, tiny, which fell to the floor. I jumped out of bed to try and find it to make sure that I wasn't hallucinating, that it wasn't a figment of my imagination. On my hands and knees, still in my pyjamas, there it was, a speck of white against the dark wood floor. Barely alive, but moving, wriggling, oblivious to the world surrounding it. I ran to the cupboard to get a hammer. I was scared that by the time I got back it'd be gone. But there it was – this tiny thing, undulating on the floorboard. I went to smash it with the hammer but stopped. I picked it up, put it in the palm of my hand, placed it on a coaster and turned a cup upside down so it couldn't escape. I went to get a magnifying glass. I could see – this little white thing, already bigger than the hole in my arm, was growing.

Pause.

Something in me said that I should let it live. This thing had come out of me – I wanted to see if it would live or die. I wanted to see what it would become. So I kept it. I put it in a cardboard box and left it in the cupboard. I figured it would die if it had absolutely nothing to feed on, which made me wonder if it had fed on me. The only thing I could think to leave it was an apple. I put it in the cupboard and I let it pupate. A few days later, it had become a cocoon. And after a week I came home to find it child-sized. Pink, green and purple and almost translucent. And inside it there was the silhouette of a head and shoulders. The next morning when I went to check on it, there was a carapace on the floor, covered with a white cream, like the maggot. And the smell was awful. I turned around and there it was. I came face to face with him. It, him – me. A mirror image. It stood there, shocked, alive, scared, hungry-eyed. We stood across the room from each other. He reached out for me, placed his hands on my shoulders and I did the same. At first I thought it was something special. But then it became a struggle. He pushed me to the floor, his face closer and closer to mine. The stench of his breath. He bit into me. Tore out a chunk of my skin, flesh and meat – and ate it. I lay there in shock, frightening pain. So painful it was numb. He ate me. He consumed me.

Beat.

That is the last thing I remember before waking up. Like this. As I am now. And now I am not sure whether he is me. Or I am him. But I am here.

Cora *rolls up his sleeve. He lets her. She examines his hand, his arm for a mark.*

Cora   That is weird as shit. I love it.

Sam   You won't tell anyone will you?

Cora   Why would I?

Two

7

The dig. **L J** *and* **Tucker**.

L J Did you feel something? When you were out there?

Tucker Feel what?

L J Did you touch it?

Tucker You're not supposed to.

L J But you did. What did you feel?

Tucker It felt like stone. Like a rock with moss on it.

Pause. **L J** *shrugs.*

L J OK.

L J *begins to leave.*

Tucker Did you? What happened when you touched it?

L J We came here once when there was an eclipse. Ages ago, before they discovered the cave and the paintings. Before they built this museum. It was just the stone circle alone in the landscape. My dad takes us to lots of places like this. Which have like – a special . . . y'know . . . *energy* or. Anyway, we had to stay up all night. My brother and sister fell asleep. There were other people who'd hiked up. Weird druidy people in cloaks, and other weird-looking people wearing North Face jackets. My dad took me up here, to the monolith. And it might feel like rock to you now, but then, in that light, this kind of magic light. Neither night nor day. In that light it looked black. Not black like . . . black shoes, or a black bag, but – *black*. Like – it absorbed colour. The absence of colour. A black void. Like you couldn't tell if it was solid, or whether you could fall through it into another dimension. My dad held me up, I reached out to touch it. And I felt . . . it seemed to change shape. It seemed to hum and vibrate. It seemed to have a kind of power. The moon and its crown. Above the stone. When I touched it, it was like I understood something from another time.

Pause.

When you touched it. What did you feel?

8

The visitors' centre. **Sam** *stands alone wearing an audio headset. Students drift in and out, looking at exhibits.* **Chris** *goes around pinging everyone wearing an audio headset.*

Ash What sandwiches did you get?

Mika Egg. You?

Ash   Hummus wrap.

Mika   Swap?

                          *

Chris   What you got?

Alex   Uh, crab.

Chris   Crab?! What you gonna do with a crab sandwich?!

                          *

Mika   Have you seen the replica? In the last room?

Ash   The monolith? It's hypnotic.

                          *

L J   Stunning isn't it.

Jude   It is. Absolutely incredible.

                          *

Ash   I'm staring at this stone with these inscriptions and I'm thinking. Isn't it mad that four thousand years ago someone wanted to write something down so much that they got a tiny little hammer and a chisel, and they carved it into stone.

Mika   What if they had bad handwriting?

                          *

Alex   Can I borrow a fiver?

Chris   For what?

Alex   A snack.

Chris *reluctantly hands over the money. Then he goes over to* **Auden** *and snaps the audio headset over his ears.*

                          *

Sam *wanders over to where* **Cora** *is. They are side by side.*

                          *

Chris   Wait, what? *Thousands of years old?*

Auden   Yes, obviously.

Chris   But like, who *made it?*

Auden   Druids.

Chris   How are they gonna be so strong

Auden   What?

Chris Them skinny old people with cloaks and beards? Are you joking? How are they gonna be so strong to lift up those stones and *sink* one right down into the earth? Nah. You'd need a spaceship. That is a mystery. That is a legitimate, full-blown mystery. They should make a documentary about that I'm telling you. Proper mysterious vibes.

Auden There already is a multi-award-winning documentary.

*

Jude What do you think of the red horses?

Alex What?

Jude The red horses. In the second passageway.

Alex Um. Yeah. Are they horses? Yeah they're fine.

Alex *watches* **Cora** *standing with* **Sam**.

*

Chris I'm gonna say it was aliens, man. How come they didn't find this stuff?

Auden They . . . they did find it. They . . . Sorry, can I just ask: why are you talking to me?

Chris It's a school trip. The rules are different. I'm gonna say it. The cave paintings. They're shit. What are those supposed to be?

*

Tucker *arrives.* **Jude** *is distracted, watching* **Alex** *watch* **Cora** *and* **Sam**.

Jude That's an ibex.

Tucker A what?

Jude And those are birds.

Tucker What's so special, what does it mean?

Jude It means that you don't have any imagination whatsoever do you. They've never found cave paintings here before. These caves, like the ones at Chauvet and Lascaux, they change how we understand human history. It's miraculous.

Tucker Alright, stress. Why can't we just go in the caves? See the real ones?

Jude Because if humans were allowed in we'd destroy them.

*

Chris I don't care about ancient people. Mosaics, that's what you do in primary school. We've got toddlers making that sort of thing now. I'm not impressed. Can you imagine, at some point in time, they didn't even know what the wheel was – you know what I mean? The *wheel*. *I* could have come up with that. Oh, how do we get this from here to there? *The wheel*. Easy. Take any of us, any of us, put us back then

– we'd be geniuses. You know? Oh – I'm really cold, we're freezing – *bang*, fire. See? Genius. There's no point looking back at all this stuff. It's all broken jars, pots and pans – everyone's got pots and pans. There's no point looking at the past. You have to be thinking about the *future*. Because if you reverse what I'm saying, and you've got people in two thousand years time looking at a museum of *us*, they're gonna be saying – oh, a car, big deal – pile of shit. They'll be like – come on, invisibility cloak, where's that? Why didn't they have that then? Mind control. Lasers.

Auden   We have lasers.

Chris   Hold on – why am I talking to you?

Auden   You think there aren't any mysteries left? You're wrong. There are ancient things which we cannot possibly comprehend.

*

Chris *leaves. As he goes he snaps* **Sam***'s audio headset against his ears.* **Sam** *reacts – 'what's your problem?'*

9

A corner of the museum. **Cora** *and* **Alex***.*

Alex   Actually, I find your singing boring. You're, you're not actually that good. Like it's not, you're not, your voice isn't – you're not *remarkable*.

Cora   What?

Pause.

Alex   I'm trying to be kind. Because I'm just saying – it's not something you could *do* for a living, it's not something you could *pursue* in the future. With something like that, singing, there's always going to be someone that's better than you. That's fair. I'm being fair. I'm just saying. To be honest, maybe I'm not the best judge because I don't, I don't actually like music that much. I don't like listening to music.

Cora   Are you dead? *Inside*? Are you actually dead?

Alex   No, it's just that – I don't – I don't *get* it. They're boring after a while, songs. I get bored of them, I need to not / have sound.

Cora   They're boring? Songs? All of songs? There's literally hundreds, millions of hours of music and you're *bored*? Maybe it's because – oh – *you're* boring. You are actually very boring. If I had to describe the majority of the time I've spent with you, I would describe it as – uh – completely boring.

Alex   If I'm boring. You're selfish. You're only interested in you. You care too much about what other people think. You're not –

Cora   Arrogant?

Alex   Confident enough.

Pause.

Cora I hate that you think, for some insane reason, that you are the most important person in the room. That your feelings matter the most. I *hate* your entitlement, your *arrogance*. It baffles me. Maybe I used to think it was *impressive*, but only because it seems to come so easy to you. I won't ever get to be like that, to behave like that. I don't get to feel that way. Confident. So yes, I hate it. I hate you.

Alex Hate me? What did I ever do to you? All I ever did was think that you're amazing. Now I think you're rude. Hate me? Hate is very ugly. What did I do to deserve that? And now you're ugly. What have you done? You've made yourself ugly. I thought that would be impossible. Why did you do that? I thought you were supposed to be good with people's feelings. But you've been dreadful with mine. Horrendous. That's you actually isn't it. You look at something, you see what you want and you take it, but only for as long as it matters to you. I don't matter to you. How can I not matter? That's impossible. You don't have a soul. You don't have any emotions. You're a machine. You don't matter.

Cora Are you sure you're not confusing me with you? I see it now, I understand. I think the truth is you're scared. You're scared that you're completely, utterly unremarkable. In every way. Because you are. And one day people will find out.

Pause.

Alex You said. You'd sit with me. On the bus. So why'd you sit with him? As a joke? Don't laugh. I saw you. Sharing headphones. Singing.

Cora I can sit with whoever I want.

Alex No. I don't want you to be around him. In case *he does something*. To you, or – He's dangerous, he'll do something dangerous one day, terrible. And they'll all be like, oh nobody saw it coming. And I'll be like *I* saw it coming – look at him. Look at the way he looks. He was always gonna do something. So no, I don't want you to hang around him – I forbid it.

Cora Get fucked.

Alex I'll say you're –

Cora What.

Alex I'll say you –

Cora *What.*

Pause.

Say whatever you want to say.

10

The café. **Alex**, **Mika**, **Ash**. *Ash is eating a churro in a cone with a tube of chocolate sauce.*

Alex What do you think of this place?

Mika   Since when do you care what I think?

Alex   The re-creation of the paintings, the 3D video, it's amazing right? As if you're going through the caves.

Mika   Are you joking? It's shit.

Alex   Is it?

Mika   This place? What is this? What actually is it?

Alex   It's a museum.

Mika   Who paid for it? Who built it? Look at who the sponsors are. Rapacious environmentally destructive parasites. What do you think this is a monument to?

Alex   It's just a museum isn't it?

Mika   It's the commodification of cultural heritage. They don't give a shit about archaeology or art. It's costumes, holograms, absolute crap. If it was real, you would be able to go into the caves. This is a simulation. They're just wrapping it up into a neat little box so they can *sell* you a product. They built a facsimile of the monolith and then put it indoors. Wow. They filmed the caves and made a 3D video. You think that's amazing? It isn't real. And the graphics are shit. Look at this building. Twisting and turning, to replicate going through the caves right? La la la. And where does every single path in the museum lead? To the gift shop. They want you to spend your money. That's what this is.

Ash   Yeah, they want you to spend your money on their delicious products.

Ash *bites into a churro.*

Mika   Bullshit. Colonial. Capitalist narrative.

Ash   It's a trap.

Pause.

Alex   So I'm wondering what you've got planned.

Mika   What?

Alex   A prank. Protest. I mean to be fair, you're on academic probation so I could understand why you'd be scared / to

Mika   I'm not scared.

Alex   No, but I can understand why you / would be.

Mika   But I'm not scared / though.

Alex   No, but to be fair you don't want to get yourself / suspended.

Mika   If I wanna fuck shit up I will fuck some shit up.

Alex   You could get expelled.

Ash   We are going to fuck shit up so how do you feel about that?

Ash *points the sauce at* **Alex**. *Pause. Squirts it on the churros.*

Alex   That was so funny, that time. When we were doing igneous rocks. Every time Dr Taylor said earthquake, you got everyone to dive under the desks

Mika   You can't prove that was me.

Ash   It was you though.

Mika   Guilty. Yeah, that was dope.

Alex   And the time you got everyone to chuck their Pritt Sticks at the ceiling when he was on about stalactites and stalagmites. He had a *breakdown*.

Ash   Taylor is a cock.

Alex   Well, since it's his trip, I just reckoned you'd have something up your sleeve. As a fuck-you.

Mika   Taylor is a fucking cock. Sexist. Ancient misogynist wanker.

Ash   True.

Mika *looks to* **Ash**.

Alex   It's so sad isn't it. Taylor and his weird little teacher's pet Sam. Walking around looking at all the artefacts together.

Mika   He is so creepy. I reckon if you said his name five times in the mirror he'd appear standing at the end of your bed.

Ash   He stares at me. Gives me the shivers.

Alex   So whatever you do, just blame *him*. Say it was *him*.

11

The last room, which houses the replica of the monolith. **Tucker** *stares, anxious.* **L J** *approaches.* **Ash** *is watching.* **Mika** *skulking about. Others around.* **Cora** *is wearing an audio headset.*

L J   They found seven stone axes buried in the middle of the circle, and a body buried in the bog. A peat cutter found it. He thought it was a piece of wood and tossed it away. But when it hit the mud it came apart and he could see a flap of skin, tanned like leather. It broke in two and he could see it was a leg.

Tucker   No.

L J   Yeah. So this man, the bog man, it turns out he was a prince.

Tucker   How could they know?

L J   Oh they know everything about him. They know what he had for his last meal. They know he was being eaten from the inside by parasitic worms. And they know he had his skull smashed in with an axe.

Tucker   Is this real. Human sacrifice? I thought this was like. Paintings and stuff.

Ash Oh, we're brutal. Our ancestors thought that the Romans were gonna come from across the sea and wipe them out. End their civilization. So they made a sacrifice to the gods. To stop the invaders coming in their boats.

L J True facts. So they daubed him in sheep's blood, drugged him with mistletoe. In the moonlight, they led him to the stone circle hallucinating, bound and gagged.

Ash And then they ate him.

Tucker WOT?

Ash Yeah, cannibals. Cannibal druids. That's what they do here. That's who we are.

Tucker Wot. No. That is not true. Is that true?

Tucker *is spooked.* **Sam** *is standing there in his audio headset, drawing.* **Tucker** *notices him; he thinks he is watching him.*

Tucker What are you staring at?

Sam *stops. He puts his drawing away.* **Tucker** *shoves* **Sam**. *He tries to snatch* **Sam***'s bag.* **Cora** *watches. They are locked in a stand-off.*

Sam Get off.

Cora You've got a nosebleed.

Tucker What? No I don't.

Chris *and* **Alex** *charge through. They grab* **Sam***'s bag. Chuck it to each other.* **Sam** *runs after them.* **Tucker** *holds a tissue to his nose.* **Mika** *drifts over to a 'break glass' box on the wall. She waits for a quiet moment, then goes for the alarm.*

Auden You shouldn't touch that.

Mika Why not?

Auden It's the fire alarm, it'll set off the sprinklers.

Mika Oh, whoops. I thought it was like an information button.

They laugh.

Auden Well. Don't press it, otherwise it would be a nightmare.

Mika Yeah. I promize I won't.

She smiles at him. As we transition, the fire alarm sounds. The world drifts into a dreamlike state. Chaos and disorder. An announcement plays, asking for Mr Sands to come to the main hall.

12

Outside. The monolith. The stone circle. Moonlight. Rain.

Cora *sings. She wears headphones.*

Sam *stands, dripping wet. In one hand he holds a stone axe.*

Tucker *cowers at a distance from* **Sam**.

The sense of the monolith. Its presence felt somehow. Gargantuan, incomprehensible. The monolith begins to hum and vibrate.

An ethereal, pure sound, like a gigantic tuning fork, or a singing bowl.

The others are in and around the stone circle.

Sam *breathes heavily, as if he's gaining strength. As if he's becoming something else. As if possessed.*

He begins to bear down on **Tucker**. *Others join in with the singing.*

As reality seems to shake, so do some of the others. At first, small, unsettling. Then gradually growing. A collective seizure. Frenzy.

The hum of the monolith becomes profoundly deep. The vibrations intense in the bones.

The song crescendos. Ritual builds to ecstatic rapture. Everyone wills **Sam** *on.*

Sam *raises the axe. The axe is about to fall when –*

Cora *is held in the light. She finishes her song.*

Three

13

Aftermath. **Morgan**, **Ash**, **Lewis**, **L J**.

Morgan That is exactly what happened. He snapped. We used to have maths together. He was *freakishly* good. Effie told me they called the police.

Ash They didn't.

Morgan That's what Effie said and she was there. And apparently, then he went out into the fields and killed a sheep.

Ash What?

Lewis That's true. He killed a sheep. That's why they called the police.

Morgan Exactly. He slit its throat. And carried the blood back to the –

Ash How did he carry the blood?

Morgan In his – in a / water bottle.

Lewis In a bucket.

Morgan In a water bottle and a bucket.

Lewis And he poured it over all himself so his face was covered in blood, then he set off the fire alarm and all the lights went out and everyone went mad.

Morgan He stole an axe from one of the exhibits and started attacking people. And Marcus McKenzie was so scared he started fitting. That's what happened.

Ash That is not what happened. It wasn't blood. *Someone* squirted chocolate sauce on him. *Tucker* had blood on his shirt cos he picks his nose. No-one called the police, they both had to go to the medical room to get cleaned up.

Pause.

Morgan That is not believable. That is the least believable story I have ever heard. That's like – that's like a cover-up.

Lewis Exactly. You know that if someone went mad and attacked everyone they're not going to let us know the real story, they're gonna make up some tame version to stop us asking the right questions. I'm telling you – my friends were on the trip, and they are saying some mad shit like he's not human / or he's *malfunctioning* –

L J No. It's –. You know like you can grow meat in a test tube, or an ear on a mouse? Well, they've been growing whole organs like that. Livers. Kidneys. They grow human hearts in pigs, and implant them into people, did you know that? His parents couldn't have a baby so he was grown in a lab. In an artificial womb. All they had to do was grow this baby to the size of a corn on the cob and then he was OK. They took him home after that and no-one would have ever known. He was *made* in a lab. That's what it is.

Ash I don't think either of those things are true.

Morgan Exactly. L J is talking shit. He attacked Tucker. I know what happened.

Lewis He's fake meat. It's unnatural. They should expel him. Unless, wait, actually. What if they make a TV series about us . . .

Ash He's not fake meat. He didn't kill a sheep. He's not a clone.

Morgan I don't know what he is but he's *something*. And nothing you can say to me can make me think he's not.

14

Ice cream shop. **Chris** *and* **Jude**. *They both have ice creams.*

Chris Do you feel bad?

Jude No.

Chris You don't feel bad?

Jude Why? What did we do?

Chris What did we do? (We –)

Jude We didn't do anything. No I don't feel bad. Why should I feel bad? What have I got to feel bad about? I wasn't involved.

Chris You *were*.

Jude I wasn't directly involved.

Chris You were there same as me.

Jude I wasn't involved *directly*. I haven't got anything to feel bad about. Did I get in trouble?

Chris No.

Jude So then I didn't do anything wrong.

Pause.

Chris No-one got in trouble.

Jude Exactly.

Chris You made people doubt the *reality* of his whole *actual* being. Did you believe what you said?

Jude No.

Chris Then why did you say it?

Pause.

Why did you go along with it?

Jude   Alex was lying. We all knew it wasn't true. Everyone had to have known.

Chris   So why did you go along with it?

Jude   Why did *you* go along with it?

Chris   Because I didn't want to be left out.

Pause.

Jude   What if I do believe it? I do. I do believe it. I *do believe it.* I think he is a thing. He is a thing.

15

Out of school. **Cora** *and* **Sam**. **Sam** *covers his face, his eyes – a hood, sunglasses maybe.*

Cora   Does it hurt? – Sorry.

Pause.

I'm scared to sleep. My mind aches. I haven't really slept since –

Pause.

Please say something to me.

Pause.

I dreamt I was singing in a garden and a wasp landed on my arm. I watched it crawl along and I could feel it, prickling my skin. I could feel my skin tingling. I was trying to blow and shake my arm so that it would get off. But I couldn't make it go away. It stung me in my sleep, and I was scared that I would go into anaphylactic shock. I'm not allergic, but maybe I was in my dream, and my throat started to close up and I couldn't sing anymore and I couldn't breathe. And when I woke up I don't think I was breathing. My hands were numb. And I thought about you. And how much I miss you. I wish we could talk to each other again. I'm sorry. I feel *anxious* and I don't know what to do. To make it better. I just remember standing in that cave together by the sea. With the waves crashing against the rocks. And it was cold. And violent. And wet. And the wind hurt. And we held each other. I was glad that I was there with you. I feel like I have a memory of a real place, of it being real. I don't know whether it was. But I know I was there with you.

Pause.

I don't talk to any of them now.

Pause.

You probably hate everyone for what happened.

Sam

Cora   Do you hate me?

Sam

Pause. **Cora** *goes to take* **Sam**'s *hand.* **Sam** *lets her. They sit for a moment.*

Cora Your mark. Has it moved? It's on your other hand. How is that possible?

Sam I never sleep. I never dream.

16

Changing room. **Alex** *and* **Sam**.

Alex Are you scared?

Sam Stop lying about me.

Alex Why should I?

Sam Please. What's the point?

Alex Don't need a point.

Pause.

Sam This is stupid. If I had been replaced by something, an *exact* replica, how would you even know? I wouldn't be any different. How would *I* even know? I'd *still* be me.

Alex You don't get it. Even if you didn't know you'd been replaced. You'd still think you belonged here. But that's what I'm saying. You don't.

Sam You're not gonna get people to think I'm a monster. You know why? You're too thick.

Alex If I say you're a monster and everyone believes it, then that's what you are.

Sam Well, if I'm a monster, then think of what I'll do to you.

Alex What are you gonna do? You're weak. You can't hurt me, you can't turn them against me – I turn them against *you* – I turn *them* against YOU. Look at my hair, I'm popular.

Sam I won't hurt you. I'll *infect* you. I'll make you like me.

Alex *See. There.* What's this, confidence? That's not you. That's a fake you. So I'm not lying. I'm telling the truth.

Pause.

What you looking at? Don't look at me. Don't *look at* me.

Sam One day your lies will chew you up.

Alex I could beat the shit out of you.

Sam Yeah you could. You probably could. So what?

Alex She doesn't like you, you know? You? *You*? What did you think's gonna happen? You two? The two of you? Rancid. What an idea. Don't talk to her. If I see you talking to her. I will destroy you. I will make you into nothing.

17

Somewhere private. **Ash** *and* **Mika**.

Ash   What if we are changing?

Mika   We are changing, we're changing all the time. Our cells change. We're chemical reactions. Chemicals can be in balance or out of balance.

Ash   Are you in balance or out of balance? I think I'm unbalanced. I feel different. Maybe we've all been replaced – us before, and us now. We're different. Cos of what we did.

Mika   I'm the same.

Ash   Are you?

Mika   I am.

Ash   You don't feel different? You feel completely yourself?

Mika   No. I don't feel myself. I never have. I don't like myself. I don't like people. Humans are irredeemable. If we were all left to our own devices, if there weren't any rules, we'd all stab each other in the back, committing the worst kinds of atrocities to get whatever we want. That's what humans are, that's human nature. It would be better if we weren't on this planet. Don't you reckon?

Ash   No, I don't reckon.

Pause.

Mika   We'd be OK. If it was just us.

Ash   Two last lost survivors. Floating on the ocean.

Mika   Yeah. That's what I want.

Ash   It can't be like that.

18

A basement. **Cora** *and* **Sam** *are surrounded.* **Alex**, **Chris**, **Morgan**, **Tucker** *control the space.* **Jude**, **Lewis**, **L J**, **Mika**, **Ash** *orbit.* **Auden** *is in the centre with* **Sam**. **Chris** *mans a large wheelie bin.*

Cora   This is mad.

Auden   OK, well, actually, based on the way he looks –

Cora   You're *fucking mad*.

Auden   Based on the way he speaks and behaves – you can't tell.

Alex   No.

Auden   So if he were a robot, he'd have tricked you, and if he was a human, he'd have just proved it. So he passes the test.

Alex OK, the next one then.

Auden Well, the reverse Turing test is this . . .

Auden *shows* **Sam** *a reCAPTCHA picture.*

Which of these pictures contains fire hydrants?

Sam *points out the fire hydrants.*

Sam Hydrant. Hydrant. Hydrant.

I'm real. See? Twat.

A few of them laugh.

Chris This is dumb. Why does he know what to do?

Alex He's clever.

Chris You think you're cleverer than me?

Auden I don't really know you. But, yes.

Cora The idiot is right. This is a joke.

Morgan What if she's like him.

Cora I'm sorry, what?

Morgan You said you saw them together – ?

Mika That's true.

Morgan So what if *she*'s one too?

Lewis Oh my God, Cora are you?

Cora You're *delusional*.

Alex Do the next test.

Cora Fuck your test.

Auden This one, this one will work. The Lovelace test.

Chris It had better work or we're gonna put *you* in the bin.

Auden If you're not a real person, if you're a clone or *whatever* – then you can't create fiction, you can't create true art.

Mika So what does he –

Morgan It –

Mika – have to do?

Auden Tell us a story. About something familiar, but abstract, and it has to contain a sort of non-logical element, like idiom, or metaphor – something that a non-human wouldn't understand.

Chris I honestly have no idea what you're going on about.

Tucker Don't, you'll prove that you're not real. And then we'll have to bin you –

Chris I fucking am real.

Cora *We're all real.* This is so stupid. You want him to make up a story and then you'll leave him alone? That's it?

Alex That's it.

Pause.

Cora Sam?

Sam I'll make it simple so that Alex can understand.

Some laughs.

Alex (*nods, sarcastic – 'good one'*) Go on then.

Chris *thumps the bin. Others join the chant.*

Chris Bin bin bin bin.

Auden Tell us a story about an otter who lives life on the straight and narrow.

Sam I . . .

Beat.

What does that mean – 'the straight and narrow'?

Alex See!

Sam I've never heard that phrase before . . . what does it / mean?

Cora It / means –

Alex You can't tell him.

Cora Being honest, / being *moral*, like . . .

Alex You're not allowed to help.

Cora If you were a bank robber and you decided to stop committing crimes – you'd start living life on the straight / and narrow.

Sam Steven was an otter . . . and in his holt he had a secret.

Chris What's a holt?

Sam It's where an otter lives.

Jude Otters live in dreys.

Cora Squirrels live in dreys. Otters live in holts.

Alex Check it –

He has checked it on a phone.

Ash   He's right.

Sam   In his holt. He had his loot. From years and years of stealing jewels. Jewels which he had stolen from the bank which lay up river. The river bank.

Ash   See that's / good.

Jude   Quite / funny.

Cora *smiles.*

Sam   But all the jewels he had in his holt meant that he had no room for another otter. And Steven the otter –

Ash   (I love Steven.)

Sam   Steven the otter started to slip those gems, one by one, into the pockets of passing travellers – people who'd come to the forest seeking shelter, looking for food. But giving away the gems didn't make him feel better. And he was still by himself. But at least he was trying. He hoped that maybe one day he'd find another otter to share his holt with. But he knew somehow that it was the right thing to do. And that's the story of how Steven the otter started to live his life on the straight and narrow.

Pause.

Ash   Oh my God I love Steven the otter.

Auden   I mean, that works.

L J   So, he's human?

Chris   (Fuckin' hell.)

Chris *chucks the bin over.*

Alex   It doesn't count. She told him.

Cora   He didn't know what it meant.

Morgan   So that's cheating. He cheated.

Lewis   Oh my God. They're in it together.

Cora   He can draw – ask him to draw. He's amazing at drawing.

Alex   OK.

Cora   OK?

Alex   OK.

Auden   It would count. You have a minute to draw an image from your imagination. It has to be an abstract version of something. You can't just draw a chair. You have to draw a, a, more complex picture, something that only other humans would recognize. So, so . . . Draw two bears sitting on two chairs. But the chairs are made from squares. I didn't mean to rhyme just then.

Alex   Do it.

Mika Draw the bears in the chairs.

Morgan Draw the fuckin' bears.

Sam *goes to get his stuff from his bag. Pauses.*

Cora Sam. Draw. Sam. Do the drawing and they'll leave us alone.

Sam *thinks about it.*

Sam I'm not going to do a drawing.

Cora Why not?

Sam I'm not going to.

Cora Please.

Sam I shouldn't have to.

Cora *Please.*

Sam I refuse. You're not trying to prove anything. You're trying to humiliate me.

Pause.

Morgan We should take out his eye.

Cora What.

Morgan His eye. He's delaying. It's a tactic. I saw it in this old film my dad likes. They look in their eyes. They ask them all these questions – to try and make them react, or make them angry, make them have an um –

Mika Emotional response.

Morgan That *reveals* they're not human.

Alex Like a lie-detector.

Mika Like an empathy detector.

Morgan Exactly.

Auden So we ask questions.

Tucker Make him snap.

Chris Yes, mate, love it.

Alex What kind of questions?

Morgan All kinds.

Tucker Make him glitch.

Chris Like what? Like

Jude Are you who you say you are?

Morgan Who do you say you are?

Jude   Are you you?

Sam   Am I *me*?

Pause.

Cora   Stop it.

Alex   Keep going.

Tucker   He glitches, we know he's a fake

Jude   Do you remember your first birthday?

Morgan   Do you remember your birth?

Jude   If you don't remember, how can we be sure?

Sam   Of what?

Jude   That you're you.

Morgan   What are you if you're not you?

Sam   I am *me*.

Cora   Please.

Auden   More abstract.

Tucker   *Glitch*, you dick.

Morgan   It's gotta be more *poetic* like . . . Have you ever seen the sea? Have you ever seen snow? Did you walk here? Did you wash up on a beach?

Auden   I've got it – You're in the Arctic. You come across a penguin, alone and tired. Instead of walking towards the sea, it is walking inland, towards the mountains, where it will surely perish. What do you do?

Sam   Why would I be in the Arctic?

Auden   An expedition.

Sam   How did I get there?

Auden   You just are. What do you do? Do you help the penguin? Or do you let him get eaten by a polar bear?

Pause.

Well?

Sam   I – I don't get it.

Morgan   *What do you do*?

Chris   He's confused.

Sam   It doesn't make / any (sense).

Tucker   He's gonna / snap.

Morgan This is it –

Alex DO YOU HELP THE PENGUIN OR WHAT?

Sam There are no penguins in the Arctic.

Cora Penguins live in the southern hemisphere, dipshit.

Pause. Everyone looks to **Auden**. **Ash** *has looked it up.*

Ash He's right.

Auden Yeah, it was . . . it was a trick question.

Cora He's not going to *glitch*, what is wrong with you? You made this up. All because you're a fragile little twat who feels threatened by a person who's nice. If you ever cared about me, if you had any respect for me, leave us alone.

Alex Why should I?

Cora He's my friend.

Alex Care about him do you?

Cora Yes I do care.

Alex Cos I didn't make this up did I? You told me. You said he told you he thought he wasn't real. That he's got maggots in his brain. That's true isn't it? We wouldn't be here if you hadn't told us in the first place.

Pause. **Sam** *looks to* **Cora**.

Sam What did you do?

Cora I –

Alex He lies. He hides. He won't tell us about what happened to him before. Why? Maybe he doesn't have any real memories. He isn't human. He said it himself.

Sam What did you (tell him . . .).

Cora I *didn't* . . .

Lewis Oh my God is it *actually* true.

Alex You all know there's something wrong. Maybe they're doing it for attention? Maybe we don't know what exactly it is but there's something. He *looks at you*. He's hiding *something*. He's *inhuman*.

Jude Alex. Look, *we* . . . maybe this is too far.

Beat. **Alex** *comes close to* **Jude**. **Alex** *takes* **Jude**'s *hand, gently.*

Alex Don't worry.

Mika Oi leave her, let her speak.

Alex I'm not doing anything. She can say whatever she wants.

L J   What were you gonna say?

Jude   Nothing.

Alex   See?

L J   We should get an adult.

Alex   What's an adult gonna do?

Morgan   You saw. He lost – lock him in.

Morgan *grabs* **Sam***, he drags him to the bin.* **Chris***,* **Tucker** *thump on the bin.*

Cora   Put him in that bin and I will bite your ear off. He can prove it, he's a person. He's got drawings in his bag –

Morgan *releases* **Sam**. **Cora** *grabs* **Sam***'s bag. She starts rifling through it.*

Sam   That's mine.

Cora   Show them.

Sam   Give it back.

Cora   *Sam.*

Sam   It's *mine*.

Sam *snatches the bag back from* **Cora**.

Sam   I don't want your help.

Cora   Fine, fuck you.

They stare at each other.

Alex (*to* **Cora**)   You're embarrassing yourself.

Morgan *takes the bag from* **Sam**.

Let's have a look for this *art*.

Alex *tips out his bag onto the floor.*

This?

He unravels a rolled-up drawing. Looks at it.

I dunno what this is.

Alex *tosses it to* **Chris***,* **Morgan***,* **Tucker***. They destroy the picture.* **Sam** *faces* **Alex** *down, feral.*

Sam   No matter how many times you hit me, I won't go down.

Alex   See. There is something dark inside you. Living there. A parasite.

Coda (19)

The beach. The entrance to the cave. **Cora** *and* **Sam**.

Sam What did it say up there?

Cora Danger of Death.

Sam So why are we down here? We might literally die.

Cora *laughs.*

Cora Did you know what it said?

Sam Yes.

Cora So if you knew you might die, why did you come down here with me?

Pause.

I wanted to see if you were OK.

Sam I didn't mean to be out of order.

Cora You didn't do anything wrong. You stood up to them.

Pause.

If we went further in, do you think we'd see the paintings?

Sam I think we'd fall to our deaths and be killed in a terrible spelunking accident.

Beat.

Why did you speak to me today? You barely knew I existed. I'm amazed you're even talking to me now. Everyone likes you.

Cora They don't know me. They have an idea of who I am. I don't want to be who they want me to be. My parents are dicks. Divorced. Self-obsessed. My family's a mess. Everyone wants me to be *normal*. But what if you're not. I'm strange.

Sam Oh, I know that you're strange.

They share a laugh.

Cora I sat next to you because I felt that. We might be similar.

Sam Similar? You don't want to be like me. I don't *connect*. I don't have any feelings. No-one really knows me. I think I'm empty inside.

Cora *laughs gently.*

Sam Why's that funny?

Cora Cos it's not true. You don't have no feelings – you have too many feelings – you're afraid cos your feelings are so strong. They overwhelm you don't they? So you hide them.

Sam *nods.*

Cora What am I feeling now?

They look at each other.

Big feelings are not bad feelings

Sam I feel disappointed, most of the time. Damaged. I feel like something is ending

Cora Do you feel that now?

Sam No.

Pause.

(But) I'm not OK, really. Ever.

Cora Nor am I. Can it not just be OK to be not OK?

Sam Yeah, it can. And to be quiet. I like being quiet.

Cora Me too. Actually that's not true, I'm usually very loud – everyone always tells me to be quiet. I just think if someone's telling you to be quiet it's because they don't want to know who you are. They're not saying 'be quiet' – they're saying 'don't be who you are'.

Sam I like who you are

Cora I like who you are

Sam I get told to speak up. I think I speak exactly the right amount at exactly the right volume.

Cora I'm either too loud or too quiet. There's no in-between.

They laugh.

Sam I wish we could climb down and see the paintings. I thought the handprints, the red horses running side by side were astonishing. I was just like . . . wow, this is what we do isn't it. Humans. We've been doing it since forever. It made me feel connected. And I thought . . . the people who tell us to stop doing that, who want us to do *serious* things with the rest of our lives – they're wrong. That isn't what we're here to do. You can't change thousands of years of existence. You can't change reality. I want to be part of that. That's what being human is, I want to be human. I don't want to fall into a black hole.

Beat.

Wait, did you think the paintings were boring? Was everything I just said total rubbish? I take it all back.

Cora No don't take it back. I didn't think they were boring, I thought they were properly, genuinely, properly incredible. Imagining someone making those paintings, thousands and thousands of years ago, and here we are seeing them now, and there's sort of a line drawn between then and now. I thought yeah, like you say, it is amazing that we've been doing that for all of time, but also it's like – someway, somehow, that person was reaching out for some reason. When they made those paintings, they were reaching out. To say like – I'm here. Or maybe just to say like there are horses over there. Or whatever. I think that's what we do.

Pause.

I like this.

Sam   What?

Cora   The mark on your hand.

She examines the mark on his hand. They hold hands. They are close.

Sam   Shall we go back up?

Cora   Or we could stay here.

Sam   We could.

Cora   We could wait here till it gets dark.

Sam   The tide will come in.

Cora   And the cave will flood with water.

Sam   And what will we do then?

Cora   We'll be OK.

Sam   Will we?

Cora   We will.

Sam   We're very different.

Cora   We're the same.

Sam   We're the same.

End.

Replica

BY TITAS HALDER

Notes on rehearsal and staging, drawn from a workshop with the writer, held at the National Theatre October 2023

Warm-up games

Click game

Lead director Graham asked the group to pass a click around the circle. This is a useful game to get actors to focus on the presence of performance and reactions/alertness. Graham explained that with the basic click you can then build and get creative in a low-resourced environment by adding expression, pace and then adding the lines with the clicks.

The aim of click is to get the actors to get the actors out of their heads, focus on the others in the scene and pass the energy between them. It helps build the foundations for receiving and responding.

Bin ball

Bin ball consists of trying to keep a ball in the air as a team whilst moving it towards the bin to score. This is again a useful game for actors to appreciate the energy needed within a scene and how that should feel.

Why this play

Graham asked the group to write down the answer to the following questions, which were then placed in different areas in the room:

1) Why did you choose this play?
2) What is the play about for you?
3) What is it that scares you most about the play?

Some of the group's responses were:

Question 1: Why did you choose this play?
- Students connecting with the characters
- The playwright is challenging the company: the answers aren't all obvious or easy to find
- Representing young people in a truthful way
- The universality of the story and the intertwining of the strands
- Opportunity for physical theatre and playing with archetypes

Question 2: What is this play about for you?

- What it means to be human
- Coming of age
- Pack mentality
- Stigma and hysteria
- Paranoia and persecution
- Malleability of truth

Graham then invited the room to consider how these might translate into themes, some of which included:

– Identity
– Stigma
– Truth
– What it is to be human
– Paranoia
– Storytelling
– Growing up

Graham explained that when she begins to direct a play, she focuses on the themes. As a director, you can't control feeling, but you can ask the questions: how do I tell this story in a way that my central themes come through? What can I do in the production, rehearsals and choices I make with the actors to tell the story I want to tell?

Graham encouraged participants to include actors in discussions about what the story is you want to tell, so that everyone can be united in the vision of the production.

Question 3: What scares you the most about this play?

- Will the audience understand it?
- Will actors understand it?
- Sitting with ambiguity, and knowing that this is OK
- The chronology of the story and making the character journeys clear
- The monolith

Graham encouraged the group to model the director position of 'I don't know': it is a superpower. In inviting a leadership that empowers your actors to help you answer the questions and solve the challenges the script brings, rather than be didactic in your vision of the play, you are enlisting all the minds in the room to be creative rather than just one. *Replica* relies on the actors playing confidently together and being responsive to one another, so however short your process is, it is important to allow your actors the opportunity to play and feel confident in this. Games like Click will help.

Writer Titas Halder commented on the monolith moment (scene 12): it is an offer to use your imaginations – it could be the whole company singing, for example. This is a directorial choice, feel free to capitalize on the abilities in the room and the actors' instincts.

You can start tackling the monolith sequence with a clear direction of 'this is the purpose of the scene' and then you can build on this by using references and inspirations from film, television and other materials the young people might have.

Short scenes can be daunting because you have to maintain pace. Be sure to communicate the story beat, but know that the pace can be found after the clarity of the scene is discovered. In this vein, Graham encouraged getting the lines off book by halfway through the process so you have time to work on pace and energy.

Halder added that although scenes can be challenging, in each of them there is a simple choice for the actor to make: what are they *doing* to the other person?

Graham used the metaphor of *Ready Steady Cook* for a rehearsal process. You only use what is in the fridge so how can you make the best of that? Canadian director/writer/actor Robert Lepage talks about how restriction brings creativity: if your budget is tight, you can come up with some extraordinary, imaginative and creative solutions.

Text, line feeding and intentions

Line feeding for line learning

The group looked at the apple monologue. Someone quietly speaks the line to the actor, who then says every line and imagines the line in the space as they say it aloud; e.g.:
'as I went to take a bite'
'I could see it was soft'
'I could feel it going rotten'
Graham encouraged the line-feeding exercise for any parts that include imagery for students – this will help with line learning because you are inviting the actor to see the image, which will help with the vividity of the storytelling.

Line feeding is particularly useful for actors with dyslexia.

Finding the intentions

Graham invited the group to get into a circle, and asked participants to read Chris, Alex and Jude in Scene One.

Graham then asked: What do the characters want from each other? All intentions in the first instance can be drafts and can evolve as you get to know the play more. The only rule is they have to be about how they want to change the other character. The group made the following suggestions:

– Alex wants Cora to doubt her relationship with Sam
– Cora wants to bring Alex down a peg or two
– Chris wants Alex to let him be the general
– Alex just wants Chris to do his job
– Jude wants Alex to choose her over Cora

Graham encouraged the group to look for places where there is strong conflict between the intentions, because in conflict there is drama.

Intention Exercise

The room divided into groups to work out the intentions of each of the characters in the play and to title the scenes accordingly.

Graham gave an example for Scene One:

Cora cannot stop the tide of doubt that begins to dehumanize Sam

Creating titles for scenes, can help clarify for the actors what story you are telling. The group came up with the following suggestions for each scene:

1. Cora cannot stop the tide of doubt that begins to dehumanize Sam.
2. Lewis goes 'fishing', Cora can't be caught.
3. Mika wants to tear down the system, confides in Ash. Ash wants to come clean.
4. Auden imparts factual knowledge that enables Alex's mission to disinform.
5. Cora fails to fight the growing fire.
6. Sam explains his distress to Cora through a dream/Sam's distressed dream.
7. L J makes us (and Tucker) believe the monolith has supernatural power.
8. Piercing the characters' personal views of the museum.
9. Alex takes it too far, Cora fights back aka Your Singing is Shit.
10. The false flag operation. Alex manipulates Mika to discredit Sam.
11. L J and Ash scare Tucker whilst Sam and Cora isolate themselves. Auden attempts but fails to stop Mika, causing chaos (Ash and L J pour gasoline).
12. The mythology of the monolith (with Cora singing).
13. Fantastical horror or science – no one's letting go.
14. Chris's conscience vs Jude's ambivalence.
15. Cora begs for reconciliation with Sam. Sam has shut down.
16. Alex confronts Sam. Sam exposes Alex's weakness and finds cracks in his behaviour.
17. Ash and Mika try to make sense of their place in the world.
18. The trial: The question of the parasite takes over the whole group, who keep re-living the circle of life.
19. Despite the danger, Cora and Sam make their connection.

This exercise gives a clear idea of what story you are telling within the scene and to give clarity and united purpose in the telling of it.

Chronology

The room split into groups and discussed what order the play would be if it was played out chronologically. Graham then asked the groups what they discovered when trying to find out the chronology of the play. Some responses from the group:

- Cora experiences time differently.
- It feels that there is a real specialness to time – e.g. sitting next to the person you wanted to on the coach has a different quality of time to a whole day of school.
- The characters' changing opinions of Sam really help as a through line to the play.
- You as individual directors might have different ideas about the order, but you and your own company must agree on a chronology to have a shared understanding of the play.
- Knowing what has happened is so important for characters, intentions and strong choices to show that time has passed.
- It is also possible that some of these scenes are happening at the same time.

Group one ordered the play as 6, 8, 9, 10, 11, 12, 13, 19, 7, 4, 1, 5, 16, 14, 3, 2, 18, 7, 15

Group two ordered the chronology of the play as: 8, 9, 10, 11, 19, 12, 7, 13, 2, 4, 1, 16, 5, 6, 18, 3, 14, 15, 17

Group 3 ordered the play as 7, 19, 8, 10, 9, 11, 12, 2, 4, 16, 1, 13, 6, 5, 18, 14, 3, 17, 15

Graham (A), Titas Halder (T) and the Participants (P) then discussed these orders and what that brought up for them in the understanding of the process and play:

A: A fun thing to do could be to play the scenes in this order, and then improvize the scenes in between. This is so you can flesh out what happens between moments that are scripted.

T: For me it is interesting where the apple monologue goes. It can go in a number of places. There must be an inciting incident, and perhaps it is this one. In a strange way, I made a case for myself that it is the first thing that happens, but it is up to you and for interpretation!

P: Did you have any idea about the amount of time that passes over all the events in the play?

T: No, not at all. This is up to your company. I sometimes think about 'Home' and 'Away' scenes though – about what it means for a character to be on their own turf as opposed to someone else's and how this informs the way they act in those moments.

A: That is interesting – really thinking about how the locations of the scenes inform how the actors behave in the space. Time, place and relationship are three important factors, with a relationship being defined by what the person thinks of another person.

T: Just a side thought about location: in my head there are not 19 different locations; the offer in my head is that there are three different locations in the three different acts. In each act, the scenes group together and have a certain mood, feeling, sensation.

Exercises for use in rehearsals

Push, Pull, Yield and Resist

Participants got into pairs of similar size and strength.

- First A leads B around the room by pushing or pulling.
- Then without talking A leads B and then B leads A, changing between the two without speaking about it.
- With A leading, now you experiment with different levels of resistance, pushing and pulling.

With this simple exercise, you can then begin to layer and expand what you do with lines and playing the scene.

Two people can line deliver to A and B who then repeat the lines out and with every line they are given, A decides to push or pull, and then B can decide to yield or resist. This can then be played so B decides to push or pull on the delivery of the line, and A decides to yield or resist on the receiving of this line.

Reflections from the group included:

- It allowed you to connect to the text more physically.
- It presented the possibility of there being different *types* of push, pull, yield and resist which can be a total shift in mood.
- It revealed the difference between moments that were calculated and thought about by the character, as opposed to moments that were spontaneous, disjointed and passionate.

Graham suggested spending 10 to 15 minutes on a warm-up to get rid of the day, and get actors into their body – you could ask the cast to create a playlist for the play and dance for three songs, leading with different body parts (roughly three per song). Being in your body gives access to your actor's impulses and you can make choices from an authentic place.

Push, Pull, Yield, Resist is a great way of starting scene work. These exercises can also help you as a director to start seeing what the blocking and staging might look like.

A further layer is to repeat the exercise in pairs again, moving a person by pushing or pulling, but this time with no physical contact. They take turns to lead and explore the right moment to change.

Partner A and B are then fed the lines and do the same exercise but this time they are pushing, pulling, yielding and resisting without using physical contact.

Graham offered some insights for thinking about this exercise in the broader context of the rehearsal process:

- According to directing teacher Elen Bowman, all human wants can be boiled down to three core needs:

  1 I am loved
  2 I am happy
  3 I am powerful

- This exercise is a way of using intentions to help inform character. For instance, Chris wants Alex to let him be general so that he is powerful or Alex wants Cora to doubt her relationship with Sam so he is loved.
- The ideal situation is for the director to create the conditions in which actors can move freely and make their own decisions.
- If you want your actors to play distance, get them to play with a ball – they can do a scene whilst throwing the ball, and won't overthink the acting.

Question and answer with Titas Halder

Q: What was your inspiration for the piece?
A: It has inspiration from everything I felt at that time in my life. If there is a confrontation with a person, that is going to have repercussions, and everyone has these stories that happened at school that went slightly over the edge. It was the feeling that the stakes are that high. Everything is so big at that age, and I wanted to do justice to the characters that they should legitimately feel that way.

Q: What are the class differences and situations of the characters? Do you have any thoughts on this? For example does LJ have a more affluent upbringing?
A: I think that is an interesting reading, and it is open for interpretation. A good question for all the characters is at what point does their moral compass start to kick in?

Q: Do you feel that characters can be merged?
A: It's possible. As long as it really makes sense. Early on the decision was made to make a play with proper characters, with a fixed cast size. We know that with Connections plays it can be useful to have flexible characters, so it did occur to me that

you could merge people. So judiciously is the answer. There are probably clever ways of snipping together one or two characters if need be.

Q: How do you feel about multiple actors playing one character?
A: Go for it!

Q: How flexible is the cast size?
A: The play was imagined for a company of twelve actors, although there could be additional cast in Scenes 8, 11, 12, 18. It may be better to do the compact twelve, or, for example it could be cool to add extra company in Scene 12 to choreograph some sort of brilliant movement sequence, or to add extra singing voices – over to your imaginations.

Q: Are the stage directions completely set in stone?
A: It is totally OK to reinterpret or reimagine the odd stage direction according to the skills and requirements of your company or your staging. Sometimes (often), what's in my head won't be as good or as cool as what you can come up with in rehearsals.

Q: Do you have an idea of costume?
A: This is up to you, but it shouldn't change too much. Whatever gets you the character.

Q: Do you have a fixed idea about staging?
A: No. You could do the play on a bare stage, an abstract set, a naturalistic set. Minimal props, or lots. Up to you.

Q: Is Auden older than the rest?
A: He is younger actually; he was bumped up a year because he was so clever.

Q: What was the reason for asterisks in the play?
A: It is to signify different places, but really it was a priority for me to make the text as clean as possible.

Q: Can we replace the swearing with other words?
A: I would encourage you to find something that is truthful to the moment. It isn't necessarily about 'straight swaps' but finding what the moment needs.

Q: You spoke about location not mattering so much from scene to scene, but you said that the acts have different feelings. Could you speak a bit more on that for guidance?
A: Place number one is school, place number two is trip, and place three is something like 'regret'.

Q: Are you talking about acts as it is on the page or acts in the chronology?
A: Acts on the page. And I'd offer that rather than nineteen scenes; think of it as three acts with moments that you drive towards throughout the play.

Q: Do you have any useful cultural references – images, music or similar – to give access to the script in a way that is not necessarily text based?
A: There are three films, *The Thing*, *Blade Runner* and *Get Out*, that were strong reference points for me. *Get Out* really feels like a cultural touchstone. It is labelled as horror but really it can talk about society in a way that is funny and irreverent. John Carpenter's movies are shocking and lo-fi, but they are really high concept, and the genre allows them to talk about societal issues. There is another John Carpenter film called *They*

Live, which is about aliens infiltrating the human race, but actually speaks about social issues in America. Music is incredibly important to me as I write. The Trent Reznor and Atticus Ross scores of *The Social Network* and *Watchmen* in particular were very present for me as I wrote, and I would recommend the *Watchmen* (TV series) score in particular for reference.

Q: Whose story is it throughout?
A: The logic lends itself to it being Cora's story or through Cora's lens. But to build on this, I think as an actor playing any part you legitimately should look at the play and think 'it is my play'. So, each actor should be serving their own journey rather than someone else's.

Suggested references

Films: *The Thing* (1982) dir. John Carpenter, *Blade Runner* (1982) dir. Ridley Scott, *Get Out* (2017) dir. Jordan Peele.

Music: *The Social Network* score, *Watchmen* (TV series) score (both by Trent Reznor and Atticus Ross), *Stranger Things* score by Michael Stein and Kyle Dixon, *The Thing* score by Ennio Morricone, *Ghosts I–IV* by Nine Inch Nails.

From a workshop led by Graham
With notes by Sammy Glover

SAD CLUB

by Luke Barnes
with music by Adam Pleeth

Luke Barnes is an award-winning writer. Theatre includes *Freedom Project* at Leeds Playhouse; *All We Ever Wanted Was Everything* at the Bush and for Paines Plough with Middle Child; *No One Will Tell Me When to Start a Revolution* at Hampstead; *Chapel Street* at the Bush; *Bottleneck* at Soho Theatre with HighTide; *The Jumper Factory* at the Young Vic, HOME and Bristol Old Vic; *Lost Boys* at the Unity with the National Youth Theatre; *Cinderella – A Wicked Mother F*cker of a Night Out* for James Seabright Not Too Tame; *Katie Johnstone* at the Orange Tree; *The Saints* at the Nuffield, Southampton; *Eistedfodd* at HighTide; Ten *Storey Love Song and Weekend Rockstars* at Hull Truck with Middle Child; *A Wondrous Place* at the Royal Exchange Manchester, Northern Stage, the Unity and the Crucible, Sheffield; *The Class* at the Unicorn with National Youth Theatre; and *Loki and Betty* at the Almeida. TV: *Minted in Manchester* (Original Single for Channel 4).

Adam Pleeth is a composer and musician who has worked across plays, musicals and dance. As a composer, his works include *The Elephantom* at the National Theatre and in the West End; *The Sad Club* for National Theatre Connections; *James and the Giant Peach* at West Yorkshire Playhouse; *Pitcairn* at Shakespeare's Globe and Chichester Festival Theatre; *This May Hurt a Bit* for Out of Joint; *Wolves in the Walls* and *Red Riding Hood and the Wolf* at Little Angel Theatre; *Laika* at the Unicorn; *The Hartlepool Monkey* for Gyre & Gimble on UK tour; *Ballad of the Burning Star* and *Juana in a Million* for Theatre Ad Infinitum; *The Caucasian Chalk Circle* for the National Youth Theatre of Wales; *The Adventures of Curious Ganz* for Silent Tide and the Little Angel Theatre; and *Time Stands Still When I think of You* at The Place.

There are songs in this piece: if you can play the instruments live that's great. If not . . . also great.

If a section is called a song, and it is indented, then it's a song to be sung.

*The **bold** sections of the song are the 'truth' of the song. There should be a change in lighting, or movement, or . . . anything you like!*

In the 'Best Things in the World' section you can add a few of your own things if you feel that's appropriate.

For those who would like the sheet music for the songs featured, please email connections@nationaltheatre.org.uk

There is a sign at the back saying 'Welcome to the Sad Club'.

Song: 'Here We Are, We're So Happy'

    Here we are, again, right here
    All together in the sun, today
    Sitting in a field again, laughing at everything we say
    And we are so happy.

    The futures great you see, for us
    All the people who are right here, right now
    Sitting in the sun again, laughing at everything we say
    And we are so happy
    And we are so happy.

    I can't see us being anything other than happy like we are
    For all our lives
    When we are grown up so happy we'll be happy like we are
    For all our lives.

    I can't see us being anything other than happy like we are
    For all our lives
    When we are grown up so happy we'll be happy like we are
    For all our lives.

    This is temporary all this,
    Thinking this will pass and I am scared
    That this is the best it will ever be
    I am so scared.

    I can't see us being anything other than happy like we are
    For all our lives
    When we are grown up so happy we'll be happy like we are
    For all our lives.

    I can't see us being anything other than happy like we are
    For all our lives
    When we are grown up so happy we'll be happy like we are
    For all our lives.

    We are so happy
    Look we're so happy
    We are so happy
    Look we're so happy

We are so happy
Look we're so happy
Happy Happy Happy Happy!

*

Competition

Craig *is in Speedos.*

Craig   I have spent every moment of the last six months thinking about nothing else but beating David Gairn and and getting into the England junior swimming team. My entire life is a direct relation to how well he is doing. It's absolutely about competition. Swimming is the thing that I'm the best at in the whole world. I have been training for ten years to get to where I am today. Everything has been leading to this. I haven't like, stopped living, I still have friends and a girlfriend and all that. Dad insists that I'm not obsessing all the time. When I'm in Maccies I hear his voice going, 'Is David eating shit?' When I'm at dinner with my family – Dad's asking if David would have a second dessert? When I'm going to play football, Dad's asking whether David would risk a broken leg. Dad says the most important thing in the world is being the best because anything but the best isn't worth it. That is what consumes me. That is what's important to me. And now is the moment where I find out whether all my worrying about him has been worth it.

Announcer   Ladies and gentlemen, welcome to the final of the [insert county name] swimming trials.

Hurrah.

And a big round of applause for David Gairn.

Hurrah.

They line up to race.

Announcer   OK. The style is freestyle.

Craig & David   Yes.

Announcer   Great. On your marks. Get set. Go.

They race . . .

Race music plays.

David Gairn wins.

Craig   Fuck! The world around me smashes into pieces. In the stands I can see Mum and Dad disappointed. My coach can't look at me. Everyone's looking down and I'm waiting to see David Gairn flailing about laughing at me but he's not. He just walks over and he says, 'Well swam, mate,' and he gives me a hug. Fuck this. I'm so tired.

I'm so tired of thinking about nothing but him and now it's over. I fucked it. I don't care. I don't feel anything. I have wasted so much time thinking about David Garin and I'm not doing it any more. I'm not spending my life worrying about what he thinks. Dad, I'm not doing it any more. I want to have fun. He looks shocked. Like I've slapped him in the face with a fish. My shoulders become free . . . And for a second I feel like the world is laid out in front of me waiting for me to enjoy it. The world is waiting. I can't wait.

*

Things to Look Forward To

Space

Best Friend 1   I'm looking forward to meeting your children.

Best Friend 2   I'm looking forward to seeing your first bedroom that's not at home.

Best Friend 1   I'm looking forward to seeing what job you do.

Best Friend 2   I'm looking forward to seeing what degree you do.

Best Friend 1   I'm looking forward to sitting down and having dinner one day and remembering today.

Best Friend 2   I'm looking forward to meeting *your* children.

Best Friend 1   I'm looking forward to falling in love and telling you.

Best Friend 2   I'm looking forward to talking about the first time I have sex.

Best Friend 1   I'm looking forward to meeting for coffees when we're both busy and important.

Best Friend 2   I'm looking forward to Sunday dinners with our families.

Best Friend 1   I'm looking forward to you writing that book.

Best Friend 2   I'm looking forward to learning instruments and starting a band.

Best Friend 1   I'm looking forward to going on holiday together.

Best Friend 2   I'm looking forward to sharing books.

Best Friend 1   I'm looking forward to sharing music.

Best Friend 1   I'm looking forward to going to gigs.

Best Friend 1   I'm looking forward to seeing the world with you. As much as we can. All the little things and the bigs things and things that might seen as stupid or small or little but will open up everything for us.

Best Friend 2   I'm looking forward to everything.

Best Friend 1   Everything.

Best Friend 2	Everything.
Best Friend 1	Everything.
Best Friend 2	Everything.
Best Friend 1	Everything.
Best Friend 2	Everything.
Best Friend 1	Everything.
Best Friend 2	Everything.
Best Friend 1	Everything.
Best Friend 2	Everything.
Best Friend 1	Everything.
Best Friend 2	Everything.
Best Friend 1	But right now. Let's go to the park.
Best Friend 2	I'd really like that. You're the best. Honestly. You're the best friend anyone could have.

*

Song: 'Things I Do When I'm Upset'

    Things I do when I'm upset
    Things I do when I'm upset
    Things I do when I'm upset
    Things I do when I'm upset
    Things I do when I'm upset.

    Sometimes I get a hotty, get a bath when feeling rotty
    Pet my lovely dog.

    When I feel I want to scream, eat some Häagen-Dazs ice cream
    Cry to my lovely mum.

    Go for a run, things I think are fun
    Give my mates a hug.

    Yes yes it's here but not oh dear
    We know what to do.

    Cuddle up on my own, give my mates a phone,
    Pray to whoever I like.

Go for a walk, have a little talk,
Listen to 'Here Comes the Sun'.

Eat some good food, walk around in the nude
Watch feel-good TV.

Read a good book, do a big cook,
Go to bed early.

Things I do when I'm upset
Things I do when I'm upset
Things I do when I'm upset
Things I do when I'm upset
Things I do when I'm upset
Things I do when I'm upset.

*

The Internet

Australia

Terri   I saw her. Right there on the screen. In a little blue dress at the circus.

Michelle   What was she doing?

Terri   Smiling. She was smiling like with a big smile on her face.

Michelle   Are you OK?

Terri   Course I'm not OK, I'm devastated.

Michelle   Was she with him?

Terri   Yeah.

Michelle   Look. That doesn't mean she was happy.

Terri   What does it mean then?

Michelle   Well, I guess like you know . . . When you put a picture on the internet or whatever why do you put it on?

Terri   Because you look good.

Michelle   Yeah but that doesn't mean you feel good. She could be like putting it on hating herself but thinking she looks good so people like think she's happy.

Terri   You reckon?

Michelle   Yeah. It's not real is it. I mean if you think about it it's basically a bunch of people who think they're not good enough lying to a bunch of people who think they're not good enough by pretending they're good enough and making everyone else feel worse.

Terri   Doesn't make me feel any better.

Michelle   I know but it's just important to remember. Do you want a mango?

*

Partying

Stacey   I am a party girl and I don't care. I'm sixteen. Mum's sound with it so I get smashed and I'm not arsed what anyone thinks of it. I do not care. I go to every party whether it's my school, or the other schools, or the boys' school, or the girls' school, I'll gatecrash anything. Mum doesn't mind because she thinks I'm the best thing ever. I am her life. My ambition is simple. To get the most smashed there and to get off with the most lads I can get off with. I go to all the parties with Chloe. Chloe is like me but she's a bit more together but basically she likes to pretend she's like me by saying she's mad and doing mad stuff but really she's like always careful. This is where I come alive and tonight at John O'Shea's party I am alive. Me and Chloe arrive late, obviously, and we're already pissed because we've been drinking on the train. So we arrive and I am steaming like proper fucking steaming and my ex is there and he's got fat and that's great. There's a lad with a guitar and he's fit. He looks like Johnny Rotten but with Johnny Depp's head. I'm a really good singer. Everyone says I'm a really good singer and if there's a guitar out I'll sing a song like no problem I don't mind doing that because everyone looks at me and thinks I'm great. He's playing 'Wonderwall' and I love this song so I come in and I harmonize with him and I say COZ MAYBE YOU'RE GOING TO BE THE ONE THAT SAVES ME AND AFTER ALL YOU'RE MY WONDERWALL. And the boy smiles and I know I've planted a seed. I know I can come back for that later and it'll be waiting. I turn around and my ex is there.

Ex   You know no one can save you.

Stacey   YOU'RE SO WEIRD. What are you saying?

Ex   You know that no one can save you, you know that don't you.

Stacey   Go away, you ming, you stink of Babybels.

Ex   Gladly.

Stacey   I try to down a tin of Fosters to forget about it but it's a lot so I just down loads in little gulps until I feel just pissed and bloated enough to talk to people and not really care what I think. The boy with the guitar comes over. Hello, I say, doing my best smile like this – hello. I'm actually really smashed but I'm good at pretending that I'm listening and I think he's saying something like, 'I see you at these all the time,' and I'm like yeah I know obviously because I come here all the time. He tells me he plays the guitar and he asks me what makes me happy? I dunno. Like. Fun. Getting smashed. Ha. Do you want to go upstairs? He tells me I look sad. I don't look sad. I'm not sad. He says he's got to go. He says goodbye and goes to talk to someone else. I can feel my ex smirking into my back and I turn and I say what do you want?

Ex Nothing.

Stacey Then why are you looking at me?

Ex I'm not.

Stacey What's your problem?

Ex I haven't got one.

Stacey You dumped me, why are you being a dick?

Ex I'm not.

Stacey Tell me.

Ex Tell you what?

Stacey Whatever you're thinking, I can see your brain whirring like a fucking fan.

Ex What do you think I want to tell you?

Stacey That I'm running away from something.

Ex Why are you saying that?

Stacey I know you're going to say that I'm just a drunken little slag and that I haven't got anything going for me because I fucked up my exams.

Ex I literally was just going to tell you your flies are undone.

Stacey And he walks away.

*

Best Things in the World

The following is to be played over music but spoken in no particular rhythm:

Rainbows
Dogs
Kissing
Eating toast in bed whilst it's raining outside
Falling in love
Making up songs
Baking cakes
Eating cakes
Cakes
Finishing a good book
Sunday dinners
Popping bubble gum
Zipping up a tent from the inside
Getting into bed with your dog
Having dinner with your family

The future
Your best friend's future
Your best friend's wedding
Your best friend's birthday
Your best friend's children
Children
Christmas
Swimming in the sea
Falling in love.

*

How to Help Someone You're Not Close With

Greenland – 1300s

Anyu *and* **Tuuq** *are fishing.*

Anyu   Stop looking at me. We're not friends. We're just neighbours. You don't have to be bothered.

Tuuq   Are you OK?

Anyu   Yes I'm fine.

Tuuq   Do you want to talk?

Anyu   No.

Tuuq   Look. I'm just going to say one thing then I'll shut up.

Anyu   How about you just shut up.

Tuuq   OK. But before I do let me say one thing. I don't know what's going on but I'm just going to say this. It's OK. I know your head's fallen off and I just want you to know everyone's has. Everyone's mind's all over the place as well and I know I don't know you very well and that you think no one can understand but I just want to say that the world is a better place when we all understand that we're all all over the place. I understand.

Anyu   OK.

Tuuq   I'm sorry.

Anyu   OK.

Tuuq   Shall we just quietly get on with fishing?

Anyu   OK.

Tuuq   OK.

Anyu   Thank you.

*

Fear of Judgement

Cassie It's mufti day and we're all allowed to come in in our own clothes and obviously this makes me anxious. I'm here in a tartan skirt from Zara, I feel stupid. I used to be a smelly and I liked Slipknot and all that until Chelsea and Dominika made friends with me. Chelsea saw me in the changing rooms after PE and she went, 'Oh you've got a lovely figure,' and I thought it was a bit lesbiany. But she did it and you know it's Chelsea so obviously I'm going to talk to her and obviously I'm going to be friends with her and obviously I'm going to let her dress me up like a fucking rag doll.

I'm not the leader of the group but I'm definitely also present and that's enough for me at the moment. But I don't belong. I can't explain it but something just isn't right and now that I'm sitting here in this weird Britney Spears homage uniform on mufti day and I'm listening to Chelsea and Dominika talk about how much they hate smellies because they smell. They just don't get it. They don't get the culture. When I hear that music I hear the pure rage of thousands of people come out, I feel the social rejection, I feel pure anger and hurt and it's cathartic and they will never get that. I feel like I'm living in a cocoon. Like I'm a butterfly walking around in the shell of a caterpillar and I hate it. I want to be me. I want to be loud. I want to fart and own it. I want to listen to Slipknot. The smellies are laughing in the corner. I wonder if they feel like they are caged birds. I'm not alive. I'm just pretending. And I don't want to pretend to be alive, I want to live. Do you mind if I go and sit with them? Just for today? And they look at me like I have just pooed on the floor

'If you go over there we are never talking to you again.'

I know that this means stopping being invited to parties. I know that I'll never be allowed at Connor O'Neill's again. I know that it means no one will fancy me. But is it worth it? Is it worth all that just to feel like . . . like you're not real? Just because of what a handful of people who think that being thin is more important than tasting donuts think?

She tells the band to play or, if there is no band, tells the DSM to press play.

She gets a microphone.

*

Song: 'Rage'

ARGHHHHHHHHHHHHHHHH

ARRRRGGGGGHHHHHHHHHHH

ARGHHHHHHHHHHH

If this is impossible, she can mosh around the stage, waving her hair around being the absolute most free person ever.

Thank you.

She puts microphone back.

*

Song: 'I'm Great, Honest'

We're like gods we don't get hurt
We don't feel anything
We carry on
We carry on.

We're the ones that rule the night
We're going out
We're having fun
We're having fun.

Let's go let's go let's go
Let's go let's go let's go
Let's go let's go let's go
Feels like the night was made for us.

We're going to sing like the world exists for us
This world exists for us
We're going to laugh like it's all that we can do
like it's all that we can do
We're going to live like we're only here now, like we'll die tomorrow somehow
We're going to sing like the world exists for us
This world exists for us.

I'm so scared, I'm so afraid
I feel an emptiness
I won't let it show.

I'm so sad and I don't know why
I can't speak so I drag it down
I bury it inside.

We're like gods we don't get hurt
We don't feel anything
We carry on
We carry on.

We're the ones that rule the night
We're going out
We're having fun
We're having fun.

Let's go let's go let's go
Let's go let's go let's go
Let's go let's go let's go
Feels like the night was made for us.

Let's go let's go let's go
Let's go let's go let's go
Let's go let's go let's go
Feels like the night was made for us

We're going to sing like the world exists for us
This world exists for us
We're going to laugh like it's all that we can do
like it's all that we can do
We're going to live like we're only here now, like we'll die tomorrow somehow
We're going to sing like the world exists for us
This world exists for us.

*

What I Need from a Loved One

Russia

Vladimer   Look you can't say cheer up, you're my best friend, you should know better than that.

Illiyana   Why not?

Vladimer   Because I can't just cheer up, that's not how it works! You know that!

Illiyana   I'm so sorry I don't know what to do. Just get up and get out of bed and we can do something. Go to the shops.

Vladimer   I honestly can't, that's too much, please just let me be here for a minute.

Illiyana   Pull yourself together!

Vladimer   I can't.

Illiyana   Vladimer. You have homework

Vladimer   Just fuck off. I hate you. You know I hate you. I hate you more than anything or anyone that's ever lived, just leave me alone. Please don't leave.

Illiyana   I don't know how to handle this.

Vladimer   I need another few days for my homework.

Iliyana   I'll ask your mum to ask.

Vladimer   I'm sorry.

Illiyana   It's OK. I don't know what to do.

Vladimer   You're doing everything right. I know it doesn't feel like it but you are. Don't take anything I say personally, you're my best friend. I just . . . I've been better before; I'll be better again. I'm sorry.

Illiyana Do you want to play PlayStation?

Vladimer Yes please.

*

Work/Life Balance

Michael My family have very high expectations of me. The tension in my shoulders isn't a medical condition it's more of a thing that is a manifestation of my work ethic. From the day I was born I was told that achievement is the most important thing, I'm too weak to be an athlete so that all came out in my work. Mr Bulger, my tutor, tells me I'm the best student he's ever had because I do everything I'm supposed to and more and then more again and more again and I read everything, I know everything about everything and more. And today's the day it's all been leading towards: GCSEs. I have worked so hard. I have made so many sacrifices. In Year 9 Sarah Spooner asked me out and I could have said yes. One night I got a message from Sarah saying her cat was sick and that I should come round and cuddle her. Now I can't tell you how much I would have loved to have gone and cuddled Sarah Spooner. I put my book down and I got dressed and I put on my coat and I went downstairs and I thought fuck me I am going to get to touch Sarah Spooner but then I thought what if. What if I go. And I touch Sarah Spooner and I don't work tonight. What if I get addicted to touching girls and that becomes my only objective. So I don't. I don't go and touch Sarah Spooner. I sit down, I read about Walter Raleigh. When everyone else is out getting fucked I'm here reading, and working, because I'm scared of what happens next.

Mr Bulger Morning, Michael.

Michael And I say 'Good morning, sir' in my customary good morning fashion. He's smiling; he knows something I know and my parents know and that every other fucker knows and he passes me my brown envelope. My parents and I go and sit in the corner and we open it up and we sit there and as expected I've got all top grades, mostly 9s with a few 8s, and Mum and Dad aren't happy – they just expected it of me.

Mr Bulger Are you off to the party?

Michael Party? What party?

Mr Bulger Oh I assumed you knew about John O'Shea's party?

Michael No.

Mr Bulger Right, well then don't mind me, bye.

Michael John O'Shea never invited me to a party. I do some online stalking Everyone's going. Everyone. Even the smellies. And no one's invited me.

I'm sitting in the back of the Volvo with Mum and Dad. I can't stop thinking why John O'Shea wouldn't invite me to his party. I start to imagine the party and what might be happening there. I start to imagine people talking and jokes and girls . . . I've never had that. Not since Sarah Spooner. What if that was a joke? What if no one likes me? Am I so out of the loop that I wouldn't even hear about a party that even the teachers knew about? What else have I missed out on? Have I been working too hard to live? I imagine life. Having a really good group of friends. Parties. Sex on tap from Sarah Spooner. Would I swap these grades for that? Just for a minute? I get up, I walk to the bathroom, I go in, I jump out of the window and I run down to John O'Shea's house and when I'm there it's kicking off. The whole world is there and he opens the door and he says, 'What do you want?' and I say –

'I'm here for my one night of fun. From now I'm going to have one night of fun a week.'

And he looks at me weirdly and I say, 'Get out of my way.' And I march in and I grab a beer. And I switch the music off and everyone's looking at me like they hate me. 'Listen. I know most of you don't know who I am but I've wasted most of my teenage years working too hard so I'm going to make up for it tonight. Can you all please chant my name. It's Michael.'

Everyone and the audience chant 'Michael'.

Thank you.

He downs a drink.

OK now music.

Music plays.

He does a full-on dance routine – the audience clap along with him.

When it's done . . .

All work and no play makes Mikey a dull bull. Let's party!

*

Song: 'How Can I Tell You the Truth about How I Feel?'

    Taking time
    We've got homework to do
    We need to be alone now
    Yes we do.

    In our rooms
    Doing what we need to
    Yes we are
    Taking time for homework.

    It's time to do our homework.
    Do our homework.
    We can't tell you what it is.

It's time to do our homework.
Do our homework.
And we are fine
Everything is just fine.

Not coming out
Got family things to do.
That's the truth
My gran is ninety-two.

I'm staying in
It's not because of you
It's just that I
Have family things to do.

It's time to see our family.
See our family.
We can't tell you what is up.
It's time to see our family
See our family.
And we are fine
Everything is just fine.

I'm telling you
I've got homework to do
It's not true
I just can't tell the truth.

If I could
I'd tell my friends how I ama
But I can't
Because you'll cast me out.

We can do our own thing
Do our own thing
Can't tell you what it is
We're doing us.
We can do our own thing
Do our own thing
But we seem fine
Everything is just fine.
We can do our own thing
Do our own thing
Can't tell you what it is
We're doing us.

*

Jealousy

Sarah It's morning and I'm walking to school behind Stacey with her perfect hair and her face and her bum and her tits and I wish I was her – I would give anything to be as beautiful as Stacey, I would give anything to be noticed. People like me get cast as best friends and not love interests.

It's the middle of lunch. The football team are staring right through me whilst I try to catch their eye and sexily eat a peach. I'm doing it really slowly to hope that they see, hating myself for wanting their attention, and . . . Then it happens. Stacey has entered the room like Jesus coming to Jerusalem with all the boys throwing down palm leaves but instead of palm leaves it's just sexual frustration.

Why can't I be sexy? Maybe I will. Maybe I'll do something now that's so sexy the world will stop. Something that's so sexy I can be like Stacey. I'm going to do something. I mean I don't know what but I'm going to do something. I'm going to make everyone fancy me like they fancy Stacey. Right. OK. Right. Here I go. I'm going to *Legally Blonde* them. I can't believe I'm doing this. Right. Yeah. Here I go. I roll my skirt up, just here, just a little bit, just a tiny little bit, just a tiny little bit and I walk right past her, right past where all the boys are looking and I drop my pencil. And I say, 'Ooopsy,' and I bend over to get it, and I let my skirt ride up a bit, just so all the boys can get a glimpse, just a glimpse and as I do   Oh no. I fart. And it's loud. And Stacey's face recoils like a snake as she goes, 'Urgh,' and all the boys laugh and my face goes red. I'm paralysed and all I can smell is last night's broccoli. This has gone terribly.

In Chemistry everyone's giggling about me and in the corner of my ear I hear it. 'Urgh. She used to be fit,' I what?! I used to be fit?! Why did no one tell me?! My world collapses. Everything falls in on itself. I am worthless. No one talks to me. I open the chemistry book. I have literally never opened a chemistry book before. I start to read. I come across this idea. The idea is that the universe is slowly and slowly pulling away like stretching clingfilm over a jar and one day it will be pulled so tight that our earth will pull away from the sun and we will lose all the heat on the earth and we will die. And I think about death and about how when the world is dead there will be so many things I miss. Mum. Hot cross buns. Getting in bed when it's raining. Birds. Cake. All those things frozen in time and it makes me sad. I think about how much time I've wasted wanting to be Stacey and how many opportunities I've missed to enjoy it. And looking around this room; I wonder how many people have missed out on their lives, wishing they were someone else. If I'm going to be alone I'm going to live. I get a peach out of my bag. I eat it. Just for me. It tastes great.

*

Song: 'Things I Am Supposed to Be'

Things I am supposed to be

I'm supposed to be thin
I'm supposed to be funny; I'm supposed to be bouncing around like a bunny
I'm supposed to be fit
I'm supposed to good at footie; I'm supposed to throw away bread from my butties
I'm supposed to be sexual
I'm supposed to be strong; I'm supposed to never be wrong.
I'm supposed to be cute
I'm supposed to hard; I'm supposed to never let down by guard
I'm supposed to be happy
I'm supposed to be free; I'm supposed to make nothing about me
I'm supposed to be unique
I'm supposed to not care; I'm supposed to have amazing hair
I'm supposed to be happy; I'm supposed to be happy; I'm supposed to be happy;
I'm supposed to be happy

Things I am supposed to be.

*

Advice to My Younger Self

You OK so I don't know what to say to you.

Younger You You're the one from the future.

You I know.

Young You So aren't you supposed to have all the answers?

You I'm still only fourteen. I don't know anything really.

Young You So why are we here then?

You I don't know.

Young You What can you tell me?

You I know you feel sad sometimes and I still feel like that sometimes as well. I know you'll find that really isolating but I do. That feels like it could be useful?

Young You That's literally the one thing I wanted you not to say.

You Well, yano . . . I don't know. I'm still here. So even when it's really bad you won't kill yourself.

Young You Are you happy?

You Now and then yeah. I dunno. Being young feels like you're sad a lot I think.

Young You Then what's the point?

You I dunno. I guess the moments where we are happy?

Young You I want to always be happy,

You We can't always be happy.

Young You Your eyes look tired.

You I'm tired.

Young You Are you still a virgin?

You Yes and that's fine.

Young You Are you in love?

You No but that's fine as well.

Young You Oh so we break up with Jenny?

You Yes but that was always going to happen.

Young You Why?

You Because we're both children and when you get to high school you change friends and some people have other friends.

Young You Is love not real then?

You Yes, just not with Jenny.

Young You Are you in love?

You You need to work on yourself before you can even think about love.

Young You Is being as fat as you avoidable?

You I dunno. Probably. I don't think about being fat much there's more important things to think about.

Young You What's more important than not being fat?

You Loads of things.

Young You Like what?

You Like cake. Pizza with friends. Treating yourself to a chocolate bar. Why would you not eat chocolate bars.

Young You Why are things bad?

You I don't know.

Young You Am I unpopular?

You Erm . . . Not particularly.

Young You Am I popular?

You Not particularly.

Young You So I'm neither.

You Not really no.

Young You How do I become popular?

You I dunno. If I knew, I'd be popular but I've got more important things to things about.

Young You What's the most important thing I've got to deal with?

You I dunno. Life. Carrying on.

Young You Why are you saying that?

You Sometimes you think you won't want to.

Young You What do you mean?

You Well, sometimes you'll feel like you don't want to carry on. Sometimes you feel like you might just sort of end it.

Young You Why?

You I don't know.

Young You So why don't you do it?

You Because it gets better.

Young You Does it ever end?

You I don't think it does, no.

Young You Is this something I'll have to do forever?

You I think it might be.

Young You So how do I cope?

You I dunno. You just sort of. Work it out. There's lots to look forward to. Isn't there.

*

Relationships

David You don't know what love is until you've made a sculpture out of jelly of someone. I'm telling you now that that's what love is. Love is me and Dee. We've been together now for three months and it's great. She is the best. I think I would die without her. We met on a wet break in room 42 because she was drawing a giant picture of Aladdin, whilst eating jelly, and I went over and said I'm a Genie and I instantly thought after I'd said it that I was being weird but I apologized on Messenger later and she said it was OK because it was nice to be talked to and the rest is history. Today is Valentine's Day and it's my first ever Valentine's Day with a girl so I've spent I'd say four hours sculpting Dee's face into jelly. Right now I'm standing outside her house and I ring the doorbell and her dad answers. I go in, the jelly concealed in a lunch box, and we sit down and she goes . . . 'OK, I've got something . . .' and I'm like wait before you do it before you bloody show me what you've got let me show you what I've got and I open the box of jelly and I go, 'Happy Jellytines,' she cries and I have smashed it. I am the best boyfriend in the world. Are you OK? Her dad leaves the room, his belly shaking his way out with him. She looks up. These aren't happy tears. These aren't tears of years of pent-up jelly joy. She loves jelly. All she talks about is jelly. All she eats is jelly. All she ever dreams of is jelly. What's the matter?

Dee I'm moving to Spain.

David Spain? Spain? Spain? Why are you going to Spain?

Dee Dad is opening an *Only Fools and Horses*-themed bar in Benidorm after the divorce.

David Well, where does that leave us? And neither of us know. We just sit in silence like two penguins who know they're going to different zoos. She's my everything. My whole life. She's the reason I get up in the morning. When are you leaving?

Dee Tomorrow morning.

David I did wonder where all the furniture was. I assumed you were getting redecorated. Can I stay over?

Dee No. I think it's best we just cut the tether now and go our own ways.

David And before I know it I'm outside and the next thing I know I find myself in bed. When I'm in bed I'm not even thinking I'm just staring so I text her and I get nothing back and I ring her and she ignores me and I can't sleep. And –

The **Company** *step in (lights up).*

Company OK there's no way to tell you this other than stepping in because it's going to take you ages to work out.

David What do you mean?

Company Here's what's going to happen now so you're ready for the next time.

David Next time?

Company Yes, the next time. So here's how it works. You feel awful for what feels like for ever. Then you'll start to feel OK for a bit then, occasionally, you'll just like erupt into tears a bit and you won't know why, then you'll realize it's because you haven't dealt with it, then you'll just feel numb for a bit. Then one day you'll wake up and you'll feel like you again. Only not the you when you were with her, the you that was before her. Every time. It's been like that for teenagers since the dawn of time. So it's actually always fine. OK?

David   Not really.

Company   Right. Well, look at this.

*

Disgrace

Medieval England

Baron Earlsfied *has pissed himself.*

Baron Earlsfied   I just don't know what to do now I feel . . . I don't even know what I feel.

Lady Homerton   It's OK.

Baron Earlsfied   It's not though is it.

Lady Homerton   Don't worry.

Baron Earlsfied   Is this normal?

Lady Homerton   Yes.

Baron Earlsfied   I'm normally really happy. I normally sing songs and . . . yano. Do stuff. Not . . . Not this.

Lady Homerton   It's OK.

Baron Earlsfied   It's not OK.

Lady Homerton   Look, it is.

Baron Earlsfied   She's gone and I'm never going to love again.

Lady Homerton   You're being dramatic.

Baron Earlsfied   I'm not being dramatic. That's it. My social life is done.

Lady Homerton   Do you remember when Lord Harrington laughed milk out of his nose.

Baron Earlsfied   Yeah.

Lady Homerton   Is Lord Harrington popular?

Baron Earlsfied   Yeah.

Lady Homerton   Why did you get over Lord Harrington laughing milk out of his nose?

Baron Earlsfied   Because he's Lord Harrington.

Lady Homerton   Yeah but really.

Baron Earlsfied   I dunno. Just forgot.

Lady Homerton   Exactly. Everyone forgot. Because we all have our own lives and we all are busy doing our own things. We fall in love. We make tits out of ourselves.

We work. We have family problems. We get ill . . . We have lives. We forget stuff like this. And eventually . . . Eventually you'll forget about it too. Because we always do.

Baron Earlsfied So what do I do now?

Lady Homerton I dunno. Eat an ice cream, do your homework, play tennis, try and think about it less and then get over it.

Baron Earlsfied But what if I never love again.

Lady Homerton You're fourteen, you're going to love again. You want some ice cream?

*

Company See. It's always been this way. You'll be fine.

David Yeah.

Company OK. Let's move on.

*

Song: 'Things This Feeling Feels Like'

This is what it feels like

Like quicksand and stinking
Like sinking
Like suffocating and barking painting
Like sour sweets
Like bitterness and dog treats
Like blackness and dark moods
Like burnt food
Like vinegar and not knowing where to go
Like vertigo
Like vomit and crash footage
Like porridge
Like sandpapers and prison doors
Your mother doing all your chores
Like screaming and slow-burning violence
Like deafening silence
Like wotsits and ketchup
Becoming a grown-up
Like cigarette smoke and artichokes
A sheep getting lost all alone

This is what it feels like

This is what it feels like

This is what it feels like

This is what it feels like.

*

Zest

Chloe *is ill.*

Chloe I'm sick. I've been sick for a long time. I'm not going to lie to you and tell you that I don't hate it and that I don't see all the dickheads in school walk past me that don't deserve health and wish this wasn't on them. I'm invisible. It's not even that everyone knows what's wrong with me it's just that I know there's something wrong with me and I can't talk to people and because I don't talk to people no one knows I exist. I'm not pretty or clever or anything like that I just sort of happen to exist in the same space as these people. Even if I wanted to talk to them I couldn't because of . . . Because of what's going on with me I'm tired. I'm tired all the time. I can't go out. I can't make friends. I can't go to sports or clubs or anything. I can't . . . I go to school and I go to class and I go home straight away and that's my life. It's not what I'd chose, I hate it, I hate it I hate it I hate I hate it I hate it I hate it I hate it. I'm not living. I go home and I lie in my bed and my house backs onto these woods, well I say woods, but they're more like just some shrubs that sort of gather together to look like woods and at night when I'm too tired to do anything, I'm too tired to read, I'm too tired to watch TV, I'm too tired to do anything at all, I lie on my back and I just listen. Outside I can hear everyone I see in school laughing, not at me, they don't know I'm there, but they're just laughing, they're just feeling their way around being young and they're playing and kissing and falling in love and I can't . . . I can't . . . My body won't let me live. I put ear plugs in. I let my mind wander and although I can't help it, although I know the last thing I want is this, the last thing I want is any of this, I let my mind wander to things I'd do if I was healthy. I let my mind wander to things like running and walking and climbing trees and just going out. Just going to a night club and dancing and not even talking to anyone, just being there, just letting the music and the lights and sound run over me and I know, I know by the way that they walk down the corridor in their shitty tight skirts, in their shitty fucking trousers that they don't know what it is to have the opportunity to live. They don't know what it is to not be ok. When I fall asleep I dream of going home from school and going to the shop and buying fucking . . . Maoams. I dream of standing outside the shop with the sugary fucking spit rolling out of my mouth whilst laughing with some people whilst falling in love whilst looking at the sky whilst doing anything. But I can't. I'm here. And the worst thing is that I know that being here and thinking and dreaming and wondering has opened the universe up to me, full of wonder and magic and delight and fucking poetry but I can't use it and you can't see it. You don't even see it. All you see is your fucking problems and the ineffencies and the fucking boring mundane shit and you don't live! You don't live and you have the choice to live and I can't live and that's what kills me. Because if I was you I'd eat a shit ton of berries and you think that sounds weird because you think that sounds fucking mundane but until you have done without you don't get to choose what freedom tastes like. I cannot be happy. I have all this LIFE in me, all this ZEST and I want to live. If I was you I would live. I would eat berries and maoams and they'd taste amazing. I would run. I would kiss people. I would do EVERYTHING just to feel it. I would forget about your bullshit and Live. So why don't you. I know you don't. Do it. I fucking dare you.

*

Song: 'It Will Come Again But I'll Be Prepared Next Time'

You're not alone
We're in the club too
Let's go out tonight
You're not alone
We're in the club
Let's go out tonight
Everybody in the club, sing
Come on let's sing
Everybody in the club, sing
Come on everybody let's sing
Everybody in the club, sing
Come on let's sing
Everybody in the club, sing
Come on everybody let's sing.

Here we are, again, right here
All together in the sun, today
Sitting in a field again, laughing at everything we say
And we are so happy
The futures great you see, for us
All the people who are right here, right now
Sitting in the sun again, laughing at everything we say
And we are so happy
And we are so happy.

I can't see us being anything other than happy like we are
For all our lives
When we are grow up so happy we'll be happy like we are
For all our lives
I can't see us being anything other than happy like we are
For all our lives
When we are grow up so happy we'll be happy like we are
For all our lives.

This is temporary all this,
Thinking this will pass and I am scared
That this is the best it will ever be
I am so scared.

I can't see us being anything other than happy like we are
For all our lives
When we are grow up so happy we'll be happy like we are
For all our lives
I can't see us being anything other than happy like we are
For all our lives
When we are grow up so happy we'll be happy like we are
For all our lives
We are so happy
Look we're so happy
We are so happy
Look we're so happy
We are so happy
Look we're so happy
We are so happy.

You're not alone
We're in the club too
Let's go out tonight
You're not alone
We're in the club
Let's go out tonight
Everybody in the club, sing
Come on let's sing
Everybody in the club, sing
Come on everybody let's sing
Everybody in the club, sing
Come on let's sing
Everybody in the club, sing
Come on everybody let's sing.

You are not alone
Everyone is in the club
You are not alone
Everyone is in the club
You are not alone
Everyone is in the club
You are not alone
Everyone is in the club.

End.

The Sad Club

BY LUKE BARNES

Notes on rehearsal and staging drawn from a workshop with the writer, held at the National Theatre, October 2023

How the writer came to write the play

> It's really tough to write for young people, so the question I started the project with was, if I could give any advice to my younger self what would it be? What were those things that still tripped me up in my 20s? I went around schools and workshopped the play and the big answers were shame, my body, the way I look, the way I behave.
>
> Luke Barnes, 2023

Barnes also talked about what he felt the challenges were for directors of Connections plays. He said he chose to have smaller monologues and duologues, because it's often hard to get lots of people together in a room. *The Sad Club* is an offer of a selection of scenes and songs, and an order, but how you do that should be a provocation for each group.

Approaching the play

Lead director Tinuke Craig talked about how useful a director's manifesto is when approaching a play. This means asking yourself the question, what do you want the show to do? This is the start of creating a directorial magnetic north for yourself, somewhere to come back to when it's tough, or you get lost.

Craig shared three questions with the group that can help in creating your director's manifesto.

> Why this play?
> Why now?
> Why you?

Craig then shared a new set of questions to consider as a director approaching the play:

> Which are the three moments this play lives and dies by?
> What is the 'five-star' moment?
> What is your company's superpower?
> What is your company's kryptonite?

Here are some of the group's answers:

What are the live or die moments:

- Opening number – especially 'this is temporary all this. . .'
- Final song
- Swimming race
- Michael's moment
- The big rage scream
- Chloe's monologue at the end
- You and Younger You
- Happy Jelly Times

Five-star moments:

- Michael let loose
- Let's go let's go let's go
- Rage
- Jelly
- Chloe

It is also worth asking the question: What can you deploy to make sure your five-star moments land? For example, casting the best possible Chloe, or underscoring the Michael moment for full impact.

Strengths and Kryptonite (relating to your cast):

- Understanding the humour of the play – help the cast see it's about them
- Focus and being in the moment when you're not delivering a monologue – create a character and a journey for every scene they're in (see under heading 'Exercises for use in rehearsal')
- Anxiety – this led to a larger conversation about how to support wellbeing in this rehearsal process. Some reflections on this included:
  - Metaphor check-ins – e.g. what kind of drink are you, and check-outs – so they leave their 'stuff' in the room
  - Voice warm-up – good opportunity to have a good breathe (breathing in for four, holding for five, out of six) – this is great to manage anxiety and can lead into the vocal warm-up
  - Make the management of the anxiety in the room part of the fabric of the show and the rehearsal process
  - Be positive as the leader: congratulate/praise them, etc.
  - Daftness and silliness at the start of the session – making it clear that there's no judgement
  - Ball games – using objects and props

Concepts and style

Craig talked about how helpful it can be to have a clear concept when directing a show.

Examples of concepts could be:
A version that is traditional, naturalistic, in the year the playwright intended
A version which strips it back, distils the play to its purest form

Craig then shared an exercise by director Robert Icke which can help you define your concept. It is called 'The Execution Gap' and it helps you work out your concept by running the play through the following binaries or scales. With all of these, you will probably be somewhere on a scale between the two extremes, but you might decide to place your production at one extreme or the other.

You ← → The text
Literal ← → Abstract
Then ← → Now
Digital ← → Analogue
This room ← → That room

You ← → The text

Who's in charge? You or the text? If it was a Shakespeare play, is the show reverent to the text or is Shakespeare dead in your production – most of us will exist somewhere on the continuum. *The Sad Club* seems to want you to be in charge – so you might be closer to 'You' on the scale.

Literal ← → Abstract

To continue with the Shakespeare example: a literal version would be creating Elsinore photo-realistically, as much like watching it in the 1600s as possible. Abstract could be the version where the set is a white box covered in blood – maybe it's set in Hamlet's head. For *The Sad Club*, literal would be creating a super-realistic set for each scene whereas abstract might be the actors saying 'House' or 'Party' as a way of defining location. Again, you will probably be somewhere on the scale and not at an extreme.

Then ← → Now

Do you want it to be set when it was written/intended or now? With *The Sad Club* it's slightly dictated, but you could definitely play with having anachronistic elements in the historical scenes. Alternatively, could your production have the logic that everything is happening at once, or the feeling that it's timeless?

Digital ←→ Analogue

How do you want to use technology in the show? Will it be fully digital, hyper-analogue – absent of any technical elements, or somewhere in-between?

For *The Sad Club* the group suggested a version where there is a filmed scene, or an analogue version with a Greek chorus. Craig said that analogue is useful if you don't have that much access to technology. You can play with sticking clearly in one camp except for one section or scene.

This room ←→ That room

Are the audience and cast in the same room, or are the stage and the auditorium two separate rooms? This is somewhat dictated by your venue, but you could challenge it with design elements or lighting. It's worth thinking about your duty of care to both the cast and the audience – this might inform your 'this room/that room' choice – for example, if this is a really important moment for your young people to share how they feel with their parents and carers, you might want your show to be more 'this room'.

Some people shared their directorial vision for *The Sad Club*:

- A bunch of chairs and everyone's on stage the whole time
- It's set at prom, with a band on stage and streamers and then it is ripped apart. The prom design elements create the other locations
- Y2K – Paris Hilton aesthetic, *Mean Girls* style, nightclub or underground bar
- Gig theatre style – they pick up their instruments at certain points and blur the boundaries between the scenes and the songs

Directing musicals

Craig encouraged the group to think about the challenges of directing musicals. The group had a range of responses:

- Putting it all together – combining music, acting and movement altogether
- Overcoming embarrassment
- Scheduling time, getting the songs right within the time you have allotted
- Sound design – microphones, instruments, etc.
- Tech – needing longer but not necessarily having longer
- Getting them to remember to act whilst they're singing
- Choreography
- Moving from speaking to song and back

Staging 'Here We Are, We're So Happy'

Craig shared how she would approach staging a musical number using the opening song 'Here We Are, We're So Happy'.

The group made some quick decisions on the binaries – this room/that room, digital/analogue. They decided to stage it in the round.

Craig asked the group about the purpose of the scene:

What do you want the opening number to do to an audience? You could also reframe this question as, if you were sat in the audience for this number how would you like to feel?

Options suggested included:

- Ground them
- Gather them
- Energise them
- Set the tone
- Take the audience on a journey – start really happy, then depressed, then hopeful

With a cast of ten, the first thing Craig did was take suggestions for how they would enter the stage. The group decided that they're already in a tableau in the park – facing out, with teenage physicality – the group decided it would be a living breathing tableau – and the cast should have their eyeline broadly up. A fidget ripples through the tableau when the music starts.

The group worked through the song with Craig, trying out different actions and choices until every line had an action, or a way of moving. Any movement the actors do really needs to support the text – so when the cast moves, this implies what the most important word or line is. So for example, in the second line of the song, the group decided that 'Altogether' was the most important word, so that's when they shifted. Craig talked about how the music gives you clues about what you could be doing, so if the music rises, that might be the time to stand up.

Here are some of the actions or movements that the group chose for the opening song:

- Sitting around looking up
- Look at each other
- Super-relaxed
- Laughter
- Face the audience with jazz hands
- Step, turn and click
- Travel to find somewhere new
- Windmill arms travel down the line
- Flingy dancing
- Conga line
- One person sings, everyone else slow motion dissolve to the ground

- Slow motion conga
- Drop the happiness (like the *Fleabag* episode on the Tube)
- Falling to the floor
- A 'Thomas Ostermeier' moment of 'the mask has slipped'
- Playing with the rictus grin of being beyond happy and then undercutting that in the bridge 'this is temporary all this . . .'

Craig talked about either using the music to support and galvanize the audience, and at times directly opposing the music. This is a specific choice but could work. She spoke about the principle of giving it a go; it will quickly become apparent if it doesn't work.

Staging 'The Best Things in the World'

Craig asked the group if they were staging 'The Best Things in the World' what would they like to 'do to' the audience with it. Suggestions included:

- Ground them
- Good chance to bring them into 'this space' – gather them
- Let it hang in the air
- Make them emotional

Craig shared that it's one of the moments in this play which potentially hits harder if you're a grown-up than if you're a teenager. Those moments could feel a bit 'grown-up' and so there is a directorial choice over whether to embrace it or push against it.

If you decide to embrace the 'grown-up' moments, that will inform your directorial choices. These were some suggestions from the group about how you might do that:

- The cast just stand and say their 'best thing'
- One by one, coming to the front to add their bit
- A digital version where the audience type it on their phones and it appears
- Photographs of the cast when they were young or their family (like in the *Barbie* movie with the Billie Eilish song)
- Using different languages spoken by the cast
- Ask the audience to write them down on the way in and the cast pick them out of a hat
- Gather suggestions from the school/community

Craig highlighted how this is an opportunity to personalize the show to your area, those young people, this moment in time.

Staging the swimming scene

Craig spoke about how the swimming scene is a magical moment (one of the five-star moments talked about in the 'Approaching the Play' section).

The group came up with various ways they could create the world of the swimming pool.

- Using lights
- Projection
- Sound
- VFX
- Comedy green screen
- Snail race films
- VR headsets or the experience of them
- A dance-off version of the swimming race – swimming to us means dancing/running/something else
- Pens as swimmers – magnify that onto a screen
- Visualizer with little Lego figures projected onto a big screen

They then had a go at staging the scene, in groups of all different sizes.

What did the group like about the different versions which were shared?

- Characters and the exaggeration
- Breathing
- Facial expressions
- This scene is a great way of using the ensemble
- You can create the whole world with two actors or with ten actors
- Going backwards to create the impression of winning
- Using the ensemble to create the impression of movement
- The dialogue before the race sets it all up – so the race you can play and really explore
- If you anchor yourself in the text you can be free to experiment
- Could use little props like swimming floats, goggles, swimming hats, swimming costumes
- Aural experience
- The actors could be still and just make the sound effects
- You could tell the story of the race through just seeing the audience
- The actors could run around the audience (in a 'this room' version)

Craig and musical composer Ian Ross discussed some broader approaches to staging sections of the play.

Craig emphasized that if there are sections that you're not sure about how to approach, ask the young people to go and make them quickly.

Ian Ross reminded the group that when there's acting and singing, you don't need to shy away from doing something really simple. This might be just someone singing – if the song works and the lyrics work, you don't always need to pile loads on top of that.

Structuring the rehearsal process

Scheduling and managing time is a big part of the director's role. Craig talked about how she splits up rehearsals into four quarters. Here are the main things that the group thought would go in each section.

Stage 1

- Learning music
- Reading songs as text
- Establishing roles/expectations
- Blocking
- Character
- World building – exploring character, voice, space, working as an ensemble
- Read through
- Establishing theatrical language
- Trying scenes
- Movement

A note on songs from Ian Ross – if you know the songs, they're like islands, the songs give you structure and shape – so you can jump from this island to that one.

Stage 2

- Blocking
- Stumble through
- Staging
- Trial and error (all the way through but especially in this stage)
- Movement

Stage 3

- Putting it all together
- Working on choreography
- Stumble through

Stage 4

- A run-through where the directors have to keep their mouths shut and the young people have to problem solve if it goes wrong
- Problem solving
- Practice with microphones
- Run throughs

- Tech rehearsals
- Dress rehearsal

Craig acknowledged that rehearsal processes can be complicated, the group shared some worries they have about their group and their process for some team troubleshooting.

When people don't turn up for rehearsal

Use character plots to help you make contingency plans for what you can do with all the different eventualities. Also, other cast members can jump in and potentially understudy.

You're not getting through all the material fast enough

Work out what you need to compromise on, so if there was going to be a dance number at the end, maybe that has to be cut because people are absent, and the focus is more on the core elements of the text.

Exercises for use in rehearsals

Warm-up games

Company building

Move around the space, add in different qualities of movement – the most confident version of you and the least

> Find a partner and identify three things you have in common
> Now in a group of four to five, can you identify three things you have in common
> Now in a group of ten, can you identify three things you have in common
> The more interesting or unusual, the better
> Each time, ask each group to share back their three things

Focus game from Ian Ross

Circle game – the following conversation is passed around the circle with an object like a water bottle or phone:

> A: This is a ping (offering the object)
> B: A what?
> A: A ping
> B: Oooh a ping (accepting the object)

> B: This is a ping
> C: A what?
> B: A ping
> C: Oooh a ping

In the other direction – with the same structure

>A: This is a pong
>
>Z: A what?
>
>A: A pong
>
>Z: Oooh a pong

At some point the two objects will cross over and make their way all around the circle back to the leader.

Character work

For each character in the play, whether they're in the script or made up/choral characters you've added, ask your cast members to come up with answers to the following:

- three things about your character that everybody knows
- three things nobody knows about your character except your character
- three things that everybody knows apart from the character

To help identify each character's motivation, work through these questions with your cast:

>By the end of the scene Bob wants to . . .
>
>By the end of the play Bob wants to . . .
>
>By the end of the day Bob wants to . . .
>
>By the end of the year Bob wants to . . .
>
>By the end of their life Bob wants to . . .

Music exercises

Warming up the body and the voice with Ian Ross

>Stand in a powerful hero pose
>
>Take a few deep breaths, see if you can notice everyone in the room, look very pleased with yourselves and keep breathing
>
>Big deep breath, say 'oh yeah' on the out breath
>
>With the heels of your hands, massage your jaw
>
>Use your fingers to massage your temples
>
>Use your thumbs to massage your jaw
>
>Make some noises, 'oh yeah', keep breathing, keep making noise throughout
>
>Massage the neck, notice whether there's any pain or itchiness
>
>Hand over your clavicle (collarbone), let you head rock away from the hand, let your head lean away – then let your head drop back and open your mouth – with a hum close your mouth

> Move your larynx (voicebox) left to right – how does that feel? Make a noise how that feels?
>
> If it's crunchy it means you have a tense jaw – go back to the jaw and massage again
>
> Make noise at the back of the throat (a creaky, vocal fry sound)

Throughout the warm-up, Ian encouraged the group to keep breathing, and keep making noise.

> Lift one arm and use the other to reach over and massage your ribs – imagine you are your ribs, what noise would you make
>
> Put your hands straight down behind your back, clasped together, look left, ahead, right,
>
> Look at the sky and kiss the ceiling twenty times
>
> Tickle your temples – what noise do they make
>
> Massage your eyebrows – what noise do they make
>
> Gently wipe under the eyes towards your temples – imagine there's something to move under your skin
>
> Give your nose a wiggle
>
> Say the following pattern – un gee – un gay – un gah – un goh – un goo
>
> Massage the top side of your neck – these are mastication muscles – say mastication muscles
>
> Tap clavicle – say clavicle clavicle
>
> Shake your body out and make sound as you do
>
> Squidge eyebrows – say squidge squidge
>
> Behind your ears – brush down into your neck
>
> Say 'errr-eh' – roll the r sounds

Tongue twister

> I dribble the lyrical dribble,
>
> To give all the miserable people a giggle

Play with speed, pitch (higher/lower), rhythm, volume as you say the tongue twister – play with lightness and heaviness. Can you have a conductor who leads the group with the tongue twister?

Warming up voices and starting singing

Ian Ross spoke about how lots of people find singing hard, because someone once told them they were rubbish, but actually singing is just about being truthful.

Hum MMM on a note, gradually go up a scale (you could do this with a piano or instrument or using call and response)

> Open it up on a MAHHHH
>
> Hum MMMMMAAHHMMM on one note, then go gradually up a scale
>
> Sing a scale up and down on MMMM and then go up a note, you can take a breath between each MMMM scale

Remember when you are singing you can return to those massaging and non-musical sounds

To the tune of the can can:

> My dog he can do the can can
>
> Better than my cat can
>
> But my goldfish thinks it's rather complicated
>
> My dog he can do the can can
>
> Better than my cat can
>
> But my goldfish find it's rather hard

This can loop around. Each loop should go up a key – the starting note is one note higher – and get quicker.

Teaching and learning music

Ian Ross spoke about finding truthful and simple ways through the music, especially as some of it is challenging. He said the quicker people can do stuff from memory the better. There is the option of complicated harmonies, but the aim is to hear the notes, and know where you are in the story before you add any complications – it's all about clarity.

This is how the group learned 'Here We Are, We're So Happy':

Speak the lyrics in the rhythm. You can focus on just the first line initially, and gradually add more lines in through call and response.
Now think about breath. go through and decide when people should breathe in the line.
Now practise the lines with the breaths.
Now you're ready to add the tune in.

When you start singing, practise singing one note together. Get used to starting, stopping and exploring
Sing the first two lines you have already practised using just one note
Then sing to the tempo (speed) in the score

Learn the same part together to start with.
Into tiny chunks, especially for bits that are tricky to learn such as 'other than happy'

Go back and remind everyone of where to breathe, adjust based on what the performers need, and where they're naturally breathing

If you start with harmonies, people often find it hard to stick to the tune. You might need to support people with the tune and gradually introduce harmonies.

Something to notice – the backing parts are very 'straight' in rhythm (on beats one and three) and the rhythm of the songs is quite syncopated (on beats two and four)

'The Best Things in the World'

Ian Ross started by asking the group to sing a note on an 'AHH' all together. He stressed that it's not just about volume, it's also about tone. Practise creating a pleasant sound, alternating between different notes; you can practise this slowly doing little sections of scales.

Then they learned one part of the Aaahs in 'The Best Things in the World'. Ross showed the group how the tune was mostly just stepping up and down a pentatonic (five note) scale. This means it is quite intuitive.

The group then spent 30 seconds thinking about the best things in the world, and then said them out loud with no particular order and no particular rhythm.

After the group shared their 'best things', Ross asked them to restart singing the Aaahs. He pointed out that you could also play the backing track with the Aaahs.

In a moment where you want to find the sensitivity but the music is playing against that you could use the Aaahs.

Ross also pointed out that you could use the Aaahs as the warm-up.

Tips from Ian Ross about how to teach the music:
- You can use lyrics written up on a board or projected
- Clap along with the rhythm as people speak the lyrics
- Loop sections around so people can pick up the rhythm

Question and answer with Luke Barnes

Q: Are you happy for monologues/duologues to be blown up into a scene for 20?
A: If the words stay the same, yes.

Q: Why a musical?
A: Most of my work is gig-theatre based, one of the things that draws me to theatre is live-ness. And in life, people share their truth in different ways. Also, a big thing was getting young people to do stuff they enjoy whether that's monologues, scenes or singing. I'm interested in how we start sharing truths honestly, sometimes music is a way we can

tap into that. In some musicals the songs burst out of the scenes, in *The Sad Club*, the songs have an equal weight as the scenes, they're not an extension of the scenes.

Q: What's the connection between the characters?
A: All the contemporary stories exist in the same world. But the characters that seem to know each other all talk by themselves to the audience. And the characters in other worlds talk to others in the same scene.

Q: Do you have a vision of what the play looks like?
A: No – genuinely, if we end up describing how things should be done to directors, we become directors. The writer gets to give loads of fun stuff for directors and designers to do. Even if I had an idea, I'd never say it.

Tinuke Craig says – Even if a writer says what should be done, the director doesn't have to listen! In this country we're particularly deferent to writers, but directors also have something to say, or a skill which is worth expressing.

Q: Is it OK to change the genre of the music, so it is the same but in a new genre (a bit like the Bridgerton soundtrack)?
A: Ian Ross says – Adam (the composer) is open to it, there are some restrictions of tune and scansion of the words – but you could create the backing tracks or accompaniment in all sorts of ways. You could also do it a cappella. It's about what's going to give the truth of the story and the truth of the performance for your company.

Q: Why the title?
A: I liked the idea of a club that everyone's in but no one's talking about. The idea of admitting that we're always bringing something with us to various situations. I always felt I was bringing challenges with me, but I never spoke about it. And as you get older you realize that everyone else is bringing difficult situations with them too. I called it a club as we're in it together. Geographically, this club goes everywhere, through space and time. It's not weird to feel anxious, it's not weird to feel isolated, or to not feel great.

Craig added – Sadness makes you feel lonely which is the opposite of being in a club – and being in a sad club makes you less sad.

Q: Can we change the gender of the characters?
A: Absolutely.

Craig added – Make sure you know if you're changing the gender of the character or changing the gender of the actor playing the character – they are two different things.

Q: Are the scenes set in Australia/Russia negotiable?
A: Those places are chosen for a reason, but play with it, you could change it. The fishing scene is about two people feeling like they are alone and they have space, it's expansive.

Craig said – When we see that a scene is set in Russia, there's a world where you set it in Russia with signifiers (hats, accents, language) – or Russia could be a more abstracted idea.

Q: Can we remove the swearing?
A: You can change the swearing if swearing is not allowed in your setting, or if the young people don't feel comfortable – you could ask the actors what they'd rather say.

In response to various questions about specific changes:
A: Take ownership of this, please feel free, it's a provocation for whatever your group can do together to make it specifically you.

Craig added – If you are making changes, really interrogate why you're making them. If it's just because it's easier, then try and sit with it a bit longer.

Suggested references

Gloria Estefan (examples of syncopation)
Thomas Ostermeier (the 'mask has slipped' reference)
Bobby McFerrin's pentatonic scale
National Theatre YouTube Channel – Voice Warmups
Gulliver's Travels at the Unicorn Theatre
Barbie movie – photograph section under the Billie Eilish song 'What Was I Made For'
Fleabag, Series One, Episode 2: On the Tube

From a workshop led by Tinuke Craig
With musical direction by Ian Ross
With notes by Freyja Winterson

WIND / RUSH GENERATION(S)

by Mojisola Adebayo

Mojisola Adebayo BA (Hons), MA, PhD, FRSL, is a Black British performer, playwright, director, producer, workshop leader and academic of Nigerian (Yoruba) and Danish heritage. Over the past 30 years, she has worked on various theatre and performance projects in Antarctica, Belgium, Botswana, Brazil, Canada, China, Finland, France, Germany, Ghana, Greenland, India, Ireland, Israel, Lebanon, Malawi, Mauritius, Myanmar, Norway, Pakistan, Palestine, Poland, Singapore, South Africa, Sri Lanka, Sweden, Syria, the USA and Zimbabwe. She has acted in over 50 theatre, television and radio productions, devised and directed over 30 scripts for stage and video, published 13 plays and several academic articles, and led countless workshops and training courses. Mojisola Adebayo is based at Queen Mary, University of London where she is Professor of Theatre Writing and Performance Practice.

With thanks to Ola Aminashawun – dramaturg

This is a play about the British Isles, its past and its present.

This is a play written for all *young people and youth theatres to perform, regardless of their cultural background, skin colour, ability or gender.*

Characters

There is potential for doubling of roles, as necessary. The names of the characters below are in some cases historic, in other cases symbolic, playful and or deliberately ambiguous in terms of gender and culture. The play is partly an exploration of names, naming and calling things as they are . . .

Students

Six first-year university students doing a degree in History. They are a close-knit team of outsiders, aged around 18, but they can be played by younger actors, of any culture, skin colour or gender. Names are deliberately androgynous and all the roles can be played by actors of any gender. Some character traits are indicated below but don't get too hung up on these. The play is driven by the story and by storytelling.

Ola – *intelligent, religious, very anxious but brave. Their name means 'wealth'*
Zhe – *(pronounced Zee) – dynamic, driven by curiosity, extrovert*
Ali – *a playful, loveable, joker*
Xia – *(pronounced Shia) – cool, understated, sharp*
Kit – *rational, focused, caring – closest to Ola*
Jay – *gentle, sensitive, spiritual*

NB: For reasons that will become clear, it makes some sense if Ola is played by a young person of African/Caribbean descent. However, this is not absolutely necessary if there are no Black members of your youth group. Equally, if there is only one Black member of your youth group they do not necessarily have to play Ola.

Monte Rosa – an elderly German female of around a hundred years old. Each time Monte Rosa speaks she is played by a new female actor (or male or non-binary actor playing female). She may alternatively be played by one actor throughout. She is a romantic, poetic, vain, egocentric, sweet old lady with an unpleasant streak. Again, as with all acting in this play, let the storytelling drive the performance choices.

Seven Villagers

A group of middle-aged, middle-/upper-class residents of a small wealthy remote rural community, somewhere in Southern England. The character names below are just playful suggestions for the reader, but the actors do not need to do impersonations of politicians with the same name and none of the names are spoken aloud in any case.

Theresa
Nigel
Caroline
Rishi
Boris
Dianne
Jacob

Captain of *Zong* – Luke Collingwood (English, historic figure)
First Mate of *Zong* – James Kelsall (English, historic figure)
Judge Mansfield (historic figure in the *Zong* case of 1781)
Sailors on *Zong* (working men from all over Britain and Ireland, fictional names, they can be played by actors of any gender, double roles if you need to). Suggested names:

Matthew
Mark
Luke
John
Simon
Peter
James
Thomas
Andrew
Nathan
Jude
Paul

British Citizens
The words spoken by British Citizens are all inspired by real lives. However, their names have been changed for anonymity. They have been re-named in memory of various Black British/African-Caribbean people. Some died at the hands of racists or in police custody and some lived remarkable lives:

Stephen (in memory of Stephen Lawrence)
Cherry (in memory of Cherry Croce)
Bernie (in memory of Bernie Grant)
Joy (in memory of Joy Gardner)
David (in memory of David Oluwale)
Mary (in memory Mary Seacole)
Kelso (in memory of Kelso Cochrane)
Stuart (in memory of Stuart Hall)
Olive (in memory of Olive Morris)
Smiley (in memory of Smiley Culture)
Nanny (in memory of Nanny of the Maroons)
Marcus (in memory of Marcus Mosiah Garvey)
Rest in peace, ancestors.

Sam and **Sim** – two Computer Gamers: Teenage friends, they speak in a stilted rhythm, mechanically, without much emotion, like figures from a video game.

Wind – the embodiment of wind, male, Jamaican, dub poet, inspired by the likes of Linton Kwesi Johnson and Benjamin Zephaniah, played by the entire cast in chorus. The role could alternatively be played by one actor who is particularly skilled at/enjoys spoken word/rap/poetry . . .

David Lammy MP – a living figure, played by the entire cast, at least ten actors, preferably more, but not less than seven. The role needs a powerful collective voice.

Notes on Playing

- Yes poetry
- Yes rhythm
- Yes to pace, pace, pace!
- Super-fast scene changes – oh yes!
- Yes musicality
- Yes theatricality
- Yes ensemble, chorus, team, collaboration, togetherness, *ubuntu*
- Yes movement
- Yes to creative accessibility for D/deaf, blind and disabled performers and audience members – e.g. BSL interpretation, audio-description, surtitles . . .
- Yes to flexibility, experimentation, inventiveness, playfulness
- Yes to small cuts but the scissors are mine – thanks! Requests to the author
- Yes it's a challenge and yes it's challenging
- Yes to taking pleasure in playing with it and seeing what can be created

Technical Notes

There are a few sound effects but nothing hard to source. Projection of certain words is very important for the storytelling and the audience understanding. If a projector is not available, you could use an old-style overhead projector, placards or sound. Experiment. As long as the meaning is clear, you can do this play simply or high tech, raw or cooked.

Notes on the Text

- A slash like this / indicates that the following person's line crosses over the person speaking at that point, i.e. two people talk over each other.
- These brackets [. . .] indicate the sense of the line but are not heard out loud.
- Please read the stage directions carefully, they will help you as each scene/setting is very different and necessitates its own distinct style.

Scene – House of Commons

The whole cast stand and play **David Lammy MP**, *speaking the verbatim text below, powerfully and passionately together. The actors embody and magnify* **Lammy**'s *physicality on the day he gave the speech/posed the questions in the House of Commons. If you have a large cast, some actors could play opposition MPs nodding their heads and calling 'hear, hear' beside him. You could also show the then Home Secretary Amber Rudd and the government front bench, fidgeting nervously. See this link for guidance on movement and theatricality in staging: https://www.youtube.com/watch?v=Y2q2dQlsywY. You could use the recording from the real debate where the Speaker of the House selects* **Lammy**.

Speaker of the House   Mr David Lammy!

An Opposition MP   Hear, hear . . .

Lammy, *played by multiple actors, speaks exquisitely clearly and is unashamedly bold, building in vocal, emotional and physical intensity and volume.*

Lammy   Can I say to the Home Secretary that the relationship between this country and the West Indies and the Caribbean is inextricable. The first British ships arrived in the Caribbean in 1623, and despite slavery, despite colonization, 25,000 Caribbeans served in the First World War and Second World War alongside British troops.

When my parents and their generation arrived in this country under the Nationality Act of 1948, they arrived here as British citizens. It is inhumane and cruel for so many of that Windrush generation to have suffered so long in this condition and for the Secretary of State only to have made a statement today, on this issue.

Can she explain how many have been deported? She suggested earlier that she would ask the high commissioners – it is *her department* that has deported them! She should know the number! Can she tell the House how many have been detained as prisoners in their own country? Can she tell the House how many have been denied health under the National Health Service, how many have been denied pensions, how many have lost their job?

This is a day of national shame, and it has come about because of a 'hostile environment' policy that was begun under her prime minister! Let us call it as it is: if you lay down with dogs you get fleas! (**Lammy** *continues as some of the cast gradually start growling in low volume and then barking and finally howling loudly like dogs.*) And that is what has happened with this far-right rhetoric in this country.

Can she apologize properly? Can she explain how quickly this team will act to ensure that the thousands of British men and women denied their rights in the country, under her watch, in the Home Office, are satisfied? (*The dogs continue in blackout. The sound culminates in wild howling with a few whimpering in pain until the start of the next scene. The effect should be chilling.*)

Senior Common Room

Lights dimly up on the old Senior Common Room (like a communal living room) of a prestigious university. Old chairs, coffee table(s), books, a rocking chair downstage right (which remains on stage throughout the play from here on) plus pictures of old – now long dead – white male academics hang on the walls. The set, however, does not need to be naturalistic. The Senior Common Room setting could be suggested with a few well-chosen items or conveyed through projection. However, the one item that needs to be physically present is a rocking chair, downstage right. Sound of a big old wooden door creaking open. **Students** *are revealed in the doorway, some wearing pyjamas, dressing gowns, slippers, holding mobile phones as torches. They speak in hushed tones, secretly seeking out a ghost, in a space they are not allowed in . . . They are all scared, but some more so than others.*

Ola This is a bad idea.

Zhe Are we going in or not?

Ola Not!

Ali But we said:

Xia Truth or dare?

All (*except* **Ola** *and* **Kit**)   DARE!

Ola But I'm scared.

Kit *comforts* **Ola** *as* **Jay** *continues.*

Jay You've got more to fear from the living than the dead.

Ali It's true. Think Putin. Trump. (*Approaching* **Ola** *with a zombie-Trump impression.*) Aaaaamericafiiiiiiirst. . . .

Zhe Climate crisis, ISIS,

Xia (*continuing* **Zhe***'s list*)   white supremacists . . .

Zhe Much more scary.

Ola Why is this not helping me?

Jay Let's just put this thing to bed so we can all sleep at night.

Ali Nice.

Kit (*to* **Ola**)   And there'll be a perfectly rational explanation.

Zhe Let's see shall we? . . .

Jay So, we just go in and calmy *talk* –

Xia to a freaking ghost.

Jay And ask it –

Zhe *politely –*

Ali (*putting on a posh voice*) to go a-way . . .

Ola You lot don't even know what you're messing with – I'm telling you!

Ola *goes to leave.* **Ali** *is disappointed.* **Kit** *pulls them back.*

Ali Arrhh . . . we said we'd stick together . . .

Zhe You won't be able to sleep anyway!

Kit [Let's just give it] two minutes.

Ola Setting my timer. (*Sets phone timer.*)

Ali Then we order delivery! I'm hungry.

Xia Me too.

Ola Can we *please* just go back down to halls? We're not even allowed in the Senior Common Room. Let's just do a different dare!

Zhe (*to* **Jay**) You got this, babe.

Kit *starts timer. They all step cautiously into the room,* **Jay** *in the lead, others following.* **Jay** *begins to talk, louder now, into the space, slowly, gently, addressing the ghostly presence.*

Jay Hello . . .?

Ali (*comic ghost voice*) HELLOOOOOOOOOOHHHH . . .

Ola Stop it!

Xia Hey there . . . spirit thing . . .

Kit Spirit thing?

Ola (*whispering a line from the Lord's Prayer*) 'Forgive us our trespasses as we forgive / those who trespass against us . . .'

Jay (*speaking over* **Ola**) We mean you no harm . . .

Zhe (*to* **Jay**) That's good keep going.

Ali We beg you – don't hurt us!

Ola (*snapping out of the prayer*) What you giving them ideas for?

Kit (*to* **Ola**) Breathe.

Jay Thank you for . . . reaching out . . .

Ola Please. (*Begging to leave, but feeling compelled to stay.*)

Jay But the truth is . . . we are all really . . .

Kit Tired, stressed

Xia – shitting ourselves.

Jay And we are only freshers.

Zhe And we've got history assessments coming up.

Kit Our lecturers are on strike *again*.

Xia And we are paying nine grand a year.

Ali I just wanna get my two-one and done.

Zhe So . . .

Jay We respectfully ask you, spirit –

Kit – if you even exist –

Jay that you please –

Ali LEAVE US THE FREAK ALONE!

Everyone is startled by **Ali**'s *volume. They* **All** *shush* **Ali**.

Kit (*reprimanding*)   You'll wake security.

Zhe (*reminding*)   Politely.

Ola (*praying quietly but even more urgently*)   'Lead us not into temptation, but deliver us from evil . . .'

Jay (*to the ghost*)   We are very sorry if we've offended you in any way.

Ali Sorryyyyyyy . . .

Jay You can talk to us anytime . . .

Xia (*not sure if what* **Jay** *has just said is a good idea*)   Errrrmm . . .

Jay And if there's something you want from us . . . just give us a sign.

Ola What did you say that for?

Kit Rewind.

Zhe (*to the ghost*)   What *do* you want?

All *pause silently, for quite a while, trying to sense the ghost, waiting for an answer, breathing deeply, alert.* **Ali** *breaks the silence*

Ali Wiiiiiings . . . chicken wiiiiings . . .

Xia Fufuuu, nooodles . . .

Ali Humouuuus, baba ganoooooooush!!! . . . (*They all laugh except* **Ola**.)

Ola [We are leaving] NOW!

Ola *drags* **Kit** *away. They all start turning and leave with the lines below, saying goodbye to the ghost, 'job done'.*

Ali Salaam [peace/goodbye].

Xia Shalom [peace/goodbye].

Zhe Salmon.

Ola What?

Ali Nah, don't fancy that.

Zhe Can't you smell it?

Ali It wasn't me.

Ola Yeah . . . (*Repulsed.*)

Jay Fish? . . .

A sudden cold breeze sweeps in. **Kit** *is startled by feeling something brush past.*

Kit Don't touch me!

Ali I didn't do nothing!

Xia It's freezing.

Ola My phone's died!

Jay Everyone keep calm.

Zhe Can you taste salt?

Ola (*in fear*) Please Lord . . .

Xia (*confused by the taste of salt on their lips*) Urgh . . .

Zhe Oh my days – the chair! It's moving!

Rocking chair is moving of its own accord. This could be conveyed by a transparent wire on the base of the rocking chair being pulled by a stage manager in the wings, or wind machine. Sudden blackout. They **All** *scream in fear.*

All AAAAAAAAAHHHHHHHHH!

Monte Rosa 1

Lights up. **Monte Rosa** *rocks very gently in her rocking chair in the Senior Common Room. She wears a blue shawl. There is a faint memory of the German language in her speech (e.g. she says 'Ja' – pronounced 'ya' meaning yes) but don't push the accent, just focus on telling the story to the audience.*

Monte Rosa
Ja, I don't look bad
Considering
I am over one hundred years old!
I still feel so young . . .

I was born in Germany, 1920
They cracked champagne when they got me!
And named me after the second highest mountain in the Alps.
Rosa.
Blanc is the highest so I'm lucky I wasn't the first!
Blanc is no name.

I travelled the whole world
But I've never seen the Alps.
I have always preferred the sea
Or perhaps the sea preferred me.
Not surprising really
I come from Hamburg
Eine schöne Stadt [meaning a pretty city].
Such a pretty city
My heart is always in a harbour
Every port an opportunity
And the best playground
To come of age
Every day a new ship
A new face
A new suitcase
Filled with music . . .
Ja, es war ziemlich toll [yes, it was quite exciting].
Quite quite exciting
Hamburg.

Und no need for school
When there was plenty of work
Tourism was new in the 1930s
My job was to take people away
On holidays.
German folk wanted to see the world
We crossed the North Sea and the Mediterranean
Mexico, Madeira, Spain . . .
Ja, sailing wasn't for everybody
Most got sick
But I was born for it!
Rocked by the *vind*
Kissed by the sun

With moon and stars and tides for guides
One moment, you feel the ease of a breeze
Then bluster, gale and gust the next!
Such a sense of adventure,
The weather.

Ouija Board and Pizza 1

Monte Rosa *has gone and her rocking chair is perfectly still. The* **Students** *are back in the Senior Common Room. There is considerable tension amongst The* **Students**, *except for* **Ali** *who is focused on enjoying the pizza. A large pizza box with one slice left is on the table, plus a candle, matches, pen, paper and an unopened Ouija board, wrapped in a piece of cloth. Nothing need be naturalistic.*

Kit It was just a gust of wind.

Xia And the lights?

Kit Momentary power cut.

Zhe What, *only* in here? Affecting *nowhere* else on campus?

Kit I'm just saying there's probably a scientific explanation.

Zhe (*sarcastic dig*) Sorry, Professor . . .

Jay (*peacemaking*) We need to bring our energies together.

Kit What's all this 'energy' shit?

Ola Stop fighting! Let's just get it over with.

Jay *smiles a 'thank you' at* **Ola** *then slowly reveals the Ouija board from the cloth.*

Jay So, a Ouija board is just like a phone, to communicate with . . . the other side. We call and . . . if there is a spirit trying to reach us, they send us little . . . text messages.

Kit This is ridiculous.

Kit *folds their arms.* **Ola** *moves back. Deep breaths as they all stare at the box.*

Ali Ommmmmmm . . .

Ola Stop it!

Ali (*laughing*) I'm just trying to get everyone relaxed!

Jay That's not a bad idea actually. What if we do some kind of ritual before we start?

Ola Ritual?

Ali What, like, slaughter a chicken?

Xia Yummm . . . (*Laughing with* **Ali**.)

Ola That's it! (**Ola** *gets up to leave.*)

Kit Don't go without me.

Ola *reluctantly sits down beside* **Kit**.

Jay It's important that we 'act collectively'. (*Recalling the instructions.*)

Zhe How about a song?

Ali (*singing the Liverpool anthem,* **Xia** *talks over*) 'You'll never walk alone / you'll never walk alone . . .'

Xia I'm not singing that. I'm Man United.

Ola I shouldn't even be here. I'm Christian.

Jay Then you've got nothing to be afraid of.

Zhe We could do that game from drama society where we close our eyes and say our names, one at a time, randomly. If we talk over each other we go back to the start but we keep going until we get it right.

Ali If I win can I eat the last slice of pizza?

Zhe It's not about winning. It's about collective action. Hold hands. (*They do.*) Close your eyes. (*They all do except* **Ali** *who keeps one eye clearly open.*) Both of them. (**Ali** *closes both eyes. The actors genuinely play the game with their characters' names, until they get it right. We never know what order the game will go in . . .*)

Ali Nice.

Zhe That was good, guys. Really focused.

Jay Ready?

Various nods, deep breaths, swallowing in anticipation, covering faces. **Jay** *strikes a match and carefully lights the candle, then slowly and silently opens the Ouija board box. They fold out the board.* **Zhe** *picks up the instructions and reads.*

Zhe OK. 'Two or three people gently place their index and middle fingers on the planch.'

Kit It's just a stupid bit of plastic.

Zhe *offers the planche to* **Kit** *who shakes their head.* **Zhe** *puts the planche on the board and they wait for someone to place their fingers on it.*

Ola Count me out.

Ali (*making an excuse*) Er, I've got greasy fingers.

Zhe Well, my fingers are far too long.

Kit (*sarcastic*) Really?

Jay If no one else wants to . . .

Xia I'll do it too.

Jay *and* **Xia** *slowly place their fingers on the planche, on the board.*

Zhe (*reading the instructions*) 'Choose one person to scribe the messages.'

Kit OK.

Kit *takes the paper and pen. Ready waiting for letters to come through.*

Zhe 'Do not force anything to happen. Simply stay open.'

Long pause. Nothing. Then after some time the planche starts slowly moving around the board, randomly. It would be great if the audience could see the board.

Ali Shiiiiiiit . . .

Ola Are you lot pushing it?

Xia & Jay (*really focused*) No.

Kit It can't just –

Xia – I swear.

Jay It's weird.

Xia It's got a life of its own.

Ola (*fearfully*) Ohhhh . . .

Jay (*to the ghost*) Are you here? . . .

The planche rests on the word 'Yes'. This is projected.

Zhe Yes! It said YES!

Ola Mummy . . .

Ali *hugs* **Ola** *a little too tightly.*

Jay Have you got something you want to tell us?

The planche stays on 'Yes'.

Xia Do you want us to leave you alone?

Ali We really don't mind going.

Kit It's got to be a trick [i.e. it's just getting interesting]

Ali *covers* **Ola**'s *eyes and their own. The planche moves to 'No'.*

Jay NO! – It wants us to stay!

Zhe (*following the instructions*) Ask their name!

Jay What . . . is . . . your . . . name?

The planche slowly moves to the following letters, speeding up gradually. The text here and throughout is projected/shown somehow for the audience. It is important that the audience see the letters as they come through. The **Students** *repeat the letters out loud and* **Kit** *writes them down.* **Ali** *and* **Ola** *can't resist looking.*

All
P
R

O
B
L
E
M

All Problem?

Ola I told you! We don't know what we're getting into!

Jay (*to the ghost*) What is the problem?

All (*except* **Ola**)
N
A
M
E

All Name?

Kit (*reading what they have scribed*) It doesn't make any sense.

Ali We said WHAT IS YOUR NAME?!

Zhe No need to shout.

Xia They are all the way over on the 'other side'.

Ola I feel sick.

Jay It's moving!

All (*except* **Ola**)
G
U
E
S
S

Ali Funny name. Maybe it's French?

Zhe Guess! They want us to play a game!

Xia This is too weird, even for me.

The planche moves again.

Jay It's moving again.

Kit Are you pushing it?

Jay I promise [I'm not].

All
N
O

T
I
N
O
T
I

Kit (*writing*)   Noti-Noti?

Ali   Definitely foreign.

Zhe   Not I? *NOT I*!

Jay   It's moving again!

All (*except* **Ola**)
C
L
U
E

Zhe   It's giving us a clue.

Jay   Keep breathing.

All (*except* **Ola**)
F
A
R
M

Ola (*confused*)   Farm? . . .

Ali   Mooooooooooooo . . . (*Then all the others join in with the mooooooing sound. The rest of the cast mix in other farmyard sounds. The final sounds are dogs barking and howling again as the scene transitions.* **Ola** *remains on stage, watching the next scene and all of the scenes inspired by the word clues coming from the Ouija board.*)

Wind Farm

The Ouija setting quickly becomes the setting of a very heated debate at a local parish meeting in the church hall of a small remote village somewhere in rural southern England. The characters sit around the table. New actors play the roles below. The names are just playful suggestions; there is no need to do impersonations of politicians with the same name, unless you want to ☺ If need be, roles (except **Ola**) *can be doubled, to accommodate cast size. The characters are posh. A forward dash (like this /) indicates that the following line comes in at that juncture, causing an overlap of speech – this is important. The scene is naturalistic but slightly absurd* *with a quick pace. Be extremely tight on cues.* **Ola** *is visible, observing the scene and all the scenes arising from the words/clues.*

Theresa   And what about house prices? If we let them take over the land / the value of our houses will inevitably fall.

Nigel   Colonize more like.

Caroline   No one is talking about the impact on migrating birds.

Rishi   They'll put tourists off.

Nigel   We don't want tourists either.

Rishi   But if we did, one day, want to attract tourism / they would definitely be put off . . .

Caroline   What about the birds?

Boris   They kill bats!

Nigel   They're bloody ugly.

Diane   You can't say that.

Nigel   I can say what I like it's a free country.

Jacob   And we want to keep it that way!

Diane   What I mean is / beauty is in the eye of the beholder.

Nigel   I am saying it like it is. They stick out, they don't fit in and we don't want them here!

Diane   Oh, I thought you were talking about bats.

Jacob   Keep up, dear.

Caroline   Well I find them quite beautiful / in their own way.

Boris   You should have your eyes tested.

Caroline   I'm just saying it's not the way that they look that bothers me. I think there's something quite elegant about them, the way they all move / together.

Jacob   That's when they work. Most of the time they don't even work. Waste of space!

Nigel   And they're bloody loud!

Diane   You're quite loud.

Rishi   Well, I've never been up close to one.

Jacob   Keep away from them I say, you never know what they might / do to you.

Caroline   I'm not saying I want them in my field –

Nigel   Well, there you are then!

Boris Apparently each one does barely enough to power a hairdryer.

Diane We could do with a hairdresser around / here.

Boris *Hairdryer* I said!

Diane A hairdryer is quite powerful actually. Mine keeps fusing.

Rishi / Does it?

Nigel They can't even boil a kettle for a decent cup of tea!

Theresa That's decided then. We move to a vote . . .

Boris We vote NO.

Caroline We haven't discussed their benefits.

Jacob What benefits?

Nigel They'll be cutting disability benefits to pay for them, / mark my word!

Jacob A lot of them are bogus too.

Diane You just can't say that.

Nigel FREE COUNTRY.

Caroline I mean what the countryside can gain from having them here.

Theresa Whose side are you on?

Caroline I just think we should have a balanced / debate. We are still a *civilized* country.

Nigel Who's going to pay for all this? Taxes will go up, you mark my words.

Rishi Let her have her say.

Caroline Thank you. Well. They are quite. . . natural.

Nigel Primitive!

Caroline They harness a *natural* power. Lest we forget we are an island.

Boris They'll build a bloody bridge to France next.

Caroline How are we going to survive / without their energy to re-build the country?

Boris That's just scaremongering.

Nigel Stick them in the sea! If the council are so in love with them, stick them in the sea!

Rishi Or find another island.

Nigel Just not in my field!

Diane But they are modern.

Theresa They've ruined Denmark. And it was such a pretty little country. You can't get more modern than Denmark.

Jacob The whole landscape is riddled with them. Riddled! / Everywhere you look.

Rishi It's true. My cousin married a Danish man. Such a lovely family. So much style.

Jacob They'll be next to leave the EU I bet. Dexshit.

Diane What?

Jacob Danish Brexit.

Boris (*quoting Hamlet*) 'Something is rotten in the state of Denmark.'

Theresa To leave, or not to leave, that was the question . . . (*They laugh.*)

Boris Long live Shakespeare! (*Singing started by* **Boris**.) 'Rule Britannia! Britannia rules the waves!' (*Then they* **All** *join in* . . .)

All 'Britons never, never, never shall be slaves!'

Theresa All those against having a wind farm erected in our parish say neigh.

Ola (*observing, trying to figure it out*) Wind farm?

All Neighhhhhhhhhh!

All *continue with horsey farmyard sounds and dogs howling again during their exit and transition into the next* **Monte Rosa** *monologue.* **Ola** *leaves.*

Monte Rosa 2

Another actor can play **Monte Rosa**. *We know it is her because she always sits in the rocking chair, swaying gently back and forth in the same light, telling her story to the audience, alone. She wears the same clothing, e.g. a blue shawl. Eerie quiet.*

Monte Rosa
And then the Nazis came to power
And we had to fly the swastika
I'm not going to lie, why should I,
I wore it proudly.
Ja, you're looking at me like that
But you don't understand
It made us feel good about ourselves
We were *besser* than anyone else
No more hunger, no more shame
Could you blame us after the first war?
Only *pure* Germans were allowed on our holidays
No Roma, or Poles or Slavs, or Blacks or Jews
No handicapped, no homos,
No '*unter-mensch*' allowed
We were the captains now!
We ruled the waves!

From Hansa Stadt Hamburg to Windhoek Namibia
The world was ours
And it was love!
Ja, that was our only song.

You got given a medal if you had four children for the Reich
No medal for me.
I was selected for a more important job
Because of my experience at sea
I was ordered to transport passengers
From Norway
To Germany.
Jews.
All ages.
From Oslo . . .
The songs they sang were different from those
We heard before the war
Their hums hung in the air
Like the thick clouds of smoke . . .
In Auschwitz.
(*With remorse.*) The children . . .
I had no choice!
I was doing my job.

Ach, but you know the history
And because of the work I had done
I was captured by the Royal Navy as a 'prize of war'
The Britishers were not so different from us
Cousins really: same Royal Family
And their language is easy
Land, land
Buch, book
Vind, Wind . . .

Ouija Board 2

The next letters from the Ouija board are projected. **Ola** *reads them out loud, slowly.*

Ola
F
A
L
L
Faaaaaaaaall . . .

Ola *starts falling slowly to the floor. They sit and watch the next scene.*

Wind Fall

Deck of slaver ship Zong. *Year 1781. The upper-class* **Captain Luke Collingwood** *and the working-class* **First Mate James Kelsall**, *both looking rough, look out, the ship rocks. Heightened playing. High stakes. Pace!*

First Mate   We're fearfully low on water, captain.

Captain   How are we doing for rum?

First Mate   Just one bottle left, sir.

Captain   How far away from drinking our own piss?

First Mate   Not as far as we are from Jamaica, sir.

Captain   How could we miss it?

First Mate   These islands all look the same, sir.

Captain   300 miles you say?

First Mate   300 miles out of the way.

Captain   How many Blacks below deck?

First Mate   379, sir.

Captain   And how many did we have in Accra?

First Mate   442, sir.

Captain   How many was our legal capacity?

First Mate   193, sir.

Captain   And how many look like they'll live?

First Mate   Less than half, sir.

Captain   I'm a surgeon not a mathematician but that doesn't sound good.

First Mate   It don't bode well for profits, sir. And the men, sir –

Captain   Our men . . .

First Mate   Are somewhat disgruntled, sir. We should have arrived two weeks ago and . . . all this thieving, rape and torture is thirsty work.

Captain   Hmm . . .

First Mate   I have a thought, sir.

Captain   Just one?

First Mate   Just one, sir.

Captain   Go on, man.

First Mate   We are, of course, insured.

Captain   Indeed, we have to be.

First Mate   We can, alas, make no claim for goods damaged during the course of the voyage . . .

Captain   Go on.

First Mate   But if we throw the Blacks overboard, sir, to save on water for us hard-working men, the insurance company will see that we dispensed with the cargo to save our pale skins and our Christian souls.

Captain   Dispense with the cargo . . . I have an idea, First Mate.

First Mate   You have so many, Captain.

Captain   I say we begin with the children, then the women, then the men, sickest first.

First Mate   It'll be heavy work, sir.

Captain   Well, keep them in chains, and throw them in in batches. It'll be as if we were to throw cattle into the sea. Not a pleasant sight but a hearty breakfast for sharks!

First Mate   And not a scrap of evidence.

Captain   Not an eyeball. Get to it, man!

First Mate   But, Captain, who shall we say is to blame for all we are about to do . . .

The **Sailors** *creep onto the now more gently swaying deck, one by one. Cast size can be reduced if necessary. They hatch out the murder plot. Pace!*

Matthew   Let's blame this old Dutch ship – *Zong*!

Mark   Her name means 'care'. Ha! She cares for none.

Luke   She's a monster made by Nether men.

John   Full to bursting, feeding on flesh, so much more than she can digest.

Simon   The greedy Dutch bitch swallows dish upon dish of –

Peter   Ashantes, Mandinkas, Igbos, Yorubas . . .

James   Women, men, boys, girls, babies . . .

Thomas   Stuffed to the sin brim with human suffering.

Andrew   She stinks of fish, piss, shit and vomit!

Nathan   So much that when we dock at Liverpool –

Jude Cardiff, London, Glasgow, Bristol –

Paul – the ladies and gents have to cover their noses, hold their breaths.

Matthew She drags us down to her depths.

Mark She gets so drunk on flesh she makes us forget our Christian selves.

Luke She got so pissed she got lost! 300 miles off the coast of Jamaica.

John Sailed right past the dock at Black River.

Scene transforms from a ship to a courtroom. The **Sailors** *give evidence in court, swearing on the Bible, passing it one by one, rapid, testifying, feigning regret*

Simon And so many of the poor Africans died . . .

Peter But we were running out of water . . .

James And we pleaded with her! 'Carry us to safer shores!'

Thomas But instead she said –

Andrew You'll have to lighten my load.

Nathan I am too full I cannot go on.

Jude And *Zong* she spat 131 Blacks into the sea.

Paul A shark's breakfast!

Captain So we have no choice. We *must* make this insurance claim. To re-compense, to compensate.

First Mate And the judge will say . . .

Judge Mansfield (*formal, slower, concluding the case*)
These slaves were no more human than horses.
And it must have been a sorry sight
But the men tried with all their might

First Mate But it was the ship, it was *Zong*, that made us do this wrong . . .

Captain (*back in the present, slower, satisfied with the plan*)
And when we get back to Tilbury Dock,
We'll open that sweet bottle of Jamaican rum
And count our little . . .

Ola (*figuring it out*) Windfall . . .

Optional visual or movement sequence here, e.g. pound notes start falling from above. Cast members enter with scissors, snipping the notes, like the mouths of little fish. They cut out little human figures from the notes and hang them up, like bunting on a ship. Or this could be a movement sequence with music. **Ola** *watches, pained.*

Monte Rosa 3

Monte Rosa *rocks in her chair. Alone again. A new actor. Same light. Blue shawl.*

Monte Rosa
The only thing I really did *not* like is they made me change my name
They have a habit of doing that, the British
Schade! Shame!
I *love* my name:
Monte Rosa
But I had no choice *again*
So yes I worked for them
All over their Reich, their vast Empire!

Life on ship could be animated physically here by the cast.

My favourite job was back in 1948
Kingston, Jamaica to London, Tilbury Dock
Transporting the great-grandchildren of slaves
Now sailing the other way
The West Indies had fought us Nazis
And since Elizabeth was their Queen
And they were British citizens
They were invited to come for a new life in England
'Come and re-build *your* country!'
Quite a story really . . .
Ja, that was one of my favourite passages
So much hope and dancing and stories

Singing the Lord Kitchener song 'London Is the Place for Me', the cast involved in the next scene join in, singing the song in full, quietly underneath **Monte Rosa***'s speech. Song available online.*

They continue singing gently and acting out playing dominoes, cards, chatting, relaxing on the Windrush *ship, approaching England.*

What a lot people don't know
Is that I also carried Poles
Sixty-six women stranded in Mexico
Ja, Polish refugees
And when they got to England
They got passports and set up Polski shops
A new life made possible.
I heard that the British Home Office were trying to send them away (**Monte Rosa** *watches the cast*)
Not the Polish of course!
The *Blacks*
Even though some are as old as me
And worked all these years for the Mother Country

Saying 'they had no place in Britain',
'The Windrush Generation'.
A scandal!
If they ordered me to transport them back to Kingston today I would have said
Nein! No! I'm too old
And they were nice folk.
Take the Blacks back under your own steam
You're on your own now, Queenie!
I've had enough of governments
Making me move people around like cargo
There were times when I should have said no . . .
(*Thinking with regret about the Norwegian Jewish children.*) I should have said
no . . .

Ouija Board 3

Ola *reads the Ouija board letters projected again. They are still afraid but moved.*

Ola
C
H
I
L
L
CHILL . . .

Wind Chill

The voices below all speak in one rhythm. Find the rhythm. Keep in time, like a song. The word 'wind' comes right on cue. Feel it. The poem is influenced by hip hop and dub poetry. For inspiration, listen to Benjamin Zephaniah reciting 'Who Killed Colin Roach?': https://www.youtube.com/watch?v=njs3I4ECIe0 and Linton Kwesi Johnson performing 'Inglan Is a Bitch': https://www.youtube.com/watch?v=Zq9OpJYck7Y

The tempo of the speech below is different than these examples but the idea is the same, telling true stories to the audience, in rhythm. No breaks between voices/ characters. Keep pulsing forward. It can be spoken with a beat/music underscored if this helps timing. Use a little movement/gestures to animate the text. If possible, project or show the years (below) to punctuate each stanza, locating us in time.

Note on use of the 'N' word: *The 'N' word appears in the following scene, twice, as a direct quotation. The word is a weapon with a painful and violent 500-year history. It is still used to assault Black people today. It is harmful and should only ever be used in the context of the scene, where it is only used as a direct and factual quotation. Treat the word in rehearsals as you might treat a gun. It is never to be played with casually. Handle with care and caution. Discuss its use with your groups – have a* 'health and safety' briefing, as it were. Only ever use the 'N' word where it is in the script. Lock it away, like a gun, when it is not being used directly in a scene. If you wish to, the line in which the 'N' word appears could simply be projected or shown, the line spoken as is but just the 'N' word mouthed but not heard aloud. You could put a silent beat in where the word should be. This is up to you. When not in rehearsals, directors, actors and creative teams are advised to simply refer to the 'N' word. The use of the 'N' word by rappers and writers of African descent (who use a different spelling) is a different subject, for a different play, entirely.

Projection: 1948.

Nanny   Ivor Cummings walks up the gang-plank
Civil servant, gay and Black:
'Things will not be easy for you here'

All (*punctuating in rhythm, in time*)   Wind
Chill
Fact.

Projection: 1948.

Bernie   Tilbury Dock was a bit of a shock
Dirt, smog and faces flat
'Welcome party? What did you expect?'

All   Wind
Chill
Fact.

Projection: 1948.

Joy   'No dogs, no Blacks, no Irish'
'I'm not renting your kind this flat'
'But I've got no-where, to sleep tonight'

All   Wind
Chill
Fact.

Projection: 1959.

Smiley   They murder Kelso Cochrane
And yes we must fight back
They say 'riot' we say 'uprising'

All   Wind
Chill
Fact.

Projection: 1964 and 1968.

Stuart   'If-you-want-a-nigger-for-a-neighbour-vote-Labour'
The Tory election tract
Enoch comes with 'Rivers of Blood'

All Wind
Chill
Fact.

Projection: 1981.

Cherry Child-ren of the New Cross fire
They were treated like suspects
'Thirteen dead and nothing said'

All Wind
Chill
Facts.

Projection: 1993.

Kelso They called out 'what, what, Nigger!'
It was *us* who was under attack
Cops hid the names of Stephen's killers

All Wind
Chill
Fact.

Projection: 2017.

Stephen Served in the British army
Paid every penny of tax
Said I had no right to draw my pension

All Wind
Chill
Fact.

Projection: 2018.

David I've been here all my life!
Work still give me the sack
'No passport? You can sleep on the street!'

All Wind
Chill
Fact.

Projection: 2019.

Mary 'You got ten days to leave the country
It's time to go home and pack'
I was a NHS nurse for seventeen years

All Wind
Chill
Fact.

Projection: 2020.

Marcus They keep me in detention
Cos I'm African. Cos I'm Black. [Alternatively: 'Cos she's African. Cos she's Black'].
If I was Irish or a dog they wouldn't lock me up! [Or: 'If she was Irish . . . lock her up!']

All and Ola WIND
CHILL
FACT!

Poem carries straight on but now as call and response. Divide **All** *cast onstage, half of them call and half of them respond.* **Ola** *joins in everything.*

Projection: 2024.

All (*calling*) No compensation
(*responding*) Wind chill factor
(*calling*) Nor rep-ar-ation
(*responding*) Wind chill factor
(*calling*) On a plane for Rwanda
(*responding*) Wind chill factor
(*calling*) Or in Jamaican waters
(*responding*) Wind chill factor
(*calling*) Spring or winter
(*responding*): Wind chill factor
(*calling*) Fall or summer
(*responding*) Wind chill factor, wind chill factor
(*calling*) Do you feel it?

Ola (*responding alone*) Yes you feel it!
And you deal with it!

All (*just half of* **All** *the cast calling including* **Ola**) You wrap up
(*half of* **All** *the cast respond*) You rise up
(*calling*) You step out
(*responding*) Face the cold
(*calling*) Fire inside
(*responding*) Walking tall
(*calling*) Give a hand from a fall

All (*everyone together*) And CARNIVAL
(*calling*) you play on
(*responding*) you pray on
(*calling*) you march on
(*responding*) you work on
(*calling*) you fight on

All (*everyone together*) And never give up
Never give up
Never give up

Never give up
Cos come what may . . .

Pause. **All** *suddenly look at* **Ola** *to complete the line but then there is a sudden blackout. Exit.* **Monte Rosa** *gets in position.*

Monte Rosa 4

In her rocking chair. Stage directions as above.

Monte Rosa
My last trip was transporting soldiers and their families from
Korea and Japan back to England
But there was a terrible fire below
And one by one
The sailors who all said they loved me
Even my beloved captain
Abandoned me
Jumping into the sea
Left me to sink into the bed
Alone.
It's pretty cold
Down here
Even in the Med
When you're dead
It's pretty cold . . .

So many
Skulls
Skeletons
Refugee children
Left to drown . . .
I could have carried them back to shore
Just yesterday: five hundred or more . . .
So many lost souls
Calling for a home
While they sit on food mountains
Refusing to see what lies beneath
Ja, the sea is history,
It repeats . . .

Ouija Board 4

Students *take a break. It's been intense. More at ease now. Pizza box is empty.*

Kit I don't get it.

Ali   They went to the farm, they had a fall and then: chill. FarmfallchillFarmfallchill!

Xia   Maybe it makes sense if you say it slow. Farrrrrrm. Faaaaall. Chiiiiiiillllll . . .

Kit   You lot are bonkers.

Jay   What do they *want*?

Zhe   Do you think they understood the question?

Kit *and* **Ali** *take over the planche.* **Xia** *scribes.*

Zhe   Who are you?

The planche moves to N-O-T.

All   NOT.

Kit   Here we go again . . .

Jay   Who are you, *not?* . . .

The planche is still. They wait. They get tired. **Xia** *takes their fingers off the planche. Pause.* **Xia** *breaks the silence.*

Xia   Have you lot all finished your essays?

All (*not in chorus, just naturally*)   No . . .

A beat.

Jay   Shall we try again tomorrow? (*They casually respond 'yeah/yep/thank God' etc. by getting up and starting to pack away*).

Ali   Who ate the last piece of pizza?

Ola (*ignoring* **Ali**, *packing away*)   Maybe we're not supposed to know . . .

Ola *goes to pick up the planche and it suddenly starts moving wildly seemingly on its own, flinging* **Ola** *around who is trying to hold on. This effect could be created physically by the actor. They all try to help* **Ola** *who is screaming.*

Ola   NO!

The planche whirls around and lands at 'No'.

Ola (*out of breath*)   They don't want us to go!

Jay   Someone write it down!

Zhe *grabs the pen and scribes frantically. Letters are projected.*

All (*not in unison, sense of chaos*)
G
O
L
D
S

U
G
A
R
G
U
N

Ola GOLD? SUGAR? GUN?

Sudden loud sound of rapid gunfire.

Xia GET DOWN!

Ola WHAT THE HELL?!

Gold-sugar-gun Gamers

*Sound of gunfire continues. The rest of the cast run on with lollipops, firing them like weapons, laughing. They sit on the floor downstage and suck lollipops throughout the scene. The two computer gamers, **Sam** and **Sim**, also run on. They don't suck lollipops, but they sit down on the 'sofa' (or any seating indicating a sofa), also facing the audience. **Sam** starts playing a computer game, **Sim** is trying to figure out which game it is. **Sam** and **Sim** speak in a very rhythmical and electronic/mechanical way, with minimal emotion, like figures in a video game, with an urgent pulsating beat beneath it all. The scene might be animated physically but let the words do most of the work. It must have pace, rapid fire but crystal clear; nothing can be lost in delivery, just like the game. It will need a lot of rehearsal. The scene is a response to the popular video game* Resident Evil 5. *Here is a trailer. Trigger warning: it is violent: https://www.youtube.com/watch?v=xxJbz_3PKQo*

Sim What's this?

Sam Wait.

Sim Is it *Hostile Environment 6*?

Sam No.

Sim *Hostile Environment 9*?

Sam No.

Sim Looks like *Hostile Environment 3*.

Sam Wait.

Sim Or *Hostile Environment 4*. (*Beat.*) Is this the one with the swamp?

Sam Wait.

Sim The one that starts with the boat? Speedboat through the swamp to the mud huts. And it's Sheva and Chris.

Sam Wait.

Sim Chris Redland and Sheva who sounds like a cat but she's not.

Sam Wait.

Sim Sounds like a Hindu goddess but she's not.

Sam Wait.

Sim Sheva.

Sam Wait.

Sim Spelt like in Hebrew but not a Jew, Hindu or cat.

Sam OK.

Sim She's a girl.

Sam OK.

Sim She's more like some kind of mixed race.

Sam OK.

Sim 'cept her hair's really straight.

Sam OK.

Sim She's got this really small waist.

Sam OK.

Sim Nice tits.

Sam OK.

Sim Walks like this.

Sam OK!

Sim But Chris is the boss. He's the protagonist. Is that what this is?

Sam No.

Sim The one with the African villages? And they've all got some kind of mad virus.

Sam Wait.
Wait.
Wait.
Wait.

Sim OK.

Sam Thanks!

Silence. **Sam** *plays on.*

Sim Sure it's not *Hostile Environment 3*?

Sam   No.

Sim   More like *Hostile Environment 4*.

Sam   No.

Sim   Where you blow off the Africans' heads. They jump out and scream and go 'ARGH!'.

Sam   Huh?

Sim   They don't even know how to speak.

Sam   Huh?

Sim   They jump out and scream and go 'ARGH!'.

Sam   OK.

Sim   Black men, they scream and go 'ARGH!'.

Sam   OK.

Sim   Black men, no t-shirts, just trousers, bare feet and viruses jump out and scream and go 'ARGH!'.

Sam   OK.

Sim   And then you blow off their heads.

Sam   Wait.

Sim   Destroy as many as poss.

Sam   Got it.

Sim   And you're Sheva or Chris with big guns but Chris's are bigger cos he's the boss.

Sam   Yes.

Sim   And he smashes the masks and smashes the pots and takes all the gold so it's his.

Sam   Yes.

Sim   And Sheva's got really nice tits, small waist, mixed race or something like that but straight hair like a Hindu a cat or a Jew but she's not.

Sam   Yes.

Sim   Says, 'OK, thank you, watch out, help me up, over here Chris!'

Sam   OK.

Sim   'Thank you, watch out, help me up, over here, Chris!'

Sam   Yes.

Sim   She's just like this stupid sidekick but it's Chris who's the man.

Sam Yep.

Sim Blonde hair and American.

Sam Yep.

Sim Chris's got one Black friend but he doesn't blow off *his* head. Cos he's an American. Like Kanye West.

Sam OK.

Sim Not like the African Blacks in the villages, swamps to the mud huts and viruses wearing no t-shirts just trousers muscles and bare chests and jumping with 'ARGGGGGHHHH!'. Not real words but 'ARRRRGGGGGHHHHH!'.

Sam WAIT! Wait. Wait. Wait.

Beat.

Sim Is that what this is?

Sam No.

Sim OK.

Sam This game is much more advanced.

Sim Slow down.

Sam This game is way more advanced.

Sim Slow down.

Sam Makes *Hostile Environment 3* –

Sim OK –

Sam – look like a walk in the park in a town with a clock in a tower still ticking still tocking somewhere in England or Scotland or Ireland or Wales – but with jobs.

Sim OK. Can I have a go?

Now **Sim** *plays the game*

Sam OK. Just shoot.

Sim OK.

Sam The Blacks. Just shoot.

Sim OK.

Sam Muslims just shoot.

Sim Got it. Anything darker than shit just shoot.

Sam Just shoot and collect.

Sim Where? What?

Sam Gold.

Pause.

Sim Where?

Sim *pauses the game and looks at* **Sam**. *They make eye contact for the first time.* **Sam** *sounds more human and speaks more naturally now that the game is on pause, but keep a sense of urgency and internal rhythm.*

Sam There's gold in the camel sacks. The camels belonging to Musa the King. One hundred camels and one thousand Africans, Timbuktu, Mali – ready to go. Not a fictional kingdom, not Black Panther Wakanda. No. Five hundred years ago. King Mansa Musa the richest man ever is going on Hajj: it's a pilgrimage. To Mecca, Medina and maybe Jerusalem. To say 'thank you' to God. He gives alms. Not arms. Alms. He gives out his gold on the way and prays five times a day. And he's famous. More than Malcom X or Muhammad Ali. The Egyptian economy crashed cos of all the gold he gives away from his camel sacks. And that's how they hear about Africa. The white people hear about Africa's gold and then the Portuguese come. Then the French, the Spanish, the Germans, Italians, the Belgians, the Dutch, the Danish, the Brits, they don't give a shit, take gold from your hand and the land. But it's not enough. They want more gold, Black gold, Black old, Black men, Black women, Black children, take them to the soil of Chris Redland and Sheva. And they've killed the first people who lived there. Strike African names and make them cut sugar cane. Sugar to make us fat addicts who sit on sofas like this playing video games to kill Blacks.

Sim Rules?

Sam Shoot. Kill Mansa Musa the Black Muslim king who makes Elon Musk and the King look like Barbie and Ken. He's way richer than them. But if white people hear of his gold, Black people get sold or die trying years later for Europe in boats. So shoot. Before anyone hears of the gold. Before anyone comes for the land. Before they get carried away. Before we all get carried away.

Sim OK.

Sam It's not *Hostile Environment 3*. Or *Hostile Environment 4*. Or *Hostile Environment 6*. Or *Hostile Environment 9*. This is *Hostile Environment* zero. The Indians invented the zero. Or Arabs invented the zero. Someone invented the zero. Let us go back to the zero.

The game resumes: now **Sim** *shoots while* **Sam** *continues speaking.*

Sam Maybe then they will never be slaves. Maybe then they will never lose names. Maybe then there will never be race. The colour of our skins will be no more significant than the colour of their eyes,[1] my eyes, your eyes, our eyes watching the killing of Blacks from the sofa suck sucking on lollipops –

Sim (*rapid rhythm*) Pop pop pop pop pop pop pop!

Sam Too fat in the head to get up and say STOP!

The gamers freeze in their scene as the next scene immediately starts.

---

1 Paraphrasing a speech by the Ethiopian Emperor Ras Tafari Haile Selassie I to the United Nations, quoted by Bob Marley and the Wailers in the song 'War'.

Last Ouija Word/Voice of the Wind

Ola *immediately comes in as the students are blown back into the Common Room.* **Ola**, *struggling with the planche, is held by the group.*

Ola STOP! MAKE IT STOP!

The letters are spelt out boldly through projection. They don't have to just be on the Ouija board; this could be in movement in the space for example.

All
W
I
N
D

A huge gust of wind and the rest of the cast is scattered on stage. **All** *play the voice of the wind. Some can take a solo stanza – whatever is clearest and most powerful. The whole speech could also be taken by one person. Experiment. The style is inspired by Linton Kwesi-Johnson performing the dub poem 'Inglan Is a Bitch'. However, this speech is much faster in rhythm. See Caliban's speeches in Shakespeare's* The Tempest, *for reference. This speech has its own defiant pace, as unpredictable as the wind itself. A kind of hip hop, but not. Make it your own. Some stanzas are a slow breeze but the end is a wild and fast hurricane! You could choreograph it. Whatever you do, hold nothing back. The wind knows no borders.*

Wind English is a bitch
Been no escaping it
English is a bitch
I want a word with it

You named oceans 'oceans'
And earth you gave 'quake'
But what a careless noun
For me
You did make
You called forest 'forest'
'Desert', 'fire' and 'sky'
But if you did not feel me
You'd say what am I
From this name?

Ind
W-ind
A fart of a word
A foul letter word
A trump up word
Hot air
A tight little title

A mean little rival
For *vento, viento, upepo*!
Could have named me something
Arabic, Gaelic, Bantu, Asiatic
You could have had Latin but you chose Germanic: *Vind.*
Wind.

Only a *liar's* rhyme you can make with it.
Even Shakespeare couldn't much play with it.
Sinned, pinned,
Mind, kind
Kindred spirits
My name has not
Elemental insult
My name is wind up.
English is a bitch
Been no escaping it
English is a bitch
And I want a word with it

Anglo I am angry!
Long neglected by language
What kind of mother tongue
Is so lazy, limp and languid
That she can't even credit her subject
With a password he can be proud of.

My moniker makes a mockery
Of all I've done for this country
My label should be libellous
Would it really have been so onorous
To make me a lickle more sonorous
Add a lickle consonant, a lickle vowel . . .
So yes I'll howl through your doors
In a rush!
In a wind rush!
I DESERVED MORE!

This linguistic disrespect
Needs a diction fixing
Some lexiconization
Some thesaurization
A new appellation
For this misrepresentation
Proper noun reparation!
With certification.

I demand new nomenclature
Powerful elegant mature
Sounding
Reflecting the true status
Of my intrinsic Englishness
For an island is not an island
Without the weather you see
You should show me some respect
I've been here for centuries.

English is a bitch
Been no escaping it
English is a bitch
And I want a word with it

Didn't I give birth to breeze
On this land?
I delivered you the tempest
Right here where I stand.
Bluster, gale, gust – I raised a hurricane!
Yet you classify me with a mere
One syllable name.

Didn't I turn your mills
To grind your grain?
To make your bread
So you would never feel the pain
Of hunger like your empire inflicted upon
Thirty million Indians
One million in Ireland!

English is a BITCH!
Been no escaping it
English is a bitch
And I want a word with it

(*Building to a hurricane.*)
So don't blame me
When you chop too many trees
And I race across your fields
And reap devastation
Don't blame me
When you turn up the heat
And it makes me swell
And arrive unexpected
Don't blame me

If I bring the desert to your door
The waters to your window
If I bring war
If I rise up
From 'rivers of blood'
Don't blame me!
For this hostility
For this, Britannia, is your legacy
And this you must know
You reap what you sow
And despite this pitiful one-syllable name
A mere footprint on a missing document that's still a source of shame
The nature of wind
The nature of wind rush
The nature of this generation
Has changed!

Howling dogs/howling wind into the next scene.

Senior Common Room Quiet After the Storm

Quiet after the storm. Just before sunrise. **All** *look at the rocking chair.*

Jay Wind farm.

Zhe Wind fall.

Ali Wind chill.

Xia Gold rush.

Kit Sugar rush.

Jay Gun rush.

All 'Windrush'.

Ola The. Empire. *Windrush.*

A beat.

Zhe She's a she.

Xia She's a ship.

Jay Rest in peace.

Kit Why us?

Ola Why *here*?

They look around the room at the pictures of old dead white male professors. Pause for thought. **Ola** *tries to figure out the mystery, through their lines below; it is not all worked out yet, use the lines to process.*

Ola An empire's gotta have either an emperor . . . or an *empress*. Right?

All Right.

Ola Our uni is named after the same empress from when the *Windrush* set sail from Jamaica. The King's great-grandma. Queen Mary of Teck. Some German countess. Wrote an essay about her. Empress of India, all her colonies. . . The West Indies . . .

Jay . . . Head of the Commonwealth . . .

Ola (*cynically*) *Common* wealth? Universities, cities, all over, from Aberdeen to Belfast to Cardiff to this place made *untold money* off of slavery. They even got compensation when they set the slaves free. And a lot of *these people* (*referring to the portraits*) invested their dirty money in *our* universities.

Ali It's true. The SU's running a campaign about it, but our uni's staying silent.

Kit Rewind. They paid the slave *owners*?

Ola Yep. And Black people are still paying for it.

Zhe Cleaning their offices, doing security, paying the fees . . .

Ali And more time, it's the Black students getting two-twos.

Xia Really?

Jay They call it the 'BME attainment gap'.

Kit They should call it the 'white privilege gap'.

Ali I better leave here with a two-one or I'm gonna take them to court. 50k debt for a Desmond Tutu – no thank you.

Ali and **Ola** *punch fists, etc. in agreement.*

Ola And uni managers are all white guys paying themselves, like, half a million a year.

Xia Half a million?!

Ali Minimum. Plus a free flat and a bodyguard!

Kit Cab rides to the Cotswolds.

Zhe Principals with no principles.

Jay But why does Empire *Windrush* want to talk to *us*?

Ola Cos of the Windrush scandal?

Xia Cos we're all doing History?

Zhe She could have just sent us to the library.

Jay I get the feeling she's still trying to tell us something.

Kit Why?

Ola (*fearfully, though much less so than earlier*) Look . . .

Ali Oh shit . . .

The chair is rocking vigorously as if it is nodding 'yes'. The group brace themselves. **Ola** *bravely gets the Ouija board and offers it to* **Jay**. *They are all surprised but go with it, silently.* **Jay** *sets out the Ouija board and places their fingers on the planche.* **Ali** *places their fingers on it too.* **Xia** *picks up the pen and paper.* **Kit** *watches* **Ola**. **Ola** *is totally focused on the letters. Deep breaths, they summon all their courage.*

Ola Empire *Windrush*. TELL US WHAT YOU WANT!

The planche starts to move to the letters below. More quickly than at first. The group are well practised now so they pronounce the letters, making out the words.

All T-R-U-T-H O-R D-A-R-E

Silence. They look at each other. They look at the rocking chair.

Ola TRUTH.

All *look at* **Ola**.

Monte Rosa 5

In her rocking chair again.

Monte Rosa
Rest in peace?
They won't let me!
In the newspapers, on the TV
They keep calling me, calling me
Windrush Windrush
Empire *Windrush*
Naming streets after me, writing books about me
And now they want to name this room in the university after me
So the 'Windrush' name game got your attention
But now my children, I want you to tell them
THAT IS NOT MY NAME!
Mine is so much more beautiful!
Monte Rosa!
Birthed in Hamburg, 1920
I worked for the Nazis
The British captured me
And painted over my name
It is a bad habit
Not calling things as they are
The English would rather talk about the weather
They didn't have Auschwitz but *ach,*

They weren't much better
It was the *British* who invented concentration camps – in Africa!
We Deutsch were just more efficient in murder
And if they cared so much about the Jews
Why did they wave that letter, appeasing Hitler?
And let so many migrants burn and drown
Just like they are doing now
From Grenfell Tower to the English Channel
They don't like you saying it
But they were not so different from us!
Re-named me after five hundred years of crime
Rape and murder, kidnap and torture
Five hundred years of Empire
And a dirty little river running away from the Thames:
'Windrush'
Best remembered for eight hundred West Indians
Most forgotten for sixty-six Poles
Invited to come and make a home.
And what names did they call *them* when they arrived?
Tell the truth! Tell them from me:
If you want to keep dragging me up from the depths of the sea
If you want to name this place after me
Call me by my name!

Morning in the Common Room

The students lift their fingers off the planch at the same time. Stillness. Sun rising.

Jay 'Monte Rosa'...

Kit It's over.

Zhe Holocaust to Windrush.

Ola Same damn ship. Diff'rent racist shit.

Pause.

Kit So all she *actually* wants is for the university to re-name this stuffy old place the 'Monte Rosa Room' instead of the 'Windrush Room'. That's it?

Ali She kept us up all night, man.

Zhe She's just vain.

Xia Sea dog.

Jay We musn't speak ill of the dead.

Xia She wasn't even a person. She was a boat!

Ali A Nazi one!

Kit And now she's just a heap of rusty metal at the bottom of the sea.

Zhe We should care more about the people she carried inside her.

Ola The uni are no better. They think calling this the 'Windrush Room' will make us all feel better about how racist it is. Why don't they ask *us* what we wanna call it?

Xia Just some bullshit tick-box exercise. I can't stand it.

Pause.

Ali At least now maybe we'll get some sleep.

Ola (*turning very serious, bold and focused, slowly*)   We will not sleep until we expel this evil spirit.

They all look at **Ola**, *perplexed by the transformation*

Kit Ola? . . .

Jay Are you OK? . . .

Ola *has a look of determination about them, trance like. The scene immediately transitions into the next with no pause. It is an extension of this scene.*

Exorcism/Protest/Student Occupation

Bright light. **Ola** *gets on a table.* **Ola's Friends** *(***Kit**, **Ali**, **Zhe**, **Xia** *and* **Jay**) *gather round – what is happening? All* **Monte Rosas** *enter, underscoring* **Ola**'s *text with fragments from* **Monte Rosa**'s *earlier speeches. The first* **Monte Rosa** *sits in the rocking chair, the others form a ship on a stormy sea.* **Monte Rosa** *resists the exorcism through movement and text fragments building under* **Ola**'s *lines. A battle of wills and no guarantee who will win! High stakes! Important:* **Ola** *does not know what they are going to say. There is fear but they grow in courage. Search videos of the occupation of Goldsmiths University online for inspiration!*

Ola Vessel of racism
Ship of hate
Leave this space!
Go tell your sob story to the salt-water fish cos –
WE AIN'T INTERESTED!
We speak! (**Ola** *gestures for the* **Friends** *to repeat.*)

Ola's Friends We speak!

Ola In solidarity!

Ola's Friends In solidarity!

Ola With Windrush generations

Ola's Friends With Windrush generations

Ola Old and living

Ola's Friends Old and living

Ola Dead and young.

Ola's Friends Dead and young.

Ola So Nazi Monte Rosa and the British Empire of hate!
Go back to hell!
We exorcise you!
We cast you away!
Set sail!

Ola's Friends GET OUT!

All **Monte Rosas** *suddenly exit, dispersing as fast as possible. They are exorcised! The rocking chair is left gently rocking, now empty.*

Ali Wooooooooow . . .

Brief excited chatter as **Ola's Friends** *take in all that has happened, e.g. 'that was crazy', 'what just happened?', 'was that real?' etc. During this* **All** *of the rest of the cast gradually enter the Senior Common Room, playing* **Students**, *also in their pyjamas, awoken by the commotion, confused, improvising, e.g. 'what's all the noise?', 'why is* **Ola** *on the table?' etc.* **Ola** *calls them to attention with their line!*

Ola QUIET! I'm just getting started!
Now,
We who stand on land
Are seizing this room
We are occupying this space!

All Students *improvise cheering and text here and throughout this section. Not just generic sounds but individual lines as well.* **All** *back* **Ola**'s *lines up, responding, but don't let the cheering slow things down. Power through with pace,* **Ola**!

And we won't go away
Until all the money
Made from slavery
In this university
Is paid back to the descendants of African slaves! (*Cheering here and throughout.*)
We want scholarships!
Reparations!
No tuition fees!
Free education!
For EVERYBODY! (*Cheering and whooping continues.*)
We demand that all the pictures and symbols
Of slave owners are taken down! NOW!
We demand that our lecturers

And our books
Start to LOOK like ALL of the people
And ALL of the histories
Of these islands!
We demand that you DE-COLONIZE THIS SHIT!
TODAY!
WE DEMAND EQUALITY!
WE WANT FAIR GRADES!

Ali   AND FREE PIZZAS!

Laughter.

Ola   Yeah! Bring us some food!
Cos we are not going away
Like the Windrush generations –
WE ARE HERE TO STAY!

Big cheer from **All** *as the five* **Friends** *and* **Students** *gather around a smiling* **Ola**. *They are not scared anymore. Blackout then projection:*

'*Dedicated to the survivors of the Windrush generation scandal of 2018 and the victims of the Grenfell Tower catastrophe of 2017.*'

End.

Wind/Rush Generation(s)

BY MOJISOLA ADEBAYO

Notes on rehearsal and staging, drawn from a workshop with the writer, held at the National Theatre, October 2023

About the writer and their style

Lead director Matthew Xia introduced writer Mojisola Adebayo and led a short conversation to introduce the group to her and the play.

Adebayo said that she:

- Thinks of herself as more of a maker and that's where she's come from, devising work, sometimes working as a director or as a performer, doing lots of work with community groups as well as professionals, and working with youth theatre for many years – this is all still in her style of writing.
- Has a sense of playfulness and collaboration in her work.
- Recognized that sometimes you can have a big group to work with, and she likes to think about always making epic work (even with small casts) – it can still be large scale with limited resources.
- Sees herself as someone who puts together events, where we can all participate (audience as well as makers/performers).
- She offered that it might be useful to see this play as a series of devised scenes that are linked together by a theme and common goal – everyone wants to work out who this ghost is.

Describing her style, Adebayo said:

- It perhaps comes from her background, with her first love being music and hip hop.
- She loves the qualities of hip hop music: the quality of call and response, the poetry, the truth telling.
- She notes that there's something about the origins of hip hop and in terms of it coming from the streets, the bedrooms and grassroots, and it not alienating people through class or anything else.
- Adebayo says that she likes the desire of the early hip hop artists to engage their audience in playful conversation and through asking questions that are relevant to ordinary working-class people, wherever they are.
- She says that she has a desire to engage in an urgent debate.
- Collaborative and devised community and youth work has influenced her style of writing.

- Adebayo also mentioned her training in physical theatre, so she often writes with a sense of movement and a visual. She likes the idea of inhabiting the writing in your bodies – she tries to give a multisensory offer.
- Musicality is always present in her writing; she is always hearing music in the text.
- Adebayo mentioned that she also trained in theatre of the oppressed and theatre for social change (e.g., forum theatre – where the audience gets directly involved and changes the piece of theatre), so there are often interventions happening throughout her work.
- With all of this in mind there is often a sense of interruption, debate, dialogue, poetry and music inherent in her work and where she's coming from.
- Adebayo mentioned that her plays *Family Tree* (created with Matthew Xia) and *Moj of the Antarctic: An African Odyssey* could be useful reading points for working on *Wind/Rush Generation(s)*.
- She ended by saying: 'I'm interested in how I can draw from history, but I'm only interested in the present and the future, and making work that's a history of now. Relating to history, but letting history speak to the present moment that we're in.'

Xia talked about how he's noticed that Adebayo's plays are often quite kaleidoscopic – they take all these ideas and then weave them together. He said that she can take themes and things that can seem quite disparate on the page (like a ghost, a computer game, David Lammy's speech) but she then finds this connecting thread that ties it all together.

Adebayo replied that:

- She thought that this came from working with youth theatre, and how often you have to put things together and try to make sense of it with the group that you're working with, to suit the needs and requirements of the group. She recognizes that this can be a constant negotiation.
- *Wind/Rush Generation(s)* is exactly that – trying to weave things together that don't necessarily fit, but then all come together.

How the writer came to write the play

Adebayo said of the play:

- It's about our island and our country as a whole.
- It's for everybody and concerns everybody.
- There are connections in there for all. It should be something that all your groups should be able to excel at.
- My job was to make sure that the play was relevant to you, whoever your group might be.
- The impetus of the play came from watching the news and crying at the treatment of elderly people – Caribbean elders – during the Windrush scandal.

- She said that she has spent a lot of her life trying to undo racism in a very celebratory and creative way through her work and trying to address it, so not a lot about racism shocks her any more – but this news shocked her. She was shocked that our country and government could treat elderly people with such disrespect, contempt and cruelty. This made her want to say something about it, and she had the opportunity through National Theatre Connections to do so and to write something. So, it came from the response to how Windrush generation were treated.
- Unfortunately, this play is still very relevant four years on from writing it.

On the play's title:

- Adebayo had a curiosity and fascination with the words 'Windrush' and 'Empire' themselves.
- Stemming from her interest in poetry and music, she notes that both 'wind' and 'rush' have movement to them – she said that 'Windrush' is a powerful word that has a dynamism about it.
- She's been concerned for a long time about the climate crisis and has been interested in the connections between industrial revolution, the climate crisis, enslavement, and also poverty – all connecting together, and the wind as a form of weather being part of this connection.
- Adebayo says that she has come to think of racism as a kind of weather something that is always there and is a constant – but sometimes you're really conscious of it and sometimes you just move through it. Adebayo said that as a Black person, she has to dress for it [racism], prepare for it, that situations can change very quickly, and so for her this metaphor of racism as a kind of weather has become connected to her play.
- She wrote the poem 'Wind' ('Voice of the Wind' scene) before she wrote the play.
- Adebayo notes that there's something infuriating and concerning about how in Britain we can talk about the weather and make small talk, but can't talk about racism, climate change and much more important issues.
- There's an urgency in the word 'rush' and the urgency of this conversation that needs to be had.
- She also said that there's something quite beautiful about the word 'empire' and Adebayo spoke about being frustrated by the beauty of the sound of the word 'empire' – it's round and has lots of breath in it. But for her it means colonialism, genocide, famine, slavery and so much cruelty. She notes that British people were very successful at colonialism as well as at creating language, and that the English language itself was very important in colonialism. For her it's a manipulative language – it can lie and hide its cruelty. It has its own ways of covering up what it's talking about – for example, 'empire' is far too beautiful a word for what it's actually talking about.

On the history of the ship:

- Following on from Adebayo's initial interest in the *Empire Windrush* and wanting to say something about it, she began more research into the ship itself and discovered quite quickly that it had an even darker history than she had realized.
- She discovered that it had originally been called the *Monte Rosa*, that it had been birthed in Hamburg, that it had been used during the Holocaust to transport Norwegian Jewish children to their deaths, and that Britain had taken over that ship and painted over its name to rename it the *Empire Windrush*.
- To Adebayo that spoke to a lot of our issues in our country – that we can paint over the past, give it another name and feel like we've got away with it. And more than that, we even celebrate some of our terrible past.
- As an example of this, Adebayo spoke about the song and lyrics of 'Rule Britannia'. She questioned what that actually means to 'rule the waves' and referenced that these waves in this celebratory song were the same waves into which 131 men, women and children were thrown from the *Zong*.
- Adebayo knows that this is tough material for young people, but the great thing about young people is that they want the truth, they want justice, they want to know what's *really* going on in our country and with our history, whatever their background – so that's why she's so excited for them to do this play.

Xia asked, why the ghost story and why the exorcism?

Adebayo answered that:

- The ship's original name, *Monte Rosa*, caught her attention. It is a pretty name, and the fact that ships are referred to as female led Adebayo to think of it as a real person. But of course, the ship as *Empire Windrush* sank, and so essentially she's drowned and is dead, and therefore a ghost.
- There's a connection therefore with the sense of history and ghosts we haven't dealt with, with histories that we haven't dealt with. We need to deal with these histories in order to heal as a country and to create a more fair, equal and kind society. We can move on from history, but importantly how do we make sure that we don't repeat what we did in the past?
- She saw a lot of possibility in having a ghost, but a ghost that wants to be at peace. As a country we want to reckon with our past, but we also want to heal, we don't want to carry ghosts around, we want them to be laid to rest.
- Adebayo also said that in thinking about young people, she wanted to write something that had surprise, intrigue. She needed to make sure that there was one thing that everyone would all be doing – whatever the cast size – that everyone was trying to figure out who this ghost was, and once that was figured out, then working out how to get the ghost out.

Characterization and casting

Adebayo said that to her it's much more about the feel of the group, rather than the look of the characters. She wrote the play with different types of young people in mind – there are scenes and characters for young people who are super-committed and like working alone (Monte Rosa), scenes with more opportunity for banter and group work (student characters), scenes for those who don't feel as comfortable with big movement ensemble pieces (Sim and Sam), scenes for comedy actors (Captain and First Mate).

All the characters are deliberately non-gendered. It should be cast with the skills of the performers in mind rather than worrying about ensuring that the identity of the performer matches a character.

Approaching the play

Some of the reasons that the workshop participants chose this play:

- To celebrate the diversity of their school
- They loved the physicality of the play/hip hop elements/ghost story element
- To challenge the entitlement of the group and to educate them
- They were keen to challenge the audiences that they're expecting to come along and watch, with the play's content and messages
- The group were keen to learn about this part of British history
- The opportunity to say something important with a piece of theatre

Some common worries or concerns that some of the group had about the play:

- A lack of diversity in their group
- Helping the group understand the themes of the play
- Young people being worried about having to portray 'slave owners'
- How to stage the eclectic mix of scenes and historical events
- Making sure that the process of rehearsing this stays fun in amongst the heavy topics
- The triggering nature of the material for some of the group and how to look after the group (and the audience)

Dealing with shared concerns:

- Diversity of the cast/is this my story to tell?
  Adebayo said:
- This play is a play for *all* young people (as is written in the play's introduction).
- The big thing is to encourage you that you will do it right with your group, it's as much your story as anyone else's.

- It's deliberately written for anyone to do (regardless of diversity of group or director).
- On the use of the 'N' word.

  Adebayo and Xia advized:
- Please refer to the notes on the use of the 'N' word in the script before the scene 'Wind Chill' along with the 'using a gun in rehearsals' analogy in these notes.
- You can choose when and when not to use the word – e.g. 'Let's not use it when we rehearse so as not to hear it in the room 20 times in a day.'
- The two times it's used are historical quotes, and there's something about the accuracy and fact of this which is really important to acknowledge.
- There are ways of making it clear that it's a quote through gesture, the way it's delivered, etc.
- Some options of what to do if you choose not to use it (Adebayo notes here that she recognizes the trauma of using that word, so understands if you/your young people do decide not to use the actual word):
    - Bleep it out
    - Use the phrase 'N' word
    - Project word or the original poster the quote is from
    - Use a sign
- Adebayo clarified that there is of course a discomfort around the 'N' word, but also discomfort around dealing with the reality of the word and its existence. Sometimes we avoid and paint over the uncomfortable reality of our country, and people have had to deal with that reality. So at the very least you should have a conversation about the discomfort of the reality of the use of this word.
- This play is also about unpacking that it's not as simple as racism and the use of this word being about either being 'a good person' or 'a bad person', it's more complicated than that, and is about systemic racism, and colonialism and how that affects everyone. If we try to avoid the discomfort then we won't deal with the wounds and the source of the pain, so we have to deal with it.
- A concern about doing the scene on the *Zong* without any white participants to play the roles of the Captain and First Mate.

  Adebayo said:
- Maybe this is even more powerful? It goes to the heart of the question about racism in our conversations sometimes becoming simplified to the colour of our skin, and being at skin level. One of her arguments is that it was never really about skin itself, that the physical features of enslaved people were used as an excuse to say that they were less human, but ultimately it has always been about capital, money, trade, empire and accumulating great wealth. Therefore, having two young people who aren't white playing the Captain and First Mate of the *Zong* makes us really look at what's happening in this scene beyond skin colour – it's about power, money and control.

- In this scene people are treating other people as products, making a decision to throw those products overboard to save money.
- Adebayo concluded by saying that the heart of the meaning of the work is about all of us, and how we profit from racism. She recognizes that the historical trauma in this play, particularly for young Black people, is real and there needs to be a process in place to be able to perform this piece, creating safe spaces for conversation and healing.

Investigating the scenes

Xia split the group into pairs and they were given a scene to investigate, looking at the questions:

Who are the characters, who are they representing?

What is happening? What is being represented? What is the functionality of the scene?

When is this happening? Time, date? Historical moment?

Where is the location of the scene?

Why is this scene important? Why does this happen?

As well as these questions, he asked them to start to pull out facts and questions from their scenes. Xia says when he does this work (who, what, when, where, why), he tries to keep it basic, just extracting the data. Then you can have the discussions later on. Let those facts inform the questions. Otherwise you'll never make the play, just have loads of interesting discussions.

Xia said a big part of his work during this pre-rehearsal prep (the investigating) is 'spark hunting'. As well as combing the script he is always looking for sparks of inspiration, reading books, watching things, visiting places, building up inspiration for his work.

Some of the discoveries from the scenes, beyond the who, what, when, where, and whys:

The House of Commons

- The rhythm of the scene is important.
- Watching the David Lammy speech and noticing his body language and how he almost physically restrains himself is important.
- Note the contrast of a man who wants to shout and rage, but is in the House of Commons.
- Xia recommended looking at Alecky Blythe's Recorded Delivery Technique when approaching rehearsing this scene. This technique involves playing one line at a time (from the YouTube clip), with the actors then repeating exactly

what they have heard as accurately as possible (including any ticks, coughs, hesitations, etc.). Xia mentioned that it was used during rehearsals for *London Road* (National Theatre).

Monte Rosa scenes

- Could be seen as a timeless space because she's not resting in peace yet.
- Rhythm of the chair rocking might be nice to play with; calm before the storm, representing the waves.
- The metaphor of 'we can't let it rest' – because if we do it might be forgotten, this feels important.
- Potential of the ensemble creating some of the moments she mentions.
- The offer from Adebayo of Monte Rosa being played by a different actor each time could enhance the message that 'it's our (collective) history'.

Wind Farm

- What's important here is the game of the scene – the audience aren't meant to know the subject of the conversation until the end of scene.
- The trick is to play the truth of the scene – it's a group of people talking about wind turbines. The names of politicians are a joke for us (the performers). They really are talking about wind turbines. It's for the audience to read into the interpretation and the subtext.
- There is still something grotesque in these characters. *Spitting Image* could be a good reference.
- A light approach that can be taken – even though themes are deep – this is true across the whole play.

Wind Chill

- Clarity from Adebayo – the names of the characters are just for us to pay homage, the audience won't know. The lines don't correspond to the characters actual names. The lines didn't need to have 'names' assigned – Adebayo knows that actors hate to not have a name, or just be 'actor 1'. The actor playing that role can choose to investigate why this name has been assigned to the line, but don't get too hung up on this.
- There was a question about why Ola doesn't complete the line at the end of this scene:

Cos come what may . . .
(*Pause. All suddenly look at* **Ola** *to complete the line but then there is a sudden blackout.*)

Adebayo said this is because it feels like the story isn't complete yet, Ola hasn't yet figured out what the next line should be, so this is a deferment of the question.

Wind Fall

- The clue to this scene is: play the truth of the scene – this is a discussion about cargo.
- Adebayo added that no one needs to see more Black suffering on stage – this doesn't need to be shown.
- The scene isn't about Black people, it's about the slave traders and their history. That's what to analyse and focus on, and on the job – they are at work and doing a job at work. This was another day in the office – the everyday reality of people doing their job within a hierarchy (it wasn't an unusual event sadly, the *Zong* massacre became more well known because of its court case).

GoldSugarGun

- This, like nearly all the scenes in the play, has elements of desensitization – which might possibly be helpful for the actors playing it, and in saying 'hey, wait a minute, how can we be so inhumane and so desensitized to this'.
- This video game is a game to reverse time so that racism never ever exists – this is what's at the heart of the game.
- Adebayo noted that there shouldn't be an invitation to laugh in this scene – i.e. the 'nice tits' line. If you play any humour in the line it takes us to a different place.

Common Room scenes

- The contrast between this pretty or grand room, and the horrors it covers up should feel uncomfortable. There's a sense of privilege but at a massive cost.
- These scenes have the energy of a protest, student sit-ins, young people taking power of what should be theirs.
- Think about the infrastructure of the space, and who feels like they belong in it or not.

Exploring key scenes

A few of the key moments from the play were explored in small groups through tasks set by Xia.

The David Lammy speech

Offers from Xia and Adebayo:

- Listen to the speech without the visuals, and listen carefully to the intonation, pitch changes, breath, coughs, etc. How does all this detail factor into the work?
- Watch the speech with the volume off and notice the physicality. Adebayo said that the physicality of the speech actually struck her before the words.

- Play it line by line, literally what do you hear?
- Be cautious of choral speaking sounding like a drone.

Groups split off into groups to explore, investigate and stage this speech.

Exploration discoveries:
- Using just one line of dialogue spoken by the group, and then focusing on the body language and gesture that Lammy uses in his speech whilst the recording of the speech played alongside this.
- Idea from Adebayo – Lammy's physique reminded her of a figurehead at the front of a ship, so perhaps the group could form the ship behind him as the speech builds?
- Speaking in unison, but sometimes voices drop in volume, different intonations used to add texture.
- Physically looking like a pack of dogs as the group builds.
- Edging forward with each new point made (Lammy couldn't do this in the House of Commons, but it felt like he wanted to) – almost like fencing.
- Added tension by the actor at the front, representing Lammy, trying to hold back the 'inner thoughts'/constituents who join him as they push against him, trying to break through.
- Creating a sense of fear through the speech – howling, dogs, ghost story links.

Representing a Ouija board on stage

Offers from Xia and Adebayo:
- You could start by researching the historical, psychological and physiological evidence behind Oujia boards to help demystify it or contextualize the scene for young people from a religious background who might feel hesitant about playing this scene.
- Another way to explore this is to play with a pendulum and look into the 'ideomotor response'.

Xia read out some notes from a previous workshop of the play (written by Nathan Crossan-Smith):

- Adebayo noted that she has deliberately written a character (Ola) who is Christian and opposed to what they are doing, so there is space for a religious young person, who wouldn't be sinning by representing that which they are critical of.
- The group also talked through the mechanics of the Ouija board: someone puts their finger on the planchette, and the group push towards certain letters (which can be explained as something they self-direct without a conscious awareness but is understood in the context of the play as communication from Monte Rosa).

- The creative challenge posed by the scene is: how do you spell out the words (such as P-R-O-B-L-E-M) in a way that is theatrically interesting, as well as being clear?
- Adebayo asked – How does the fact that it's Monte Rosa who is sending the messages inform the stylistic choices? How might she send the messages? Remember, Monte Rosa likes to have fun (she tells us of music, champagne and good times as part of her story). Is she writing, speaking, texting or shouting? The audience won't know this, but it's good for you the company to know.

The challenge in this scene is replicating something small in reality that on stage needs to be big.

Exploration discoveries:

- Using a phone to create an overhead camera above the board that is then projected live onto a screen. In a similar way that concerts use this technique to enlarge what the audience sees.
- Adding humour, e.g. messing up the spelling, can lighten the scene.
- Vocalizing the letters by the whole group saying them out loud.
- Changing the proxemics of the scene to represent the characters and their responses to the moment.
- It did feel possible to do it just through storytelling – you don't necessarily need to see the object of the board
- It was tried in the round, using the whole space as the board with the actor's hands moving up and down for a 'yes', side to side for 'no'. There were letters on sticky notes around the space that the pair are guided to physically like they're being magnetized towards them. As the scene went on, more of the group joined the huddle of students that were moving from letter to letter.
- Adebayo's reflections were that she liked the physicality of the ideas. And the playfulness. Thinking about the use of the space – what else is in the space that you could use – table, or even a YMCA style of making letters with bodies perhaps?

Wind Farm scene

Offers from Xia and Adebayo:

- This scene should be played at a fast pace.
- The characters are not listening to each other, they are talking over each other.
- The challenge for you is not letting the audience get ahead of you in their realization of what the scene is actually about.
- Parody might be useful to explore.

Wind Fall scene

Again, Xia read through some notes from previous workshop (written by Nathan Crossan-Smith) that he felt were important considerations:

- This scene presents the 1781 *Zong* massacre.
- Adebayo on the historical event – it is one of the most shocking stories that comes out of the history of the slave trade. It's something that British people did off the coast of Jamaica and it's shocking that people don't know about it. It's a really important part of our history and an important part of insurance law. The facts in the scene are correct, though not everything is exactly as they said it. In understanding racism we need to understand an idea at the heart of imperial racism in the slave trade: the idea that humans are not humans. The Captain and First Mate don't care about the people they talk about and in fact don't see them as people.
- Adebayo acknowledged that this kind of scene work is painful and traumatic work to do, especially for those for whom this directly affects their ancestry. It's a scene that needs to be held by the director, who is positioned to look after everyone in the company in rehearsing and presenting this scene.
- Taking this into consideration, the other key note for approaching this scene, as Xia pointed out, is not to play this challenge. The work is to put aside the sensitivity of the scene and look at the robustness of the arguments, the characters' status and the mechanics of the scene. Xia observed that the Captain and the First Mate aren't thinking about the humanity of the people they are talking about. In their mindset, they effectively are trying to decide 'how many cows to take off the field'. This kind of thinking was supported broadly by Enlightenment thinking and what we would now call eugenics.
- Adebayo added that the horror for the audience is in the words themselves and so you don't necessarily have to play that horror in the performance. Pace enables the actors to dissociate a little: powering through the scene, working through the pace of it, could offer the actor a way to cope emotionally with it.
- Another key consideration in rehearsing this scene is the deliberate choice made about not repeating imagery which shows Black people in pain. Adebayo was clear in writing this scene, not to repeat those images or create a context within which Black actors would have to experience playing people who have been enslaved.

Xia also made the important note that the use of the term 'enslaved people' in place of the term 'slaves' should always be used – as this puts the onus on the person who did the act and not the victim.

Exploration discoveries:

- Standing in ship formation was a strong visual image.
- Gentle swaying to indicate a boat at sea, which builds up as the scene builds and creates a rhythm for the sailor's lines.
- Using a simple switch of orientation on stage to create a courtroom scene from the boat scene. This helped to make the link of the order of a ship to the order of court through physicality on stage. As well as both scenes having a figure at the front (Captain, then Judge).

- Thinking about tempo and timing of speech to reflect class, power and rash decision making.

GoldSugarGun scene

Xia read through some notes from previous workshop (written by Nathan Crossan-Smith) that he felt were important considerations:

- The provocation for this scene was about how you can make it feel pixelated and not as fully rendered as other scenes; how it can feel like a new performance language.
- A key note on this scene was that, though on the surface the game looks like *Resident Evil*, they are in fact playing a radicalized version of *Resident Evil*: *Hostile Environment*. The scene is about playing a game that means the slave trade and colonialism never happens. Sam is on a mission from the beginning of the scene, whereas Sim thinks it's a regular *Resident Evil*-style computer game. There is a pause in the game where the two talk about the background to Mansa Musa. They want to kill him so that no-one hears about the continent of Africa. Sim and Sam are radicals.

Exploration discoveries:

- Having a lightness of touch in the characters perhaps makes it hit harder.
- Sounds of bleeps and repetition could be fun to bring to life to add digital quality.
- Sim and Sam don't have to necessarily be in the same room as one another in the scene.
- As directors, you might want to watch the *Resident Evil* clip (mentioned in the script) to add context, but perhaps not share this with your casts.

Structure, style and transitions

Xia offered two methods for tackling the structure of the play and breaking it into more manageable bite-sized pieces.

On the Wall

(a technique that Xia picked up from theatre director Sam Pritchard)

- Physically cut and paste each scene and stick it to the wall, with one page below another if a scene is longer than one page, and a new column for each new scene (this might mean you have to cut a page of your script in half if more than one scene spans a single page). So, if you have eight scenes, you end up with eight columns along the wall.
- Visually, having this in front of you can help you to look at how much time you might need to spend on each scene or section, as you can see the size of each

column and therefore scene (as well as which roles have more significant parts to learn, etc.).
- By highlighting and/or annotating your script on the wall you can help to reveal patterns, e.g.:
  - Green highlight = Monte Rosa scenes
  - Pink highlight = common room
  - Red asterisk = sizeable ensemble scenes
  - Orange line alongside text = things that feel heightened in terms of musicality / rhythm
  - Yellow highlight = particularly tricky moments (e.g. transition within the *Zong* scene), or scary stage directions.

Scene chart table

This is something that Xia uses for every play that he works on, in order to get a full overview of it and to be able to plan out rehearsals more easily. He said that it helps to tell him how long he's got with each section, what he might need in the room, who to call for rehearsals, etc.

On the left side of the table, you list all of the **page numbers**, and then fill out the **scene titles**, **characters** in the scene (and include in this column if they exit during the scene), the **location**, then any **miscellaneous** information (e.g. props needed, song, illusions, tricky staging moment, big transition within scene).

Page	Scene Title	Characters	Location	Misc.
1				
2				
3				
4				
5	1 House of Commons	Full company as David Lammy	House of Commons	Ensemble movement Recording of speech
6				

Page	Scene Title	Characters	Location	Misc.
7	2 Senior Common Room	Ola, Xia, Ali, Kit, Zhe, Jay	Common room	Phones
8				
9				
10				Rocking chair illusion Blackout

Adebayo then offered her approach to breaking down the play to see it as a whole:

Storyboarding

- In a similar way to how films are storyboarded, do a little sketch to show how you think that action might look on stage.
- This can be as simple as stick person drawings.
- This enables her to map out things like; there's too much sitting down in this chunk of play.
- You can add a short description underneath of what is happening.
- Adebayo said that it helps her to then think, 'I want to get to that image, and then to that image – how would the images tell the story?'
- She offered that you could also make mood boards for scenes, characters, moments too.

Production, staging and design

Xia read through a series of provocations that director Sacha Wares uses when considering a production and offered these, acknowledging that each director in the room would have different levels of budget and support for their production:

- What are you told that the environment should look like and what is necessary? E.g. what is functional set and what is set dressing?
- He said that he will often read the play through a set of slightly different filters and noticing when certain things are mentioned, including: colour, light, time, weather, objects, smells, imagery, nature, etc.
- You might think about designing through limitation: How would you tell the story if you could only use light? Or if you could only use the furniture you have in the room you rehearse in?
- Imagine a brilliant theatre-maker who has a really clear style, someone whose work you know (e.g. Katie Mitchell, Rupert Goold, Ivo van Hove). How would they direct this show?
- What is the £500,000 version of this show and what is the £5 version?

Exercises for use in rehearsals

Warm-ups/Rhythm exercises

Shake banana

- This is a simple call and response. It introduces play, silliness and rhythm.
- The participants should be in a circle, and the call and response can be started by the director but then passed around the circle.
- Caller: 'Shake banana, shake shake banana' (*said alongside an action of their choice which is done in time with the rhythm of the words*).
- Response: 'Shake banana, shake shake banana' (*action is copied*).
- The next person in the circle then becomes the Caller.
- You can do whatever you want with bananas, go round the circle and each person calls a different verb with an action within the same rhythm as 'Shake banana, shake shake banana'. Some examples we had were:
  - Fry banana, fry fry banana.
  - Phone banana, phone phone banana.
  - Slip banana, slip slip banana.
  - Fish banana, fish fish banana.

Conductor's circle

- This is an ensemble music/rhythm creation exercise.
- The ensemble stands in a circle with the conductor (which could be the director at first, and then a student) in the centre.
- Led by the conductor, the group are brought in one by one, or in small groups and invited to add a sound, rhythm, base line, word – anything that can be repeated on a loop (using voice or body).
- A soundscape is built up.
- The conductor can stop/start people, change the dynamics, bring groups together to join one another's rhythm/sounds/words, or select a new conductor to hand over to. They use gestures to conduct the group, and can use their instincts to explore what to add/take away to create an interesting soundscape.
- You might choose to use words/lines/phrases from the script as well as sounds.
- You might choose to do it around a theme (e.g. 'wind' and sounds and words around this).
- You could use this idea and turn it into a soundbath, where one of the group sits in the middle of the circle and the rest of the group build up sounds, but always based around the person in the centre's name. This can feel like quite a healing and unique experience to hear lots of people surrounding you with your name.

Vocal exercises

Xia talked through two vocal exercises that could be used to explore resistance in the voice (perhaps useful during the David Lammy speech). These are exercises created by director and vocal coach Cicely Berry:

Restraining:

- A group of people hold back the actor (safely) whilst that actor talks through the speech, and tries to work against the group of people to try to get to the door/ other side of the room. The group then releases the actor and the actor must start the speech again, trying to retain some of the vocal quality they found when being restrained.

Pushing against the wall:

- The actor goes through the speech whilst they physically push against a wall. They can then move away from the wall, trying the speech again but aim to keep the quality found from pushing against the wall in their voice.

From a workshop led by Matthew Xia with assistance from Joelle Ikwa.
With notes by Kate Pasco.

BACK IN THE DAY

by Yasmeen Khan

Yasmeen Khan is an award-winning radio presenter, writer and performer based in London with roots in West Yorkshire. Khan writes comedy and drama and very much enjoys the space between the two. Screenwriting includes BBC's *EastEnders*, with over 20 episodes written to date.

Alongside hundreds of hours of live programming on national and local radio, she presents documentaries on BBC Radio 4 across a wide variety of topics.

Yasmeen Khan's theatre writing has been produced nationally, with a specialism in comedy-drama. During lockdown, her northern and British Asian-focused digital adaptation of *The Importance of Being Earnest* received a five-star review from *The Stage*. She also co-wrote *Going the Distance*, a streaming production about a struggling community theatre, starring Matthew Kelly, Shobna Gulati and Sarah Hadland.

She regularly hosts Q&As and panel discussions at theatres including the National Theatre. Her current writing includes development of two new plays.

Characters

Taz – *pupil, a girl*
Miss Mahmoud – *a woman, the teacher, British South Asian*
Remy – *pupil, a boy*
Sam – *pupil, a boy*
Marni – *pupil, a girl*

Sooz – *adult, TV presenter, a woman*
Jez – *adult, TV presenter, a man*
Ellie – *adult, band lead singer, a woman*
Lana – *adult, band member, a woman*
Mickey – *adult, band member, a man*
Young Miss Mahmoud – *teenager, British South Asian*
Mum – *Miss Mahmoud's mum, aged forty to forty-five, British South Asian*
Inner Monologue/Chorus/Adult Survey Respondents

Introductory Notes

The main cast of pupils is gendered as above, but these can be changed as appropriate to your cast, except for **Taz** who should be a girl and **Remy** who should be a boy.

The characters of **Sooz** and **Ellie** should be gendered as above, i.e. both women.

The character of **Miss Mahmoud** is a British-born woman of Pakistani origin and this visibility is important. (If relevant culturally appropriate casting, i.e. female British South Asian, is not available, do not be restricted by this – her full name is never used in the script, she is merely referred to as Miss, so change the casting as appropriate to your cast.) She should have a British local accent and wear standard Western dress appropriate to any teacher. Miss Mahmoud comes from a Muslim background but she does not need to wear a headscarf. There are additional lines in the script in Scene Five marked in square brackets which should be used if your Miss Mahmoud is indeed South Asian or from another non-white/non-British background. The questions in those lines from Marni and Taz can be asked by them no matter what background your Marni and Taz are from.

A note on interpreting the character's age: Miss Mahmoud is around 50 years old and due care should be given to relish the acting challenge this presents – what is hoped for is authenticity, based on care, observation, detail, and empathetic imagination and creativity. Seemingly easy and generic options like grey wigs and cardigans should be avoided at all costs.

Young Miss Mahmoud and **Mum** are also British South Asian, but again they do not need to be in 'traditional' clothing with headscarves, etc. If your Miss Mahmoud and your Mum are both from South Asian backgrounds, you can have Mum in something more traditional like salwar kameez with a loose dupatta scarf around her neck or loosely on her head, with the lines in the script referring to what she's wearing changed as appropriate.

And again if you do not have culturally appropriate casting, change the casting as appropriate to your cast and who you cast as Miss Mahmoud.

There are two alternative ways of representing the **Inner Monologue** members:

- They can either be one group all wearing the same costume, and move from character to character, representing that character's inner monologue as appropriate.
- Alternatively, if you have a large cast, each character can have their own individual group of inner monologues, perhaps denoted by wearing a version of that character's costume, say in a more muted colour.

Inner Monologue can also double up as audience in the TV show and other dance chorus/crowd parts.

Staging – Where there are suggestions of lighting, etc. for the roller disco scenes, these can be done as elaborately or as simply as your resource allows. For example, perhaps the chorus could be used to play 'spotlights'.

Skating – There are key characters for whom it is important to roller skate, namely Taz, Miss Mahmoud and Sam. Ideally Marni and Remi should roller skate too. For the rest of the cast, if roller skates are not possible, then achieving the same effect through creative means is fine.

Language – The text contains a small number of mild swear words but less offensive alternatives are provided in brackets for each. Finding your own alternatives is also an option. There is one instance of a more offensive swear word, but again alternatives are provided.

Local language – the play is written with no particular region of the UK in mind or indeed identified. If there are particular words or phrases that don't feel right to your region, directors should feel free to change small aspects of the way the young people in the play speak to local vernacular.

Pacing – The play is a comedy-drama and works best when the characters are fluid and pacey in the adventurous and fun parts, leaving room to breathe in the more emotional moments and turning points.

Music – The 1980s songs referred to in the play are the preferred options – for the purposes of legal rights and permissions you may have to find alternatives. If you can use the given suggestions, then perfect, but if you have to find alternatives, try and be as faithful to the original suggestion as you possibly can but please do stick to 1980s tracks. Ultimately, whatever choice you go with, you are responsible for securing the necessary rights. Rest assured there will be further advice and guidance on this matter from the National Theatre in the Company Handbook.

Scene One

Lights up on **Taz** *in the classroom. Laid back, waiting for class to start. She looks bored. Suddenly the* **Inner Monologues** *appear next to her.*

Inner 1   You should tell someone, you know.

Inner 2   You absolutely should not!

Inner 3   What would you even say?! Er, I feel so miserable sometimes that I can barely get out of bed?

Inner 2   Like, who even would care? So no, don't say anything.

Inner 1   Are you sure?

Inner 3   Unless you want to look really stupid?

Inner 4   Oh God, what's that song?! It's on the tip of my tongue.

Inner 1   We've got more important things to worry about right now, like telling someone how you feel.

Inner 2   No! I said no way!

Taz *has enough of the voices.*

Taz   Shut up!

The **Inner Monologues** *retreat.*

Enter **Sam**.

Sam   Who shut up?

Taz   What? Oh, nothing, it was just something on my phone.

Sam *takes centre stage; a track ready on his phone, he hits play and strikes a pose. The first beats of the intro of Hall and Oates' 'You Make My Dreams' start to play, loud, thumping, the promise of a joyous tune, and* **Sam** *starts his clearly pre-prepared routine.* **Taz** *regards him, eye-rolling, shaking her head.* **Miss Mahmoud** *enters.* **Taz** *grabs* **Sam**'s *phone, the song gets as far as the first lyric before she hits stop.* **Sam**'s *routine is cut off just before he's about to fully launch into it.*

Sam   Taz! You can't stop an artist once they've entered the zone! Tell her, Miss.

Taz   I'm doing us all a favour.

Miss Mahmoud   You can do your TikTok or whatever it is in your own time.

Sam   It's not for TikTok.

Taz   What's it for then?

Sam Just . . .

Taz Just what?

Sam I don't know, just. Like, for fun?

Taz Lame! What even is that track?

Sam It's one of my mum's favourites. (*Enthusiastic.*) It was released in –

Taz (*across*) Alright, alright, don't start your walking Wikipedia crap (alt.: rubbish).

Miss Mahmoud Right, we need to start. I want everyone in a circle.

Taz Not the circle chat again!

Miss Mahmoud Yes, the circle.

Marni *comes on, having overheard.*

Marni (*singing*) The circle of liiiife! *Lion King* vibes, Miss.

Taz (*being contrary*) Doesn't have to be a circle. We could sit in a square.

Miss Mahmoud Fine, fine sit in a square then!

Marni No, Miss . . . *Lion King* wasn't the square of life though was it? That would've been a rubbish song.

Taz Marni, I swear you get weirder every year.

Marni (*pleased*) Ah thanks, Taz!

Miss Mahmoud You shouldn't call people weird, Taz.

Taz She likes it!

Marni I actually do.

Remy *comes on, serious, busy doing something on his phone.* **Inner Monologue** *go to him.*

Inner 1 (*re. what's on his phone*) I don't understand this!

Inner 2 But don't tell anyone.

Inner 3 Cos no-one will get it. No-one. Especially not this lot.

Inner 4 (*re. the song they can't remember*) The song sort of goes dum dum dum de dumm . . .

Inner 1, 2 & 3 Shut up!

Inner 1 No-one cares about the song you can't remember!

Inner 4 *looks hurt.*

Sam Remy, guess what, you know where your dad used to work? That building, yeah?

Remy (*distracted*)   What about it?

Sam   It used to be the old town hall. And I'm talking proper olden days, like when cars were basically horses.

Remy   So?

Sam   Imagine all the people that would have used that building all those years ago. Don't you think that's interesting?

Taz   There is nothing interesting about anything around here.

Miss Mahmoud   Always so negative, Taz.

Sam   It's still a beautiful building! It's just that nobody notices now. Because it's a Sports Direct. Where does your dad work now, Remy?

But **Remy** *is still on his phone.*

Remy   I'm busy.

Marni   The triangle of life! That would've been a good song.

Miss Mahmoud   Right, come on, all of you. In a circle, now. We're going to sit and talk.

Sam *immediately obediently sits down.*

Sam   Love it! What are we talking about? Oh, we could talk about the history of local architecture –

Taz (*across*)   Give it a rest.

Miss Mahmoud   We're talking about the same thing we did last time we got in a circle – mental health.

Taz *hates the idea – not this again!*

Taz (*fast*)   Actually, Sam, architecture sounds pretty good.

Miss Mahmoud (*pressing on*)   More specifically, how we're all feeling.

Taz   We're fine! (*To everyone.*) Everyone's fine, right? Great, let's do something else.

Miss Mahmoud   No. Remy, put your phone away.

Remy   I can't.

Taz   He's gaming, innit. Always.

Remy   I'm not!

Miss Mahmoud   Well whatever it is, do it later.

Remy, *vexed, puts his phone away.*

Marni (*still musing*)   The parallelogram of life.

Miss Mahmoud *is desperate to get started.*

Miss Mahmoud   Circle. Circle is fine. Right come on, all of you.

Sam Maybe future generations will look at old photos of Sports Direct and think that they were beautiful.

Miss Mahmoud *loses patience.*

Miss Mahmoud Can you all just sit down, please! Taz, that means you as well.

Everyone except **Taz** *sits down.*

Taz I don't need to talk about anything. I could just watch, take notes?

Miss Mahmoud And what if the others want to talk, what if they've got things on their mind?

Taz What's talking going to do? It's like my mum says, you just get on with it, right? Honestly, Miss. I'm fine. Like . . . totally fine. Can't we go and actually do something? Like, get out of here, go somewhere interesting?

Miss Mahmoud *is frustrated but then makes a decision.*

Miss Mahmoud OK, Taz. We'll play it your way. You can stay out of the circle.

Taz*, pleased, sits on her own.*

Miss Mahmoud I wanted to sit and talk today, check in with everyone. And decide who should be the school's next Mental Health Ambassador.

Sam I'd be up for that.

Miss Mahmoud I know, Sam. (*Beat.*) But I've made my decision. It's Taz.

Taz What? Me?! No.

Miss Mahmoud You'll get exactly what you wanted, to get out and do something interesting.

Taz I don't want to do it!

Miss Mahmoud And that's exactly why it should be you.

Taz *huffs.* **Marni** *takes it all in.*

Marni That's the hypotenuse of life right there.

Scene Two

Taz *is with a bunch of other pupils out on the street, outside a once grand old building, taking a survey – the survey respondents being the cast playing adult members of the public.* **Taz** *is holding a clipboard and steps forward downstage to ask someone a question.*

Taz Excuse me –

Sam *appears from off stage, on roller skates and out of control, also holding a clipboard. He almost runs into* **Taz** *as he whizzes past her.*

Sam Excuse me! Arrrgh!

He crashes into the other pupils at the end, dazed and confused.

Taz (*annoyed*) Sam!

Sam *struggles to stand up.*

Sam Sorry, sorry! I just thought it'd be faster, you know, with skates?

Taz This stupid survey's bad enough without you nearly knocking me over.

Sam I just thought I'd be able to get round more people – Miss Mahmoud's got targets of how many people she wants us to survey.

Taz (*impatient*) I know.

Sam Probably should have tried skating before actually, you know . . . skating. 'Cause I've never actually –

Taz Skated? (*Sarcastic.*) Yeah . . . you'd never tell. Not like you to be whizzing around. Thought you preferred standing still and staring at buildings.

Sam *gets excited and pulls some notes out of his pocket.*

Sam Actually, this building here dates back to –

But he's interrupted by a chorus of groans from all the pupils except **Marni**.

Remy Don't set him off!

Marni But it might be really interesting!

Taz The only interesting thing about this town is how to get out of it. Bad enough we have to live here let alone stand in the middle of it and do this stupid survey.

Dejected, **Sam** *puts his phone/notes away and takes the skates off, helped by sympathetic* **Marni**. **Taz** *sighs and attempts to do the survey. The others don't look very interested.* **Remy** *is particularly annoyed by the whole thing.*

Taz Come on, we better get on with it, Miss is gonna be back any minute.

She stops two passers-by.

Taz (*awkward*) Hello . . . excuse me, sorry . . . I'm doing a survey . . . about how people are feeling . . . so . . . do you mind if I ask you . . . how are you?

Woman Fine?

Man Um . . . what?

Taz How are you?

Man Right . . . fine. Yeah, fine thanks. You?

Taz Fine. Thank you. How are you?

They get stuck in a loop. **Remy** *watches, incredulous.*

Woman Really fine. Yeah, fine, thanks. You?

Taz Fine. Thank you. Fine, yeah fine.

The two passers-by leave.

Remy Are you joking?! This is painful!

Taz I don't want to do it either, but she's going to be here any minute checking up on us.

Another **Woman** *passes by,* **Taz** *stops her.*

Taz Excuse me . . . how are you?

Woman Fine, thank you.

Remy How is this important?

Taz Look, don't do it if you don't want, but I don't have a choice, because –

Remy Don't start.

Taz What?

Remy Going on about being Mental Health Ambassador.

Taz You know I didn't ask to be, she made me!

She continues to silently ask people how they are and notes their answers – everyone says fine.

Remy It's not a real thing, it's not important.

Marni Mental Health Ambassador? Course it is. Just cos you waste all your time gaming.

Remy No I don't! You don't know anything. I reckon Taz likes it, makes her feel important.

Taz As if! I don't care.

But part of her does . . . **Taz** *perseveres as* **Remy** *gets bored and scrolls on his phone to one side. As he does, his* **Inner Monologue***, slowly rises and stands behind him.* **Remy** *is unaware of their presence. The group all look at each other, uncertain.*

Inner 1 Will people know?

Inner 2 Do we want them to know?

Inner 3 I thought the whole point was that we were not, you know . . . outside?

Inner 4 Yeah but sometimes I feel like we do want people to know . . . that we are . . . The INNER MONOLOGUE.

He bows deeply. The others look annoyed.

Inner 3 You're not supposed to tell people!

Inner 1 (*a put-down*)   I've always thought you had very *outer* monologue tendencies.

Inner 4   What?! No. I just think we need to point it out. Because they don't know. Them. Everyone out there.

Inner 1   So now you've told them . . . what do you want to say?

Inner 4   Oh God, nothing.

Inner 2   Good, because I think there are some things we should keep private!

Inner 3   Especially this!

Inner 4   But what if . . . maybe we should? Someone could help!

Inner 3   NO! It's embarrassing.

Inner 1   Tell her how boring this is! Tell her. Tell her we should go.

Inner 2   Go, we should go.

Inner 3   Because we've got places to be.

Remy *stands suddenly.*

Remy   Taz, seriously, I'm done here.

He slopes off. **Inner Monologue** *goes with him.*

Inner 4   Do we have to go?

Inner 2   You know we do.

Inner 4   We could . . . we could tell someone?

Inner 3   How many more times?! NO! Why would we tell anyone? What can they do?

Inner 4 (*defeated*)   You're right.

Remy *stops suddenly, away from* **Taz***; for a moment he looks older than his years.*

All Inner Monologue   I'm so tired.

Remy *goes.* **Inner Monologue** *go over to* **Taz***; she is unaware of their presence. She looks at her clipboard, fed up.*

All Inner Monologue   Am I pointless? Yes. You. Are.

Taz *tries to drown out the voices in her head. Lights lower on* **Taz** *and the others as they quietly continue their survey. Lights up on* **Miss Mahmoud** *as she enters. The* **Inner Monologue** *go and stand behind her. She's downbeat.*

Inner 1   Remember to be upbeat in front of the pupils.

Inner 2   Remember why you went into teaching.

Inner 3   Shut up, shut up, shut up! People will think you're stupid.

Inner 1   Maybe I am a bit stupid. Maybe I'm a loser. Maybe –

Miss Mahmoud *has had enough of the voices in her head.*

Miss Mahmoud   Shut up!

Taz *jumps, noticing her.*

Taz   Miss?

Inner 1   Remember, pretend to be happy, happy, happy!

Miss Mahmoud   Taz! How's it's going?

Taz *takes a beat, looks at her survey answers.*

Taz   This is . . . Miss, it's pointless!

Miss Mahmoud   What have I told you about being negative?

Taz   Can't we do something somewhere else? Go on a trip or something? 'Cause this is rubbish. Everyone just keeps saying 'fine' . . . they're fine, all fine, everyone is just . . . 'fine'.

Sam *gets excited to tell* **Miss Mahmoud** *about the building they're standing outside.*

Sam   Miss, this building dates back to 1850. It started life as a sort of community centre and then in later years it became a picture house.

Remy   Picture house? Lame. Just say cinema, innit.

Miss Mahmoud   Really, Sam? That's interesting. When I was growing up it was a roller disco.

Taz   A what?

Miss Mahmoud   Don't tell me you don't know what a roller disco is?! You know . . . roller skates, music, fun.

Taz *looks blank.*

Taz   Ummm, sounds . . . great?

Miss Mahmoud   It was! Well, at least it looked it from the photos.

Taz   Closed down before you could go?

Miss Mahmoud   No, I was never allowed to go. Strict parents and all that. But roller discos were really popular. It was just one of those things that was better back then.

Taz (*teasing*)   Oh here we go . . . things were better back in the day, yeah? You going to one of your vintage fairs again soon?

Miss Mahmoud   Well, actually yes.

Taz (*sarcastic*)   Sounds fun.

Miss Mahmoud   Some things about the past were fun. I grew up without the pressure of social media. I grew up with great music! (*Remembering.*) And Saturday morning TV was brilliant! It was actually for children and young people, not just all cooking shows. It was so exciting, you could see all your favourite pop stars being interviewed, maybe even get through on the phones and ask them a question.

Taz   What, rather than just slide in their DMs? (*Teasing*.) Miss, you ever slid into anyone's DMs?

Miss Mahmoud (*telling her off*)   Taz . . .

Taz   So did you never go to the disco?

Miss Mahmoud   No. It would've been nice. But no.

She looks fondly at the building.

No point looking back, it's not like you can change the past. (*Beat*.) Anyway, the survey. What has the experience shown you so far?

Taz *shrugs.*

Miss Mahmoud   You've must've learnt something?

Taz (*fed up*)   Yeah. That 'How are you?' and 'I'm fine' are probably the two most over-used phrases in the English language . . . and neither of them mean anything!

Miss Mahmoud (*guiding her through the thought process*)   So these are strangers on the street, right, members of the public?

Taz   Yeah . . . randoms, so they're not gonna tell me anything anyway. Why did you make us do this, Miss?

Miss Mahmoud   So strangers aren't opening up to you. Do you think your friends and your fellow pupils will be any better at opening up to you?

Taz   Joking, aren't you?! No way.

Miss Mahmoud   And do you think they are all 'fine', or that maybe some of them do need to share their problems?

Taz (*thinking*)   Yeah . . . I reckon they do, Miss.

Miss Mahmoud (*prompting her*)   So as Mental Health Ambassador . . .?

Taz   I need to find ways of encouraging pupils to open up?

Miss Mahmoud   Absolutely. You really need to think about how you can get people to feel comfortable and supported and not embarrassed.

Taz (*getting it*)   'Cause that's why everyone just says 'fine' right? No-one wants to seem like they've got a problem.

Miss Mahmoud   Exactly!

The **Inner Monologue** *rush to* **Miss Mahmoud***.*

Inner 1   Success! Look what you just did.

Inner 2   Don't delude yourself. You. Are. Pointless.

Miss Mahmoud *winces, as if trying to drown something out.*

Miss Mahmoud   Shut up . . .

Taz *looks at her, wondering who she's talking to.*

Taz   Miss? Are you OK?

Miss Mahmoud   What? Oh, yes, I'm fine. (*Beat.*) And you, Taz, how are you?

Taz   I . . . I'm fine.

But neither of them mean it. **Inner Monologue** *stands between them both and gently chants.*

Inner Monologue   Not fine, not fine, not fine.

Miss Mahmoud (*gentle*)   Things can be hard some days, Taz. And like we've just said, it's not easy to open up. But once you do . . . it does help to talk about it. If you ever want to, I'm here to listen.

Taz   I don't know what you're on about. I'm fine. Like, really fine.

Miss Mahmoud   I hope so, Taz. But if you weren't, I'd say sometimes doing something for someone else can make you feel better. Help you forget about your own troubles for a bit.

A couple of beats as **Taz** *thinks about this. But defensiveness takes over.*

Taz   Yeah, well, like I said, Miss. I'm fine.

Miss Mahmoud *knows this isn't true but goes along with it for now.*

Miss Mahmoud   OK, well, good . . . even more reason for you to be Mental Health Ambassador, you can help everyone that really isn't 'fine'. Because like I said, do something for someone else and you really do forget your own troubles. (*Beat.*) Right, come on, all of you, let's get back.

Everyone gathers to leave. **Taz** *notices* **Miss Mahmoud** *looking up at the roller disco. As the others leave,* **Taz** *looks at the old building a moment. The* **Inner Monologue** *surround her again.*

Inner 1   She's right, you know. About doing something for someone else.

Inner 2   Why would someone care about anything you did? You don't count.

Inner 3   Yes, you do.

Inner 2   You don't count. And no-one even notices you.

Inner 1   Well, they will if you do something for someone else. Something big.

Taz *takes one last look at the building before leaving. Lights change.*

Scene Three

Taz is in the classroom with **Remy**, **Marni** *and* **Sam**.

Remy   It's a dumb idea.

Taz   You shit (alt.: crap/dump) on everyone's ideas.

Marni   Imagine . . . imagine if you did actually shit (alt.: crap/dump) on someone's ideas . . . not that you can actually, you know, touch an idea, cos ideas are, what do you call it –

Sam   Intangible.

Marni   Intangible! That's it. Ideas are intangible. So you can't shit (alt.: crap/dump) on them really. But, like, figuratively.

Taz *despairs.*

Remy   I'm not doing it.

Taz   I can't do it on my own.

She looks to **Sam** *and* **Marni**.

Marni   What do you need us to actually do? Like, actually, *tangibly* do.

Taz   Help me set it up, decorate it a bit?

Remy   A bit?! It's not exactly a small job.

Sam   I think it's a good idea. I could do, like, a mood board!

He starts to look things up on his phone, gets inspired.

Taz   That's great.

Sam   For my vision.

Taz   OK – wait, what? Your vision?

Sam   It needs a vision, an idea like this.

Taz   Fine, great, whatever, as long as you're helping me.

Remy   Why you even doing this?

Taz   For Miss, innit.

Remy   Lame.

Taz   Well, at least I'm doing something for someone else.

Remy (*sarcastic*)   Someone get her a certificate. (*Dismissive.*) I'm not getting involved.

Taz   OK, fine, don't help. But come, at least?

Marni   Might be alright?

Sam, *who's been pacing and coming up with ideas, stops suddenly.*

Sam   My vision is starting to take shape! It needs people. Loads of them.

Taz   Please, Remy?

Remy   Depends what time.

Taz   What, you got something better to do?

Remy   I got places to be.

Taz   Yeah, right. Forget it.

She starts to leave. **Remy** *feels bad.*

Remy   Alright, I'll come to your stupid thing.

Miss Mahmoud *enters.*

Miss Mahmoud   What thing?

Taz *shushes everyone; she doesn't want to give it away.*

Taz   Nothing, Miss. Just a . . . thing.

Sam   A brilliant thing!

Taz   Shut up, Sam.

Sam   With so much vision! And history! This is gonna be an immense –

Taz *jumps in to stop* **Sam** *giving it away.*

Taz   Study group!

Miss Mahmoud *has no idea what they're talking about.*

Taz   We were wondering if you could join us?

Miss Mahmoud   What, in your study group?

Taz   Yeah, we could do with some help. We're a bit stuck with some . . .

Marni   History stuff.

Miss Mahmoud   OK. When?

Taz   Friday lunchtime?

Sam   Friday?! I need more than two days for my vision!

Taz *tries to stop him giving it away again.*

Taz   Shut up, Sam!

Marni   Revision. He meant he needs more than two days for revision.

Miss Mahmoud   I was planning on popping into the vintage market on Friday lunchtime . . .

Taz Please? We really need the help.

Miss Mahmoud (*giving in*) Fine. OK.

Scene Four

Outside, by the door of the old roller disco, **Taz** *is with* **Remy**.

Taz (*stressed*) Everyone's here, right? They're ready?

Remy For the third time . . . yes. Look, is this gonna take long?

Inner Monologue *stand by* **Remy**.

Inner 1 Late, late, late, late, late.

Inner 4 That song's still bugging me . . . what is it?!

Inner 1, 2 & 3 Shut up!

Inner 4 *looks hurt.*

Taz Shh, she's coming!

Miss Mahmoud *approaches.*

Miss Mahmoud So, why are we meeting here? I thought we were going to the library.

Taz The thing is, Miss . . . I wanted to –

Sam *and* **Marni** *burst out of the old building.*

Sam & Marni Surprise!

Miss Mahmoud You nearly gave me a heart attack! What are you doing in there?

Sam Oh, Miss Mahmoud. You're gonna love this.

Taz We're going to the roller disco!

Miss Mahmoud What?

Taz You said you'd never been, right? So . . . we're going.

Miss Mahmoud When I said do something for someone else, I meant the survey. Finding ways to get pupils to open up and talk.

Taz Yeah but, Miss, this is so much better! You said you never got to go. And now you can.

Miss Mahmoud It closed down years ago.

Taz Sam's dad is an estate agent, he pulled a favour that got us in.

Miss Mahmoud To an empty building?

Sam No . . . to my vision!

He flings open the doors, we enter the world of the roller disco . . . a glitterball hangs from the ceiling, spinning slowly. Multi-colour lights, streamers, balloons, etc. decorate the room in a riot of colour. **Miss Mahmoud** *is shocked.*

Miss Mahmoud   What . . . how did you do all this?

Sam   Googled it. And asked my mum. She said it basically needs to look like a rainbow threw up.

Miss Mahmoud   It looks . . . it looks. . . . brilliant!

Taz   It's just missing one thing . . .

Sam   Music. Marni?

Marni *hits play. The lights change and KC and the Sunshine Band 'Give It Up' starts to play.* **Inner Monologue** *chorus form a line and begin to do a formation dance.* **Taz**, **Sam** *and* **Marni** *take* **Miss Mahmoud** *and transform her into an eighties look (on top of what she's already wearing is fine) – placing deely boppers on her head, putting leg warmers on her, a bright top, a skater/puffball skirt, etc. and finally hand her a pair of roller skates. As they do this,* **Remy** *stands, not interested.* **Miss Mahmoud** *holds the skates, overwhelmed, as the dancers continue their routine.* **Taz**, **Marni** *and* **Sam** *join in.*

Taz   Come on, Miss!

Unable to resist, **Miss Mahmoud** *puts the skates on and joins in. The whole cast turn into a dizzying riot of colour and fun as the song peaks, all skating forward.*

Miss Mahmoud   This is brilliant!

Taz   You having fun?

Miss Mahmoud *feels like a teenager unleashed, spinning and turning and free.*

Miss Mahmoud   I love it!

The track lowers, the rest of the cast quietly skate on as **Miss Mahmoud** *and* **Taz** *come to the front and slow to a stop to talk.*

Miss Mahmoud   Thank you, Taz. It's really kind of you.

Taz (*shy*)   Whatever, Miss. It's just cos you said you never got to go.

A warm moment.

Miss Mahmoud   Well, I'm very grateful. And everyone seems to be enjoying it. Except Remy.

Miss Mahmoud *skates over to him.*

Miss Mahmoud   Remy?

Remy   I don't have time.

Miss Mahmoud   You don't even know what I'm going to say.

Remy Yeah I do. You've got that face you do. Your therapy face.

Miss Mahmoud I'm just worried about you.

Remy Why? I'm fine.

Miss Mahmoud *gives up.*

Miss Mahmoud OK. Good. Well, try and enjoy it at least, Taz's gone to a lot of trouble.

She skates off. **Remy** *gets up, as if to go after her, but he can't.* **Miss Mahmoud** *turns round.*

Miss Mahmoud Come on.

She holds a hand out to encourage him.

His **Inner Monologue** *jump up behind him.*

Inner 4 Go, go, go, go . . . you're allowed to have fun.

He roller-skates over to join everyone and they skate forwards in a circle together.

Taz This is easier than I thought . . . can you skate backwards, Miss? We should all do it! Hey, everyone –

Miss Mahmoud No! Don't.

Taz What?

Miss Mahmoud It's . . . well it's stupid. But . . .

Sam Go on.

Miss Mahmoud I was never allowed to come here. My parents were worried about alcohol and boys and all that. But I always knew there was a . . . well I suppose you'd call it an urban myth.

Marni A what?

Miss Mahmoud Sort of a rumour, something a bit weird but that people start repeating and it somehow does the rounds –

Marni You mean it goes viral?

Miss Mahmoud Well, yes I suppose.

Sam And then do you get cancelled?

Miss Mahmoud No, that was never a thing.

Marni Wait, what do you mean? You couldn't get cancelled in the olden days?

Miss Mahmoud The eighties isn't the olden days! But no, there was no such thing.

Taz So what's the rumour thing, the urban myth?

Miss Mahmoud They used to say that if you all skated backwards together here three times round . . . you'd end up back in time.

Silence from everyone; everyone stops and stares at **Miss Mahmoud** *before they start laughing.*

Taz   Miss, that is jokes!

Marni   Tangible jokes.

Miss Mahmoud   Well, I did say it was silly.

Sam   Imagine if you could go back in time though! Miss, when would you go to?

Miss Mahmoud   I don't know, a simpler time perhaps. No responsibilities. No social media. Less stress.

Taz (*joking*)   Come let's go then.

She slowly starts to skate backwards; others join her.

Taz   Imagine if we could really go!

Miss Mahmoud   The thing with urban myths was that they were usually about bad things happening.

Taz   Nothing bad is gonna happen if we skate backwards. You gotta stop being so scared all the time, Miss!

Miss Mahmoud   Go on then . . .

The rest of the cast except **Remy** *join her.* **Remy** *gets a text, reads it, gets stressed.*

Remy   I need to go.

Sam   Come on, Remy, it should be all of us.

Remy   This is dumb.

Taz   You can do your flippin' gaming anytime! Come on.

Remy, *frustrated, gives in.*

Taz   Right everyone, backwards three times, yeah?

Everyone starts to skate backwards together. As they complete a circuit, the lights and music get brighter and louder, like the tornado in The Wizard of Oz.

Taz   One . . . Two . . . Three!

Everyone stops suddenly. Out of breath and tense.

Taz   See, Miss? Nothing's changed.

Sam *goes over to the door and opens it . . . and quickly slams it shut again.*

Sam   Oh my God . . . everything's changed!

But no-one believes him.

Remy   Right I really have to go now.

He goes to the door.

Sam I wouldn't go out there if I was you.

Remy Move.

Sam Fine but don't say I didn't warn you.

Remy *opens the door, stares a moment, shocked, and then slams it shut again.*

Miss Mahmoud What's wrong?

Remy Outside . . . is not outside.

Taz What are you on about?

Remy Look!

He flings open the door. **Miss Mahmoud**, **Taz**, **Marni** *and* **Sam** *go to look.*

Taz What . . . what is that?!

Marni Woah. That is tangibly different to outside.

Sam Stop saying tangibly!

Remy What's happened? What is that?!

Miss Mahmoud (*in shock*) That . . . is 1987.

Sam I think I might have taken my vision a little bit too far.

He nearly faints, the others fan him/give him water, etc. He sits up.

With great power comes great responsibility . . .

He stares at his hands, unable to believe what he's done.

Taz Shut up, Sam, this wasn't you, this was the disco! The urban legend thing was true!

Remy We need to get back!

Taz You're joking?! We've time travelled! Like we're not gonna go check out 1987.

Miss Mahmoud 1987 . . . (*Sudden realization/remembering something.*) We can't. We have to get back home.

Taz What for?! This is amazing – we've gone back in time, who gets to do that?! We've gotta go look . . . please, Miss? Please?

Marni How do you know it's 1987, Miss?

Miss Mahmoud *looks at what's through the open door.*

Miss Mahmoud Because that's the set of a TV show that was big that year . . . 'Go, Go Saturday!' I used to watch it every –

Marni Friday?

Miss Mahmoud Saturday! It was brilliant. So upbeat and the presenters were so much fun, you wanted to be their best friends.

Taz We're going in, right? Miss?

All eyes on **Miss Mahmoud**. *A beat.*

Miss Mahmoud OK.

Taz, **Sam** *and* **Marni** *celebrate.*

Remy Miss, I need to get back!

Miss Mahmoud Taz is right, who gets to do this? We can't not. BUT. We're just going there, and that's it, right? (*Firm.*) Because you shouldn't mess with the past. So just the show, then straight home. If we even know how.

Taz Course, Miss. Just the TV show.

Scene Five

The lights change as they all step into the studio of 'Go, Go Saturday'. The presenters, **Sooz** *and* **Jez**, *are interviewing an enigmatic pop band, StarSign. Behind* **Sooz** *and* **Jez** *are a bunch of kids making up the studio audience. The band are in a bad mood; the lead singer Ellie is wearing sunglasses. All the action goes on without anyone realizing* **Miss Mahmoud** *and the others are there; they mix in with the other kids in the studio audience.*

Sooz And finally now the moment we've all been waiting for, everyone please welcome Ellie, Lana and Mickey from StarSign!

Whoops and cheers from the studio audience, including **Miss Mahmoud**, *who is a bit too loud.* **Sam**, **Taz** *and the others stare at her; she calms down.*

Sooz *is over-the-top enthusiastic.*

Jez So, guys, so great to have you here.

Sooz Yeah, amazing!

Jez We've got lots of questions for you, including some from our audience at home. But let's start with one from our audience here today . . . Lee? Lee what's your question for StarSign?

Lee Hi! Ellie, you mostly write the songs, don't you, so where do you get your inspiration?

Lana Actually we all write them.

Mickey (*trying to keep the peace*) It's a team effort.

Ellie Well, sort of. I mainly write them and the guys chip in.

Lana (*annoyed*) Chip in?

Mickey Collaborative chipping in!

Ellie But the ideas, the main stylistic thrust of our lyrics, that's all me.

Lana Pretentious –

Jez (*across* **Lana**, *trying to stop the argument*) So when you wrote the lyrics for your huge hit 'Love Spell', the lyrics 'I love you, you love me, love times two makes us free' –

Sooz Amazing. Inspiring.

Jez What was the inspiration for that? Because it seems like a simple love song.

Ellie See, you've fallen into the trap of thinking that's what it's about, when actually – subliminally – it's about communism and the plight of the working classes.

Mickey Is it?

Ellie Coming from a working-class background myself –

Lana You went to private school!

Sooz What's the new vision? Because you said your new album is going to take the band in a new direction.

Ellie Yeah, I'm calling it post-pop, you know?

Sooz Oh, amazing.

Jez So . . . less poppy?

Ellie With pop undertones. Post-pop pop.

Sooz So amazing!

Taz That lead singer's an idiot!

Sam Oh my God I love her vision.

Miss Mahmoud I can't believe I'm in the studio with StarSign!

Taz They don't seem to like each other.

Marni Tangible creative differences vibe.

Miss Mahmoud Shhhh!

Sooz Let's take a question from the phones. Line two, Sarah from Doncaster, Sarah what's your question to StarSign?

The band pick up landline phones but **Sarah**'s *voice comes from off stage/speakers.*

Sarah I'd just like to ask StarSign why they're so fucking (alt.: bloody) crap (alt.: dire).

[The F word can be beeped as it would be on TV if this is preferred.]

Sam Woah.

Marni I didn't know you could swear on TV back then!

Miss Mahmoud You couldn't!

Sooz and Jez desperately try to be in control again.

Sooz Well, that wasn't very clever, was it, Sarah? Has anyone got a sensible question?

Jez And apologies for the bad language.

Ellie There's no such thing as 'bad' language', language just . . . is.

Sooz (*awkward*) Hahahaha. . . . let's move on, shall we?

Lana Sarah's right though, we are a bit crap (alt.: dire).

Mickey (*trying to calm his bandmates down*) Let's not argue, think of the kids.

Sooz Seems like we've caught StarSign on a bit of a bad day.

Lana You can say that again.

Sooz We all have them!

Ellie Yeah, except this time, I'm done.

She gets up.

Mickey What are you doing?

Jez Yeah . . . what are you doing?

Ellie I'm quitting the band. As of now,

Sooz Ummm . . . let's go to a break while we get all of this sorted out. Nothing to worry about, just a little tiff. We'll be right back after this.

Taz Woah . . . this must be blowing up online!

Miss Mahmoud There was no social media, remember? I heard about this happening but I never got to see it . . . this was the one week I missed the show.

Marni Why didn't you watch it on catch-up?

Miss Mahmoud Because there was no such thing!

Remy No social media, no catch-up . . . what was the point of the eighties, even?

*Lights low on **Miss Mahmoud** and the children as they watch what's unfolding in the TV studio.*

Lana What are you doing, Ellie?! Just because me and Mickey said we wanted as much say in the band as you, you just quit?!

Ellie It's been a long time coming.

Jez Do you maybe want to take this backstage?

Ellie I don't want to do anything you tell me.

Sooz is desperate to keep the peace for the sake of the audience.

Sooz (*re. the studio audience*) The children, remember the children!

Mickey You can't leave!

Ellie Watch me.

Mickey No lead singer, no band!

Lana We don't need her!

Mickey I mean, we do, we actually do! Come on, mate.

But **Ellie** *leaves. Lights up on our gang.*

Taz Must be weird, Miss, never seeing it and now actually being here?

Miss Mahmoud Yeah. Though I kind of wish I wasn't. Never meet your heroes . . . Ellie's a bit of an idiot. I had posters of her all over my walls. Used to buy every magazine they were in. Wished I was allowed to go to their concerts.

Remy *stands suddenly.*

Remy Let's get out of here.

Miss Mahmoud Shh, they'll hear you.

Taz *looks at the studio audience then stands; no-one notices.*

Taz They can't hear us . . . because they can't see us.

Sam Oh my God.

Marni We're not tangible!

Remy I need to get back.

Sam We're having like a proper adventure! Why would you want to leave?

Miss Mahmoud My heart broke when the band split.

Sam Maybe you could get them back together?!

Marni (*very confident*) You can't mess with the space-time continuum.

They all stare at her; where did she get that from?!

Marni I dunno what that actually means. I heard it on *Doctor Who* or something.

Miss Mahmoud Actually Marni's right, you shouldn't change the past.

Remy Look can we just go now, I'm done with 1987.

Taz No way! What is there to go back for?!

Remy Fine, I'll go back on my own.

Taz How are you going to do that? The urban legend thing only worked when we all did it together.

Remy What time is it?

Sam Who cares what time it is, it's flipping 1987, mate!

Marni It's . . . oh, where's my phone?

The others look for theirs.

Taz Haven't got mine either.

Remy *is freaking out about not having his phone.*

Remy I need my phone! I can't . . . this can't be happening.

Marni How am I going to post about this with no photos?

Miss Mahmoud You don't need photos, you just need to be in the moment – just use your memory.

Marni Miss, you keep saying really weird stuff.

Remy I just want to go home.

Taz What's so great about 2024 that you want to get back for? Miss, we can go somewhere else, right?

Miss Mahmoud Remy's right, we should get back. (*Hesitant, thinking it through.*) Although . . . the thing is, when are you ever going to get a chance to do something like this? It's actual living history.

Sam I want to see it! I want to go outside and see more!

Remy But I want to go home.

Taz Nothing ever happens at home!

Miss Mahmoud I just want to watch this . . . just a few more minutes and then we'll decide what to do.

Their side of the stage goes to black as they sit and watch. We go back to the studio.

Sooz We've had to go to an extended break because of you!

Ellie Don't blame me, you're the one who wants to keep on –

Sooz Don't say it! Don't say I'm living a lie.

Ellie Well, you are.

Sooz You know I can't. I'll lose everything. And it's the same for you. Those screaming kids are the ones buying your records, paying your mortgage.

Ellie I don't care anymore.

Sooz You won't be saying that when you've tried and failed to go solo and you're struggling to pay your bills.

Ellie It won't come to that, come on, please! Let's do this together, now, live on television. Tell everyone who we are, what we mean to each other.

Sooz Are you insane?!

Ellie I could just go over there, look straight down the camera . . . it'd be like ripping a plaster off. Yeah, OK, so the papers would run a few stories –

Sooz They'd have a field day! 'Female pop star and female TV presenter in secret relationship!' We'd never work again.

Ellie You can't live like this. I know I can't.

She gets up and storms off.

Sooz Ellie . . .

But **Ellie** *has gone. Their side goes dark. We go back to* **Miss Mahmoud** *and the others.* **Miss Mahmoud** *is surprised.*

Taz Woah.

Sam No actual way.

Marni That was intense.

Sam So wait, they were –

Miss Mahmoud Together. Well, it looks like it. But I didn't even know either of them was gay.

Taz They never came out? Why?

Miss Mahmoud Things were very different. It wasn't so easy to be openly gay, there was a lot of prejudice. I know there still is, but it was much worse then.

Taz But couldn't you just own it, ignore the haters?

Miss Mahmoud It's not like now. That level of hate could be enough to crush anyone, let alone someone in the public eye with a career to protect. Sometimes the newspapers outed people and it would be devastating for them.

The children are shocked and saddened by this.

Sam That's awful, Miss.

Miss Mahmoud No wonder Ellie and Sooz were living a lie. I do remember reading that Ellie had a breakdown a few years later. Makes sense now.

See Introductory Notes on the following lines of speech in square brackets – these should be used if you have culturally appropriate casting

[**Marni** So some people didn't like you if you were 'different'. I guess some people still don't.

Miss Mahmoud And obviously it wasn't just about someone's sexuality. Being Asian wasn't always easy.

Taz Were you bullied, Miss?

Miss Mahmoud Not bullied, but sometimes people made nasty comments. But bullying did happen to Asian kids in other schools. And sometimes things happened in town in the street to my parents and some family friends. People shouting racist things. Once someone attacked my uncle simply because of the colour of his skin.]

The children are appalled.

Marni   Are you sure you want to see more of 1987, Taz? Seems pretty rough.

Miss Mahmoud   Yes maybe it is better if we go home.

Marni   Though . . . I kind of like not having my phone.

Miss Mahmoud   How does it feel?

Marni   Lighter. I don't just mean the weight of it in my pocket. I mean . . .

Miss Mahmoud   I know. I get it.

Taz   Yeah I get it too. And I've just realized something else . . . I can't hear all the thoughts that go round and round in my head. Sometimes they literally do my head in! (*Trying to think of how to describe it.*) I feel more . . . peaceful. (*Feeling stupid.*) That probably doesn't even make sense.

Miss Mahmoud   It does. Because I feel it too.

Taz   It feels good here, Miss. I know you said we shouldn't mess with the past – and we won't, but . . . maybe we could stay a bit, see outside, like proper outside?

She enlists **Sam**.

Taz   Sam . . . all that history, all those buildings . . . you could actually see it, instead of just reading about it.

Sam   Yes! It'd be amazing! Let's stay?

Remy   No! We should go.

Taz   Please, Remy. Miss is right, who gets the chance to do this? Don't you want an adventure? Don't you want to have some actual fun?

Remy *is torn; he thinks about it.*

Remy (*relenting*)   It would be nice to do something different.

The other pupils celebrate.

Miss Mahmoud   That settles it then.

Sam   How would we even get there?

Marni   Yeah, because no phone, no Uber.

Miss Mahmoud   Marni, Uber was not a thing in 1987.

Marni   My head can't even process that. What, did you go on, like, bicycles and that?

Miss Mahmoud   Sometimes, yes.

Marni   Penny-farthings?

Miss Mahmoud No! We had taxis.

Marni Let's get a taxi then.

Remy (*sarcastic*) Yeah because that's gonna be easy.

Stage Manager Taxi for Ellie at the stage door!

A taxi appears.

Marni That was way faster than Uber. Some things are better in 1987, Miss.

Remy How are we going to get in a taxi?

Sam No-one can see us.

Remy We don't even know where it's going.

Miss Mahmoud Only one way to find out!

They all start to follow **Ellie**. *The lights change as they get into the taxi next to her; she's unaware they're there.*

Scene Six

In the taxi.

Taz She looks really sad. (*To* **Ellie**.) Are you OK?

Sam She can't hear you.

Taz Mate, are you alright? Hello?

Miss Mahmoud (*gentle*) Thought you didn't believe in asking people how they are, Taz?

Taz *shrugs.*

Taz Yeah, but . . . can't be easy, living like she does. Living a lie.

Miss Mahmoud And none of us fans ever knew. Thirteen-year-old me would have been so excited to even be in the same building as Ellie, let alone the same taxi.

Marni Oh my God, look.

A gaggle of young fans flock around the taxi, screaming **Ellie**'s *name. She puts her dark glasses on again and hunches down.*

Miss Mahmoud She hates it, doesn't she.

Sam She's famous and popular, what's bad about that?

Taz Everyone knowing you, getting up in your face in the street.

Ellie Train station please and can you put your foot down?

The children, **Miss Mahmoud** *and* **Ellie** *all move in unison as if in a taxi. They comment on things as they pass them.*

Taz Wait, 'Go, Go Saturday' wasn't filmed in our town was it?

Miss Mahmoud No, and yet . . . we're somehow in our town.

Taz But it looks . . . really different. All those shops that are boarded up now . . . they're all open.

Miss Mahmoud It looks how I remember it.

Sam I recognize some of the buildings. Not the shops though.

Marni Miss, what's Our Price?

Miss Mahmoud I loved Our Price! Used to rush down there when I'd saved up enough pocket money to get the latest LP, or a limited edition gatefold single.

Marni *stares at her a beat.*

Marni I don't know what most of that sentence meant.

Miss Mahmoud (*amused*) It wasn't that long ago! Don't you listen to any of the stories your parents tell you?

Taz My mum doesn't tell me much. Apart from how tired she is from working and how much the bills are.

Miss Mahmoud Is that why you don't want to go back, Taz?

Taz *shrugs, embarrassed.*

Miss Mahmoud I know you don't believe in talking about things . . . but trust me, it helps.

Sam Me and my dad talk a lot. He's the one that got me into all the history stuff. He always says everything's got a story, you just need to find it.

He is peering out.

This is where we were born and now we get to see what it was like before we even existed.

Remy And it's sort of . . . buzzing. I've never seen it so busy. I never go in to town . . . no reason, innit.

Miss Mahmoud There wasn't always a lot to do for people my age – well, your age. A lot of it was just hanging around. But if you wanted to see anyone, or buy anything . . . you had to go to town.

Remy People are . . . they're talking to each other, like properly talking.

Miss Mahmoud *is amused by the children's wonderment at something so simple.*

Miss Mahmoud (*lightly sarcastic*) Whatever next!

Ellie (*to the taxi driver*) Cheers, mate.

She pays the driver and leaves. The rest of them get out of the taxi.

Sam Can't we just stay in the taxi? See some more.

Taz Driver can't hear us, remember.

Marni So what do we do now?

Taz Miss, didn't you say you used to live near the train station?

Miss Mahmoud Not far.

Taz So . . . we could go to your house!

Miss Mahmoud Absolutely not.

Taz Miss . . . if we can see other people like we saw all that lot in the studio . . . maybe you could see yourself!

Miss Mahmoud I'm not sure that's a good idea. Some things are better off left in the past.

Taz Aren't you even a bit curious, Miss . . .? See what you were like when you were our age?

Miss Mahmoud *struggles, tempted.*

Remy How would we even get there?

Miss Mahmoud The old-fashioned way.

Marni I don't know how to ride a penny-farthing.

Taz Walk, Marni, we're going to walk.

Sam Yes! That way we can really see things up close. Come on.

Scene Seven

The lights change, the Pet Shop Boys' 'Suburbia' plays as they walk.

Headlines from 1987 flash up on screen or are held up by the **Chorus***. Everything from unemployment (three million) to 'one person a day dies from AIDS in the UK' to 'Black Monday economic crash' should be included alongside positive ones such as 'Aretha Franklin becomes the first female artist to be inducted in the Rock & Roll Hall of Fame', 'Martina Navratilova wins her eighth Wimbledon singles title', 'George Michael releases debut solo album,* Faith'*. Other pertinent ones can be added.*

Taz, **Remy**, **Marni** *and* **Sam** *stop to take in things that they pass and the headlines, as* **Miss Mahmoud** *leads the way. They eventually come to a stop outside a house with a garden. The track fades.*

Miss Mahmoud This is it. I'm home. Though maybe this is a bad idea . . . Maybe we should go.

Taz We just got here!

Miss Mahmoud (*nervous*)   Yes, but –

Sam   Miss! Is that you?!

They all stare as a fourteen-year-old **Young Miss Mahmoud** *appears, back from the shop with a small bag of groceries.*

Suddenly, from within the house, the sound of glass smashing. **Miss Mahmoud** *jumps.*

Young Miss Mahmoud   It's alright, Mum, I'll clear it up! Don't want you getting glass in your foot.

Young Miss Mahmoud *rushes into the house.*

Miss Mahmoud *gets upset.* **Marni** *misunderstands.*

Marni   Your hair wasn't that bad, Miss.

Taz   Shut up, Marni!

Young Miss Mahmoud (*offstage*)   All done. I'll get you another glass, you need to take your tablets and then I'll get your lunch ready. You go and sit in the garden, Mum.

As **Remy** *watches, he realizes something.*

Remy   Miss . . . were you –

Miss Mahmoud   Shhh, wait . . . she's coming. . . .

Miss Mahmoud *watches with bated breath as her* **Mum** *appears.*

Miss Mahmoud   Mum!

But **Mum** *doesn't respond. She tends to a pot plant as* **Miss Mahmoud** *and the children watch her.*

Taz   I don't know what's weirder, seeing your younger self or seeing your mum.

Miss Mahmoud   My mum . . . because she died a few years later.

Taz   Miss . . . I'm so sorry.

Remy (*hesitant*)   You were her carer, weren't you?

Miss Mahmoud *gets upset and nods.*

Taz   That's why you didn't want to come to the house, isn't it? I'm sorry, Miss . . . if I'd known I wouldn't have pushed it.

Miss Mahmoud   It's OK . . .

Remy   What was up with your mum?

Miss Mahmoud   She started dropping things one summer. That's why I had to clean glass up. The summer of 1987 was when it got worse. At first we just thought she was tired, needed time off work. But then other stuff started happening and then it was just doctors' appointments and scans and more appointments and more scans and then tablets and more tablets and . . .

Sam Must've been awful.

Miss Mahmoud I never thought I'd see her again. Now I wish I had my phone to take pictures.

She is now very upset.

Marni No . . . it'd just be in the way. Like you said, be in the moment. Remember it . . . remember the details. Five things . . .

She scrambles to go right up to **Mum**. *As she describes the five things,* **Miss Mahmoud** *slowly starts to calm down.*

Marni She's wearing blue jeans and a red top.

[Change the line above as appropriate to your casting; see Introductory Notes.]

Miss Mahmoud She loved that top.

Marni Her hair's in a scrunchie.

Miss Mahmoud Always.

Marni She's got pink nail polish on her toes.

Miss Mahmoud I used to put it on for her! When she couldn't do it anymore.

Marni She's watering the plants . . . potting the one with the white flowers.

Miss Mahmoud Chrysanthemums. Her favourites.

Marni And she's humming.

Miss Mahmoud Yes . . . (*Beat.*) And she's beautiful. Thank you, Marni.

Taz (*to* **Marni**) How did you do that?

Sam That was cool, Marns, I could feel myself relaxing.

Marni I got taught it. In counselling. If you're stressed, you stop and notice five things about where you are – anything, just all the details. And by the time you've done it you feel calmer.

Taz You never said you're having counselling.

Marni *shrugs.*

Marni Not that easy to talk about.

Taz (*heartfelt*) Not when I've been taking the mickey about mental health stuff. Sorry, Marni.

Marni It's OK.

Taz And I'm sorry I said you were weird.

Marni What?! No, I told you, I like it!

A warm moment between them.

Remy *hesitates.*

Remy I . . . (*Trails off.*)

Taz Yeah, yeah we know, you want to go home now. Gaming thing.

Remy No. Well, yeah I do want to go, but not because of gaming. (*Beat; he looks at* **Miss Mahmoud**.) My dad needs his tablets, Miss. And I need to get his dinner ready. And I'm stressing out without my phone in case he's trying to get hold of me.

Miss Mahmoud Oh, Remy. Why have you never said you're your dad's carer?

Remy *shrugs.*

Remy One of them things, innit.

Miss Mahmoud How long has it been?

Remy A year now. That's why he left his job, cos he got sick.

Miss Mahmoud Have you got any help?

Remy We're trying, But there's so many forms and whatever . . . that's why I've been on my phone so much. Trying to figure it all out with the information online. And I always check my phone in case my dad's trying to message me or call me. He needs me.

Miss Mahmoud School and your dad's GP can help you access some help, for you and your dad.

Taz (*feeling bad*) You're always in a mood, Remy, so we thought –

Remy (*across*) You'd be angry and all! You don't know what it's like!

Taz No, I know, I'm sorry. What I meant was 'cause you didn't want to talk and you were always on your phone, I thought you were gaming or whatever. And I just kept going on at you about it. I'm really sorry, Remy.

Remy *shrugs.*

Remy You didn't know. It's OK.

Feeling vulnerable he moves off to a corner.

Sam Makes sense now, why he's been tired in class.

Taz Should I go after him?

Miss Mahmoud Give him some time.

Young Miss Mahmoud *comes back.*

Young Miss Mahmoud Is beans on toast OK?

Mum Sounds good to me, love. Aren't you going into town today? I can manage a couple of hours on my own. You've got your friends' party, haven't you, at the roller disco?

Taz You said you weren't allowed to go!

Young Miss Mahmoud *watches as her* **Mum** *tries to get up but stumbles.*

Young Miss Mahmoud (*covering*) It's fine, I don't really fancy it. Rather stay with you.

Taz *watches* **Miss Mahmoud** *as she watches her younger self.*

Taz That's why you never went? You're a good liar, Miss.

Miss Mahmoud I'm not sure that's a compliment.

Sam I know everyone thinks I'm obsessed with history and old buildings and all that. But I've always wondered . . . if you could go back in time, to just one moment. . . . would you go and relive the best thing that ever happened to you, or change the worst thing that ever happened to you?

Miss Mahmoud You can't change the past.

Sam We thought you couldn't go back in time 'til this morning!

Miss Mahmoud And yes, we are actually here in the past . . . but we're just onlookers. And I'd take reliving the best bits over anything.

Taz This isn't a best bit though, is it?

Miss Mahmoud Watching my mum water the plants and sing to herself? Oh it really is. I want to remember her like this. It got harder once it was all hospital beds and tubes and monitors and drips.

Young Miss Mahmoud *brings through two plates and hands one to her* **Mum**. *They sit and eat together, enjoying each other's company.* **Miss Mahmoud** *goes up to them, watching them closely. She talks to her younger self.*

Miss Mahmoud Hey, hello, you. Well, I mean . . . me. People say, don't they, 'What would you tell your younger self?' And I'd never known how to answer that. But I do now. (*Beat.*) It gets hard . . . but you'll be OK. You really will.

Taz *joins her.*

Taz And what you become. . . . what you are . . .

Taz *and* **Miss Mahmoud** (*together*) Is enough.

Young Miss Mahmoud *looks around as if she's just heard something.*

Young Miss Mahmoud Can you hear something?

Taz *and* **Miss Mahmoud** *hold their breath.*

Mum Mmm?

Young Miss Mahmoud Thought I heard voices?

Mum Probably just next door's telly.

Young Miss Mahmoud No . . . didn't sound like the TV.

Mum She had it on pretty loud earlier.

Young Miss Mahmoud She must've been watching 'Go, Go Saturday'.

Mum Didn't you watch it today?

Young Miss Mahmoud (*covering*) Me? Nah, didn't fancy it. Better out here, isn't it, just me and you having a chat.

Mum *gets upset, knowing she's lying to make her feel better.*

Mum You're a good girl.

Taz *steps back a moment, leaving* **Miss Mahmoud** *to take one last look at her* **Mum** *and her younger self.*

Miss Mahmoud Everything's going to be alright.

She turns away and then quickly turns back.

Miss Mahmoud One last thing . . . just in case you can hear me . . . don't over-pluck your eyebrows in the nineties . . . they never grow back properly.

She looks at them one last time as her younger self and her **Mum** *pick up their plates and head inside.*

Miss Mahmoud (*soft*) Bye, Mum.

Mum *turns around, as if she's heard something . . . but then shakes her head; it was nothing. She leaves.* **Miss Mahmoud** *watches her go and in that moment finds her peace. She takes a deep breath.*

Miss Mahmoud It's time to go home.

Remy Don't you want to spend more time with your mum?

Miss Mahmoud I didn't remember today – this particular day. Just an ordinary day in the garden, eating beans on toast. While she could still walk. An ordinary day but it turns out . . . the ordinary days are the brilliant ones. I didn't remember it, because of all the pain and sad things that came after. But I will now. (*Beat.*) Time to stop living in the past. And Remy, it's time to get back to your dad.

She looks to them all.

Miss Mahmoud It's time . . . to go back to the future!

She looks really pleased with herself. They all stare at her.

Miss Mahmoud Oh come on, don't tell me you don't know the film?!

They all stare at her before **Taz** *breaks the silence.*

Taz Just winding you up.

Sam Course we know it. It had vision, that film.

Marni Tangibly different vision.

Remy One of my dad's favourites.

Marni Wait! Are we going to need a flux capacitor to get back to 2023? And do we have to go at 88 miles per hour?

Miss Mahmoud Pretty sure we won't need a flux capacitor. And if we do we're in trouble, I've got no idea where we'd get one.

Marni Maybe that Our Price place sells them.

Miss Mahmoud (*amused*) I'm pretty certain it doesn't.

Sam Surely we just need to get back to the roller disco?

Taz Do you think anyone's going to believe us, when we get back?

Sam Maybe we won't be able to remember.

Marni Dorothy remembered. In *The Wizard of Oz*.

Taz That wasn't time travel.

Miss Mahmoud But she was trying to get back . . .

Sam So maybe we should try it . . .

Remy Try what?

Taz You know . . .

They all stand in a circle. **Remy** *realizes what they're doing and joins in.*

Miss Mahmoud I think we should close our eyes.

Eyes closed, they click their heels and chant 'There's no place like home' three times. They open their eyes to find they haven't moved.

Sam Well, that didn't work.

Marni Major anti-climax vibes.

Taz So now what?

Miss Mahmoud We walk.

Marni We can time travel by skating backwards, but we can't teleport back to the disco? That's messed up . . .

Taz Wait . . . what if we didn't go?

Remy What are you on about?

Sam You want to stay here?

Marni With the landlines and the penny-farthings?

Taz Would it be that bad?

Remy You're mad.

Miss Mahmoud We can't stay, Taz. We don't belong here. And you wouldn't like it . . . it's too different.

Taz But I'm happy here. Like . . . I don't feel like I do at home.

Miss Mahmoud Not now you don't. But that feeling doesn't just go away because you're in a different place.

Taz But what if I was a different person here?

Miss Mahmoud Without your friends, your family?

Taz *knows she's right.*

Miss Mahmoud You don't need to be a different person.

Marni Taz, I felt like that before I went to counselling. Like I needed to be someone else. Someone better. (*Beat.*) I don't feel like that now. Cos now I think I'm pretty great. I went full circle, innit. (*Beat, smiling.*) Circle of life.

Miss Mahmoud (*to* **Taz**) If you want, I can put you forward for some sessions with the school counsellor as soon as we get back.

Sam Well, this is all lovely, but am I the only one worried that we might not actually be able to get back?

Taz Alright, buzzkill.

Sam I'm just saying we should get a move on.

Remy (*kind*) Yeah . . . cos Taz's got a survey to finish.

Taz (*kind*) And Remy's dad's needs him.

They share a nice moment.

Marni Tangible nice moment vibes!

As they all smile, Huey Lewis's 'The Power of Love' begins to play as the gang make to walk back to the disco. As they walk in a circle and change back into their roller skates, the lights change and we're back at the roller disco. They begin to skate forwards in a circle together. The lights change, the track fades.

Scene Eight

Taz Are we back?

Sam *opens the door to look.*

Sam Outside . . . is outside.

Marni *checks her pocket.*

Marni   And I've got my phone back.

The others check for theirs.

Remy   Me too.

Taz   And me.

They all feel apprehensive.

Marni   Maybe we could go back one day?

Miss Mahmoud   Maybe. Or maybe we won't need to.

Taz   Because everything we need is right here?

Miss Mahmoud   Time to find out.

She leads them towards the door. The lights change.

Scene Nine

Taz *is taking her survey again, much more upbeat this time, asking people how they are and also giving them a leaflet.*

Taz   Hi, excuse me, I'm just doing a survey . . . how are you?

Boy   Umm . . . fine.

Taz   That's great. (*To the girl.*) What about you, do you mind if I ask how you are? (*Beat.*) That's great! I really hope you mean that.

She hands them a leaflet.

But if you're not, or even if you are . . . you could come to that? If you like?

The **Girl** *and* **Boy** *look at the leaflet, unsure.*

Taz   I promise you, it's brilliant.

The **Girl** *and the* **Boy** *nod and take the leaflet and leave. The* **Inner Monologue** *appear by* **Taz**.

Inner Monologue (*upbeat*)   We are cooking on gas!

The **Inner Monologue** *whoop, cheer, celebrate, etc.*

Miss Mahmoud *enters.*

Taz   Miss!

Miss Mahmoud   How's it going today?

Taz   Well, they're all still saying 'fine', but at least I'm getting to give them a leaflet and so far no-one's said no.

Miss Mahmoud   Sounds good.

Taz Where are you off? The vintage market?

Miss Mahmoud No . . . maybe it's time to stop spending too much time in the past and surrounding myself with old things. I was going to tell you all in class on Monday . . . I'm leaving.

Taz What?! Why?

Miss Mahmoud I just want to expand my horizons. Try somewhere new.

Inner Monologue *appear behind her.*

Inner Monologue So excited, so excited, so excited . . .

Taz But . . . will you ever some back?

Miss Mahmoud 'Course! (*Re. the leaflet, smiling.*) Maybe even once a month . . .

Miss Mahmoud *makes to go.* **Taz** *turns but then stops.*

Taz Miss?

Miss Mahmoud Yes, Taz?

Taz (*with meaning*) How are you?

Miss Mahmoud *smiles. Her next line is said in unison by her and the* **Inner Monologue***, who stand between her and* **Taz***.*

Miss Mahmoud (*heartfelt*) I'm fine. How are you?

Taz*'s next line is said in unison by her and the* **Inner Monologue***.*

Taz (*heartfelt*) I'm fine.

A moment. The lights change.

Scene Ten

Lights up on an empty chair. **Taz** *comes and sits on it. She talks as if a therapist is asking her questions.*

Taz How've I been since my last session? (*Beat.*) I've been . . . good. Actually yeah. I've been good. (*Beat.*) I've been keeping a diary, like you told me, about how I feel every day . . . actually writing it down. (*Beat.*) But . . . I've been talking to my mates more, about you know . . . stuff. (*Beat.*) Sometimes I feel a bit stupid, but mostly . . . it feels good.

She leans forward.

I know you're the therapist, so you ask all the questions, but . . . can I ask you something, for once? Is that allowed?

She waits for a response.

It's just, I was wondering . . . if you could go back in time to just one moment, one day . . . what would it be? Would it be like, a day where something amazing happened . . .

or . . . (*Thinking of* **Miss Mahmoud**'s *day with her* **Mum**) just an ordinary day? (*Beat.*) Why am I asking? (*Smiles.*) I just wondered.

Scene Eleven

The lights change. **Taz** *has left and now* **Remy** *is on stage. He's nervously preparing to do a talk to his class, reading off notes. The rest of the cast are in front of him as classmates. Much of the following is hard for him to say – he's nervous.*

Remy I didn't know what to write for my end of year presentation. But Miss said write what you know about. So . . .

He takes a deep breath, pushing down his nerves.

The Children's Society says there are approximately 800,000 young carers in the UK. (*Beat.*) I'm one of them.

And with that, a weight is lifted from him. He slowly starts to tell his story.

I became one when my dad got sick last year and my mum had to go back to work full time. The Children's Society also report that nearly 40 per cent of young carers said that nobody in their school was aware of their caring responsibilities. (*Beat.*) So I thought I should tell you. Because sometimes I bail on mates. And sometimes I miss school. And people wonder why, they think I'm a letdown, flakey, whatever. (*Beat.*) Thing is . . . some days I feel . . . well, it's hard. But how I feel doesn't feel as important as how my dad's doing. But he said I need to tell you all. That I need to look after myself. Ask for help. (*Beat.*) So anyway, yeah. Like don't get me wrong . . . mostly, I'm fine. Except some days . . . I'm not. And that's OK.

His classmates applaud him and cheer.

The lights change.

Scene Twelve

Lights up on **Sam** *outside the roller disco. Only his top half is lit so we don't see what he's wearing on his feet. If lighting not possible, perhaps he could be stood behind a box, with the box covering his feet. He talks directly to the audience or to a group of pupils on stage, but none of main characters should be in that group.*

Sam Thank you for coming to my first ever guided tour of the town! I've really enjoyed it, I hope you have too. I wanted to end it by this building here and tell you a bit about it and . . . give you a bit of a surprise. It used to be a town hall and then a picture house and then . . . well, it's been empty for ages and they're supposed to be knocking it down to make way for flats. But look at it, it's beautiful. They don't make places like this anymore. Anyway . . . my dad says the developers ran out of money, so for now no-one wants it. (*Beat.*) Except me. Because I had a vision! A vision of a brilliant place where there were bright colours and actually quite decent music and where everything was glorious! OK, well, actually somethings were terrible . . . but I took the good bits! And I got my dad to ask the landlord if we could hire this place once a month for, like, really cheap. Told them it was for kids who want to use it to help promote good mental health. Because it is! (*Pulls one of* **Taz**'s *leaflets and holds it out.*) So welcome . . . welcome, all . . . to our monthly roller disco!

Light fully up on **Sam**/*or he skates out from behind the box to reveal he's wearing his roller skates and we're now inside the roller disco, decorated as it was before, with glitterball, etc.*

Sam   Taz? Cue the music!

Taz *skates on. She hits play on her phone. The lights change and the same track from Scene One, Hall and Oates' 'You Make My Dreams', starts to play as* **Sam** *finally gets his chance to dance to it.* **Inner Monologue 4** *suddenly appears in the middle of everybody, exuberant.*

Inner 4   This is the song I couldn't remember!

All the cast join in with the dance; the mood is exuberant and fun. The **Inner Monologue** *are having a riotous time together.* **Taz**, **Sam**, **Miss Mahmoud**, **Marni** *and* **Remy** *skate forwards.* **Miss Mahmoud** *and* **Taz** *move forward together. The tracks dips as the rest of the cast continue to skate behind them.* **Taz** *and* **Miss Mahmoud** *speak out to the audience.*

Taz (*upbeat*)   I heard this rumour once . . . you should never skate backwards together three times . . .

Miss Mahmoud (*upbeat*)   Because you never know where you might end up!

She and **Taz** *rejoin* **Sam**, **Remy** *and* **Marni**. *The track reprises and they continue their formation dance.*

The track fades.

Curtain.

Back in the Day

BY YASMEEN KHAN

Notes on rehearsal and staging, drawn from a workshop with the writer, held at the National Theatre, October 2023

Introduction

Lead director Justine Themen asked the group to identify elements of the play that excited them.

Themen asked the group to come up with some challenges and questions the play presents.

Some of the challenges/questions included:

- How to approach locations when there is no or limited set?
- How to approach the play with a large cast? How does the play allow for ensemble work?
- How to balance the topics of mental health – not making it too heavy but also not glancing over it?
- How to ensure safeguarding with young people when tackling the heavier topics?
- How to utilize rehearsal time efficiently?
- How to represent the inner monologues on stage?
- How can transitions be smooth (and allow for skate changes)?
- How to look at the scale of the transition into the 1980s?
- How to roller-skate or represent roller-skating creatively?
- How to ensure health and safety for young people when roller-skating?
- How to approach the ethnicity of the characters sensitively if the company doesn't have performers of South Asian heritage?
- What should a non-Muslim performer know about the background of Miss Mahmoud to understand and represent the character as truthfully as possible?
- How strict are the genders of the characters? Is it possible to change them?

This is an exercise you could do with your cast after a read-through to identify the challenges and questions the young people might have at the beginning of the process.

Warm-up

Exercise: Walking and Moving as an Ensemble (seeding 1980s music and dance)

Gear shifts
Justine invited the group to start walking around the space, filling any empty spots by walking through them. The group started at a neutral, everyday walking pace which she

called Gear One. This was followed by a series of stopping and starting walking again as a group to sharpen the group's ability to fill the space. Slowly Themen asked the group to raise their tempo going to Gear two (a walk that has more purpose), Gear three (a quicker pace) and then into Gear four (a light jog). Once the group had gone through all four gears Justine asked them to stop, start and change the gear they were walking or jogging in by listening to each other, rather than by responding to her instruction. Throughout the exercise she also reminded everyone to check in with how they were feeling, and to meet the exercise where it felt comfortable and possible (for example, if a jog doesn't feel comfortable then find the pace of walking that works for them in that moment).

From moving in pairs to ensemble dance

Themen then asked the group to keep walking and to find a person to walk behind and to follow their steps – moving in tandem with them. She also reminded the group to keep filling any empty spots in the space. Then she asked the group to slowly start moving clockwise in a circle. Once the group was walking in a circle, Justine asked them to start jogging again and to slowly create two smaller circles. She then asked the group to spread out in the space walking again.

Justine put on a song and asked everyone to find their best 1980s moves, and then to share these moves with a partner and dance with them. She then asked the pairs to find small groups and create a dance circle together. In their circles everyone was invited to move into the middle to offer their movement, which the group then performed together. Once everyone had danced it out, she turned the music off and asked the group to starting moving around again and do any stretches that they might still need. At the same time, she asked everyone to take a couple of deep breaths in and out, gradually coming to a standstill.

Themes

Mental well-being: Highlighting, encouraging and empowering conversations about mental ill health and mental well-being.

Nostalgia and yearning for the past: Writer Yasmeen Khan shared that nostalgia used to be looked at as a mental illness in the 1700s. It was an illness about yearning for things in the past, a sense of displacement and isolation (as a result of people fighting away from home). Considering nostalgia now, the past has so much to offer us, but it is also worth reflecting why we feel the need to escape into the past, and whether looking back is held in balance with being in the present moment and looking forwards to the future.

Young carers: Bringing visibility and highlighting the challenges of being a young carer. Young carers are often not visible, their stories are not told, making people unaware of the weight of responsibilities on their shoulders and the challenges they face daily.

Mental well-being and safeguarding

Justine asked participants to have a conversation in groups around the question, **what does mental well-being hold for you?** She asked each group to nominate a scribe to write down their thoughts on a piece of flip chart paper.

She then asked the groups to have a discussion around the question, **what does mental ill-health hold for you?**, also recording their thoughts on flipchart paper.

The groups shared back some of their key thoughts with the wider group.

Justine then asked the group to think about the question, **where do you see mental-wellbeing and mental ill-health in the world?** Possible concentric circles to focus on, from close to home to macro: in own experience (where comfortable), in school, in media, in politics, in entertainment, in the country, in the world. Starting from the smaller and then going through the wider circles. Justine reminded the group to only share what they were comfortable with, and to keep it observational rather than personal.

Responses included:
Mental well-being

- Balance
- Building resilience
- Self-care/understanding yourself
- Finding a sense of enjoyment/self-expression/creative outlet
- Letting oneself feel
- Accepting oneself/being authentic
- Music and art
- Friendships and family
- Safeguarding and well-being
- In nature
- Finding a community/sense of belonging
- Sports
- Trust
- Positive interaction with strangers (on the bus, in the shop, etc.) is how our brains reassure us that the world is safe and that we are welcome. Connecting with people to support mental well-being.
- Change in perception:
  o Teaching young people early on in schools about how to look after themselves, ways to learn how to calm themselves down or how to express emotions in a healthy way

- Celebrities advocating for mental well-being and drawing boundaries to look after themselves. For example, athletes and artists taking breaks to look after themselves
- A shift in language and recognition about the importance of looking after our mental well-being

Mental ill-health

- Overwhelm/overthinking/inner critic/self-doubt/overstimulation
- Imbalance – of private space and social opportunities
- Isolation and loneliness, including isolation due to living in rural areas
- Pressure – especially pressure about achieving (the myth of 'perfect mental health')
- Constant social media and news – no way to switch off and impossible to remove yourself from events
- Physical ill-health (disconnect between mind and body) – exhaustion and burnout
- Relationship breakdowns
- Bullying
- Substance misuse
  Fear of asking for help
- Lack of support
- Other people's fears and expectations
- Stressful home environment
- Guilt
- The disconnect with nature and people. Young people being lost in digital world with lack of in-person connection or being in nature. People not spending enough time outdoors.
- Theatres having a hypocrisy talking about mental health, but not actually reaching communities and not impacting the well-being of those communities

Themen then asked the group to respond to the question, **where do you see these two concepts in the play?**

Some of the responses included:

- Seeing Remy's struggles and challenges of being a young carer, and how he attempts to mask these (mental ill-health)
- Miss Mahmoud masking her mental health challenges (mental ill-health), but also drawing on her own experiences to advocate for the young people to talk about their emotions and struggles – creating trust for the students (mental well-being)
- Sam's confidence in his own character, being proud of his geekiness and his love for architecture. He has real self-confidence and resilience. He has a strong

relationship with his dad which enables him to have this confidence (mental well-being). He has setbacks from his peers, but they end up understanding him and letting him dream up the roller disco at the end. Yasmeen also mentioned that in the 1980s it was easier to find your 'tribe' in person (e.g., being a goth), now it's a bit harder in person as so much has moved online

- The queer relationship in the 1980s and how it affects the mental health of the two characters through them not being able to come out in the open about their relationship (mental ill-health due to societal discrimination). Recognizing how things have changed for the better in this respect. On the other hand, in the 1980s there was the peace and quiet of not needing to be on your phone all the time (mental well-being).

These questions can be good tools to use with young people and offer an approach to talking about the topic of mental health within the text. They allow conversations to happen without needing to share anything personal and rather focus on the wider world as well as on the specifics of the play.

One participant mentioned that the question **what does mental ill-health hold for mean to you?** might be challenging for some students. Teachers and youth leaders shared some of their practices in creating safe spaces. These included the following: Creating context before the conversation can be useful, as well as creating a system where anyone can take a few minutes out in a discrete way. For example, you could use a stack of empty sticky notes as a visual pass that a student can pick up and place on the teacher's/director's table without needing to explain that they need a moment outside the room. You could also do a check in where you ask the young people to rate how they feel day to day: an idea to ask this in an open way was to ask 'if you were an egg today what kind of egg you would be?' Allowing young people to interpret this in any way they want.

Themen talked about what an important space youth theatre is for young people to connect their own experiences with the wider world around them, making it vital to allow for these conversations to happen in the space.

Approaching the play

Justine said that like education (which comes from the Latin words 'ex' and 'ducere' meaning 'to draw out'), directing is about drawing out and building on what's already within the group. The young people will have so much expertize that you can draw out by creating a space where they are able to play and share.

Uniting

Uniting is a great tool to approach a text and to find the shape of every scene. The group looked at the first scene (from Sam's entrance on p. 515). Whilst volunteers read the scene, Justine asked the rest of the group to note any changes in dynamic within the scene as they listened. The group was told, in addition, that almost any time a character enters or leaves the space creates a unit change. The participants were put into small groups to discuss where the key changes occurred – where each unit ends and a new one begins. A unit is signalled in the text by a straight line after the last moment of a unit and before the first moment of the new unit across the page.

Sometimes a change might be an intensification of a unit's dynamic rather than a full unit change – for example, Sam walking on stage is a unit change, but him immediately afterwards turning the music on is not a new unit, but an intensification of the same one. Justine signals these intensifications with a dotted line across the page.

The next step after finding the unit changes is to give titles to each unit. This can be a useful tool in remembering what happens in each unit. For example, who is pushing the change in the scene – identifying the character and placing them in the title can be useful in finding the focus and drive of each unit. An example of a title one group found was, 'Remy is distracted' – this referred to a section about Remy's inner monologues bombarding Remy, while he tries to continue a conversation with Sam.

This is work you can do with your young people, or you can do at home and bring into rehearsals if you have limited time. Justine Themen always explores/shares the units with the companies she works with to ensure a shared understanding of points of change for clarity of storytelling.

Titles can be useful to remind a cast about what the focus of each unit is. If your rehearsal time is short, you might just do the work for yourself and bring out the specifics only when the company doesn't naturally find the moments of change by themselves. Finding units is a great way of digging deeper into the text, and revealing out more about the characters and the world of the play. It is also an incredibly useful tool to ensure clarity and pace. It can be used as a first approach to the play with the company or it can be used alongside other exercises and approaches such as super objectives and character backstories.

Exercises for use in rehearsals

Character backstory and daily routine

Justine divided participants into groups, each focusing on a different character from the play. She asked everyone individually to think about what the daily routine of this character might be, and to decide on one thing that the character might spend time doing on a regular basis. She then asked everyone to find a space on their own in the room, and to spend time carrying out the daily activity that they had decided on. The activity can be really simple, for example the character doing their shopping for their dad, listening to music, doing their make-up, or completing their homework. The group then spent around five minutes in the space non-verbally doing the tasks they had chosen for the characters they were given.

Tasks the group explored included:

- Scrolling through social media on their phone
- Napping
- Meditating
- Writing their homework
- Stretching / doing yoga
- Writing
- Listening to music
- Waiting for the bus
- Practising dance moves

Justine then asked the group to reflect on what they discovered about the characters by doing one of their daily tasks. Discoveries included: Taz needs to charge up on alone time so she can handle when she has to be social; Sam feels hyper-focused, and wants to learn everything off by heart; Miss Mahmoud is incredibly organized and prepares a lot for her teaching; Remy is never able to stop, he is constantly switched on in case his dad needs him; and Marni feels incredibly present and connected to anything she is doing.

Yasmeen really resonated with all the discoveries and added that perhaps Sam always wants to be able to explain what he has learnt about the buildings; Miss Mahmoud's needing to be organized could be rooted in her having been a young carer; Remy always needs to be in two places at once, dealing with split screens constantly. She also reminded us that Marni has learnt how to calm herself through therapy, which enables her to be much more present.

This exercise can be done with larger ensembles by dividing them into groups and giving each group a character to focus on. This would allow everyone to explore different characters even if they are not the ones performing them, providing them with a way to engage further with the text and the other roles.

What does a character want? (Super-objectives)

Justine asked participants to discuss what their character wants for the whole play: what do they want to achieve by the end of the play (this is often known as their 'super-objective')?

After a few minutes, she asked the group to apply this 'want' and see how it works with the actions of the characters in the initial scene of the play – what their objective (want) is in each scene and how it's connected to their overall 'wants'. Justine encouraged this 'want' to be articulated in the positive (something they do want) rather than in the negative (something they don't want), because visualizing the thing that you want makes you much more driven to achieve it, and much clearer for performers to play it.

The super objectives the group found for characters included:

- **Taz:** She wants to be OK/more centred.

  Yasmeen added that Taz is a complex character who is battling a lot of different anxieties. Taz doesn't necessarily have a specific mental illness, it's more about the constant battle with her inner voices and this is what undermines her mental health.

- **Sam:** He wants to enthuse others with the things that enthuse him.

  Yasmeen added that his passion for creating a community is incredibly important to her (the theme of community is often present in her writing). She also said that Sam would have been a great 1980s music video director – a go-getter who makes things happen and gets people excited.

- **Miss Mahmoud:** She wants people to fulfil their potential (which includes herself).

  Justine Themen added how for people to be able to fulfil their potential they need have good mental well-being which connects her overall 'want' to her actions in the play.

- **Remy:** He wants to be Remy again.

  Yasmeen agreed that he wants to find himself again.

- **Mani:** She wants to connect (with people and with the world).

An additional exercise: Ask the young people to think about what a key memory for their character might be. This can be a task done almost as freewriting, asking the young people to write for 5 minutes straight without stopping.

Reminiscence Interviews about the 1980s

Justine split the group into two – interviewers (those who hadn't lived through the 1980s) and interviewees (those who had). The interviewers had to come up with a list of questions they had about the 1980s. The interviewees set up the space and had a quick discussion about their experiences of the 1980s. Justine then asked one half of each group to merge with one half of the other, so that there were interviewers and interviewee in each new group. With a nominated facilitator, the groups conducted interviews with each other about life in the 1980s.

This is a good research exercise for young people to go away and interview their parents or other adults in their lives to learn about the 1980s and then bring their findings back to the rehearsal room.

Some of the questions and responses that came out of the conversations included:

- How did interpersonal relationships work differently in the 1980s? Now everyone is in each other's pockets all the time with mobile phones and social media, in the 1980s you had to use the landline and you could only chat at specific times (calls were cheaper after 6pm!).

- In the 1980s what were you nostalgic for and why? Not much nostalgia in the 1980s for the decades before, people seem to have been more present (having a great time).
- How did you explore your sexuality in the 1980s? People were shocked to hear about Section 28, about not being allowed to talk about homosexuality. There were also conversations in the room about how homosexuality was handled by the government in the 1980s and parallels with trans rights now.
- The shock of how little things cost back in the 1980s, and the difference between then and now.

This is a great opportunity for young people to connect with their parents and others from their lives to start intergenerational conversations.

Headlines for 1987

Themen asked the group to spend five minutes looking up a few headlines from 1987. She asked everyone to write down some of the headlines on sticky notes and to put them up on the wall, creating a sea of headlines. Two participants read the news headlines as if they were reporters on the news.

Some of the headlines included:

- 'Smiths split'
- 'Fire at King's Cross, 31 fatalities'
- 'Riddle of the open doors' (Zebrugge ferry disaster)
- 'New London AIDS danger'
- 'PANIC! Dow plunges through floor'
- 'Search ends for the Loch Ness monster'
- 'Lester Piggott imprisoned for tax evasion'
- 'Boy George banned from British TV show – suggested he would be a bad influence'
- 'Black Monday – Wall Street Crash'
- 'Kylie Minogue Releases First Single – "The Loco-Motion"'
- 'Police crack down on football hooligans.'
- 'Hungerford Massacre – 14 people killed before a shooter takes his own life'

If doing this with young people, it's important to think about how the headlines are curated for Scene Seven, where the characters wander through their town. Each group might choose to focus on a mix of local news stories, news from the music scene, national and international politics, etc. It will all inform how the young performers inhabit the world of the 1980s.

Transition into the 1980s and roller-skating

Justine asked participants to form groups to stage the moment when the play shifts from the present day into 1987. She firstly asked the whole group to read the moment of transition together on p. 530. Themen's provocation was to start from the moment of the opening of the door into the movement of the roller-disco and then back in time to 1987. She put a playlist of 1980s tunes on and asked the groups to come up with an initial staging for this transition.

The transition ideas included:

- Group one: Going from stillness and conversation into music and synchronized movement, miming the putting on of the roller-skates in the foreground, and using movement to represent roller-skating.
- Group two: Creating the magic of transition by circling around Miss Mahmoud as she walks into the space, then starting to dance around her until she is caught by the joy and joins in.
- Group three: Creating a line of dancers with Miss Mahmoud being transformed into an 1980s outfit behind them; and once the transformation has happened, starting skating all together as a group around the space.

Reflections:

- Realizing that creating the feeling of being at a roller-disco can be easily accessed and portrayed just by using ensemble movement, it doesn't necessarily need actual roller-skating!
- Creating the moment of putting roller-skates on meant it was clear to an audience what was happening.
- Creating a chain of people and moving in a synchronized way in a row evoked a sense of roller-skating.
- Using energy – clapping, movement, whooping is the most effective and powerful transformation. It instantly lifts and changes the world of the play!

Exploring your young people's ideas for this transition, with you curating, editing and structuring their ideas alongside your own, will create a moment that is unique and rich as well as being owned by them. The way in which your actors move from outside the door to inside the door is key to this moment. Keep it fluid, rather than stopping one scene and starting another. Continue this sense of fluidity between scenes also (Justine advised against blackouts and advocated for smooth, more film-like transitions from one scene to another).

Staging exercise: Inner monologues

Justine divided participants into groups of different sizes (from five to twelve people) and gave everyone the middle section of Scene Two to look at, when Remy and Taz's inner monologues are incredibly loud. She asked each group to find a way to stage the inner monologues, dividing the lines up between themselves. Her provocation was to be as inventive as possible in their staging and by how the text is allocated between them.

The staging ideas included:
- Inner monologues moving as an ensemble around the character whose inner monologues they were (though attention needs to be paid here to where the focus is on stage at any one time)
- Standing in a half circle around the character
- Moving in a line behind the character as they move around the stage, and jumping out when they have a line as inner monologue
- Standing in a vertical line behind a character, and leaning out to the side when they have a line
- Inner monologues sometimes delivering lines singly, sometimes sharing a few lines to add emphasis (lines read by one to six members of the ensemble at the same time). One of the groups played with echoing lines – the dissonance created by the voices not all being synched up was effective.

Reflections:
There is exciting potential in the fluidity of the inner monologues and in the doubling up of voices, which is a great tool for companies with larger ensembles.

Justine pointed out how composing the space and finding the rules of a set choreography for how the inner monologues interact with the external characters is really important. This is to make sure that they don't pull focus from each other and to help an audience know what to pay attention to in each moment. For example, she thinks that the chorus and the characters' movement influencing each other could be powerful, but them physically touching might break the illusion.

Where do the inner monologues exist? What's the rule of them existing on stage? These are useful questions to ask, especially if the inner monologues are on stage all the time. Justine suggested this should be devised and figured out in collaboration with the young people. In case of limited rehearsal time, she suggested finding a way to streamline the decisions (maybe bringing two offers) to still give creative agency to the young people.

Characters and casting – gender and ethnicity of characters

Gender of characters

The script suggests the specific gender of each character in their character descriptions.

Some of the gender decisions were to reflect how wider society perceives gender roles. For example, Remy being a boy and struggling to talk about his mental health resonates with how our society doesn't permit men to open up about their mental ill health. Another example was Taz and Miss Mahmoud's relationship; in Taz we have a girl who is defensive when it comes to talking about mental health, showing that, contrary to some stereotypes, it's not necessarily any easier for a young woman to navigate the issue. In a further instance, the choice to make the TV presenter and singer both female and to make their relationship 'problematic' is to highlight the lack of visibility of female queer stories, particularly in the past.

Yasmeen is open for gender and ethnicities to be changed and made specific for every cast as long as the original through-line of the intentions above and in the introductory notes are kept in mind and carried through wherever possible.

Ethnicity of the characters

There are three roles for British South Asian women in the play – Miss Mahmoud, Young Miss Mahmoud and Mum. A question that came up several times throughout the day was about how to approach this sensitively if the company doesn't have South Asian young people. In the introductory notes of the text, Yasmeen mentions that the casting of these roles should be made specific and can be changed to fit each company. It was important for her to write British South Asian characters for representation and visibility, and it is important that, as British Asians, Miss Mahmoud and Young Miss Mahmoud are shown in Western dress, or something that gives a nod to their heritage (eg a Kurta top with jeans, etc.) but she is happy for these characters to be played by young people who are not of this heritage. Yasmeen and Justine suggested two ways to approach this – one was to do some slight signalling as a nod to the South Asian heritage of the characters, for example via costuming (but important to say that not all people from one community dress the same). It is all about approaching this with care – for example, your company could reach out to a local South Asian community to get their support and advice to navigate these characters.

Another approach is to change the characters' ethnicity and make it specific to your company. Yasmeen talked about how all these characters are rooted in code switching – having to switch between two worlds, which will be an experience shared by people and communities who have a heritage of migration, are mixed race, multilingual and much more. There may be young people in the group who will resonate with this even if they are not from a South Asian background. For example, if a lot of the young people have Eastern European heritage, you could make the characters specific to that.

Justine highlighted the importance of holding a character's heritage, their experiences, and the stage representation of this with respect. It is also important to hold with care the diversity (and specific needs) of the members of all the groups. This should be balanced and approached with care.

Question and answer with Yasmeen Khan

Q: Did you have any simple ideas about staging?
A: I always imagined it being done with minimal set. For example, if your company doesn't have stage lights you could just get some fun small lights the cast can hold in their

hands or just mime the door. Small props or even just the performers' reactions to the space can support the creation of each location. Anything goes – it's about embodying it!

Q: Did you have anything specific in mind about what the health issues are that Remy and Miss Mahmoud's parents have?
A: No, I deliberately left it open. The only specifics are about what the responsibilities placed on the young people are (e.g., Miss Mahmoud's mum's dropping things.)

Q: Did you always imagine them actually roller-skating or just miming it?
A: Originally, I thought that it might not be practical or possible for all groups to have actual roller skating, much as I would love it! But the Connections team encouraged me to keep it in, so I did, but it can be done in creative ways.

Q: Does Sam have autistic tendencies? Is that something to explore within a production?
I didn't write Sam with autistic tendencies in mind, the aim was for him to be self-confident, knowledgeable and unashamedly passionate about his love for architecture. I don't want this enthusiasm/'geekery' to be given a label other than what it is – a hobby/interest/passion. If Sam had been written via a neurodivergent perspective, the other characters' responses to him might have been written differently.

Q: Why did you choose to set the past scenes in 1987?
A: There was a whole bunch of reasons. Partially it was the music, but also it felt like it was a period of change in society. A lot of creativity as well as a lot of societal kick back and protests. Also, the economic crash (Black Friday) happening without completely understanding what that means as a teenager but feeling it, but then switching focus by turning back to favourite bands and magazines etc. It felt like a brink of change moment.

Q: Why aren't there any inner monologues in the 80s scenes?
A: They are quietened because the characters are so involved with what's happening, making them incredibly present. They don't have to get rid of their inner monologues, but they are lighter because they found something they truly engage with.

From a workshop led by Justine Themen
With notes by Júlia Levai

Participating Companies

#TeamDrama, Roding Valley High School
20Twenty Connections
Aberdeen Academy of Performing Arts
Aberystwyth Arts Centre Youth Theatre
Acorn Young People's Theatre
Actors Workshop
Alderbrook School
All Saints Secondary School
Amersham School
Andover College Performing Arts
Angmering Connections
The Archbishop Lanfranc Academy
Ardclough Youth Theatre
artsdepot Young Company
Artz Centre
Ashford Youth Theatre Company
Atlantic Coast Theatre Co.
Attleborough Youth Theatre Company
Aureus School
BACstage Youth Theatre
Benton Park School
Berkshire College of Agriculture
Bishop Fox's School
Bishop Luffa School
Bishopshalt School
The Black Cherry Youth Theatre
BLAS, Pontio
The Boaty Theatre Company
Bodmin College
Boteler StageCraft, Sir Thomas Boteler
    Church of England High School
Bournside School
The Boury Academy CIC
Bright Minds Collective
Brockhill Park Performing Arts College
Burton College
Buxton Opera House Young Company
Cabot Learning Federation Post 16
Calderdale Theatre School
Callywith college
Carmel Performing Arts, Carmel College
Cast Doncaster
The Charter School East Dulwich
Chatham and Clarendon Grammar School
Chaucer School
Chelsea Academy
Chetwynde School
Chiltern Hills Academy
Churchill Theatre Young Company
City of Westminster College
Cockburn John Charles Academy
Cockburn Laurence Calvert
Coleg Gwent Performing Arts
Company BA, Bedford Academy
The Conquest Youth Theatre
Coombe Girls School
CORE Principals
Corn Exchange Young Performers
The Costello School
Crescents Arts Youth Theatre (CAYT)
Crewe Lyceum Youth Theatre
Cromwell Community College
Croydon Youth Theatre Organisation
    (CYTO)
The Customs House Youth Theatre
Demesne Community Youth Theatre, in
    partnership with Tracing Steps Theatre &
    Dance Company
Denny High School Drama Club
Derby Theatre
Devizes School
The Dorset School of Acting
The Drama Studio
The Earl's Courtiers
East London Theatre School Young Actors
Echo Theatre
The Edge Young Actors Company
ESC Hastings Theatre Company
Ever Unique Productions
Felpham Community College
Flourish Youth Theatre
Flying High Young Company
Folkestone School for Girls
Footlights
Fowey River Academy
Framingham Earl High School
Fred Longworth High School
Freedom Academy Actors Company
Friern Barnet School
The Garage
Gladesmore Community School
Glenthorne Theatre Company
The Grand Young Company
Griese Youth Theatre

568 Participating Companies

Guild of Players Youth Theatre
Gulbenkian Young Company
Hackney Shed Collective
Harris Willesden
Hatch Youth Theatre
Hatton Youth Theatre
Havant & South Downs College
Hillhead High School
Holyrood Academy
Hoxton Hall
Hungry Wolf Visionary Youth Theatre
Imaginarium Young Actors Company
In the Round Theatre
Inverclyde Youth Theatre (Kayos)
Ipswich High School
The Island Free School
Jarrow School
JFS Theatre Company, The John Fisher School
JK Acting Platform, JK Theatre Arts
John Ruskin School
Kensington Arts
Kesteven and Grantham Girls' School
King Edward VI Community College
KGArts, Kingsbury Green Academy
Kildare Youth Theatre
Kindred Youth Theatre
The King Edmund School
Kings Theatre Arts Academy Youth
Kingsford Seniors
The Kirky Playhouse, Kirkintilloch High School
Knightswood Secondary School
Kola Nuts
Light UP
Lipson Cooperative Academy
The Loft Arts
Longfield Hall Trust
Love Theatre Ltd
The Lowry Young Company
Lowther Youth Theatre
LSC Expressive Arts, Leyton Sith Form College
M.A.D Youth Theatre
MAAD, Malcolm Arnold Academy
Make Sense Theatre Company
Make Your Mark Theatre Company
Mary Hare School
Mayflower Youth Theatre
Momentum Theatre, CAPA College

Mulberry UTC Theatre Company
Multiplicity Theatre Company, Northampton College
Murray Park Community School
Netherthorpe School
Newcastle Performance Academy Acting Company
Norbury High School for Girls
North Lindsey College
Northampton School for Boys
Northamptonshire Music & Performing Arts Trust Young Actors Company
The Norwood School
Notre Dame High School
Nottingham College
Nottingham Playhouse Connections Company
Oldham College
Ormiston Rivers Academy
Oslo International School
Ousedale School
OX2 Collective
Oxford Playhouse Youth Theatre
Page2stage Youth Theatre
Penistone Grammar School
Pensby High School
Perfect Circle Youth Theatre
Pike and Musket
Plashet School
Platform Theatre Arts
PlayActing Youth Theatre
Plympton Academy
The Point Ensemble Youth Theatre
Porthcawl Comprehensive School
PQA Burton
PQA Wolverhampton
QEGS
Queen Elizabeth's School
Queen's Park High School
RCS Juniors Performance Company, Royal Conservatoire of Scotland
REC Youth Theatre
Rednock School
RHSC Drama Club, Reepham High School and College
Riverside Youth Theatre
The Robinson Drama Academy
Roundwood Park School
Royal & Derngate Young Company: Connect
Rugby Connected Youth Theatre

Rushcliffe Spotlight Ensemble
Saint Aidan's Church of England High School
Salford City Academy
Sandbach School Theatre
Saracens High School
Shazam Theatre Company SCIO
Shenfield High School 6th Form Theatre Academy
Sherman Youth Theatre
Simon Langton Grammar School for Boys
Sir Henry Floyd Grammar School
The Sir John Colfox Academy
Sir Robert Pattinson Academy
Sir William Ramsay School
SM6 Acting Company, St Mary's College
Small But Mighty YPT
South Hunsley School
South Side Theatre Academy
Southwark Playhouse Young Company
Spalding Academy
Spires Academy
Spotlights Community Youth Theatre
SRWA Theatre Company, Sir Robert Woodard Academy
St Brendan's Sixth Form College
St Christopher's School
St John Plessington Catholic College
St Laurence School
St Paul's Way Players
St Richard's Theatre Company
St Saviour's and St Olave's School
St Thomas More Catholic High School
St Thomas More Catholic School
stage@leeds Young Company
Stagedoor Learning
Stockton riverside College
Straffan Drama Club
Stratford School Academy
Strode College
Suffolk New College Performing Arts
The Swanage School

The Sydney Russell School
Taunton Brewhouse Youth Theatre
Team RTMAT, River Tees Multi Academy Trust
Telford Priory School
Theatre Peckham
TheatreWorks Deal
Titchfield Festival Theatre Youth Associates
Torch Youth Theatre
Towers School and Sixth Form
Tramshed
Tribe Theatre
Trinity Youth Theatre
Twyford School
Varndean Studio Theatre Company
The View from Here, Sawston Village College
Washington Youth Theatre
Westfield Arts College
Wheatley Park School
Wimbledon College
Winstanley College
Wollaston School Theatre Company
Worcester Theatres Young REP Company
Worcester Youth Theatremakers
The Workshop
Worthing College
Wyke Sixth Form College
Wykham Park and Futures
Wymondham High Academy
Yew Tree Youth Theatre
York Theatre Royal (1)
York Theatre Royal (2)
Young Actors Club, Green Shoes Arts
The Young Actors Company
The Young Creatives Havant
Young Dramatic Arts
Young Octagon
Young People's Theatre
Ysgol Aberconwy
Ysgol Gyfun Gwyr

Partner Theatres

Aberystwyth Arts Centre
artsdepot
Beacon Arts Centre
Bristol Old Vic
Buxton Opera House
Crewe Lyceum
Derby Theatre
The Garage Norwich
The Grand Theatre Blackpool
Gulbenkian Arts Centre
HOME Manchester
Lighthouse Poole
The Lowry Salford
Lyric Theatre Belfast
Lyric Theatre Hammersmith
MAST Mayflower Studios Southampton
North Wall Oxford
Nottingham Playhouse
Pitlochry Festival Theatre
Queen's Theatre Hornchurch
Royal & Derngate
Sheffield Theatres
Sherman Theatre Cardiff
Soho Theatre
Southwark Playhouse
Theatre Peckham
Theatre Royal Plymouth
Tramshed
Trinity Theatre, Tunbridge Wells
Washington Arts Centre
Wiltshire Creative
Worcester Theatres
York Theatre Royal

National Theatre Connections Team

Kirsten Adam	*Head of Young People's Programmes*
Ola Animashawun	*Connections Dramaturg and National Theatre Associate*
Finley Neilens	*Young People's Programme Assistant*
Jenny Wilkinson	*Project Producer, Connections*
Alice King-Farlow	*Director of Learning and Partnerships*
Virginia Leaver	*Deputy Director, Operations*
Liza Vallance	*Deputy Director, Programmes*

Production notes edited by Kate Budgen

National Theatre

National Theatre
Upper Ground
London SE1 9PX

Registered charity no: 224223

Director of the National Theatre
Rufus Norris
Executive Director
Kate Varah

Performing Rights

Application for permission to perform, etc. should be made before rehearsals begin to the following representatives:

For *Age Is Revolting* and *The Sad Club*:
42M&P Ltd of Palladium House
7th Floor, 1–4 Argyll Street
London W1F 7TA
info@42mp.com

For *Shout*:
Casarotto Ramsay & Associates Ltd
3rd Floor, 7 Savoy Court
Strand
London WC2R 0EX
agents@casarotto.co.uk

For *Orchestra* and *The Periodicals*:
The Agency (London) Ltd
24 Pottery Lane
Holland Park
London, W11 4LZ
info@theagency.co.uk

For *Your Name Is Dead/Dy Enw Marw* and *Back in the Day*:
Permissions Department
Bloomsbury Publishing Plc
50 Bedford Square
London WC1B 3DP
performance.permissions@bloomsbury.com

For *Kiss/Marry/Push Off Cliff*:
United Agents
12–26 Lexington Street
London W1F 0LE
gsmart@unitedagents.co.uk

For *Replica*:
Dalzell & Beresford Ltd
Paddock Suite
The Courtyard
55 Charterhouse Street
London EC1M 6HA
KaraFitzpatrick@42mp.com

For *Wind/Rush Generation(s)*:
2 John Kings Court
67 St Johns Grove
London, N19 5QR
hello@team-artists.co.uk

www.ingramcontent.com/pod-product-compliance
Lightning Source LLC
Chambersburg PA
CBHW051801230426
43672CB00012B/2594